Wing Chun Masters

Jose M. Fraguas

EMPIRE Books
P.O. Box 491788, Los Angeles, CA 90049

WING CHUN MASTERS
by JOSE M. FRAGUAS

EMPIRE BOOKS
Los Angeles, California

Disclaimer
Please note that the author and publisher of this book are NOT RESPONSIBLE in any manner whatsoever for any injury that may result from practicing the techniques and/or following the instructions given within. Since the physical activities described herein may be too strenuous in nature for some readers to engage in safely, it is essential that a physician be consulted prior to training.

First published in 2013 by Empire Books/AWP.

Copyright (c) 2013 by Jose M. Fraguas.

All rights reserved. No part of this publication may be reproduced or utilized in any form or by any means, electronic or mechanical, including photocopying, recording, or by any information storage and retrieval system, without prior written permission from Empire Books/AWP.

Library of Congress Cataloging-in-Publication Data

Fraguas, Jose M.
  Wing chun masters / by Jose M. Fraguas.
      pages cm
  Includes index.
  ISBN 978-1-933901-52-7 (alk. paper)
 1. Martial artists--Interviews. 2. Martial artists--Biography. 3. Kung-fu. I. Title.
  GV1113.A2F757 2013
  796.8092--dc23
                              2013036096

EMPIRE BOOKS
P.O. Box 491788
Los Angeles, CA 90049

First edition

13 12 11 10 09 08 07 06 05 04 03 02 01
Printed in the United States of America.

"We shape clay into a pot, but it is the emptiness inside that holds whatever we want."

— Lao Tzu (c.604 - 531 B.C.)

Dedication

To the memory of Wong K. Yuen, who taught me my first kung-fu kuen and helped me to understand Chinese culture as way of life, work and art.

Acknowledgments

I would like to express my gratitude to those who provided valuable assistance in the preparation of this book. Assistance is an inadequate term for all the patience, time and knowledge that my numerous colleagues and friends so generously provided.

Special thanks goes to Arnie Friedman, the editor of the work. Also of particular assistance were Ed Ikuta (one of the world's greatest martial arts photographers), Greg Rhodes of London, England (a long-time friend, martial artist and photographer), the late John Steven Soet (director and writer), France's Thierry Plée (President of Budo Editions); Bey Logan (my long-time English friend now resides in Hong Kong), and finally Curtis F. Wong, the man who carried martial arts in America on his shoulders for more than 30 years, and who was ever-willing to share his expert knowledge on Chinese kung-fu.

I would further like to give my heartfelt gratitude to all the masters appearing in this book. They not only generously gave me an enormous amount of personal time for the long interviews, but also provided wonderful photographs to illustrate the book. Without their work ethic, sacrifice, and commitment to preserve Chinese culture, this book would not exist.

I would be also remiss if I did not recognize the many writers, philosophers, and martial arts masters whose works I have read but whom I have never met. Through the written word, their lives and spirits have greatly impacted me and given me invaluable insight. These people are treasures and my life is far richer because of them.

Finally, this book would never have been completed without the support of my family.

—Jose M. Fraguas

About the Author

Born and raised in Madrid, Spain, Jose "Chema" Fraguas began his martial arts studies with judo, in grade school, at age 9. From there he moved to taekwondo and then to kenpo karate, earning a black belt in both styles. During this same period he also studied shito-ryu karate under Japanese master Masahiro Okada. He began his career as a writer at age 16 by serving as a regular contributor to martial arts magazines in Great Britain, France, Spain, Italy, Germany, Portugal, Holland, and Australia. Having a black belt in three different styles allows him to better reflect the physical side of the martial arts in his writing: "Feeling before writing," Fraguas says.

In 1980, he moved to Los Angeles, California. His open-minded mentality helped him to develop a realistic approach to the martial arts. Seeking to supplement his previous training, he researched other disciplines such as kali, jiu-jitsu and muay Thai. His training in the Chinese martial arts for more than a decade mainly included hung gar kuen and wing chun kung-fu, although he occasionally trained in northern Shaolin methods as well. In his first struggling years he managed to meet numerous martial arts greats such as Jun Chong, Wally Jay, and Dan Inosanto.

In 1986, Fraguas founded his own book and magazine company in Europe, authoring dozens of books and distributing his magazines to 35 countries in three different languages. His reputation and credibility as a martial artist and publisher became well known to the top masters around the world. Considering himself a martial artist first and a writer and publisher second, Fraguas feels fortunate to have had the opportunity to interview many legendary martial arts teachers. He recognizes that much of the information given in the interviews helped him to discover new dimensions in the martial arts. "I was constantly absorbing knowledge from the great masters," he recalls. "I only trained with a few of them, but intellectually and spiritually all of them have made very important contributions to my growth as a complete martial artist."

However there were some drawbacks to his position as a publisher, Fraguas acknowledges, that directly affected his personal martial arts development. "Of course, some people taught me because of my position as a publisher and not because who I was as a person. Even though I recognize that, I'm still grateful for the knowledge they shared with me."

Steeped in tradition yet looking to the future, Fraguas understands and appreciates martial arts history and philosophy and feels this rich heritage is a necessary stepping stone to personal growth and spiritual evolution. His desire to promote both ancient philosophy and modern thinking provided the motivation for writing this book. "If the motivation is just money, a book cannot be of good quality," Fraguas says. 'If the book is written to just make people happy, it cannot be deep. I want to write books so I can learn as well as teach."

Introduction

I've been both lucky and fortunate. Some of my best days were spent interviewing and meeting the masters appearing in this book. There is little I enjoy more than "gnawing" on a great interview while time slows and sometimes even seems to stop. Having the opportunity to meet and interview the most relevant and prestigious martial artists of the past four decades is something that every martial artist doesn't have the chance to do. Hopefully, in some small way, this will help make up for that.

Meeting the masters and having long conversations with them that were published in magazines around the world allowed me to do more than simply "scratch the surface" of the technical aspects of their respective styles, but to also research and analyze the human beings behind the teachers. Some of the dialogues and interviews began by simply commenting about the superficial techniques of fighting, and ended up turning into a very uncommon spiritual conversation about the philosophical aspects of the martial arts.

Although they are all very different, considering their respective styles and backgrounds, they all share a common thread of the traditional values such as discipline, respect, positive attitude, dedication, and etiquette.

For more than 30 years I've faced the long odds of interviewing these martial arts masters, one-on-one, face-to-face, and with no place to run if I asked a stupid question. Many times, it was a real challenge to not just make contact with them, but also how to make the interview interesting enough to bring out the knowledge that resided inside them. In every interview I tried to absorb as much knowledge as I could, ranging from their training methods, to their fighting methods, and to their philosophies about life itself.

Their different origins and cultural backgrounds heavily influenced them but never prevented them from analyzing, researching, or modifying anything that they considered appropriate. They always kept an open mind to improving both their arts and themselves. From a formal philosophical point of view many of them follow the wisdom of Zen and Taoism, others just use common sense.

They devoted themselves to their arts, often in solitude, sometimes to the exclusion of other pursuits most of us take for granted. They worked themselves into extraordinary physical condition and stayed there. They ignored distractions and diversions and brought to their training a great deal of concentration. The best of them got as good as they could possibly get at performing and teaching their chosen art, and the rest of us watched them and, leading our "balanced lives," wondered how good we might have gotten at something had we devoted ourselves to whatever we did as ferociously as these masters embraced their arts. In that respect they bear our dreams.

It would be wonderful to find a single martial artist who combined all the great qualities of these fighters-but that's impossible. That, however, was one of the things that inspired me to write this book. I wanted to preserve some things that were said a long time ago, of which not many people today are aware.

If you read carefully between the lines, you'll see that none of these men were trying to become a "fighting machine" or training in order to create the most devastating martial arts system known to man. They focused, rather, on how to use the martial arts to become better human beings. There are many links that, once discovered, open a wide spectrum of possibilities, not only to martial arts, but to a better existence as individuals.

The interviews often lasted as long as three or four hours of non-stop talking. I would begin at their schools and finish the conversation at a restaurant or coffee shop. A lot of information in these interviews had been never published before and some had to be trimmed, either at the master's request or edited to avoid creating senseless misunderstandings later on. It is not the questions that make an interview. An interview is either good or bad depending on the answers given. Considering the masters in this

Bruce Lee & Ip Man.
"Photo courtesy of Bruce Lee Estate."

book, I had an easy job. My goal was to make these masters comfortable talking about their life and training-especially those who trained under the founders of original systems. In modern time, there are not many who have had the privilege of living and learning under the legendary founders.

"The masters are gone," many like to say. But as long as we keep their teachings in our hearts, they will live forever. To understand the martial arts properly it is necessary to take into account the philosophical and psychological methods as well as the physical techniques. There is a deep distinction between a fighting system and a martial art, and a general feeling in the martial arts community is that the roots of the martial arts have been de-emphasized, neglected, or totally abandoned. Martial arts are not a sport-they are very different. Someone who chooses to devote himself to a sport such as basketball, tennis, soccer, or football, which is based on youth, strength, and speed chooses to die twice. When you can no longer do a certain sport, due to the lack of any one of those attributes, waking up in the morning without the activity and purpose that has been the center of your day for twenty-five years is spooky. Martial arts can and should be practiced for life. They are not sports, they are a "way of life."

A true martial arts practitioner-like an artist of any other kind-be this a musician, a painter, a writer or an actor, is expressing and leaving part of himself in every piece of his craft. The need for self-inspection and self-realization of "who" he is becomes the reason for a journey in search of that perfect technique, that great melody, that inspiring poetry, that amazing painting or that Academy Award performance. It is this motivation to reach that "impossible dream," that allows a simple individual to become an exceptional "artist" and "master" of his craft.

Many of the greatest teachers of the fighting arts share a commonly misunderstood teaching methodology. They know the words that could be used to pass their personal experience to their students have little or no meaning. They know that to try "self-discovery" in quantitative or empirical terms is a useless task. A great deal of knowledge and wisdom (the ability to use knowledge in a proper and correct way) comes from what are called the

Bruce Lee practicing Kung Fu.
"Photo courtesy of Bruce Lee Estate."

"oral traditions," which martial arts, like every other cultural aspect, has. These oral traditions have been always reserved for a certain kind of student and have been considered "secrets." I believe these secrets are such because only few very special students, perspicacious and with a keen sense of introspection, have the minds to attain them. As Alexandra David-Neel wrote: "It is not on the master that the secret depends but on the hearer. Truth learned from others is of no value, the only truth which is effective and of value is self-discovered...the teacher can only guide to the point of discovery." In the end "The only secret is that there is no secret," or as Kato Tokuro, probably the greatest potter of the last century, a great art scholar, and the teacher of Spanish painter and sculptor Pablo Picasso (1881-1973) said: "The sole cause of secrets in craftsmanship is the student's inability to learn!"

As human beings, we are always tempted to follow straight-line logic towards ultimate self-improvement-but the truth is that there are no absolute truths that apply to all. You have to find your own way in life whether it be in the martial arts, in business, or in cherry picking. Whatever path you pursue, you have to distill your personal truths to what is right for you, according to your own life. The quest for perfection is actually quite imperfect and is not in tune with either human nature or human experience. To have any hope of attaining even a single perfection, you have to concentrate on a single pursuit and direct all your energies towards it. In this sense, perfection comes from appreciating your endeavors for their own sake-not to impress anyone-but for your own inner satisfaction and sense of accomplishment.

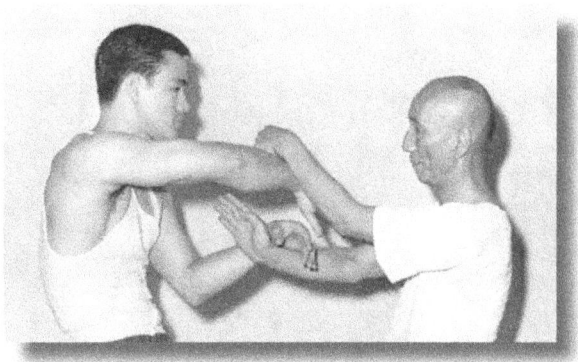

Bruce Lee practicing Chi Sao with Ip Man.
"Photo courtesy of Bruce Lee Estate."

Martial arts are a large part of my life and I draw inspiration from them, both spiritually and philosophically. I really don't know the "how" or the "why" of their affect on me, but I feel their influence in even my most mundane activities. It's not a complex thing where I have to look deep into myself to find their influence. All human beings have sources or principles that keep them grounded, and martial arts is mine. I believe that is when the term "way of life" becomes real. In the martial arts, the self-discipline required to pursue mastery is more important than mastery itself-the struggle is more important than the reward. A common thread throughout the lives of all the masters is their constant struggle towards self-mastery. They realized that life is an ongoing process, and once you achieve all your goals you are as good as dead. But this process is not all driven by action. Often the greatest action is inaction, and the hardest voice to hear is the sound of your inner voice. You need to sit alone and collect your thoughts, free from all forms of technology and distraction, and just think. It is perhaps the only way to achieve mental and spiritual clarity.

I don't believe that great books are meant to be read fast. I've always thought that really good writing is timeless, and that time spent reading doesn't detract anything from your life, but rather adds to it. So take your time. Approach the reading of this book with either the "beginner's mind" or "empty cup" mentality and let the words of these great teachers help you to grow not only as a martial artist but as a human being as well.

Wing Chun's History

Chinese Martial Arts are full of exciting stories of the origins of the various systems. Wing Chun is no different. Finding the true history of Wing Chun, or many other Chinese Kung Fu systems is difficult due to the lack of written records. Stories of the origin have been passed down orally from master to disciple for centuries. Thus it is possible that names, places and events are inaccurate.

The stories handed down through the generations hold that the Wing Chun system was developed in the famous Siu Lum (Shaolin) Temple. The system was said to have been taught to a young woman named Yim Wing Chun by a Siu Lum nun named Ng Mui. Yim Wing Chun eventually married a Martial Artist named Leung Bok Cho, to whom she taught the method. Leung Bok Cho in turn taught Leung Lan Kwai, Leung Yee Tai, Wong Wah Bo and others. Leung Yee Tai and Wong Wah Bo taught Leung Jan who became a famous fighter and Chinese doctor. Leung Jan taught his son Leung Bik as well as a merchant named Chan Wah Shun. Ip Man was passed the system first by Chan Wah Shun, and then later in Hong Kong by Leung Bik.

There are many books and articles which debate the history listed above. As we have pointed out, with the lack of written records, there is no way of knowing just how accurate this account is. There is also nothing to be gained by arguing over it. So instead of debating the uncertain history of this great system, we will concentrate on what we know to be fact. The Wing Chun system as it has been passed from the late Grandmaster Ip Man up to the present generation, through the teaching of his many students.

Ip Man was the first to openly teach Wing Chun. He began his teaching career in Foshan, China and then later in Hong Kong. It was through Ip Man's teaching that Wing Chun has spread throughout the world. Ip Man had many students, but it was Bruce Lee, the famous movie star and "King of Kung Fu" who was the most notable. It was through the fame brought by Bruce Lee that the world became aware of Wing Chun and Lee's teacher, Grandmaster Ip Man.

According to the accounts given to Ip Man's sons Ip Chun and Ip Ching by their father, Ip Man began his training as a young boy.

Ip Man (1893-1972) was born at Song Yuen of Foshan, China at the end of Qing Dynasty. Foshan was situated at the most prosperous region of the Guangdong province. Well known masters of the Southern kung fu schools, Wong Fai-hung, Cheung Hung-Shing, Leung Jan, Leung Siu-Ching etc. came from Foshan. So Ip Man grew up hearing the stories of the exploits of these great Kung Fu men. It's not surprising that he would develop into one of the legendary masters himself.

Ip Man's education in Wing Chun began as a youth when he became a student of Chan Wah Shun, who was a student of the famous Leung Jan. Chan Wah Shun rented the Ip family clan hall on the main street of Foshan in order to teach kung fu. He accepted Ip Man as a student towards the end of his teaching career when he was quite old. Master Chan was a big man by Chinese standards. So his Kung Fu was powerful. Ip Man learned from Master Chan until the masters' death, and continued his training with his Sihing (Senior) Ng Chun So until Ip Man left Foshan for Hong Kong in 1941.

Ip Man moved to Hong Kong at the age of 15 to attend St. Stephens College. There he had a chance meeting with an old gentleman who was a martial artist. This old man crossed hands with Ip Man and beat him soundly. This disturbed Ip Man very much as he had developed his kung fu to a high level and considered himself to be quite proficient. As it turned out, the old gentleman turned out to be Leung Bik, the son of Ip Man's Sifu, Master Chan Wah Shun's teacher, the famous Leung Jan.

Master Leung Bik's Wing Chun was much more refined that what Ip Man had learned from Master Chan. While Chan Wah Shun had been a big man, Leung Bik was much smaller. There was also a pretty wide gap in the education level between the two masters. Chan Wah Shun was not very well educated, while Leung Bik was the son of Leung Jan, who was a well educated doctor of Chinese medicine. This education was passed to his son. This meant that Leung Bik was better able to understand the underlying principals of the Wing Chun system. This knowledge was passed to Ip Man.

Upon learning all that Leung Bik had to teach him, Ip Man went on to explore ways to simplify Wing Chun, making it easier to understand. In addition to his education in "Wing Chun", Ip Man received an advanced formal education in his youth. He learned the theories and principals of modern science and could therefore make use of modern technological knowledge such as mechanical and mathematical theories to explain the principals of Wing Chun. Ip Man even changed terminology such as the Five Elements and Eight Diagrams (Ba Gua) which were commonly used in metaphysics. This helped to demystify Wing Chun, thus making it easier for the common student to understand and apply the system.

After completing his Wing Chun education under Leung Bik, Ip Man returned to China. Back in Foshan Ip Man began teaching a small group of students, including Kwok Fu and Luen Kai. In 1949 Ip Man returned to live in Hong Kong where he eventually began his public instruction of Wing Chun.

In July 1950, through Lee Man's introduction, Grandmaster Ip Man started teaching in Dai Lam Street, Kowloon. The first Wing Chun Kung Fu class was for the Restaurant Workers Association. When he opened the class there were only 8 people including Leung Shang and Lok Yiu. All these were restaurant workers, but later he was joined by Chu Shung Tin, Yip Bo Ching, Chiu Wan, Lee Yan Wing, Law Peng, Man Siu Hung and others. Grandmaster Ip Man also taught in the Restaurant Workers, Shang Wan branch, Union HQ in Hong Kong. Students included Lee Wing, Yue May Keng, Lee Leung Foon and others.

Over the next 20 years Ip Man would leave his mark on the world of Martial Arts by teaching those that would spread Wing Chun across the globe. Some of those who became students of the Grandmaster were Wong Shun Leung, Bruce Lee, and of course Ip Man's sons Ip Chun and Ip Ching.

The Ip Man Wing Chun system has today become one of the most popular Martial Art systems in the world. Bruce Lee was initially responsible for bringing Wing Chun to the attention of the world, but it has been propagated through the teaching of today's WING CHUN MASTERS!

Wing Chun history
by ip Man

The founder of the Ving Tsun Kungfu System, Miss Yim Ving Tsun was a native of Canton China. As a young girl, she was intelligent and athletic, upstanding and manly. She was betrothed to Leung Bok Chau, a salt merchant of Fukien. Soon after that, her mother died. Her father, Yim Yee, was wrongfully accused of a crime, and nearly went to jail. So the family moved far away, and finally settled down at the foot of Tai Leung Mountain at the Yunnan-Szechuan border. There, they earned a living by. All this happened during the reign of Emperor K'anghsi (1662-1722).

At the time, kungfu was becoming very strong in Siu Lam Monastery (Shaolin Monastery) of Mt. Sung, Honan. This aroused the fear of the Manchu government, which sent troops to attack the Monastery. They were unsuccessful. A man called Chan Man Wai was the First Placed Graduate of the Civil Service Examination that year. He was seeking favour with the government, and suggested a plan. He plotted with Siu Lam monk Ma Ning Yee and others. They set fire to the Monastery while soldiers attacked it from the outside. Siu Lam was burnt down, and the monks scattered. Buddhist Abbess Ng Mui, Abbot Chi Shin, Abbot Pak Mei, Master Fung To Tak and Master Miu Hin escaped and fled their separate ways.

Ng Mui took refuge in White Crane Temple on Mt. Tai Leung (also known as Mt. Chai Har). There she came to know Yim Yee and his daughter Yim Ving Tsun. She bought bean curds at their store. They became friends.

Ving Tsun was a young woman then, and her beauty attracted the attention of a local bully. He tried to force Ving Tsun to marry him. She and her father were very worried. Ng Mui learned of this and took pity on Ving Tsun. She agreed to teach Ving Tsun fighting techniques so that she could protect herself. Then she would be able to solve the problem with the bully, and marry Leung Bok Chau, her betrothed husband. So Ving Tsun followed Ng Mui into the mountains, and started to learn kungfu. She trained night and day, and mastered the techniques. Then she challenged the local bully to a fight and beat him. Ng Mui set off to travel around the country, but before she left, she told Ving Tsun to strictly honour the kungfu traditions, to develop her kungfu after her marriage, and to help the people working to overthrow the Manchu government and restore the Ming Dynasty. This is how Ving Tsun kungfu was handed down by Abbess Ng Mui.

After the marriage, Ving Tsun taught her Kungfu to her husband Leung Bok Chau, and he passed his kungfu techniques on to Leung Lan Kwai. Leung Lan Kwai passed it on to Wong Wah Bo. Wong Wah Bo was a member of an opera troupe on board a junk, known to the Chinese as the Red Junk. Wong worked on the Red Junk with Leung Yee Tei. It so happened that Abbot Chi Shin, who fled from Siu Lam, had disguised himself as a cook and was now working on the Red Junk. Chi Shin taught the Six-and-a-half Point Long Pole Techniques to Leung Yee Tei. Wong Wah Bo was close to Leung Yee Tei, and they shared what they knew about kungfu. Together they correlated and improved their techniques, and thus the Six-and-half-point Long Pole Techniques were incorporated into Ving Tsun Kungfu.

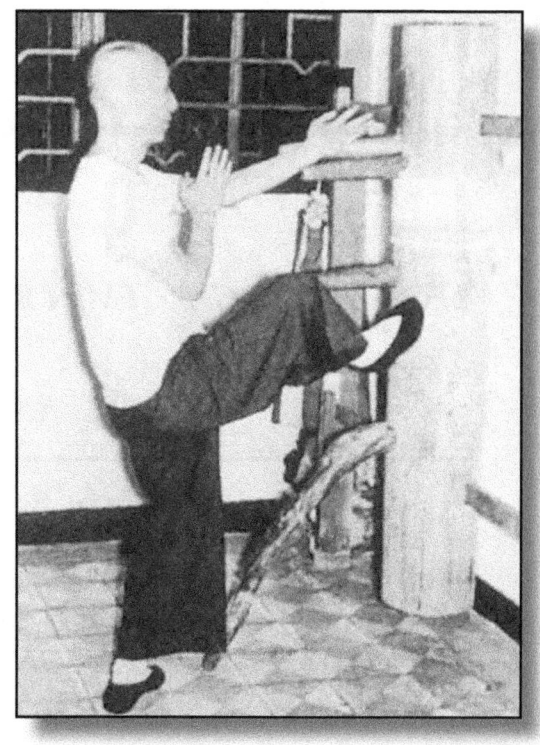

Leung Yee Tei passed the Kungfu on to Leung Jan, a well known herbal doctor in Fat Shan. Leung Jan grasped the innermost secrets of Ving Tsun, and attained the highest level of proficiency. Many kungfu masters came to challenge him, but all were defeated. Leung Jan became very famous. Later, he passed his kungfu on to Chan Wah Shan, who took me as his student many decades ago. I studied kungfu alongside my kungfu brothers such as Ng Siu Lo, Ng Chung So, Chan Yu Min and Lui Yu Jai. Ving Tsun was thus passed down to us, and we are eternally grateful to our kungfu ancestors and teachers. We will always remember and appreciate our roots, and this shared feeling will always keep our kungfu brothers close together. This is why I am organizing the Ving Tsun Fellowship, and I hope my kungfu brothers will support me in this. This will be very important in the promotion of Kungfu.

Contents

1 LEO AU YEUNG

9 EMIN BOZTEPE

19 STEPHEN CHAN

27 HAWKINS CHEUNG

43 WILLIAM CHEUNG

49 IP CHING

59 ROBERT CHU

79 CHUNG KWOK CHOW

89 IP CHUN

99 AUGUSTINE FONG

111 FRANCIS FONG

123 JIM FUNG

137 VICTOR KAN

149 KEITH R. KERNSPECTH

165 SAMUEL KWOK

183 ALAN LAMB

199 GARY LAM

207 JIM LAU

219 ALAN LEE

239 GORDEN LU

257 TONY MASSENGILL

277 DAVID PETERSON

301 SHAUN RAWCLIFFE

319 WONG SHUN LEUNG

327 LEUNG TING

335 RANDY WILLIAMS

351 LIN XIANG FUK

LEO AU YEUNG

Bringing Yip Man to the World

LEO AU YEUNG GREW UP IN HONG KONG. IN 1995, MASTER YEUNG STARTED HIS WING CHUN TRAINING WITH THE ELDEST SON OF THE LEGENDARY IP MAN AND GRANDMASTER IN HIS OWN RIGHT, IP CHUN. AFTER TWO YEARS TRAINING WITH GRANDMASTER IP CHUN, MASTER YEUNG CAME TO ENGLAND FOR ACADEMIC STUDY BUT STILL WENT BACK TO HONG KONG TO TRAIN EVERY SUMMER.

MASTER YEUNG DID THIS FOR A NUMBER OF YEARS UNTIL HE STARTED WORKING IN PRESTON, ENGLAND WHERE HE BEGAN TRAINING UNDER GRANDMASTER SAMUEL KWOK ON RECOMMENDATION BY IP CHUN. SINCE 2002, MASTER YEUNG HAS TRAINED UNDER THE SUPERVISION OF GRANDMASTER SAMUEL KWOK. AFTER THREE YEARS OF INTENSIVE TRAINING WITH GRANDMASTER KWOK, HE BECAME ONE OF SAMUEL'S TOP STUDENTS AND CHIEF INSTRUCTOR IN THE LONDON AREA.

MASTER LEO AU YEUNG HAS GAINED MUCH RESPECT OVER THE YEARS FOR HIS HIGH LEVEL OF SKILL AND UNDERSTANDING OF WING CHUN – SO MUCH SO THAT IN 2008, MASTER YEUNG WAS ASKED TO BE ONE OF THE FIGHT CHOREOGRAPHERS ON THE HONG KONG BOX OFFICE SMASH "IP MAN". NOT ONLY DID HE GET TO WORK ON THE MOVIE, BUT HE ALSO GOT TO WORK WITH TWO HONG KONG MOVIE LEGENDS, DONNIE YEN AND SAMMO HUNG.

h ow long have you been practicing Wing Chun and who was your teacher?

I have been practicing Wing Chun for more than 20 years. I have studied this form of Martial Arts from Sifu Ip Chun (the oldest son of Ip Man), Sifu Samuel Kwok (United Kingdom), and Sifu Sin Kwok Lam (Hong Kong).

I have also trained in Tai Chi (Yang's style), Hung Gar, Chinese kickboxing, and various weaponry methods.

What are the main principles intrinsic to the Wing Chun forms?

Well, the form Siu Lim Tao mainly focuses on stance, relaxation, hand position, structure, and power generation. Chum Kiu emphasizes turning, weight transfer, footwork, stepping, and isolating the stance using your upper body in order to produce more power when you are moving. And the last empty hand form, Bil Jee, focuses on elbow strikes, opponent takedowns, learning how to defend and attack from multiple angles, using up and down body positions, etc.

Wing Chun Masters

Do you teach Westerners?

Yes I do. Many of my students are Westerners; they are very keen to learn Chinese kung fu and they train very hard. I will teach anyone as long as he or she is willing to learn and has the right attitude. I disregard their nationality.

ho w has your personal kung fu has developed over the years?

From my experience, kung fu movements never came easily to me; I had to practice all the movements over and over again until they became "natural." The words kung fu to me mean training until something goes from being "unnatural" to becoming "natural."

When I first started training kung fu, I was only able to use my hand to block or attack from a certain distance. Over the years, I have learned to understand that we have to be able to use any part of our body to defend or attack. In addition, I realized we cannot just master one form of fighting or be happy to fight just within one particular range. In fact, I have become familiar with all kinds of fighting ranges, and I believe you have

"The most important point in my teaching method is to be able to bring out the Martial Arts interest from the student."

to be able to deal with any style of fighting in order to become a good Martial Artist. As Bruce Lee said, "You have to be flexible and adaptable like water."

What are the most important points in your teaching methods and what are the most important qualities for a student to become proficient in the Wing Chun style?

The most important point in my teaching method is to be able to bring out the Martial Arts interest from the student. If I can make the students interested to learn kung fu, then they will automatically want to learn more and devote more time to practice. In this way, they will have the chance to become proficient in the arts.

In terms of the most important qualities for the student to become proficient in Wing Chun, I think they have to have an open mind. For example, I always tell my students to see more of how other people practice Wing Chun (or other forms of Martial Arts) and try to understand how and why they do it differently. I encourage them to try to compare, point out where their training can be improved or how you can counter attack their movements. To understand the way other people practice is useful, as you can use it to improve and adapt it into your own training. This way enables you to always learn more and can constantly improve on what you've got.

Do you think there are still "pure" styles of kung fu and more specifically Wing Chun?

I think it is hard to define "pure," as different people will have different interpretations of this. I think if the technique works on any size of your opponent, and still follows the basic Wing Chun principles, then it is good Wing Chun.

From my point of view, different "styles" is equivalent to different forms of combat, and since we are all different in size, build, and mentality, we need a variety of "styles" to fulfill each different requirement. In addition, each "style" offers a slightly different way of training; it would be beneficial to be aware of all the different types if you want to achieve all-round training.

What is your opinion of Full Contact kung fu tournaments?

Good. All the tournaments are good because you will have the chance to put what you have learned into practice. You can also participate in tournaments to test what your skill level is compared to others doing the same Martial Art.

how different from other kung fu styles do you see the principles and concepts of Wing Chun?

I have learned and taught a few different forms of Martial Arts. I found there are some similarities between Wing Chun and other Martial Arts. Of course there are differences in terms of techniques but the overall objective in attack and defense is the same. The three hand forms are like a database of all the techniques in Wing Chun, but Chi Sao is like a writing program to identify the solution from the database.

Do you feel that there are any fundamental differences in approach or physical capabilities of Chinese kung fu practitioner in comparison to European or American practitioners?

I think the Westerners' approach to Martial Arts is more focused on the result and efficiency but a Chinese kung fu practitioner is more focused internally – the psychological effect and health of body and mind. I have met many great Wing Chun practitioners from both sides of the world, and some who can still improve, so I think it depends on your luck and who you meet.

Kung fu nowadays often is referred to as a sport (Wu shu). Would you agree with this definition?

I do not really agree with this definition as, for me, kung fu and Wu shu are two different things. Kung fu is for practical self-defense but Wu shu is more for competition.

how do you see Wing Chun kung fu in the world at the present time?

I think Wing Chun kung fu has a very bright future at the moment as there are many people practicing/teaching Wing Chun all around the world.

Does the weaponry aspect of Wing Chun enhance the student's empty hands ability or are those two completely non-related skills?

My point of view is that any kind of training is beneficial to practitioners as long as they get a full understanding on what they are doing and can relate that into enhancing their ability.

how does the Wing Chun style differ from other kung fu methods when applying the techniques in a real situation?

Wing Chun style concentrates on the centerline, close-range combat, and does not encourage meeting force with force. More importantly, it focuses on using hand and leg movements at the same time to maximize fighting efficiency. If you follow the correct traditional way of teaching, this way will lead the students to be able to defend themselves and gain good health at the same time.

Forms and Chi sao, what's the proper ratio in training?

There is no proper ratio on that because when you first begin to train Wing Chun, you will need to spend more time on hand forms in order to practice the stance, hand position, and power, etc. However, when you have achieved a certain level in Wing Chun, you will need to concentrate on applications more, like Chi Sao training. Of course, that doesn't mean you don't need to train your forms anymore. I would say it depends on what level you are at.

"Wing Chun style concentrates on the centerline, close-range combat, and does not encourage meeting force with force."

some people think going to China or Taiwan to train is highly necessary. Do you share this point of view?

If you are really keen or serious about kung fu, I think you should do it at least once in your lifetime. Firstly, you can see how other people over there do it and secondly, to understand how and why it's different and use it as a benchmark to improve your training.

Who would you like to have trained with that you have not?

Bruce Lee and Ip Man.

What would you say to someone who is interested in starting to learn Wing Chun kung fu?

Do some research about Wing Chun first and try a few different schools and compare them before finally making your decision, and then commit to who you would like to train under. Always challenge on what you already know and always ask yourself how you can do it better. The last thing is, always practice and practice again.

Wing Chun Masters

"Always challenge on what you already know and always ask yourself how you can do it better."

What is it that keeps you motivated after all these years?

My genuine interest in Martial Arts, because this is something I really like and enjoy doing. Don't forget that you are training to make something impossible become possible, and from possible to become easy and effortless. I ask myself every day, "Is there any way I can improve my Wing Chun and take it up to another level?" I don't think you can ever reach a level and stop and be done with it. It is not constant, and I will always be involved in some sort of training every day. I see constantly improving myself as a lifetime development. Never give up and always improve on what you already have.

What is your opinion about mixing kung fu styles? Does the practice of one nullify the effectiveness of the other or, on the contrary, can it be beneficial to the student?

I have nothing against mixing kung fu but only on the condition you can deliver each style properly, as each style requires a slightly different approach and set of skills. If you can master a few different arts, then it will only ever be an advantage rather than a disadvantage.

is there anything lacking in the way Martial Arts are taught today compared to how they were in your beginnings?

Yes. In the old days, you had to really show respect and learn how to build up a good relationship between your sifu and other senior students before you could learn kung fu. But nowadays, a lot of students just come and learn, then go home.

ha ve there been times when you felt fear in your kung fu training?

Never. Kung fu training is like a friend of mine; will you ever feel fear to see you friend?

Tell us about your experience in working on the "ip Man" movies.

Of course our biggest challenge was how to make Wing Chun look good on the screen, as you know most of the Wing Chun moves are very small and simple. Therefore,

"I want the people around the world to give a chance to the art and to share what I know in terms of Wing Chun, and to be open-minded."

sometimes we had to exaggerate the movement a bit, or use close-ups on the movements, in order to make them look impressive onscreen. However, we still have to keep the accent of Wing Chun. In the end, we still spent more than seven days to choreograph just three minutes in the movie.

What would you like practitioners to know about Wing Chun and Leo yu yeung?

I want the people around the world to give a chance to the art and to share what I know in terms of Wing Chun, and to be open-minded. I fully recommend the Ip Man movies and welcome anyone to come and learn from me. They will see that I am a very different from other sifus in the way I teach and what I teach.

EMIN BOZTEPE

A Delicate Balance

EMIN BOZTEPE IS SEATED IN THE CORNER OF HIS KWOON, RELAXING AFTER A FULL-DAY'S SEMINAR. CLAD IN FADED, BLACK SWEATPANTS AND A RED TEE-SHIRT, THE GENIAL AND UNPRETENTIOUS MARTIAL ARTIST IS AWARE THAT ANYONE WHO STRIVES FOR PERFECTION TENDS TO HAVE A VERY NARROW FOCUS. HE ALSO KNOWS THAT WHEN A PERSON REACHES THEIR PEAK, IT'S NOT ACCEPTABLE TO GO BACK AND JUST BE ACCEPTABLE. HE SPEAKS WITH A SOFT, GERMAN-ACCENTED WORDS AND DISPLAYS A ROBUST LAUGH. A PERPETUAL STUDENT OF CHINESE PHILOSOPHY AND ITS DEEP RELATIONSHIP WITH KUNG-FU, BOZTEPE PREFERS HIS STUDENTS KEEP IN CONTACT WITH THE "REAL WORLD," INSTEAD OF PURSUING THE GLAMOUR AND GLITTERING TROPHIES OF MODERN SPORT COMPETITIONS. HE'S BEEN CALLED EVERY NAME IN THE BOOK, BOTH GOOD AND BAD. HE HAS STOOD FACE-TO-FACE WITH SOME OF THE MOST FEARED FIGHTERS IN THE WORLD AND HASN'T BLINKED AN EYE.

A RESTLESS, SOLITARY TRAVELER EQUALLY AT HOME IN TURKEY AS HE IS IN NEW YORK, GERMANY, SPAIN, OR ITALY BOZTEPE KNOWS HOW TO ADAPT TO THE TEMPER OF A PLACE BUT YET, AT THE SAME TIME, RETAIN HIS UNIQUE IDENTITY.

What got you interested in WT and when you decided to begin to train?

I was interested in martial art since I was age 14 (1976), but later about 16 I start to look for things which could be more effective in a street fight situation. On those days I was reading the legendary "Real Kung Fu Magazine" the Chief editor was my Si-gung Mr. Leung Ting. Most I was looking at the pictures since I couldn't speak English. Then in a German martial art magazine I saw some translated articles of real kung fu specially about Wing Tsun or Wing Chun. And about two years later February 1980 I joint a Wing Tsun School in Kassel Germany under my si-hing Frank Krueger which became my personal friend and still today I'm happy to consider him as my best friend.

Why do you think your teachers took such an interest in you training?

Well, it is not easy to talk of about yourself, but I guess I was not only the fact I have always been gifted for sport but I did worked very hard on everything I got involved into. And why I was training so hard most of my WT classmates really didn't know? It was because I was always the most of the time a target of racial conflict in Germany as a Turkish person. Interestingly enough that racial feeling has not changed even to day for a Turkish or any

Wing Chun Masters

"I think that the origin or nationality of an instructor doesn't matter!"

foreigner with different cultural background in Christian Europe.

To go back to your question, I try to help and encourage a young hard working student to becoming a better fighter or one day an instructor. I believe in the Taoist way of "learning by doing" so he didn't gave much instruction just showed you and you have to figured it out for your self, in other words if you don't get it by yourself then…too bad for you! This gave me an extra will power to try to succeed, and I'm still that way under pressure and a challenge I'm at my best.

some people think going to hong Kong or China to train is highly necessary to fully develop yourself in the arts, do you share this point of view?

I think that the origin or nationality of an instructor doesn't matter! It matters that if the instructor has a good education in that particular art and did he over come his personal physical and mental weaknesses like ego, jealousy, greed etc, only with an open mind and his gola is to develop good student that one day become masters in the art. When the right time comes the you, as a grandmaster should ask yourself if you are ready to accept the fact that your students are on their won now and they have the knowledge and ability to go ahead by themselves. Many top-masters in the martial arts world are not ready to accept this fact due to other hidden reason such as monetary interest or personal ego.

I definitely encourage my students to travel to Hong Kong or any other country. I truly believe this is the only way they can keep their mind open to others and help themselves to overcome their limitation of any kind of judgment you may have to make over another style or person.

What do you consider to be the major changes in the art since you began your training in kung fu?

That's a good question but I ask myself if the arts have changed or it is me who has changed? Definitely there is an evolution in the technical part of any art but also this change in increased by the practitioner maturity process and personal experience. You perception and understanding of a basic punch or technique changes with your level of education and expertise in the art. You may find new ways of doing some techniques but it doesn't necessary you change the art.

Who would you like to have trained with that you haven't?

There are a lot of masters out there with great personality and a tremendous understanding and experience in the styles they teach. They have reached levels of skill that others can only dream of. I definitely would have liked to have meat the late Bruce Lee and Alexander Fu Sheng, but I guess it is a little bit late for that.

What would you say to someone who's interested in starting to learn what you're teaching?

Welcome to my Family. Be honest to yourself and train hard. I like people who dedicate themselves to whatever path they have chosen. Honestly it's an extremely important word for me and I try to show that in everything I do in life, not only in martial arts. On the technical aspect I would say Wing tsun is very economical and you're more protected in the way you fight in this style. In most other styles you're more open to outside attacks. I don't want to hurt the feelings of other practitioners, but if you look at karate, for example, you use outside blocks while we in wing tsun stress the importance of protecting the body to a much greater extent. We focus on protecting all of the vital, living organs of the body. I carry a passion for wing tsun and I think people feel this when I teach.

What can you tell us about your beginnings in the arts and how you have evolved as a martial artist?

Germany was not the healthiest of places for a young Turk in those days of growing racism and neo-Nazi movements. It was very frustrating for me and there were times when I really felt I was ready to kill! I was always tense, never relaxed and constantly prepared to protect myself. I had problems communicating with people and very often I was simply at the wrong place at the wrong time. Today I understand that I'm lucky to be alive. Wing Tsun was, really, love at first sight and it fit me. For whatever reason, I was a natural at it. I was always looking to prove myself on the streets and I was very aggressive because of the way I lived back then. But the thing that really got me hooked on the art was the technical aspects of the style. It doesn't really matter how good you are; it always boils down to the techniques. It's important to point out that I have never started a fight and I have never boasted about my victories. I'm convinced that I would never have become such a versatile fighter and successful martial artist without the painful experiences of my past. Later on, I became interested in the philosophical side of the martial arts and I began reading books on the topic, thus allowing me to search for and bring forward the sensitive side of my personality. Most people get started in the martial arts because they're insecure, they're afraid of things that you have to deal with in life in general as well. If you go into the martial arts, you deal with your fears and your complexes right away. There's no escape. It's hands on. You're forced to use your brain differently, you're forced to open up yourself and you're forced to learn how to deal with your own problems. Too many are afraid of such an insight and instead they fall into the trap of drugs and crime. Aspects such as these are the essence of the martial arts.

What is it that keeps you motivated after all these years?
Well, first it was the need to survive under very strenuous circumstances. Of course, as you grow up and you go deeper in the martial art way, the reason for training is not fighting anymore. The art becomes part of your life and is a way of expressing yourself and do something that you love in this world. For me martial art are a way of life, they are my life.

Do you think it is necessary to engage in free-fighting to achieve good fighting skills in the street?
I don't really think you need to go to free-fight tournament in order to be a good fighter. Of course if you do this will benefit your skill and experience but we need to differentiate between a free-fight championship and a real fight. They are two separate things that even of the participants use martial arts, the environment is not the same. In a championship – regardless of how tough it can be, there are always a certain restriction for the fighter's safety. These are necessary. In a real fight you are 'out there', no rules, no restrictions, everything is a tool to be used and there is no referee or training partner who can throw the towel or protect you from major injuries. Championship fights are ok, if you like them but the feeling your get in these competition has nothing to do with what you feel in a real fight. And I can talk about what real fights are. I believe in going through extreme situation but in a save environment for students until they are skilled enough and understand the risk of getting injured badly. This will increase their level of understanding without going to free-fight tournaments. No everybody wants to be champion. There are many people out there that only want to defend themselves and do not care about tournaments or championships.

Are you proud of being a fighter?

Let me put it this way; I don't like to fight. I don't look for people and start fights. It's not my personality. I'm a martial art teacher than can fight. I don't talk bad about anyone but if someone talks bad about me then I'll confront him. I don't look for trouble but sometimes people give you this kind of trouble. So in order to answer your question, yes, I'm proud to be a fighter because you have to be a fighter in life to defeat the odds. Fighting is not only done with the fist but also with other qualities such as dedication, perseverance, focus, et cetera. And as you probably guessed, I'm not talking about a physical confrontation.

"Experience is a very important factor in life."

What's your opinion about mixing martial arts styles? Does the practice of one nullify the effectiveness of the other or on the contrary, it can be beneficial for the student?

You have to be extremely careful or you may end up with a "chop suey". We all have two hand and two legs so the key and secret lies in using those in the most efficient way regardless of style prejudices. You have to find a way or style you like and learn how to use it in many different situations. There are certain principles or methods that can be interchanged but you have to be careful since you may end up 'confusing' your own body.

What is-was your philosophical basis for your kung fu training?

In the early years I was only interested in fighting and being physically fit, in top physical condition, but due to personal problems with my parents and being always targeted by racial conflicts I needed to find a mental balance for my inner peace. I found it in philosophy and self-help books that teach you how to use your brain and how to direct your emotions. On other side, all my friends are about 10–15 years older than me, if there is a older person telling a story I carefully listen and pay undivided attention to what he is saying. Experience is a very important factor in life. I remember to have read that in a non-martial arts book that a good master should protect his students from his own bad habits – meaning that a master how truly care

Wing Chun Masters

"A true teacher should not misuse his position as a mentor!"

about his students should not allow himself to do bad things due to ego or greed. A true teacher should not misuse his position as a mentor!

Do you have a particularly memorable training experience that has remained with you as an inspiration during all these years?

I have a fair amount of these! I had studied Tae Kwon Do before I started Wing Tsun and Escrima, there was this instructor who was very self-centered and quite arrogant. I remember that he was teaching a group of beginners and was talking about the real street fight situation. I knew this instructor that he has actually never had a real fight out side the Dojo. However he was pushing quite hard on one of the beginners and basically challenged that beginner who did not accepted the answer to the question he had presented to the teacher. The instructor got really mad and lost the control challenging the student in front of everybody. The beginner just walked up to him and punched him in the face and knocked him flat out! I thought that's funny! This is where arrogance brings you if you underestimate anyone in life even if he is just a beginner.

After all these years of training and experience, could you explain the meaning of the practice of martial arts?

For me the most important goal is inner peace. Martial arts is a journey into yourself and it is form of research and introspection especially through the hard times. It give you focus and perspective of things. In the end, martial arts is something you do for yourself, it's something you can take with you no matter where you go, no matter what your environment may be.

ho w do you think a practitioner can increase his-her understanding of the spiritual aspect of martial arts?

Everyone may use different approaches to this but personally I tried to understand the basic and fundamental principles of the arts I practice and then move to the higher level where I apply those principles in my life. In training you go from the principle to the physical technique but in life you strive to behave according to the very essence of the art your practicing.

is there anything lacking in the way martial artist are taught today compared with those who were being taught in your day?

I don't think we lack of anything in particular, maybe we have too many 'great masters' who are only interested in money and feeding their won ego. The scientific approach to training and fighting is better than ever, there are more practitioners around the world than never before but this growth also brings other negative aspects. The old relationship teacher-student is being lost, money is the reason to teach, not love for the art. I guess like in everything else in life...expansion brings good and bad things at the same time.

Regardless of style, flexibility and adaptability is the most important aspect to survive in both combat and life.

What advice would you give to students on the question of supplementary training?

Well, I don't do much weight training. But I recommend have a good cardiovascular program and any kind of isometric power training with your own body since this is great for your tendons and ligaments. You have to do the extra training in order to have the 'edge'. Just don't get caught up with the supplementary training and believe that because you have big biceps or you look good on swimming trunks, you can fight. Supplementary training is an addition to your martial arts training not a substitute for it.

What do you see as the most important attributes of a student?

His loyalty. The teacher has to earn that loyalty and respect from the student. Loyalty is a two way street but unfortunately many instructors demand it from there students but they do not give it back. They only 'take' and 'demand' but never 'give' and 'earn'. Interestingly, they preach all the traditional values in the martial arts but in the end these "philosophical speeches" are simply a bunch of word used to brain wash the student's brain and take his/her money for classes and affiliations. Don't misunderstand me, there is nothing wrong with paying for something you want, be a car or martial art training. In the old days it was not accepted the fact that a martial arts teacher could ask for money. And I don't know why because a great number of the old masters were asking either money or other kind of services from the students. Historical facts of great masters having their private students cleaning, cooking, and buying food or other kind of expensive gifts for them are documented. The important point here is the student gives

Wing Chun Masters

things to the teacher and the teacher is responsible for the student. There is a mutual obligation between them. As I said before is a two way street.

Why is it, in your opinion, that a lot of students start falling away after two-three years of training?

There are many reasons for that and they apply to every student who leaves a martial arts training center in a very different way. It can be the quality of the instruction that the teacher gives that makes a student to quit. There are cases when the politics involving the art and the people teaching the art make the student 'sick' and he decides to move on or practice other system where he finds joy and pleasure instead of friction and hard feeling everywhere he goes. Politics may seem to be fun at first sight and in the beginning of a situation but after a while only bring the art and the teachers of the art together with the students down the drain. The student only wants to train and enjoy the practice of the chosen art. And that's what the teacher should give; high quality instruction. In order to do that the teacher need to keep training and improving. An instructor should never train less of that what he expects from his students. Training is training regardless of your level of skill.

"An instructor should never train less of that what he expects from his students. Training is training regardless of your level of skill."

ha ve been times when you felt fear in your martial arts training?

All the time, when I hit the wall bag or the punching ball or I do free chi sao training or lat-sao training. I believe fear is the key that help the individual to find a lot of answers about himself – and I'm not strictly speaking about martial arts. But fear is also a dangerous ally is you don't know how to have a 'relationship' with it. Fear is your 'blood brother", it's always there, no matter where you go and the tricky part of there are many reason why the fear appear in our lives. You can't get rid of it so better embrace it and find the right way to use it.

you have added anti-grappling and groundwork training in your classes, why is this?

I did Turkish wrestling before even I decided to start learning Wing Tsun and Escrima. I never underestimated a wrestler because I always knew what a good grappler can do to you once he passes the striking distance and takes you to the ground. The current deserved respect in the martial arts world that we see these days for the grapplers is not a revelation for me. A grappler may not know how to strike – although today the grappler are excellent strikers - but once you are in a close range and wrestling with him, then you'd better be in a good shape because these guys are extremely tough. I have lots of friends in the international wrestling circuit, great guys and amazing grapplers whom helped me not to underestimate anyone. My anti-grappling is based on the WT concepts and works fantastic for the average person and even for someone who is a wrestler or grappler. This approach would greatly help him to improve what he already has. Some people may say I'm way too modern of a martial artist because adding this aspect in the arts. I see myself as both traditionalist and modernist. I adhere to the traditional values and the 'traditional' principle of using what it works. In order to do that a constant modification and experimentation is required to catch up with the times.

"I see myself as both traditionalist and modernist. I adhere to the traditional values and the 'traditional' principle of using what it works."

how would you like to be remembered?

As a good martial artist and a loyal person to his teachers and students. As someone who followed his dreams and work hard to make them true regardless how many times people tried to stop him. As a man who left a legacy of knowledge behind and, treasured his students' dedication and friendship as much as they treasured his passion and instruction.

STEPHEN CHAN

Sharp Punches

STEPHEN T.K. CHAN AS BEEN REFERRED BY MANY KNOWN WING CHUN MASTERS AS AN "ECLECTIC MAN OF THE WING CHUN METHOD". IN SIFU CHAN'S OWN WORDS, "THERE IS NO ALTERATION FROM THE ORIGINAL ROOTS OF WING CHUN KUNG FU WITHIN MY INSTRUCTION. ALL MY TECHNIQUES FOLLOW THE PRACTICE OF THE GRANDMASTER YIP MAN AND ULTIMATELY FROM MY TEACHER - CHOW SZE CHUEN. MY SYSTEM MAY SEEM TO BE DIFFERENT, BUT THIS IS ONLY DUE TO THE CHANGES IN MY PHYSICAL BODY. AS A YOUTH, I WAS SMALLER THAN THE REST OF THE STUDENTS AND WAS TRAINED BY GRANDMASTER CHOW SZE CHUEN IN HIS OWN APPROACH TO THE WING CHUN METHOD, WHICH IT WAS BASED ON HIS HEIGHT AND WEIGHT. SINCE I WAS OF A SIMILAR SIZE TO HIS, I PRESENTED A PERFECT SUBJECT FOR GRANDMASTER CHOW SZE CHUEN TO RELATE TO."

SIFU STEPHEN T.K. CHAN HAS ALWAYS BELIEVED IN THE PRACTICAL SIDE TO KUNG FU TRAINING. THIS MEANS THAT WHILE THE ESSENCE OF WING CHUN KUNG FU IS RETAINED, FIGHTING TECHNIQUES HAVE BEEN ADAPTED TO THE TRUE REALITIES OF REAL COMBAT AGAINST MULTIPLE OPPONENTS OR ARMED ATTACKERS. HE EMPHASIZES A 'REALISTIC' APPROACH DURING TRAINING WITH FREE-SPARRING AGAINST BOTH WING CHUN SYSTEM OPPONENTS AND PRACTITIONERS FROM OTHER MARTIAL ART SCHOOLS.

h ow long have you been practicing Wing Chun and who were your first teachers?

I have been teaching Wing Chun Kung Fu for more than three decades. I started teaching Wing Chun Kung Fu in 1976 in London, England. I founded the "Stephen Chan Wing Chun Kung Fu Association" in 1977 in England. Wing Chun Great Grandmaster Chow Sze Chuen is the only Wing Chun teacher in my life and I started learning under him in 1970. Mr. Chow is known openly to be Yip Man's closest student. He learned Wing Chun under Yip Man since 1957. And for your information he was the only person chosen by Yip Man to learn the Bart Cham Dao, or how we call it the "Butterfly Knives" techniques. The other two person's names are Ng Chang and Wong Jok. Both are deceased unfortunately.

What are the principles intrinsic to the three empty hand forms? Do they interrelate with each other?

Of course they are interrelated! The first form Siu Lim Tao is fundamental to everything else. You have to start off with fundamentals. It is a station-

Wing Chun Masters

"In the early days it was very difficult to learn under Mr. Chow because his teaching was non-systematic at all."

ary form that teaches the student the basics of special breathing exercises like internal strength, etc. As time goes by the student will gain strength from these breathing exercises naturally. Chum Kiu is the second form and it emphasizes the footwork and kicking techniques of the Wing Chun system; the basic ones of course. And after these two forms, the Bil Jee form only focus on attacking moves. There are eight attacking moves in Bil Jee: the elbow strikes, the Man Sao, the Bil Sao, Kan Sao, the Lap Sao and the Chop Kuen. Chop Kuen you use the fist - Kuen is the fist and it is a semi-circular movement kind of punching technique that is special and unique in Wing Chun. You have to learn the three forms before you approach the wooden dummy because the stances that appear within the three forms are interrelated to the leg movements in the 108 wooden dummy techniques. The wooden dummy form has 8 sections. Within these 8 sections there are 8 kind of kicking techniques, the highest of the kicking techniques will not go up beyond the waist level. It is all groin kicks and knee kicks.

Would you tell us some interesting stories of your early days in Kung Fu?

In the early days it was very difficult to learn under Mr. Chow because his teaching was non-systematic at all. You have to be very smart to learn things from him and the school was situated in a very poor area in the city called the Sham Shui Poo district. There were normally forty or fifty students learning during the evening and I always went to train with Sifu Chow during the day and during the evening too because during the daytime there were less people there and I thought that you could learn more. I think I was only one of the few handful of students to be taught by Sifu Chow personally about the secrets of the Wing Chun kicking techniques. Sifu Chow is known in the Wing Chun circle to be the successor of Wing Chun kicking techniques taught by Yip Man. Because of his physique, when GM Yip Man would demonstrate his kicking techniques in front of

"I think I was only one of the few handful of students to be taught by Sifu Chow personally about the secrets of the Wing Chun kicking techniques."

his students, Sifu Chow was always the chosen one because they had similar physical built, and of course he learned it directly from Yip Man. During the afternoon, Sifu Chow emphasized the kicking techniques, and he would allow us wear protective gear that would give us more confidence and more targets to attack so he could teach us the correct angle of attacking. These were great training sessions with him and I learned a lot from him on how to kick freely without hesitation.

After all these years of training and experience, could you explain the main goal of Wing Chun?
My Wing Chun system has only one goal; to destroy the opponent. A lot of people think that if you are good in Chi Sao or sticking hands, you are a automatically a "fighter". But I emphasize in all of my seminars and classes that if you are good at Chi Sao that doesn't mean that you are a good fighter! Open hand fighting in Wing Chun is a different world. It is

Wing Chun Masters

"When you involve yourself with martial arts for more than 30 years I would say that it is built into you. It is part of your life."

totally different and they are not interrelated. When you involve yourself with martial arts for more than 30 years I would say that it is built into you. It is part of your life.

What advice would you give to students on the question of supplementary training?

I train Wing Chun seven days a week with the help of weight training. I do emphasize the weight training because I actually practiced weight training since I was about 18 years old. I was very skinny then and I use them to built my physique up. It was believed that weight training slows you down, but I proved differently and I encourage students to train with weights alongside with Wing Chun training. You must train alongside with it. You just can't do weights and then stop Wing Chun training because it has to go together. Wing Chun Kung Fu is a pure street fighting art. I would not suggest that you use it in any ring fighting with rules and protective gear. Because Wing Chun actually attack the human's weakest part of the body like the eyes, throat, groin, knee joints, sternum, rib cage, etc. Wing Chun Kung Fu as an art suffered drastic changes throughout these last thirty or forty years to be a more lethal and effective martial art with an introduction to MMA and also with an instruction of other media tools that gives the students more chances to contact with other people around the world. Thus, you can compare the Wing Chun masters or so-called "masters" and their skill on the screen. It is good news to the real masters and bad news for the "so-called" masters and grand masters.

Do you feel that there are any fundamental differences in the physical capabilities of Chinese practitioner in comparison to European or American practitioners?

Teaching and developing Wing Chun Kung Fu is a very personal thing. It does not depend on the color or race of the student but totally rely on the built and the learning ability of the student. The technique applied differs depending of the student's physique. If you are smaller, I would suggest that you use more kicks, if you are a stronger tall guy than I would suggest that you use a lot of knee blocks and knee strikes and long kicks. It is very personal and unlike Tae Kwon Do and Karate where you can train together in one class. We don't do that. Everybody knows that the basic theory of Wing Chun is the straight line and the centerline theory. The shortest distance between two points is a straight line. We base on this theory to build up our fundamentals. And the student is taught to react with the autonomic reflex action. This kind of reaction enables you without using the brain to react directly when you contact with the opponent. That's why sticking hands or Chi Sao comes into use. But it's only an exercise. Unlike Tai Chi's pushing hands we tend to go direct instead of going through circles around the opponent. We use the "simultaneous block and hit" principle that enables us to win in nearly all

"Teaching and developing Wing Chun Kung Fu is a very personal thing."

Wing Chun Masters

"The shortest distance between two points is a straight line. We base on this theory to build up our fundamentals."

kind of fights within a very close-quarter range of fighting.

What can you tell us about the weaponry method of Wing Chun?

The Butterfly Knife technique we call it Bart Cham Dao, it is unique to our style and is regarded as a jewel of the Wing Chun system. Although a lot of people claim that they learned the method itself, the truth is that according to Sifu Chow, the form was only been taught by Yip Man to 3 persons. The Butterfly Knife form is 8 sections total and it encompasses all of the Wing Chun hands and feet techniques, which you learn from the three forms and wooden dummy method. The form introduces us to "Bil Bo" or thrusting footwork and "Bik Bo" and "Chui Cham", which is also a footwork method. Chui it means "chasing" and cham is "chopping". The Chui Cham footwork is a combination of Bil Bo and Bik Bo together. Normally when our students reach the instructor level they will be taught the skills of knife techniques. And usually when you've learned the knife techniques, then I would suggest that you use a pair of 5 pound knives to train with, that means 5 pounds in each knife. The knife is used to train the wrist and waist power of the students. Different horse stances are introduced which are totally different than the ones you learned in the three forms and the wooden dummy techniques; we call it Sai (four) Ping (flattened) Ma (horse stance). It is a very low horse stance similar to the one used in Hung Gar Kung Fu. It is a low horse stance and a lot of waist movements are involved with the knife techniques. This is the first time the student is introduced to the uniqueness of the Wing Chun long range fighting skills with the knife techniques. Actually, the knife techniques are integrated with the fighting skills in the Wing Chun system. They are very closely related.

And what about the Long Pole method?

We come to the Wing Chun six and a half point pole. I would suggest that the pole has no relation whatsoever to the Wing Chun family fighting system at all or to the Wing Chun family. It is 12 foot long with one end thicker than the other. The main benefit to those who learn the pole tech-

"Actually, the knife techniques are integrated with the fighting skills in the Wing Chun system."

nique is purely to increase the wrist power and strengthen the forearm muscles of the students. It was known that the pole technique was a gift from exchanging forms with other styles of martial arts in the early days. That came from the time when people were traveling in a boat called "hung shu". We called it "hung shu" which was a boat that usually took the Chinese Opera from one point to another. It was of red color and translated to English is "red boat", "hung" means red "shu" means boat. And during these times the people had nothing to do so they talked about Kung Fu on the boat and that is how they exchanged the skills and the pole technique became part of the Wing Chum system.

What are your thoughts on the future of the art?

Wing Chun system is here to stay. It is the most practiced Kung Fu style in the world and it is proven to be highly effective and practical in real self-defense situations. I only see a good future for the art.

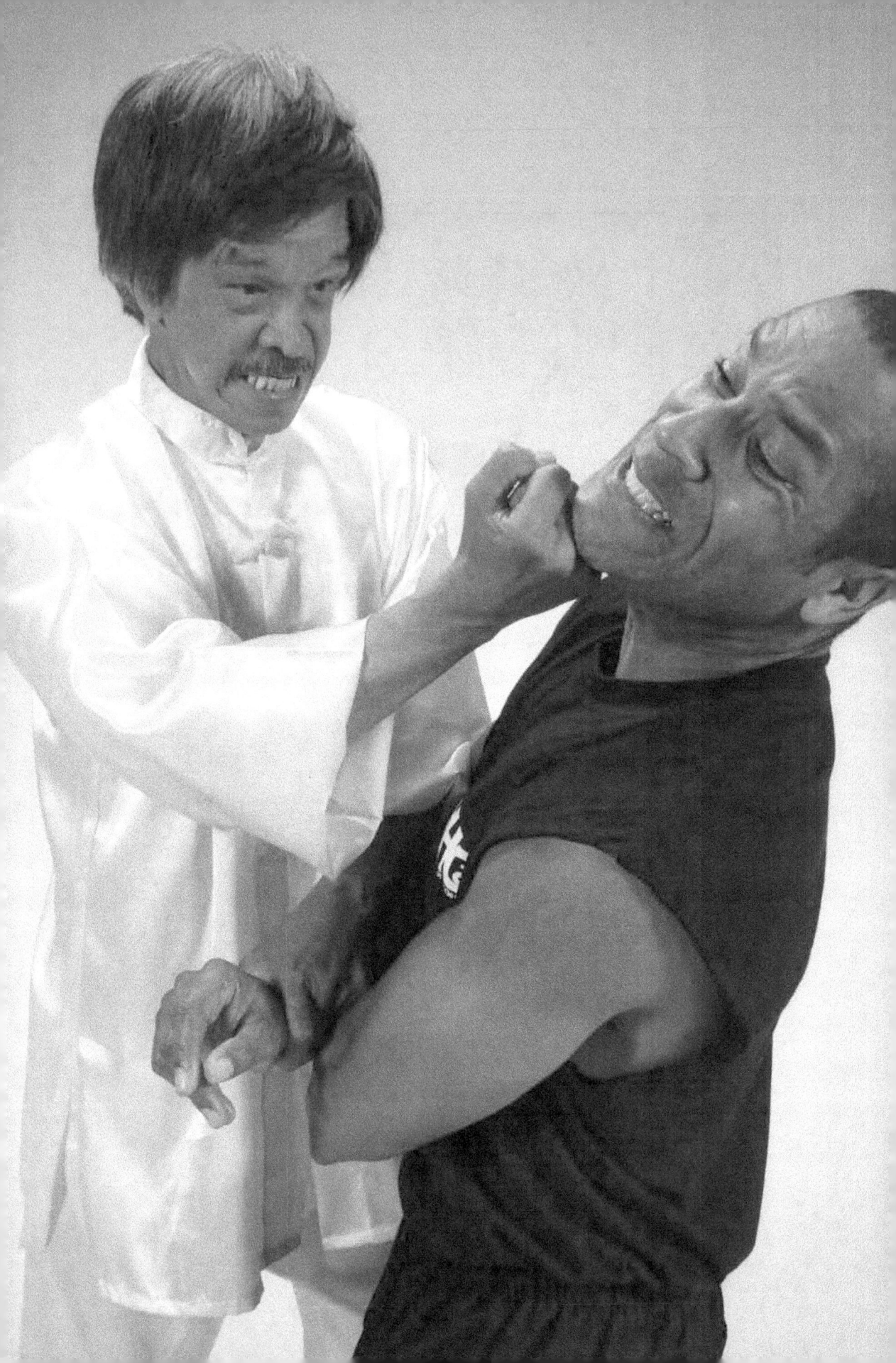

HAWKINS CHEUNG

The Invisible Thread

HAWKINS CHEUNG IS RECOGNIZED AS THE MOST SENIOR YIP MAN INSTRUCTOR IN THE U.S. TODAY, AS WELL AS ONE OF THE TOP PRACTITIONERS IN THE WORLD. HE BEGAN HIS EXTENSIVE MARTIAL ARTS TRAINING WITH GRANDMASTER YIP MAN IN HONG KONG AS A YOUTH AND CONTINUED HIS TRAINING OVER A SPAN OF ALMOST TWENTY YEARS, UP UNTIL THE GRANDMASTER'S DEATH IN 1972.

SIFU HAWKINS CHEUNG IS WIDELY KNOWN IN THE MARTIAL ARTS WORLD FOR TESTING AND PROVING HIS PRACTICAL WING CHUN SKILLS "ON THE STREETS" IN HONG KONG, ALONGSIDE BRUCE LEE AND WONG SHUN-LEUNG IN THE 1950'S. SIFU HAWKINS CHEUNG ALSO HOLDS A THIRD DEGREE BLACK BELT IN GOJU-RYU KARATE. IN THE LATE SEVENTIES, SIFU CHEUNG MOVED TO THE U.S. TO HELP PROMOTE THE ART OF WING CHUN.

THROUGHOUT HIS CAREER, SIFU CHEUNG HAS INSTRUCTED MANY STUDENTS FROM VARIOUS LAW ENFORCEMENT AGENCIES, INCLUDING THE F.B.I., AS WELL AS MEMBERS OF SOME ELITE U.S. MILITARY SPECIAL OPS - CAPABLE UNITS, SUCH AS THE MARINE CORPS' FORCE RECON.

HE HAS ALSO AUTHORED MANY ARTICLES IN MARTIAL ARTS MAGAZINES ABOUT THE ART OF WING CHUN AND HIS PERSONAL RELATIONSHIP WITH THE LEGENDARY BRUCE LEE.

how would you describe the Wing Chun system?

Wing Chun is designed as a combat system. For this reason, the system emphasizes confidence, timing, intercepting, capturing the centerline, shocking the opponent, setting up for consecutive strikes, and trapping. But the most important weapon in Wing Chun is the mind. The mind is the center, the "referee" that the system revolves around. Having a calm mind will determine your success in combat. The Wing Chun mind is the mental frame of mind you need to survive.

The basic drills "pak sao" (slapping hands), "lop da" (grabbing and striking) and "dan chi sao" (single sticking hands) give a beginning student a sense of facing an opponent. The first form, Siu Nim Tao, advises the student to 'not think too much,' and gives the basic tools and how to utilize them, as in learning to drive a car, which you eventually do without having to think. The Wing Chun system was designed to develop a person with no knowledge of martial art to eventually become a proficient fighter.

Wing Chun Masters

"The system was founded by a lady and as a result, the art requires mental strategy and physical skill and timing."

Anyone can learn the entire Wing Chun system in a short time, but it is difficult to master. I often ask my students, "You can learn so and so, but can you do it?" Being a close-range art, Wing Chun is based largely upon timing. Hitting a person just as he is attacking requires perfect timing. The question is, "can you do it?" The boxing jab is perhaps the fastest punch, and coming in on it is dangerous. By utilizing the proper timing, you can score a blow just as the jab is retracting or about to be launched.

Wing Chun is a mental, rather than physical martial art. The system was founded by a lady and as a result, the art requires mental strategy and physical skill and timing. Wing Chun requires that the mental be ahead of the physical. It is a system to develop skill, not a style.

how was hong Kong when you started to train?

Hong Kong in the 1950s was a depressed place. Post-World War II Hong Kong had suffered from unemployment, a poor economy, over-crowding, homelessness, and people taking advantage of each other. Gangs roamed the street, and juvenile delinquents ran rampant.

how do you see the characteristics of the Wing Chun system?

Each martial arts style or system goes into battle believing it has all the answers. Any classical style deals with the imparting of a fixed knowledge that becomes alive when it is mastered. It is up to the disciple to use that knowledge to develop and carry that knowledge to the point of free expression. Bruce did that. Every martial art master created something new and alive. His followers, later changed the system, intentionally or unintentionally, and made it deviate from the founder's original intention. What was passed on from then was a dead system.

With Wing Chun, you still have the tools and concepts intact. Some individual in each generation that applies the tools and concepts will make Wing Chun alive. No one can say he has the "original Wing Chun," as it has undergone generations of refinement, but if you apply the tools and concepts and can use it in combat, then you are using "live Wing

Chun." In applying Wing Chun, you have to change to keep up with your opponent's change; your target is always moving. Wing Chun is a system that has no particular style.

Any expert in his system or style has spent years continuously training the basic movements to discover the most effective movement. Every expert has to find a way to make his movements simple, direct and economical. If you have a lot of fundamental movements, you have to test out each movement to discover how to refine them and make them simple, direct and economical. This process will take years and years to refine.

When did you meet Bruce Lee?
I met Bruce in intermediate school; he had been expelled from the famous European LaSalle Intermediate School to the Eurasian Francis Xavier Intermediate School which I attended. I used to make fun of him and call him "Bad Boy" because he was expelled. That was the beginning of our friendship. There was a real political situation in 1950s Hong Kong. The British led the colony and would sometimes treat the Chinese like dogs.

We were good buddies. We wouldn't openly share our knowledge, but we tried to steal each other's card. Whenever we learned a new method or technique, we would add it to our repertoire. Bruce would use a new trick on me, the next time I would throw it back to him first.

William Cheung and Wong Shun Leung were Bruce's source of information on Wing Chun. They were our seniors, but we couldn't openly let them know what level we were at for fear they wouldn't show us more. If a senior got into a street fight, however, and lost, we could find out his standard. If we couldn't figure out a problem, we would have to ask the old man (Yip Man) from different angles.

Tell us some stories about Bruce and his Kung Fu training.
Bruce said that his father would support him and pay for his expenses in the U.S., but he wanted to be independent. To make money on the side, he said he would teach Wing Chun. I replied that he didn't have much to teach at that time; we had both only learned up to the second Wing Chun form, chum kiu, and 40 movements on the dummy. We had a friend whom we called "Uncle Shiu" (Shiu Hon Sang), who taught northern styles of gung-fu. Bruce thought it would be a good idea to learn some of the more pretty, showy styles before he left. Bruce learned northern style for showmanship.

We went to Uncle Shin's gung-fu club at seven every morning. We began to learn "lam ad" (a northern style gung-fu set). I hated master Shin's dog, and his dog hated me equally, as he would bark at me every time I visited. Finally, the early mornings and the loud dog made me drop out. Bruce continued for two months more and learned "gung lik kuen", "bung bo kuen", and "jeet kuen", all northern style sets.

you mentioned once that he got you into trouble before leaving h ong Kong. What happened?

Prior to any Hong Kong resident leaving for a new country, you had to check with the police station to make sure your record was clean. Bruce applied for this certificate, and found that our names were on a blacklist of known juvenile delinquents. He called me at home. "Hawkins, big trouble," Bruce exclaimed. "Our names are on a known gangster list. I'm going down to the police station to clear my name, and while I'm there, I'll clear yours, too." I thanked him.

A few days later, a police investigator came to my house and questioned me about gang relations. Bruce's efforts to clear me actually got me more in trouble. My father had to pay off this investigator to have my name wiped from the record, or else I wouldn't have been able to attend college in Australia.

Did Bruce mention anything to you about his evolution in the us A?

Yes, he said that in the United States he didn't have any good training partners to practice Wing Chun with. He said, "You can say that my Wing Chun is better than any so called Wing Chun masters there. I can't go any further. But I have had a lot of challenge fights. My opponents are fast, so I have to be faster; they're strong, so I have to be stronger than them. There's no other way, because in the U.S., I'm a 'gung-fu' guy. Because my Wing Chun is limited and my structure can't hold up against larger opponents, I have to use no way as the way, no limitation as the limitation."

I realized that Bruce felt frustration in his martial arts training. Although Bruce was becoming Westernized, he still felt pride that he was Chinese and he never wanted to appear inferior when comparing Chinese gung-fu with other nations' martial arts.

Change and adaptation are essential to survival. That is why there are so many types of martial arts. He insisted that like an immigrant, you have to change your ways to adapt to your new environment A good Wing Chun player is a great pretender. He can adapt and change his tactics. You must change and adapt to circumstances to survive! That is the Wing Chun mind.

Wing Chun is a trap too, because many practitioners get hung up thinking Wing Chun is the only way to fight. Many Wing Chun men are in the process of still developing the tools, so they can't begin to conceptualize how to apply them properly in combat. Changing to survive is universal, not just in Wing Chun. The frustrating part of Wing Chun is learning how to enter. This skill takes years to develop.

In Asia, we practiced Wing Chun to defend mainly against body blows, so you'll have to emphasize crossing the bridge, gaun sao and other techniques. In America, you have boxers, wrestlers and other martial arts, each with their strengths, so you have to keep aware and adapt.

A master can only be a master today. You can't tell what the future is, as the situation may change. You can only be a master up to the present. An individual has to develop, continue with his own research and grow everyday.

"A master can only be a master today. You can't tell what the future is, as the situation may change."

sifu, how important is Chi sao for Wing Chun?

The Chi Sao training is a famous feature of the Wing Chun system. Many Wing Chun practitioners overemphasize the drill. They find themselves unable to use the sticking hands in combat. Sticking hands is for contact sensitivity. At long range and no contact with your opponent, you must have eye sensitivity. The problem with most Wing Chun practitioners is they have trapped themselves with only relying on contact sensitivity; you must have both. Both eye sensitivity and contact sensitivity follow each other, where one leads off, the other follows to continue.

Chi Sao training is for you to get information on your opponent, but if you don't have the contact and are at a distance, you must rely on your eyes. Eye sensitivity takes over when you don't have the contact with your opponent; contact sensitivity takes over when you're jammed up and/or in close. If you don't develop this, you will never be able to use Wing Chun.

"When I saw Yip Man stick hands with others, he was very relaxed and talked to his partner."

how was your Chi sao when you were training in hong Kong?

I always got pushed out when I practiced chi sao with my bigger seniors. Everyone who learned Wing Chun always wanted to prove that they were better than the others. Most of the practitioners concentrated on the offensive side of sticking hands. They tried to learn how to first hit the opponent. The practice became a sport fighting game. Whoever was stronger would win. Egos ran wild and every one wanted to be the best. In Wing Chun we say we don't have any seniors because we strove to become better than the seniors and even better than the founder. If you look at your art this way, you will certainly improve.

During that period, I had a hard time. I thought of quitting a few times, until I finally went to the old man (grandmaster Yip Man). He always told me, "Relax! Relax! Don't get excited!" But whenever I practiced chi sao with someone, it was hard to relax, especially when I got hit. I became angry when struck. I wanted to kill my opponent. The sticking hands game became a fight, with both parties getting hurt. The question was who got hurt more. Because I was smaller, I was the one who usually hurt more.

When I saw Yip Man stick hands with others, he was very relaxed and talked to his partner. I never once saw Yip Man take a step backward during chi sao. I kept watching his perfect Wing Chun body structure. Whenever he took a step forward, his opponent was thrown back. No matter how big the student was, Yip Man never exhibited a killing attitude. The students would swing his hands, and Yip Man would smile and merely control the movements.

I really felt hopeless, so I asked sifu what should I do to further myself. He told me, "Why do you always want to be the same as the others? You know it won't work, why don't you change? Do the form more, don't even play sticking hands for a while. Do the form slower." I was confused; I wanted to learn Wing Chun to fight. I wanted new ways and new techniques.

So I reviewed all the forms with him and he corrected them during private lessons. I did stick hands with him slowly. He just coached me and guided my hands like a baby sitter. In this manner, I learned the softer, defensive side of Wing Chun.

When you do chi sao, you should not attack first, but rather try to collect as much information as you can on your opponent. Many Wing Chun practitioners want to attack first without gathering information. Attacking first is to give your opponent information on yourself. The forms of Wing Chun are for you to know yourself; chi sao is the way to knowing others.

When Yip Man faced a larger opponent, his skill was so high that he would shut off his opponent's move or never let it start. When you're old, you have to adapt this way to survive. Yip Man's skill in the 1950s was the epitome of sensitivity; he could immediately read his opponent's intention.

What about the aspect of trapping hands?
Trapping is the heart of Wing Chun. Sun Tzu wrote that all warfare is based upon deception, and to trap an opponent is to deceive him. When I trap your hand, your leg, or your body, your mind instantly freezes and considers the options. There is a psychological breakdown, and my opponent begins to lose his sense of confidence. When I don't allow you the time to solve your immediate problem, I frustrate you, and therefore trap your emotions. You then have two opponents against you-- me and yourself.

If your opponent is fast, you be slow. If he is slow, you be fast. You must always keep in control of a fighting situation. If a motion is too fast for the eye, it can be a trap, and if it is too fast for the hand, it may be a trap. In these circumstances, you must use your eyes to zoom in, or cut your opponent's motion by rushing in and use your contact sensitivity.

If I can trick you, I am controlling your mind if I make believe there's no pressure in my right hand, you may believe I'm not paying attention and want to attack there. But since I'm deceiving you, I want to draw your response so I can set up the next shot.

You never allow your opponent to feel comfortable, that is the essence of trapping.

sifu, yours is a very personalized method of using Wing Chun, can you explain this concept?
Wing Chun is not a style, but a system of preparation for combat. Wing Chun gives you the information to be one step ahead of your opponent.

Wing Chun Masters

Wing Chun is not better than other systems of martial arts, but it offers a practitioner some unique advantages. No matter what style or system of martial arts, to defeat your opponent you must land your tools. I can fight using Wing Chun tools. But I express my own Hawkins Cheung style based on my experience. As a martial artist, one must stand on his own credit, not his master's. When I teach Wing Chun tools to my students, I coach them to find which way best fits their character. Some students are very emotional, yet I can't force them to relax. So I teach them the offensive way of Wing Chun.

Wing Chun is very simple to learn. The system contains only three forms, a dummy set, the 6 1/2-point staff and the double knives set. It is also very easy to teach. The question is if you have tested it out yourself. Can you use the skills in application? Have you forgotten how many fights or whom you have fought before? Each style of martial arts is defensive, so you use what is useful and reject what is useless for the particular stylist. You have to find what is useful for your style of fighting. It may be useless to other stylists, but you have to change the order of using your Wing Chun tools according to circumstances.

In my Wing Chun concept, I like the opponent to start first. I will initiate my timing from my opponent's start. To my experience, this movement is a trap. When you approach me indirectly, you must have a reason why. I have to first discover your intentions. I just wait calmly. My mind becomes a "referee." To wait is better than changing. I listen to my own music or rhythm. I pay no attention, and that means that my emotions are not involved in fighting. The big question is when to start. Of course, this takes time to develop.

You will see in the "Westerns," when there is a gunfight, no one dares to start first. In Japanese samurai movies, during the sword fighting scenes, the opponents may wait for a long time. If you can't wait, your mind has to find your opponent's rhythm and starting point. From here you have to find your opponent's intentions with an "asking hand."

Wing Chun was the gun that Yip Man gave us; the frustrating part was that you had to learn how to aim and shoot. The problem was your target always moved, you couldn't get a fix on it. Wing Chun is a problem solving art. You can say that Bruce and I were given a problem from the "old man" to solve. In fact, the "old man" didn't explain things unless he saw you work for it.

how would you describe a real fight?
Having a fight is like arguing with someone. When you're engaged in an

argument, you and your adversary are emotionally charged and each side wants to speak his point of view. But in Wing Chun, the idea is to let my opponent speak first, and I will initiate my timing from his start. From that point, I shock or scare my opponent and initiate my "say-so".

Fighting is based on shocking attack. To shock the opponent with a blow or through surprise will slow or stop his attack.

A Wing Chun player captures the centerline first, which means he has the opponent targeted. If I am pointing my gun at you, and you move, even slightly, I'll shoot. Other systems want to shoot as soon as possible, but with Wing Chun, you want to be the one that draws first, then shoot if necessary. If you can strike your opponent at his moment of entry, the results can be devastating. Impact is virtually doubled.

You have basically two methods of capturing the centerline: the first is to have superior speed over the opponent, and the second is to start entering just as the opponent attacks. The key determining factor is timing.

"The centerline is the fastest line of entry between two opponents facing each other."

how important is the principle of the centerline?

The centerline is the fastest line of entry between two opponents facing each other. The centerline concept is what differentiates Wing Chun from other systems of martial arts.

In other styles, movement originates from outside toward the center. Other styles choose to use the curved line. Wing Chun is different in that movement originates from the center outward. Wing Chun is designed to cut the motions from other systems, and timing is the means to occupy the center first. It's not Wing Chun if the movement doesn't originate from the center.

One must capture and control the centerline to occupy a superior position. To occupy the centerline in an instant is the mark of expert skill, by controlling it you have immediately developed a sense of what the oppo-

Wing Chun Masters

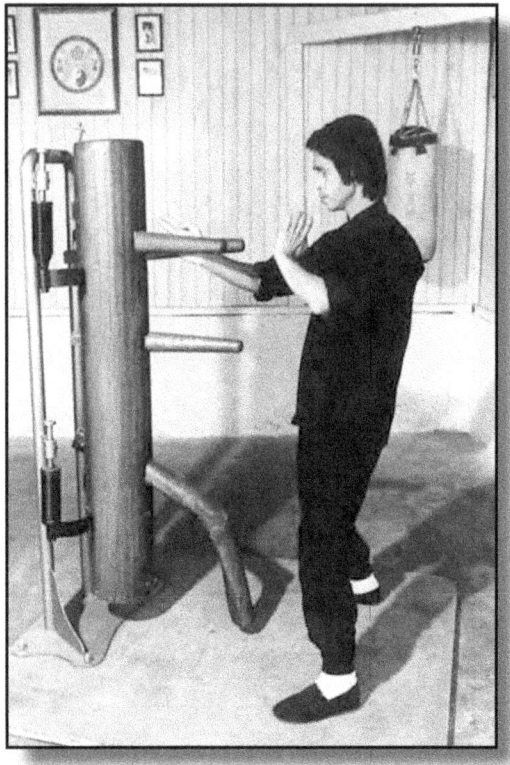

"To shock your opponent, you can use "pak da" (slapping strike), "lop da" or any other tool."

nent can or cannot do. You have, in essence, presented a question or problem for the opponent to answer.

In Wing Chun, the term "centerline" not only refers to the line in fighting, it also refers to your mind, the things you do, the problems you solve, the way that you live your life. If you stray too far to the right or left, it takes some time to return to the center. The center has no opinion.

Are you supposed to 'crash' inside the opponent's territory?

Well...pretty much so!

If you're facing an opponent, you must have the confidence to walk straight in on his punch or kick! There is no retreating step in Wing Chun; the idea is you have to 'eat up' your opponent's space and step in. It's not Wing Chun if you take a side step or retreat from an attack.

Newton's law of physics states that *only one body can occupy a space at a time*. You must rush in with absolute confidence because if a practitioner can't fulfill this requirement, he may as well study another style.

Many Wing Chun men ignore the skill of closing the gap and distance fighting. Wing Chun's famous motto explains, "Stay as he comes, follow as he retreats; rush in upon loss of contact." To "rush in" means to overwhelm the opponent with a blast An analogy of the pressure of a river behind a dam suddenly opening its gates should help you understand this feeling of 'rushing in." Seeing a whole body charge at you has a totally different mental reaction than a fist coming at you. A fist is small, but an entire body is big. This mental shock can be unbalancing to my opponent.

To shock your opponent, you can use "pak da" (slapping strike), "lop da" or any other tool. You must catch your opponent with the correct timing. When you shock your opponent, you cause him to blank out, and in that instant he loses himself and his surroundings, and there is an opportunity to destroy him! Anytime a martial artist, regardless of style, throws a punch or kick, he is blanking out because of the focus and emotional commitment. This blanking out gives you the time to strike your opponent.

how did grandmaster yip Man train the students of your generation?

Back in the 1950s, Yip Man trained us to fight, not be technicians. Because we were so young, we didn't understand the concepts or theories. As he taught us, Yip Man said, "Don't believe me, as I may be tricking you. Go out and have a fight. Test it out." In other words, Yip Man taught us the distance applications of Wing Chun. First he told us to go out and find practitioners of other styles and test our Wing Chun on them. If we lost, we knew what we should work on. We would go out and test our techniques again. We thought to ourselves, "Got to make that technique work! No excuses!" We learned by getting hit. When you are in a real fight, you find out what techniques are good for you. Just because your technique may work for one person doesn't guarantee it will work for you. When you test your techniques on someone you don't know, you experience a different feeling than when training with your friends. If you discover through your own experience, it's much better than relying on another's experience. In this way, you won't be in his trap.

For this reason, physical and strong tool development is more important than the techniques. The way you apply techniques comes from your courage or confidence. You gain courage and confidence through your experience. For application, you have to ask yourself, "How much experience do I have? How many ways can I use this technique?" There is an old Chinese saying that in real fighting, you must have three points: courage, strength, technique. Technique comes last, unless you have superior timing to deliver techniques. These qualities are of personal development; they have nothing to do with styles. Through your fighting experience, you can check your system's concepts and theories.

As I reflect, I think that if Yip Man first taught us [the students] the concepts or theories, we would follow them based on their requirements and rules. We wouldn't need to test them out, simply because the Wing Chun system already had generations of testing. We would try to make the art as perfect as Yin Wing Chun displayed. Perhaps Bruce and I would have become perfect technicians.

We wanted to find out what is important and not important when we fought outsiders. This is why we fought a lot when we were young. Only through application can you prove if the theories are valid. Techniques without timing are dead techniques. Display timing without power and the results are equally disastrous. Nowadays, many Wing Chun people have the same techniques, but how many Wing Chun people have gone through Bruce's and my development?

sifu, what really happened between grandmaster yip Man and Bruce Lee?
During one of his visits to Hong Kong in the mid 1960's, I ran into him and he said: "I have to train very hard to beat my opponents. So I've come back to further my training in Wing Chun, and I hope to learn more of the dummy techniques from the old man (Yip Man). Hopefully, sifu will let me film him on 8mm so that I may show my students in the U.S. I'm on my way to see the old man now."

A few days later, Bruce gave a demonstration on a popular talk show on television. Bruce didn't mention anything about Wing Chun, but referred to his art simply as "gung-fu." I realized that something must have happened between Bruce and Yip Man.

I found out that the "old man" refused his request to be filmed doing the dummy set. I knew that the "old man" was very Chinese tradition minded and that Bruce was very direct and Western in his thinking. Bruce wanted to learn everything overnight, but the 'old man" felt you had to train to get it. Later on, I found that Bruce formed his own method and called it 'jeet kune do."

Every martial arts student has to solve the problem of applying the physical portion. All martial arts styles tend to be theoretical in application. Bruce may have abandoned some Wing Chun tools' but he didn't abandon Wing Chun development. He changed the art for himself, not for you or me. Bruce used the concept of intercepting and "modified the gun" for his own needs. I kept the traditional gun and made it work for me. Yip Man posed the question, it was up to us to solve the problems.

What are the characteristics of a Wing Chun fighter?
The best Wing Chun players can combine both offense and defense simultaneously in one beat if offense and defense are separate, you're not adhering to Wing Chun principles. Many Wing Chun men don't realize the importance of timing which makes the concepts come alive. You have to make the opponent blank out if you don't make the opponent blank out, you have lost the superior one-beat timing. A common reason is because you have jammed up your own timing because the shock has reverberated to you. If a Wing Chun practitioner can master superior timing, he can be free from the style. If you master timing, the style is secondary. You can use the opponent's technique at that point .You have to train

to reach that point. It takes years of hard work; you literally gamble with timing.

Being physically small, I can't take a punch or a kick. Using timing and these methods of attack, I never had to draw my last card. If I had a body like Mike Tyson's, I could afford to wait and play the defensive role and wait for my opponent.

Offense is based on attack, defense is based on body structure. Offense is only 50 percent of the art. Many Wing Chun men only concentrate on the offensive portion because offense is the best defense. Mastering the defensive portion of the art requires that one develop a strong stance and correct body structure. Defense means that you have to depend upon being a half-beat slower and follow your opponent and respond from there.

For the Wing Chun practitioner, defense relies upon the correct structure of the body. The Wing Chun body structure holds back the rushing in of an opponent, much like a dam holding back a river. Again, we come to Wing Chun's motto of "Stay as he comes, follow as he retreats; rush in upon loss of contact". Your body must stay and be able to receive your opponent's rushing in.

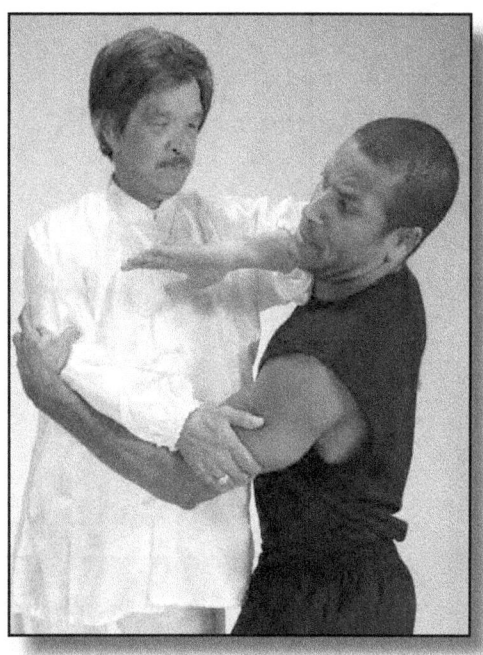

"Offense is based on attack, defense is based on body structure. Offense is only 50 percent of the art."

The principle of 'bridging' is very important in Wing Chun but how relevant is it in actual combat?

Very important! What is paramount is to learn is to control your opponent's bridges and set him up for the next shot. Good Wing Chun is like playing billiards, you must always look for the next shot. Make your opponent follow you, if you are fast, make him catch up to you. If he is faster, make him slow. If he is hard, defeat him with soft. If he is soft, defeat him with hardness. If you can master the Wing Chun principles of stay as he comes, follow as he retreats; rush in upon loss of contact, you will realize the essence of Wing Chun.

After setting up the opponent with a shocking strike you must follow up with consecutive strikes. One of the most often drilled punches in Wing Chun is called "lien wan kuen". It is a quick burst of straight -in punches

Wing Chun Masters

"Don't fight it if you have too much to lose. If you must fight, you must destroy your opponent and not stop until he is defeated."

along the centerline that continues until an opponent is downed. Translated loosely in English, lien wan kuen means "chain punches" or "consecutive striking."

Lien wan kuen is a major application of the Wing Chun principle, each one of your shots scores and sets up for the next shot. You do not give your opponent a chance to breathe. You strike and set up the opponent for more strikes until he is unconscious. You act like a butcher, cutting and hacking away at your opponent. Never stop until your opponent is down. That is the Wing Chun attitude.

What about the fear factor?
Don't fight it if you have too much to lose. If you must fight, you must destroy your opponent and not stop until he is defeated. You must have the fighting spirit and attend to the job on hand. Don't have fear, let your fighting instinct guide you in destroying your opponent. This is the kind of confidence you need to face your opponent.

What about if the principle of 'interception' is used against you?
In the Wing Chun system, whenever we want to attack, the legs have to step out before you extend your arm or punch, so you won't lose your bal-

ance. If your arm gets interrupted or "intercepted" by your opponent's pressure or power, you can still continue your attack because your body equalizes the pressure placed on you. You can still continue to extend your arm or punch while being intercepted. This is how a good Wing Chun man can use the power twice in one motion, rather than having to reload the power. You reload by extending the punch.

Wing Chun's energy is on the legs more than the upper body. Because the Wing Chun hands are used to feel the opponent's hands and read his intentions, the hands must be soft. It is analogous to a baseball catcher. You have to be soft to hold up and receive the incoming pressure. You must feel comfortable. The legs are used to throw the whole body forward, like a hammer striking a nail (a "nail" is your tool striking your opponent). This is what is called the Wing Chun structure power. If we use the analogy of a hammer and nail, the nail must be positioned in the center of the hammer, otherwise your nail will be broken or bent crooked while the hammer hits it. In Wing Chun, this means the hand is jammed or has no power transference. A good Wing Chun man first aligns the nail to the target, while the target waits to move. The hammer then follows up.

In order to accomplish this first, you have to connect your body as one unit. Then you should develop it with a partner who tries to interrupt your unit by pulling, pushing and other types of physical interruptions. If you can manage physical interruption without disrupting your body unit, then you can talk about separating your unit into individual parts. If you don't like physical interruptions (i.e., punches, kicks, etc.), then you may move your unit away before the punch or kick arrives. If you can do this, you can then move on to attacking techniques. You can also speak of unit attack with the body or either individual parts (arms or legs).

Finally, are there any secrets in the Wing Chun method?
There are no secrets. To me, the Wing Chun techniques are of secondary importance. Techniques can be learned from any Wing Chun teacher. However, without body connection and physical development, the techniques become useless. Confidence and experience go hand-in-hand. If you're not confident, you will be a disaster in driving or fighting.

To Confucius, *the centered mind sees clearly*. In life, your yin and yang must be balanced for you to be in the center.

William Cheung

A Life Vision

WILLIAN CHEUNG (CHUK HING) BEGAN HIS WING CHUN TRAINING UNDER GRANDMASTER YIP MAN AT THE AGE OF 10. A MEMBER OF THE HONG KONG SWIM TEAM, CHEUNG DECIDED TO JOIN YIP MAN'S KWOON AFTER A CONVERSATION WITH A FRIEND OF HIS, THE LATE WONG SHUN LEUNG. FOUR YEARS LATER HE DECIDED TO MAKE WING CHUN HIS WAY OF LIFE AND MOVED TO MASTER YIP MAN'S HOUSE TO STUDY FOR ANOTHER FOUR YEARS UNTIL 1959, WHEN HE LEFT FOR AUSTRALIA. TRAINING UNDER YIP MAN, HE BECAME ONE OF THE THREE "FIGHTERS OF WING CHUN" IN THE STREETS OF HONG KONG – WONG SHUN LEUNG AND BRUCE LEE BEING THE OTHER TWO. THEY ACCEPTED AND WELCOMED EVERY CHALLENGE, SPREADING THE WING CHUN REPUTATION FAR AND WIDE.

IN 1964, CHEUNG ENTERED THE AUSTRALIAN NATIONAL UNIVERSITY IN CANBERRA, WHERE HE OPENED THE WING CHUN KUNG FU CLUB. TEN YEARS LATER HE FOUNDED THE AUSTRALIAN WING CHUN ACADEMY, IN MELBOURNE, AND ALSO THE AUSTRALIAN KUNG FU FEDERATION. LATER, HE WAS ALSO APPOINTED AS A CHIEF INSTRUCTOR FOR UNARMED COMBAT AT THE US NAVY BASE IN YUKOSUKA, JAPAN. HE CAUSED A HUGE CONTROVERSY IN THE WING CHUN WORLD WHEN HE OPENLY PROCLAIMED HIMSELF TO BE THE ONLY MASTER WHO LEARNED FROM GRANDMASTER YIP MAN, AND THEREFORE TAUGHT THE ONLY ORIGINAL AND TRADITIONAL VERSION OF WING CHUN. HE HAS AUTHORED SEVERAL BOOKS ON THE WING CHUN SYSTEM AND ALSO STARRED IN MANY INSTRUCTIONAL TAPES.

When did you begin your training?

Well, in the early '50s, Yip Man began accepting formal students. Wong Shun Leung and myself were both swimmers. Wong Shun was practicing a different kung fu style. He decided to visit Yip Man´s kwoon and challenge him. After being beaten up, he signed up for Yip´s classes. He mentioned to me how good Yip was, so I signed up too.

Why did you move in with yip Man?

Some of us at Yip Man´s kwoon began to accept every challenge issued to us from other schools. My reputation as street fighter became very big and my family was not happy with that. I didn't feel very comfortable being at home – I couldn't find much warmth in the house.

Wing Chun Masters

"The wing chun system was developed by a woman, so it avoids meeting force with force."

Did you tell yip Man?
Yes. I needed a place to go, so I told him that I would do the house chores if he let me stay at his house. He said that I didn't have to do anything, just move in. I slept in the corridor in a canvas bed and ate whatever he did.

how long did you live with him?
It was around three years. He used to teach me before or after the classes and I used to help teach other students.

Was Bruce Lee one of them?
Yes. Wong Shun Leung was my senior and I was Bruce's.

Why is your wing chun different from other wing chun teachers?
Yip Man learned wing chun from two different masters. The first was Chan Wah Sun. This version was based on the centerline and it is the wing chun version that you see in most schools today. But there's an older version of the art that is not based on the centerline, and this is the version the late Yip Man learned from Leung Bik, his second master. This is the one I learned from Yip Man while I lived with him. This simple but relevant concept changes the whole art. The wing chun system was developed by a woman, so it avoids meeting force with force. In the traditional version of wing chun, the practitioner deflects rather than stops a blow. This is the reason why positioning and footwork are so important.

Did yip Man tell you not to teach that version?
He said to me that what he was going to teach me I shouldn't teach to anyone. That was his secret and his knowledge. The day he passed away that knowledge would be mine and only I had the right to teach it.

What are the strengths of wing chun?
Wing chun specializes in close-quarter combat. I teach three stages of combat: the pre-contact stage, the contact stage, and the pursuit and retreat stage. For the first stage, the most important aspect is to focus on the opponent's elbow. For the second stage we use chi sao techniques, and for the third we focus on special footwork for pursuing and retreating.

Do you think full contact sparring is important?

You can learn a lot of good things from it, but it's not necessary. Also, you have to wear gloves and that limits the versatility of empty-hand techniques. In sparring, you need to know how to improvise – that's why I use the most advanced innovations to upgrade the training methods I teach.

you mentioned focusing on the opponent's nearest elbow. Can you elaborate?

People do not know that they cannot see a punch coming because it moves so fast. With a fast punch, the fist is so close to the eyes that you cannot focus. But you don't have to stop the punch by blocking the fist, you stop the elbow. Then you don't have to worry about the fist, just the elbow because it travels much slower than the fist. Also, if you stop the punch at the elbow, the force is less, so it is easier. The elbow is easy to watch and block and will always indicate the movement of the punch.

h ow were your training sessions with Bruce?

Bruce always looked on me as a role model in wing chun. This can be a problem because you don't let your own potential come out naturally. You're always thinking about somebody else. Also, I was his senior, I had more experience at that time and it was easy for me to play with him. I was bigger than him and I knew the original version of the art as well.

What was Bruce Lee like at that time?

He was a little bit of immature and I'll dare to say that he had more or less some kind of inferiority complex. This is the reason why he trained so hard. He was constantly practicing and very hungry for wing chun knowledge.

Did yip Man tell you to teach Bruce?

Master Yip told me to take care of Bruce because we were always involved in fights and I was his senior. I had the responsibility of leading him a little bit.

Did you see his evolution over the years?

He became very analytical, very scientific. If something doesn't make sense with scientific logic, it must be wrong. He also did a lot of research on physical conditioning. Just look at the screen – he had a great physical appearance. He realized that if you're not in shape then you're out of business in martial arts.

Do you think he was ahead of his time?

Bruce was 100 years ahead of all other martial artists. Read his notes and look at what he was doing. Even today, people don't understand things he said a long time ago. Big principles, approaches, or revelations that are "in" these days, were things that Bruce was studying 30 years ago! You can see his influence in almost everything related to martial arts and physical fitness. I really think this is his greatest contribution.

What do you think about his art, Jeet Kune Do?

Bruce found what it was useful for him and he used certain logical philosophy. I don't think the name "Jeet Kune Do" is that important.

Would he have keep evolving?

He was very clever and knew that when you're young you have to use speed, but when you're older you have to find something to compensate for the speed you're losing. That's nature. I'm sure he'd be doing research to find new ways to improve his ability and gain more knowledge.

Do you think his art and philosophy was simple?

You can discard and simplify when you already have something. Probably some people have oversimplified some things and the art is getting too thin. Bruce had a lot of knowledge and there are certain things that won't work unless you have that knowledge too. You might have Bruce's physical technique but lack the knowledge he had to make it work. So what's the use of trying to copy him?

Do you think Bruce would have created Jeet Kune Do if he had known the complete wing chun system?

It's hard to tell. Bruce Lee left Hong Kong when he was 18 years old and he only knew part of the modified version taught by Yip Man. Perhaps Bruce had to look for answers and solutions outside wing chun because he didn't know enough wing chun and had to fill the gaps. Wing chun has solutions for some of the problems Bruce had. Maybe he didn't know that wing chun had a way of dealing with those tactical fighting problems he struggled with. If you know them, you don't have to go outside of wing chun to look for solutions.

What were his biggest qualities as a fighter?

I think his speed. He was very fast. He trained for that speed but it was very natural. However, I'm sure he'd change his training regimen because after 30-35 you have to change the way you train, because your body changes too. You can't go against nature. Speed and power were his greatest assets but even the level of those would decrease over the years and he would definitely compensate with other attributes in order to keep his level up.

Who do you think would be a good fight for Bruce?

I really think that there was no one his size in the world who could have beaten him. But if I have to pick one person I guess I would say Benny Urquidez. He could give Bruce a good fight. But who knows what the outcome would be.

What's your philosophy of fighting?

My philosophy of fighting is that if you can avoid a fight, do it. I don't recommend that anyone fight. But if you have to do it, watch your opponent's nearest elbow.

"My philosophy of fighting is that if you can avoid a fight, do it."

Do you think it is good for students to analyze different fighting systems?

Definitely, I encourage students to get out of the system and come back so they know the others.

These days there are many jealousies, not only in Wing Chun, but also in Jeet Kune Do and many other styles. What do you think about this?

As far as wing chun goes, I personally felt this problem. I'm sure that people like Yip Man, Bruce Lee, and other legendary masters would be very upset seeing people and students inside their families fighting and bad-mouthing each other. A junior must always respect his senior. And if the senior does wrong then the teacher will correct him, not the junior. The discipline in martial arts comes from respect and integrity. Unfortunately, some people seem to have forgotten what those are all about.

IP CHING

The Passage of Knowledge

IP CHING WAS BORN IN FOSHAN, CHINA IN 1936. HE IS THE SECOND ELDEST SON OF YIP MAN. AT A YOUNG AGE IP CHING STARTED HIS TRAINING UNDER HIS FATHER YIP MAN. HOWEVER THIS WAS SHORT LIVED AS HIS FATHER HAD TO LEAVE AND TRAVEL TO HONG KONG IN SEARCH OF A BETTER LIFE FOR HIS FAMILY. IN 1962, IP CHING AND HIS OLDER BROTHER IP CHUN WERE REUNITED WITH THEIR FATHER IN HONG KONG. IP CHING RESUMED HIS TRAINING UNDER IP MAN'S DIRECT GUIDANCE. IP MAN TAUGHT FROM HIS HOME AND TODAY THIS IS WHERE IP CHING RESIDES. AS WELL AS LEARNING WING CHUN AT HIS FATHER'S HOME IP CHING ALSO WAS AN AVID OBSERVER OF HIS FATHER TEACHING OTHER STUDENTS. IN TURN GAINING VALUABLE INSIGHT ON HIS FATHER'S TEACHING METHODS. IN 1972 GRAND MASTER IP MAN DIED. IP CHING CONTINUED TEACHING WHILST RUNNING A MANUFACTURING BUSINESS. IN 1994 HE RETIRED FROM HIS WORK AND DECIDED TO OPEN HIS DOORS TO FULL TIME, TEACHING WING CHUN ACROSS THE GLOBE. A WISE MAN WITH GREAT EXPERIENCES AND HISTORY, IP CHING TAUGHT IN IP MAN'S CLASSES FOR MANY MULTIPLE YEARS AND AFTER HIS FATHERS LAST DAYS. SIFU IP CHING IS A TREASURE AND HONOR TO THE TITLE OF MARTIAL ARTS.

how long have you been practicing the martial arts and who were your first teachers?

I began training with my father as a child, and continued training when my father went to Hong Kong. I resumed training with my father when I joined him in Hong Kong in 1962. My father was my only teacher. During the 10 years between the time I arrived in Hong Kong and the death of my father, I trained and lived with him. During that time my father taught privately a lot and I was usually the assistant and training partner of those he was teaching.

how many styles of Martial Arts have you trained in?

I was born in Foshan, China. This is a very famous area for Kung Fu. The area was not only the home of my father Ip Man, but also famous masters from other systems, such as Wong Fei Hung from the Hung Kuen system. So, being from this area I had the opportunity of seeing a lot of Kung Fu methods. But, because of my father and the practicality of Wing Chun, I chose to ground my studies in that method. So my background is just in Wing Chun.

Wing Chun Masters

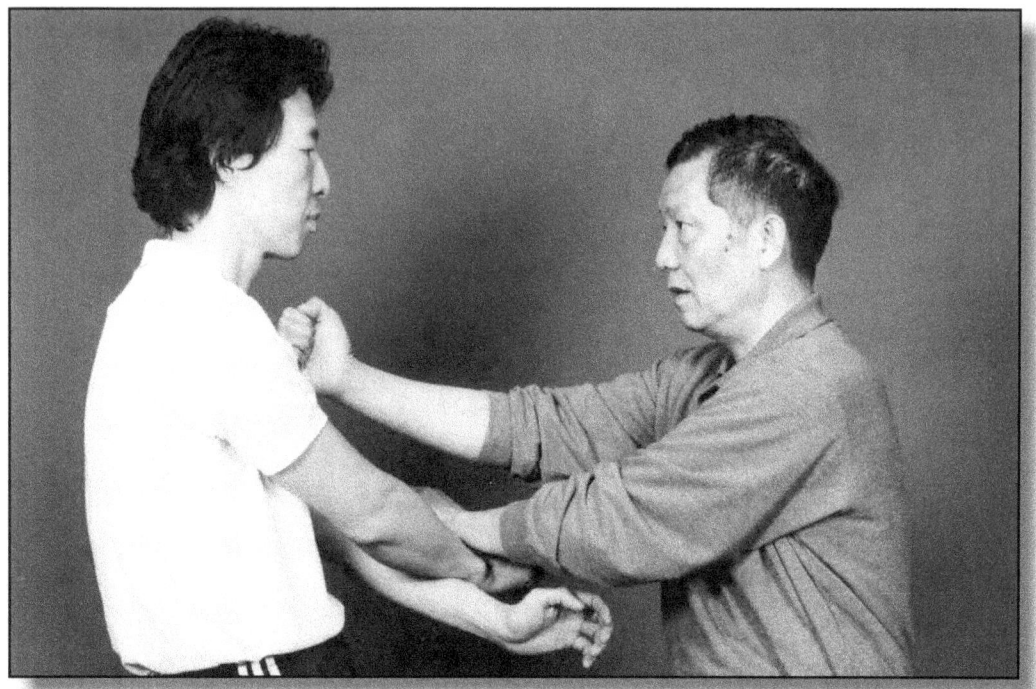

"There really is nothing new in Mixed Martial Arts. It goes all the way back to the Greeks, and they had what we are calling Mixed Martial Arts now."

What are the main principles intrinsic to siu Lim Tao, Chum Kiu and Bil Jee? Do they interrelate with each other?

The empty hand forms lay the structural foundation for the Wing Chun system. Each one builds on the foundation laid by the previous form. In Siu Lim Tao, the student is given the introduction to the defensive and offensive tools as well as the root stance from which the fighting footwork will be based.

In Chum Kiu the student learns how to apply the tools developed in the first form against an opponent. In this form footwork is trained and the student encounters the principle of Yiu Ma - "Waist Energy". It is here that the student begins to learn the power base of Wing Chun.

The third form, Biu Gee teaches the student the power of relaxation in application of technique. Here they will learn about Whipping Energy and recovery from a lost position. These forms all come together in the training of Chi Sao. Chi Sao is the bridge between forms and fighting. Chi Sao is the skill of Wing Chun.

how did you find the Westerners respond to traditional Chinese training?

Some westerners do well but many do not have the patience to train in a traditional sense. Too many are more interested in having a title (Master, Sifu) rather than developing the knowledge and skill necessary to earn those titles. The eastern student is generally more willing to follow the teachers timetable for advancement, where the western student seems to want everything "Right Now", and if they do not feel they are advancing fast enough, they will start trying to learn from other students, or the internet. This creates a problem for the teacher, who is trying to make sure all of the key points are understood and the student has gained the necessary mastery of the foundation methods upon which more advanced methods are built.

how has your personal kung fu has developed over the years?

Naturally as you mature, your understanding matures as well. I have learned to rely on structure more and more as I have continued to study Wing Chun. One of the main keys to learning Wing Chun is learning not to rely on muscular strength in the application of technique. One must learn to use the body as a whole to provide the needed power for the method. Learning to apply Yiu Ma - "Waist Energy" and not muscle makes a great difference in power and control of the opponent.

With all the technical changes during the last 30 years, do you think there are still 'pure' styles of kung fu?

I don't believe there are any pure systems. I believe every system evolves somewhat with each person who learns it. Everyone will perform differently based on a number of factors, such as body type, height, weight, past experience, and reason for learning.

Do you think different 'styles' are truly important in the art of kung fu? Why?

I guess different people have different needs. Having a variety of different systems fulfills the needs of different people.

What is opinion of Full Contact kung fu tournaments?

Anytime you have rules, and you must have rules in any kind of sporting events in order to protect the competitors, you must understand that it is not real. Even if the contact is real, rules make it much less than real fighting. We train to develop conditioned reflex. If those conditioned reflexes are based on a sport with limiting rules, you may not respond as you need to in a real situation

how different from other kung fu styles do you see the principles and concepts of Wing Chun?

Wing Chun is based on efficiency. There is no wasted motion. Wing Chun is simply about being efficient in a real fight. As far as other systems are concerned, I have only trained in Wing Chun so I will not make a statement about systems I have not trained in.

Do you feel that there are any fundamental differences in approach or physical capabilities of Chinese kung fu practitioner in comparison to European or American practitioners?

The standard of Wing Chun in Europe is very high. In the United States the level is very inconsistent. Some are good, but many are not. Unfortunately there have been many instructors who have misrepresented their background and knowledge of Wing Chun and have not been teaching a very high standard. While this is not the fault of the student, they have been the victims of unscrupulous people who have set themselves up as instructors without a thorough knowledge of the system. I think the differences are more in quality of instruction available rather in ability of the students themselves.

Kung fu is nowadays often referred to as a sport (wu shu)… would you agree with this definition?

Real Kung Fu was and still is a Martial system. A method of beating the opponent in a real and violent encounter. Sporting rules dilute the real systems and make them less than the originally were.

Do you feel that you still have further to go in your studies of the art of Wing Chun?

As long as one is alive, they have the opportunity to increase their understanding of Kung Fu. So I feel that I will continue to understand better as time passes.

how do you see Wing Chun kung fu in the world at the present time?

The system is very popular, however the standard is very inconsistent. What my father taught has been diluted in many cases and the integrity of Ip Man's Wing Chun is in danger of disappearing if we can not standardize his teachings.

Does the weaponry aspect of Wing Chun enhance the student's empty hands ability or are those two completely non-related skills?

The pole training develops the students power and understanding. The

"Reflex action is built by way of sensitivity training drills, which make the application of defense and attack much more reliable."

knives have footwork and principles not found in the empty hand system. These things will enhance the students empty hand skills.

how does the Wing Chun style differ from other kung fu methods when applying the techniques in a self-defense situation?

I can only tell you how Wing Chun is applied in a fight. I cannot speak of systems I have not trained in. Wing Chun is built on a foundation of simplicity and efficiency. Kicks are to low targets, application is at close range, which is where real fights occur. Reflex action is built by way of sensitivity training drills, which make the application of defense and attack much more reliable.

When teaching the art of kung fu – what is the most important element; self-defense, health or tradition?

I believe all are equally important. You can not fight if you are not in good health. You may loose your health if you can not protect yourself. And without tradition, you will have no understanding of what you are learning. So I believe all are needed to form a complete martial system.

Wing Chun Masters

"Without proper dedication to training, people can not progress and develop the skill of Wing Chun."

Forms and chi-sao, what's the proper ratio in training?

The forms give the student the proper structure for the techniques employed in Chi Sao. Chi Sao teaches the student application, use of energy, direction of energy and sensitivity. Chi Sao teaches the student how to control the opponent. So after developing the structure in the forms, Chi Sao should be a major portion of training. My father considered Chi Sao to be the genius of the Wing Chun system. I would have to agree with this opinion. In a fight, you may be able to get lucky and hit the opponent, but if you can control the opponent, you can hit him easily.

Do you have any general advice you would care to pass on to the practitioners in general?

Practice. Too many students neglect their training time. Without proper dedication to training, people can not progress and develop the skill of Wing Chun. There are several things needed to become good at Wing Chun. The student has to find a good instructor who not only understands the system, but is concerned with passing that knowledge to their student. The student has to have a good work habit. The teacher can present the knowledge, but he cannot develop the skill for the student, that is up to the student.

some people think going to China or Taiwan to train is highly necessary, do you share this point of view?

Training in Hong Kong is very educational for foreign students. Here in Hong Kong the student gets a glimpse of the culture and history of the system. Visiting Foshan is also very beneficial. The Ip Man Tong (museum) in Foshan is a wonderful experience for those following my father's method. But visiting China is not necessary to learning the system. The student needs only to find a good teacher. Fortunately, there are competent teachers all over the world, but the student must be sure to find a good one, as there are a lot of bad ones as well!

What do you consider to be the major changes in the art since you began training?

The art hasn't changed a lot, just my understanding of it. One thing that has improved the ability to learn the system is the invention of the video camera. Today the student does not have to rely only on his memory, but can easily film the lesson from the teacher, and is able to catch more details of the lesson.

What would you say to someone who is interested in starting to learn Wing Chun kung fu?

Wing Chun is a very good method for someone interested in realistic Martial skills. Just train hard and gain an understanding of the principles of the art.

What is it that keeps you motivated after all these years?

I want to see my father's method survive into the future. My wish is to maintain the integrity of the Wing Chun system.

Do you think it is necessary to engage in free-fighting to achieve good self-defense skills in the street?

Wing Chun is a fighting system. Free-fighting or Chi Sao is necessary in order to develop an understanding of the proper timing, pressure, energy and application.

What is your opinion about mixing kung fu styles? Does the practice of one nullify the effectiveness of the other or on the contrary, it can be beneficial to the student?

I have never found it necessary to mix anything with Wing Chun.

What is the philosophical basis for your kung fu training?

Kung Fu originally is about being able to protect yourself. This is the chief aim of Wing Chun training.

Wing Chun Masters

"Chi Sao is the skill of Wing Chun, and control of the opponent is the skill of Chi Sao."

how are chi-sao aspects of training related to the practical application of the Wing Chun techniques used in the three empty hands forms?

As I explained earlier, the forms are the structural frame work of the system, but Chi Sao is the skill of application. Chi Sao is the skill of Wing Chun, and control of the opponent is the skill of Chi Sao. Too many trainees concentrate too much on hitting each other rather than in controlling the training partner. The most important point for a student to become proficient is that of patience. They must thoroughly learn the method and underlying principles of each step, and not rush on to more advanced training than they are ready for. Relaxation is also a major key to developing Chi Sao. Many students use too much muscular strength and turn Chi Sao into a wrestling match rather than the reaction and sensitivity exercise it is designed to be.

is there anything lacking in the way martial arts are taught today compared to how they were in your beginnings?

Patience. Students today do not seem to have the patience that was required in the old days. Respect is also a virtue that seems to be lacking in many students in today's world.

Could i ask you what you consider to be the most important qualities of a successful kung fu practitioner?

Having a genuine love for the art. Without that the student will not last long, and will be unwilling to do the training necessary to develop the skill.

What advice would you give to students on the question of supplementary training?

Conditioning is important to ones health. But in a real self-protection situation as opposed to a sporting contest, knowledge and skill are more important than conditioning.

What do you see as the most important attributes of a student?

Patience, dedication to training, and honesty.

Why is it, in your opinion, that a lot of students start falling away after two-three years of training?

A lack of a real love for the art, and as mentioned before, a lack of patience. Many people today who begin training in the martial arts do so as a hobby. In times past, people trained out of a true love of the martial arts, or out of a need for self-defense. Today however, many people go out and see a martial arts movie and think it would be a fun thing to do. They do not have a deep interest, but see it just as any other recreational activity, so they lose interest quickly. Today, true martial artist are very hard to find.

What are your thoughts on the future of the art?

It is important that we maintain proper standards if the Wing Chun system is to survive. It would be very sad to see this system become extinct after just a few generations. Unfortunately we can't stop people from teaching improper methods and poor standards. We can only ensure that our Wing Chun is of proper standard.

ROBERT CHU

The Perfect Balance

ROBERT CHU (CHU SAU LEI) BEGAN PRACTICING THE MARTIAL ARTS IN THE EARLY 1970S. HE SPECIALIZES IN COMBAT APPLICATIONS AND HEALTH ASPECTS WITH A FOCUS ON THE YIP MAN WING CHUN KUEN SYSTEM AS TAUGHT BY HAWKINS CHEUNG AND THE YUEN KAY-SAN AND GULAO WING CHUN KUEN SYSTEMS AS TAUGHT BY KWAN JONG-YUEN. A WRITER ON HIS OWN RIGHT, HE IS THE CO-AUTHOR OF COMPLETE WING CHUN, AND HAS WRITTEN NUMEROUS ARTICLES FOR SEVERAL MARTIAL ARTS PUBLICATIONS. IN ADDITION TO HIS WING CHUN TRAINING, SIFU CHU HAS INSTRUCTOR RANKINGS IN HUNG GAR KUEN AND LAMA KUNG FU. ALSO A LICENSED ACUPUNCTURIST/CHINESE HERBALIST, ROBERT CHU CURRENTLY TEACHES WING CHUN PRIVATELY IN THE PASADENA, CALIFORNIA AREA.

A FACULTY TEACHER AT SAMRA UNIVERSITY OF ORIENTAL MEDICINE AND A FACULTY PROFESSOR OF TAI JI QUAN AND QIGONG AT LOYOLA LAW SCHOOL, AND CHIEF INSTRUCTOR OF TAI JI QUAN AND QI GONG AT THE ST. VINCENT HOSPITAL CENTER FOR HEALTH AND HEALING IN LOS ANGELES, ROBERT CHU IS ONE OF THE MOST RESPECTED INSTRUCTORS IN THE MARTIAL ARTS COMMUNITY, NOT ONLY FOR HIS INSIGHT IN THE COMBATIVE ARTS BUT FOR HIS DEEP KNOWLEDGE OF THE HEALING TECHNIQUES AS WELL – A PERFECT BALANCE.

h ow long have you been practicing the martial arts?

I started martial arts during my youth, about 7 years old. My grandfather was a practitioner of Shaolin martial arts and tai ji quan and several times when I acted up, I was punished by having to stand in a corner in a horse stance. Little did I know that was basic training in the martial arts.

I trained primarily in Shaolin, hung gar, and wing chun kuen in my youth. As I matured, I became interested in xing yi, tai ji quan and ba gua, and Mi Zong lama quan. I was also one of the last disciples of the late master, Lui Yon Sang, the grandmaster of the fei lung fu mun (Flying Dragon/Tiger System). I was fortunate to have received the complete transmission from him personally. Despite all my cross training, I view my personal style as wing chun. I practice and teach tai ji quan also, but I feel wing chun is more closely suited to my personality.

Who were your primary instructors?

I studied with many teachers in New York Chinatown, and wanted to

Wing Chun Masters

"I was also seeking a system that suited me best personally, and I wanted to sample what I could."

explore the Chinese martial arts as extensively as I could. I thought all systems had their good and bad points, and I thought to cross train and improve myself with the various systems. Also, as young man, I was also seeking a system that suited me best personally, and I wanted to sample what I could. New York Chinatown had all systems - 7 star praying mantis, white crane, Lion Fist, hung gar, bak mei, lung ying mor kiu, hung fut, Northern shaolin kung fu and many other systems. Some masters in Chinatown were masters of legitimate systems, some masters just made things up. At age 14, I studied some wing chun basics with a friend of mine, Jeung Ma Chut, who studied the Jiu Wan system. Later another friend, Eric Kwai, who was a student of Moy Yat, and I had a gong sao match, and although I beat him, his close quarters fighting skill was apparent, so I wanted to learn some of his basics in exchange for some fighting techniques. Eric suggested I continue my studies with one of Moy Yat's top students, so I learned from Lee Moy Shan. Because of a falling out with Lee Moy Shan, I left to study the Gu Lao and Yuen Kay Shan systems of wing chun under Kwan Jong Yuen, a good friend and generous teacher. I later went to seek out Master Hawkins Cheung in wing chun and have been with him since 1988. He is truly a master and an honorable man and it is his methods that I primarily use.

I trained in hung gar under Yee Chi Wai (Frank Yee). Yee is the successor to the Tang Fong system of hung gar, and I studied the major forms and weaponry of this system with him. He also introduced me to mi zong lama pai master, Chan Tai Shan, with whom I studied.

I studied Yang style tai ji quan and hebei xing yi under Kou Min Tang General and Chiang Kai Shek's personal bodyguard, Wang Shin Liu. Wang Lao Shi was a General in the KMT army and studied military science in Japan. He was a student of Yang Cheng Fu's disciple, Zhu Gui Ting. When the Japanese invaded China, Wang led many troops to do battle with the Japanese. Wang was also a master of Xing Yi which he learned from Zhu Gui Ting, who studied with Li Cun Yi, so I am proud to have learned these martial arts from a man who used the arts in the battlefield. Wang went to Taiwan when the Communists took over China, then later retired in New York City.

I also studied briefly under the late Kenny Gong, exploring his xing yi. Master Gong taught me the Five Elements, za shi chui and 12 animal forms, and I was very interested in the internal power that was cultivated in xing yi. Master Gong influenced me to seek internal power in all the arts I studied.

I was one of the last disciples of fei long fu mun under the late Lui Yon Sang. Master Lui was 83 years old at that time and many of the top young masters in New York Chinatown studied with him. He was interesting because his art primarily consisted of weaponry, most notably the pole and the spear. His fist art came from one of the greatest Southern fist masters of all time -- Leung Tien Chiu. Lui taught primarily san sao and two man work when it came to empty hands. His art was simple, yet very devastatingly effective.

Since most of Lui's students were experts in other systems of martial arts, I was introduced to yin fu ba gua under my fellow training brothers, Chan Bong and Thomas Lee, who studied under Wang Han Zi. I later continued more studies of yin fu ba gua quan under He Jing Han of Taiwan.

Would you tell us some interesting stories of your early days in kung fu training?

New York Chinatown was a mecca of Chinese martial arts and it was always exciting to meet other practitioners. I would often go and visit my friends from other schools and we would engage in "gong sao" (fighting matches) and exchanges with others. Most of the time, we would want to see the forms of the people we fought against – this led to comparison and trading arts. For example, I would fight a guy and if I didn't do so good, then I would study fighting methods and a set with him so I could improve my weakness. In this way, I became familiar with the strong points of many styles, and saw how each approached their training from. It was real exciting and fun. Also, there are a lot of family associations in Chinatown – Oak Tin, Jung Shan, Chinese Restaurant Worker's Association which sponsored spaces for visiting or local masters and I might have some friends who were studying or practicing there. I would often go and visit other martial artists and try to pick their brains on how to improve, or just to compare how their martial arts were practiced.

Were you a "natural" at martial arts – did the movements come easily to you?

I was no natural – in fact, I was rather skinny and uncoordinated when young. I was tall and lanky compared to the average Cantonese. I did have one advantage -- I had great flexibility with my legs, and usually beat most Southern fist practitioners with my legs. In martial arts, natural athletes rarely last. The martial arts are an acquired skill; they have to be learned. Some people learn things quickly and just burn out quickly. I also think if you have a burning desire to learn, then you will excel and continue practicing. There's a saying in Chan (Zen) – "No doubt, no attainment; little doubt little attainment; big doubt, big attainment." I'm a firm believer in that. Today's experts and masters all had to study real hard to get where they are today. No one just gets it handed to him. Some think they can buy martial arts knowledge. I think money may open up the doors, but when it comes to using it, you have to have it in your body, so hard work is essential.

h as your personal martial art changed over the years?

I think it develops as you mature. For example, in my youth fighting was something that was natural – you did it for survival or for the sake of ego. Martial arts were something that led to big delusions – jealousy, hatred, ignorance. I see most practitioners still stuck there today. I saw a lot of guys get involved with the secret societies and with underground activities, and saw many lives ruined. I think that ultimately in martial arts, a small Dao (Way) should lead into a big Dao (way) – you use the arts to temper yourself and as a method to cross over from greed, anger, stupidity. This way you can be more in harmony with yourself and your world.

Physically, one has less time to train when he gets older, so one has to continue to practice basic "gung" (work) - that is, basic exercises to maintain strength, flexibility, and timing. Nothing leaves the basics. Advanced work is just the basics applied.

With all the technical changes, do you think there is still a "pure" system of kung fu?

Pure? I think there is no such thing as "pure" – it's an illusion. For example, everyone has his/her own personal style – you eventually express it when you reach the highest level where art and personality match. Martial arts are both an art and a science. In wing chun, the art is scientific because it gives you tools and if you properly replicate them, you can have the same results. The art is flexible in that it allows for personal expression. Personal expression is the art part. You learn the tools, then apply them; you don't learn the fighting forms of your master to copy their style. For example, no one in Yip Man wing chun fights exactly the same as Yip Man did - it is not a style that you learn to fight with and duplicate your master. The system is based on the most effective use of human body and proper timing and positioning. Everything is dependent upon the moment and the energy that the opponent gives us. People are not entirely correct when they think that wing chun is only scientific and based on physics - the basics are the science, but the expression in application is the art. In wing chun, nobody teaches you step by step what to do in "chi sao" (sticking hands) or what to do when attacked spontaneously -- you have to develop yourself to utilize it. We're not a paint by numbers system.

"The art is flexible in that it allows for personal expression. Personal expression is the art part."

Wing Chun Masters

"You study martial arts for you – not for what names you can drop."

All of the founders of the above martial arts must have had some training elsewhere in order to create their system, so only people under that rigid thought of "lineage" try to be pure. Ed Parker said it best – "When pure fist meets pure flesh – that's pure." Too many Chinese people are hung up with pure lineage, authentic transmission, from the grandmaster. I see Americans buying into that also, because they were trained in that way. I think it's rigid. You study martial arts for you – not for what names you can drop. All those names and credentials don't help when you're being attacked. This is why I have a motto, "Let application be your sifu; let function rule over form." In that way, you really weed out the non functional and learn to use your core system.

Would you talk about different wing chun styles or methods?
Sure. There are many schools of wing chun. There's Yip Man, Yuen Kay Shan, Gu Lao, Pao Fa Lien, Chi Sim Weng Chun, Pan Nam and others. Of course, the best known is the school of Yip Man, and within it, there are many branches based on what the first generation students of Yip Man interpreted. For example, Leung Ting's association is known worldwide

and reflects his teachings. William Cheung is also very famous and teaches his interpretation of what Yip Man taught him. I was lucky and was able to study many wing chun systems in the Yip Man family, but I concentrated on studying more of what Hawkins Cheung taught me. Hawkins' style I feel is unique, his wing chun emphasizes body structure and stresses combat applications. When I went to him, I already knew the entire system and had practiced wing chun for over 11 years. Hawkins told me that knowing forms wasn't enough – I had to concentrate on application. I thought, who is this cocky guy? Later I found out that he could back up everything he said.

When I studied with Hawkins, I found that the real DNA of wing chun is body structure, and this is what permeates in the application of it. What I was lacking in my previous study was how to use body power. When I learned this, it made sense, for after all, Yip Man was a small man - how could he beat bigger, huskier people like Leung Sheung, Tsui Sheung Tien, Lok Yiu and Wong Shun Leung, unless he had a mastery over body structure?

Some have speculated special or secret techniques, or another secret system, but this is not so. The truth is one either develops body structure or doesn't. With advanced practitioners of wing chun – the lineage isn't important -- what I noticed was only a small handful of people had body structure. Most didn't. Even experts with 10 or 20 years practice still topple over during "chi sao" or go flying around the room. It's a shame.

Anyway, I also went to Hong Kong and Taiwan visited the elders of the system, including Wong Shun Leung, Tsui Sheung Tien, Lo Man Kam, Koo Sang and others. I also studied with William Cheung for a while. So my grounding is based mostly on the Yip Man system. I've also had the opportunity to study the Yuen Kay Shan system thoroughly, under my Sifu, Kwan Jong Yuen, and through my co-author, Rene Ritchie. I think the Yuen Kay Shan system is very rich in teachings and tradition. I was also fortunate Kwan Sifu also passed on the Gu Lao wing chun to me, a system that was brought to Gu Lao village by Leung Jan, wing chun's most famous fighter. The Gu Lao system, as you might expect, lays emphasis on combat application. Through the years I met people open and willing to share their systems. For example, the outstanding exponent of Chi Sim wing chun, Andreas Hoffman, taught and showed me his version of weng chun, which is a completely different system than wing chun. His stances are wider and deeper, and their body and pole work are excellent. I was fortunate to learn his applications of throws and joint locks first hand.

Wing Chun Masters

Through Hendrik Santo, I have been fortunate to study completely the Yik Kam siu lien tao system, which in my opinion, is probably the forerunner to today's version of wing chun. This system is unique because it emphasizes the body structure, much as I do in my wing chun, and that it is composed of one set that embodies the three forms in Yip Man wing chun. The siu lien tao system is comprised of movements from Fujian White Crane boxing as well as Emei 12 Zhuang – an esoteric Buddhism health/combat/meditation system. Yik Kam Siu Lien Tao emphasizes the 36 Tian Gang hands which can be used to cure or injure. The system also has a short dummy set, pole and knives sets and features sticking hands, although from a different platform than what is seen in the Yip Man and Yuen Kay Shan systems.

Do you think different schools of the same method are important?

Not really, as I think it is the practitioner who cultivates his martial art is most important. In the end, everyone develops his own personal style and if he has followers, a "school" ensues. For example, one of my early wing chun teachers was a very mediocre teacher, but I persevered and studied real hard and was not afraid to experiment with what suited me. Of course, I also consulted with other practitioners, seniors, and elders. Hawkins taught me something great, he said, "Yip Man would tell us not to believe him regarding application of the art, but to test out our wing chun for ourselves." I think this statement had a profound effect on me. Prior to studying with Hawkins, I was always concerned if I learned something correctly, but Hawkins said it's the application that counts the most. In other schools people always care if they were passed down the art correctly, but I find even if it is transmitted "correctly", but if one cannot make it work, it's worthless. This is why I laugh at all the claims of "original" wing chun - if you can make it work, then it is "original". If you can't make it work, then it is BS. Even wing chun has a saying passed down from our ancestors, "Sao Gerk Seung Shiu, Mo Jit Jiu" (hand and feet defend accordingly, there are no secret unstoppable techniques.) When people come out with secret lineages of wing chun, I question their intentions.

One thing I must say is that in the United States, many come out of the woodwork with secret family systems which claim to be "original" or the most "traditional". Often these claims are just a form of puffery, based on greed or ignorance. In China, we used the marketing claim, "Old, original, or traditional", whereas here in the US, we say "new and improved". Often these individuals claiming their wing chun is the first or oldest is a load of crap – people just want to gain money or fame through the "secret lineage". There are a lot of giveaways and contradictory statements when people come up with this stuff, but often, people are gullible and want to really believe in this fake stuff. I guess some people can't tell the difference between "chop suey" and Peking duck. I guess unless one is scholarly and actually takes the time to look things up, one can fall for the tricks and advertising.

Wing chun probably developed most in the 1850's, although some say that it has it's roots are connected to events in Southern China to overthrow the Qing Dynasty that began 150 years earlier. In my opinion, all historians are speculators, since they weren't there. The late Dharma Master Hsuan Hua, the 45th Dharma successor to Chan (Zen) Buddhism said, "Historians are just people having nothing to do and looking for something to do." They want to investigate history, in other words, to discover what era this person lived in and what period that person lived in. It is like having eaten one's fill, one has nothing to do, so one putters around with meaningless things. In my opinion, these kinds of people are undesirable. The more they research, the more trouble they create, saying, "This is counterfeit, that is real." What is real in the world? What is counterfeit? Nothing! If you think it is counterfeit then it is counterfeit. If you think it is real, then it is real.

"If you want to believe your lineage is real and you cultivate it and develop it to a high level, then it is."

"The secret society origins are also fables, popularized through myths and powerful images of Chinese culture."

I think this scolding is full of Chan flavor. If you want to believe your lineage is real and you cultivate it and develop it to a high level, then it is. Who is to say something is legitimate or not? What historians try to do is to prove their hypothesis based on facts they gather and create a paradigm for you to believe in. Pay your money and take your pick! When I looked into the history of wing chun with Rene Ritchie, the first thing I told him was every branch will say they're the first, most original and best. You can't avoid the politics. And practically every branch of wing chun has said they are the oldest, most original. This is all human nature.

They all say that to bolster their egos or want fame, after all, Chinese think the most original is best. So in a sense, this is just a marketing ploy. Chinese knew and understood the power of myths and legends, knowing that the Chinese mind enjoys a mystery and likes to find things out if they are real or not. In fact, in Chinese culture, it is often a custom to exaggerate a friend's credentials when introducing him to another friend. It's a kind of puffery - the only thing is you have to find out whether it is real or not and in what context. It's the same with wing chun or any other martial art. For example, the origins of the Shaolin Temple - Damo (Bodhidharma) went to shaolin, he didn't found the temple; it was already there. Nor did he create Zen or Chinese martial arts. People (usually retired warriors and generals) brought the arts to the temple. The saying "all martial arts are from Shaolin" is an exaggeration. The secret society origins are also fables, popularized through myths and powerful images of Chinese culture. I think even the average Chinese knows the fables and take them with a grain of salt, but the average American has no idea of the culture and lore of the Chinese, so take things as fact. And you know what? You can tell when these people are trying to say their style is special and most original exclusive of every other related style, after all, they're the ones trying hard to promote that lineage. If a person says that wing chun is over 300 years old, then it is true for all the branches as well, not just one branch, after all, they all are linked through one important period of time -- the time of the Red Boat Opera people of the King Fa Hui. I realize what I say might be offensive to some, but if we have our differences, then I salute you! I can only say these things after I have looked into so-called secrets revealed and researched the history of China from the Ming to the Qing Dynasty period.

Personally, I think it is despicable when people lie and talk about their made up origins as real, but if a style has merits, then I try to focus on that. I think some people just want to fill their rice bowl with food and make a living, keep their business open, attract more students, keep their wives happy and put their kids through school.

What is your opinion of other sport competitions like kickboxing and of other fighting events such as the u FC? Do they represent the real martial arts?

I think these events are still basically sports, because the level of contact is agreed upon and there are rules. I would call these events "martial sports", just like boxing, but they do not reflect martial arts. I think these sports produce superb athletes with excellent condition and good all round skills, but the intent to kill someone is not there. True martial arts deal with a life or death situation and it also looks to heal the body, mind and spirit. Too many are practicing to be brawlers or fighters, but a true martial artist develops the soul of a Jun Zi – Confucius' idea of a nobleman – not necessarily in prestige or rank, but rather in character.

Do you think that kung-fu in the West has caught up with the East as far as skill level?

Yes. We've probably even surpassed them. The best people always come over here as this is the land of opportunity. I also think that people in Asia struggle to make a living and have less free time to cultivate and develop themselves. I used to think the skill in Hong Kong or China must be superior to here, but after I visited in 1987 and later saw people who trained on the mainland, I was not impressed with the level of skill.

Basically, if you're good here, you're also good there. I think one can always improve. The most important thing is to maintain my level and improve daily. One can get better in timing and positioning and with regards to experience, and in this way, intuition can take over. But it must be grounded in logic, and mastery of your arts.

Martial art are nowadays often referred to as a sport. Would you agree with this definition?

The way most people practice is a sport, a recreation. I think martial arts is not a sport, but rather an art form. It is in a unique category. Martial arts is still the best name, rather than being classified as a sport.

Do you think weapons training helps kung fu physically?

Definitely. The weapons skills are a complement to the empty hand skills. They teach you how to move with weight and how to dynamically apply your power and momentum through an apparatus. Few people train today with the intent to fight with a weapon. Most wing chun people use the pole as a form of weight training, and the knives as an exercise with weights; I think this is wrong in a way, as it does not develop the thought of application with the weapon – how to really cut, or disarm an opponent, and how to finish him with your weapon. In essence, the martial intent behind the weapons is lost. Weapons skills in the United Sates have degraded into a show; basically everyone wants to dazzle people – but it's empty. In Southern China, one had to be proficient with a pole – to really protect oneself.

Do you think the practitioner's personal training should be different than his teaching curriculum as instructor?

Yes. But I do think teaching is also a form of training. When you have learned your art inside out and spent enough time, you begin to move within the context of the art – therefore, everything you do is training. You stop just using arm power when you use a wrench or hammer – your body, your intent - everything is behind your movement. I change my son's diaper, I have to use a 'wu sao' (wing chun guard hand) to protect myself from his squirting me. I use my steps to walk through crowds, I time my entry into a revolving door. All of these are daily activities that train us.

Do you have any general advice you would care to pass on the martial artist?

Yes, don't fall for Chinese marketing BS of "original" this or that! But seriously, everyday is training and find ways to train in everything you do.

Try to study with as many people in your field as possible and concentrate on that. Then, get perspectives from outside your area of expertise. I would also say the core of real skill, the DNA of wing chun, is body structure. A person wanting to really master the art ought to get some real instruction in that.

More information is available today, and slowly, all the secrecy is going away. Andreas Hoffman said something good to me, "In the future, there will be no secrets, all that people have to do is train hard and they will have it all". I think that is very true. More and more, teachers today are willing to share their fine points with you through books and videos. Of course, the majority of the stuff out there is mediocre.

With whom would you like to have trained, but could not?

Yip Man, mostly because he was such a character. I could

"Always think of how to improve and you eventually will attain a high level of skill."

also ask him whether or not he really taught some of today's people, especially the knives forms I have seen. I'd also like to have studied with Yuen Kay Shan because he had a great mind and he was always trying to improve. I've often thought of Leung Jan, because he was an expert in Chinese medicine, as well as a fighter and teacher. I regret not having enough time to visit with Si Bak, Wong Shun Leung, who's passing has left a hole in the wing chun family. I would also like to travel back in time and meet with the founders of wing chun, so I could really discern who was the real founder of system.

Wing Chun Masters

"Teachers shouldn't teach you theory, but rather they should teach you principles that work."

What would you say to someone who is interested in starting to learn martial arts?

Find something that you like and stick with it. Also, don't be afraid to try something else new if you don't like it. Try to get as much advice from elders and seniors. Always think of how to improve and you eventually will attain a high level of skill. You have to leave techniques and theory behind and really dig deep to reveal the principles and concepts behind your systems. That is real training.

What is it that keeps you motivated after all these years?

I believe that the wing chun method I practice is a very complete system. It has stimulated my mind to working out the variations, changes and combinations for many, many years. It stimulated my sensitivity to touch and pressure, with timing and directions so that I can develop my tactile sense. The guiding principles always kept me motivated, as this was advice from our ancestors. The spiritual, moral aspects of the art made me want to study Chan (Zen) deeper. The health aspects led me to study Chinese medicine and acupuncture and the body better. Johnny Wong, a fellow Yip Man wing chun practitioner once said to me that Yip Man told him, "The great secret in wing chun is that it develops your mind and makes you smarter." I think that comment is very telling. If you can apply that mind set to anything else you study, you can be very successful. Speed, strength, accuracy, timing and cruelty are the basic requirements to get the job done, and a student has to learn how to apply things under stress. I think free fighting is just a means to develop proficiency under stress, but it is not everything. For a student to excel, students need to master timing positioning, concepts and principles. That they need the method, as well as the training behind it. Teachers shouldn't teach you theory, but rather they should teach you principles that work. Instructors shouldn't just teach techniques, but the concepts needed to create techniques. The difference is whether a person has gone through the experience or not.

What is your personal training schedule nowadays?
I do a little something every day. I generally practice the wing chun basics – stance work, form, stepping, and basic combinations. For me, wing chun is very natural. All movement I do embodies wing chun. For example, if I have to change a flat tire, I use body structure, not my shoulders. This is the way it ought to be. I also train a lot with the long pole, as I feel it is the best way to train for power in wing chun.

What is your opinion about mixing styles (karate with kung-fu, kickboxing with jiu-jitsu)? Does the practice of one nullify the effectiveness of the other or on the contrary, it can be beneficial for the student?
I am a big advocate of cross training, but I believe you have to have a strong root and basis in one system you identify with. I firmly believe that you win with your basics and what you trained in the most. Not try to be a "jack-of-all-trades", simply because you've studied a bit in all of them. For example, in wing chun, we finish a guy with our intercepting strikes. They try to strike us, and we intercept their attack with our own attack. Once we land, the opponent's reaction time is off, and we can further strike him to further slow his reaction time. This allows us time to win with multiple blows. If we can't win with that basic requirement, then our training in basics is crap.

What is your philosophical basis for your martial arts training?
Since I am a Chinese doctor, I believe very much in Taoism and the harmony of yin and yang. The philosophy of yin and yang extend into the si xiang (4 corners), and later the ba gua (8 trigrams), and within this, all of the balance of body, mind and spirit are embodied. The core of this philosophy is balance. This is what wing chun stresses - neutralizing and balancing, and adjusting to fit in with your opponent. That is the highest skill. I also think very highly of Chan/Zen Buddhism. I find myself reading the Sutra of the Sixth Patriarch (Hui Neng) quite a bit, as I find that the essence of Zen is there, and it is the core of the Chinese martial arts. One of the passages in the Sutra that sticks with me is when Hui Neng was confronted by Hui Ming, he taught Hui Ming the essence of the Dharma in one sen-

tence, "Not thinking of good or evil, where is your original face?" Hui Ming became enlightened at these words, and asked, "What other secrets did our master give to you?" Hui Neng said, "If you look into your heart, you know there are no secrets." I think these words can alleviate the frustration one encounters when trying to master a martial art. I also think that Zen is the root of the wing chun mind.

Do you have a particularly memorable martial art experience that has remained with you as an inspiration for your training?

I have been so fortunate to see many unique things and study with some real masters. I guess I can share some rather unique stories. For instance, when Yee Sifu practiced the hung gar system, you could really see the expression of the five animals come out. When he did the Tiger form, he looked like a tiger. When he did the crane form, he really looked like a crane. Yee was fast and explosive and extremely talented. In my opinion, he was the best hung gar man I have ever seen. His ba gua Pole was fantastic! Yee displayed all the strong, flexible and explosive power and deep stances of Hung Ga.

Lui Yon Sang at 83 asked me to attack him with a pole, but no sooner than I attacked him with a Biu Gwun (Darting staff), he disarmed me and struck me five times before the 8 foot staff hit the ground. He was amazing!

Kwan Jong Yuen always encouraged me to learn medicine, as he felt that martial arts knowledge was never complete unless you knew Chinese medicine. He felt you had to learn the body, the weak and strong points, the range of motion, and how to cure. Kwan Sifu taught me Dim Mak, and how to really injure a person striking their vital points, but he was also balanced, as he taught me how to treat someone if you injure them. This influenced me to study acupuncture and herbology, and I am a Licensed Acupuncturist with my own clinic today. In fact, most of my teachers were expert at acupuncture or herbs, including Yee Chi Wai, Chan Tai Shan, Lui Yon Sang, and Kenny Gong.

One time, Hawkins Cheung and I were discussing fighting techniques and I threw a punch at him. With one crashing slap, he used "pak da" on me and left an incredible expanding welt on my forearm. I was literally stunned at the power of this small man!

Wang Shin Liu was very accomplished in internal cultivation and stressed the internal feeling and movement of Qi in the practice of martial arts. But he was more than a warrior, he was always soft spoken and a kind gentleman. I was always impressed by his humbleness. He was truly a balanced warrior cultivating wen (scholarly) and wu (martial). All in all, I have been fortunate to meet so many talented individuals.

After all these years of training and experience, could you explain the meaning of the practice of kung fu?

Kung fu means to cultivate. Every day cultivate a little and improve a little. Soon all will be clear.

h ow do you think a practitioner can increase their understanding of the spiritual aspect of the arts?

I think a person has to get away from all the violence and worry about kicking butt and really have to find the inner wisdom. Avoid three things – greed anger and stupidity. Don't ever think you're a master or a Buddha. You have to always be a student of life. One thing I don't get is why people want to be teachers – lawyers and doctors have to be practitioners, so should martial artists. What's so great about being a teacher? It's hard work! Perseverance and an open mind are very important for improving in the arts. A martial artist can't be too smart, or else he won't persevere. If a martial artist is close-minded, he will never have greatness in his expression of the art.

"If a martial artist is close-minded, he will never have greatness in his expression of the art."

What advice would you give to students on the question of supplementary training?

I think all training is good, but you have to have a goal in mind. For example, if you train with weights, it may enhance your strength, but it doesn't really enhance your knowledge of body mechanics and application

Wing Chun Masters

"I think because students are of a fickle nature they tend to stop training after few years. In our modern society, things come easy."

of strength in martial arts. I also think supplementary training is to overcome boredom in martial arts training, so I think if a student can cultivate something, then it's good. One of my students in Long Island, Michael Manganiello, owner of the "Ling Nam Siu Lam Academy" in Long Island once asked me of the peripheral equipment in wing chun like the sand bag, wall bag, iron palm, bag, and spring arm. I told him, basically, this is for dumb students - when a Sifu doesn't like someone or really doesn't want to teach him one on one, he directs a student to a piece of equipment to get him out of his hair! Of course, I'm joking, but there is a truth to what I am saying.

I think because students are of a fickle nature they tend to stop training after few years. In our modern society, things come easy.

We all study broadly and not deeply. So it is with studying martial arts. But I also think it is the fault if the instructor for not being a partner with the student and helping a student achieve his goals. I think the secrecy of the Chinese martial arts is also a detriment and causes much student drop off. When sifus have a scheme of withholding secrets or levels of training until a certain ceremony is held or a certain sum of money is ascertained, I think this is also a big turn off. Most Chinese know that Chinese hold secrets, and would prefer to study foreign martial arts like karate do, judo and tae kwon do in Asia. I think this is a laugh for people who hold too many secrets. I think also, it is a fault of commercial schools offering belts, certificates, testing, phony titles - they're all geared to make a teacher money and inflate the ego. People look at that and can see right through it. Of course, some people love that external accomplishment, but real martial arts training is better than that commercialism and money making scheming. Wouldn't something that preserves your health and offers you peace of mind be better than all of that commercialism? Of course, student can always choose with whom they want to study.

have been times when you felt fear in your training?

I don't think fear is something you have while training - most training never escalates to a point where one is in danger. As long as an instructor teaches a student confidence, I think it will permeate in their demeanor. Fear is something good when you are in a dangerous situation -- it heightens the senses and makes the body ready for fight or flight, so I think it is a good thing to be introduced to during training.

What are your thoughts on the future of the martial arts?

I hope martial artists can study the martial arts to avoid delusion, stupidity, greed, envy, anger and hatred. It's a good medium to develop friendship and understand more about life. I'd like to see secrecy abolished and the ego and puffery of stylistic superiority be rid of. I think martial artists need to see others and try to understand people from their context, and avoid the negative politics, which breeds negative thoughts that lead to destructive actions.

"I don't think fear is something you have while training - most training never escalates to a point where one is in danger."

CHUNG KWOK CHOW

Winds of Change

Sifu Chung Kwok Chow was born in Hong Kong in 1951. Because he grew up in a rough neighborhood, fighting was just another part of life. As he reached his teens, he started to look seriously for martial arts training and joined Carter Wong's class in a YMCA. However, his passion for the martial arts drove him to study further. By age 20, Sifu Chow had already studied karate, judo, Hung Gar, Loon Ying (Dragon style), and Wing Chun. He studied the latter art under Master Ng Wah Sum, one of the seven disciples of legendary Master Leung Sheung. Leung Sheung's Wing Chun was original and unique because he studied from both Yip Man and Yuen Kay-San back in the '50s. In fact, it was Yip Man's idea for him to study under Yuen Kay-San.

Sifu Chow immigrated in 1971 to the United States, where he stayed with his parents on the East Side of Manhattan. The popular martial arts at that time were judo and karate. Soon afterward, Bruce Lee's kung fu movies flooded the country, and Wing Chun became very popular and in demand. At first, Sifu Chow was just teaching a couple of friends. Then, more and more people wanted to study under him. The following year, he opened his Wing Chun school between Soho and Chinatown on Lafayette Street. It was the first of its kind on the East Coast in the United States. In 1973, Fu Jow Pei Master Ng Wai Hong invited Sifu Chow and many other masters to join his Eastern United States Kung Fu Federation. Sifu Chow was the secretary and other members were Tai Chi master William Chen, Eagle Claw master Shum Leung, Praying Mantis master Chan Pei and Hung Gar master Frank Yee. This position gave Sifu Chow many opportunities to travel the country, city to city, promoting the art of Wing Chun.

Dedicated to Wing Chun, Sifu Chow is the founder of "Integrative Wing Chun", which teaches not only the traditional Wing Chun, but also covers a wide range of martial arts training, including long-range entry, close-range trapping, takedowns, and ground submission.

Wing Chun Masters

how long have you been practicing the martial arts, and who were your first teachers?

I've been practicing martial arts for almost 40 years. My first two teachers were kung fu instructor/actor Sifu Carter Wong, and Wing Chun "Lightning Hands" Sifu Ng Wah Sum. I've been trained in Hung Gar, Karate, Wing Chun, Dragon Style, JKD, Thai boxing, Kali, Brazilian Jiu-Jitsu, and Tai Chi.

When I was 14 years old, there was a bully in my neighborhood in Hong Kong who always picked on me and others. One day, I realized that I would have to fight him to make him stop. An adult who saw the confrontation waited to see the fight start. I took a deep breath and swung my fists at him. In a few seconds, the bully got a bloody lip and backed away. The adult smiled at me and said, "Well done." After that incident, everybody in the neighborhood looked up to me.

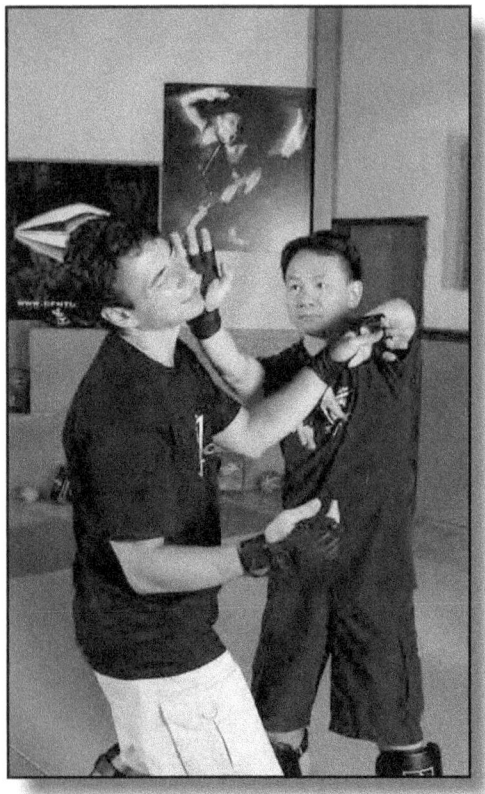

"I took a deep breath and swung my fists at him. In a few seconds, the bully got a bloody lip and backed away. The adult smiled at me and said, 'Well done.'"

Another story happened after I came to the U.S. in 1971. In order to retain my skills in Wing Chun, I started to teach near Chinatown in Manhattan. About the same time, other Wing Chun sifu came to teach Wing Chun. One of them, who I will call Sifu A, invited me to his school for tea one evening. I visited his school and we chatted about the art in the old days of Hong Kong. Later, he asked me to spar with his students. I declined in the beginning, but after awhile, I got off my chair and sparred with them. After exchanging a few moves, I finished the first fight with a stalking bong-sao, followed by a lop-dar. That student backed away and a second student came in. I also took care of him. I thought that would be the end of it, but then came a third student. This time, I instinctively struck the third one much faster and harder. I saw the left side of his face swell up to the size of a melon. Afterward, I couldn't believe what had just happened. Sifu A wanted a true test of my skill, and the result was something he didn't expect.

Luckily, I was a natural with two skills necessary for kung fu — my observation skills, and my hand/leg coordination. I developed them early in my life by playing and learning in the streets, where everyone made a living by using their eyes and hands. It was also because I started to train in kung fu when I was a teenager. However, other aspects of kung fu didn't come too easily — it has always been a learning curve for me. Traditional Chinese kung fu training takes time.

h ow has your personal kung fu changed and developed over the years?
It has been non-stop development. Wing Chun was invented by a woman (probably the only martial art invented by a woman) who solved problems by maximizing her power, speed, and sensitivity. My most important points of teaching are based on "Wing Chun's Eight Theories". The most important point is sensitivity. Without sensitivity, you could have hundreds of techniques but not know how to use them. Sensitivity tells you when to use something (timing), how to use something (leverage), and what to use (technique). Although I have been practicing martial arts for 40 years, I am always looking for better ways and setting higher goals. I believe Wing Chun has one of the best theories, so it deserves to be expanded to other fighting ranges, especially the ground range, which I call chi-sun, which means "sticky body."

With all the technical changes during the last 30 years, do you think there are still "pure" styles of kung fu?
Thousands of years ago, the Chinese already knew that nothing stayed the same forever. They wrote the book "I-Ching", which means "the way of change." So, the "pure" always evolves. Not to mention that "pure" is only an interpretation by a certain group of people at that specific time. Nobody can stop the evolution of something "pure."

I think styles are important, since they represent kung fu's skills and history. There are so many ways in fighting. Some are good in long range, so they are best using longer limbs. Some are good in close range, so they strike with shorter limbs. Some are good in clinching, so they are good in takedowns. Some are good in the ground range, so they are best in body control. There is no one style that has the best of all ranges. I try very hard to train in all ranges, because I recognize the value they contribute.

What is your opinion of full-contact kung fu tournaments?
I think they should have more of those and keep developing and improving them, especially their regulations. I am also a big fan of

"PRIDE" and "UFC". Free-fighting training is the closest "fighting" situation a sifu or a school can offer. I am training a couple of law enforcement officers, who give me good feedback on this type of training. When I was young, I looked for training and techniques that could help me to fight better. Today, I am still looking for training and techniques that can help me to fight better, except I am also looking for better strategies as well.

how different from other kung fu styles do you see the principles and concepts of Wing Chun?

Most kung fu styles focus on long range, while Wing Chun focuses on close range. Some of them focus on showmanship, while Wing Chun focuses on practicality. In general, most kung fu styles focus on power and speed, while Wing Chun focuses on sensitivity for leverage and timing. Siu Lim Tao means "little idea," which trains your basic stance and your arm mechanics. In that basic stance, you understand the centerline theory and your base structure. It is also the first time students have a chance to practice generating and releasing energy. Chum Kiu means "bridging the gap," which trains you how to coordinate the hand techniques from Siu Lim Tao with footwork. Bil Jee means "thrusting fingers," which trains not only the finger techniques, but also includes powerful close-range techniques, like elbow strikes, cutting blocks, underhand strikes, and takedowns. By training in this order, students develop the fundamentals of Integrative Wing Chun. Wing Chun is best when techniques are used in close range, especially in a defense situation. Other kung fu methods tend to be better in longer range and offense.

Do you think that kung fu in the West has "caught up" with the technical level in China?

Physically, yes—even better in some ways. Internally, we could use more help.

Because of their culture, Chinese kung fu practitioners can pick up certain concepts or moves quicker than European or American practitioners. On the other hand, Europeans and Americans usually have bigger builds, so they have better physical capabilities. Generally, I think Chinese kung fu practitioners are more agile, while European and American practitioners are physically stronger.

Wing Chun became one of the most popular kung fu styles in the world because of Bruce Lee, and it still is. There are more Wing Chun practitioners than ever. Unfortunately, there are not enough Wing Chun instructors. Kung fu is a sport when you use it in regulated competitions. It is an art when you practice it. It is a tradition if you study the history. It is a way of life when you think about it all of the time.

Does the weaponry aspect of Wing Chun [long pole and butterfly knives] enhance the student's empty hands ability, or are those two completely unrelated skills?

Weapons are the extension and enhancer of hands. The long pole is for long range, while butterfly knives are best for close range. They are two completely unrelated skills. The pole is single-headed and relies on both hands to manipulate, while butterfly knives are manipulated by one hand and can be used individually or in a pair. Originally, one of the Wing Chun masters traded his butterfly knives form for the long pole form by the Red Boat opera performers. Long poles were used by them for paddling and pushing the boat. They are not very practical on land. Butterfly knives can execute techniques just as the hands can. For example, tan-dar with hands becomes tan-dao (chop) with knives, gaun-dar becomes gaun-dao (chop), and bong-sao becomes bong-dao.

"Advanced practitioners should spend more time on chi-sao, which gives you sensitivity training that forms can not."

When teaching the art of kung fu, what is the most important element—self-defense, health, or tradition?

Different strokes for different folks! I believe Americans set their priority order as self-defense, health, and tradition. In Asia, I believe the order is tradition, health, and self-defense. In Wing Chun, there are three empty-hand forms and a Wooden Dummy form. All the Wing Chun techniques are from those four forms. Chi-sao is the application of the forms. Beginners should spend more time on the forms. Advanced practitioners should spend more time on chi-sao, which gives you sensitivity training that forms can not. To me, forms are the ingredients, chi-sao is the recipe, and sensitivity is the chef.

Wing Chun Masters

"I designed Integrative Wing Chun because I want to bring traditional Wing Chun to another level."

What do you consider to be the major changes in the art since you began training?

When I learned my style of Wing Chun in Hong Kong in the late '60s, my sifu always emphasized the importance of being soft, which took me a long time to achieve. Today, most students are fast-results oriented. I had difficulty in training them the way I used to train, so I designed more interesting and effective ways instead. There is more than one reason to keep me going. There are personal reasons, such as keeping in good shape, both physically and mentally. We know there is no one style that covers all four ranges in fighting (long range, close range, takedown range, and ground range). Mixing other kung fu styles with yours helps you to understand about different situations of fighting. It is the positive thing to do.

On the other hand, my students and my fans are other reasons to keep me motivated all of the time. I often receive e-mails and phone calls from my fans to tell me how much they appreciate a good teacher like me. I designed Integrative Wing Chun because I want to bring traditional Wing Chun to another level. My job is not done yet.

Who would you like to have trained with that you have not had the chance to?

The founder of the Wing Chun style, since Wing Chun is probably the one and only martial art style invented by a woman. She was probably five feet tall and less than 100 pounds, so with her physical disadvantages, she had to fight smarter, not harder. I am interested in understanding more about her and the development of her art.

What would you say to someone who is interested in starting to learn Wing Chun kung fu?

Don't jump in impulsively. Find out about as many nearby Wing Chun schools as possible. Then, compare them by visiting them, observing a class or two, talking to the sifu and even talking to his students. I would suggest paying more attention to sensitivity training. There are two kinds of sensitivity—non-contact (long range) and contact (close range). Again, sensitivity tells you when to use it, what to use, and even how to use it.

Do you have a particularly memorable kung fu experience that has remained as an inspiration for your training?

I have many memorable experiences with kung fu training. For example, watching Yip Chun—who was already 70 years old, stands 5-feet-2 and weighs 115 pounds—do the butterfly knife form. His pair of butterfly knives moved like paper fans in his hands. Finally, the most memorable kung fu experience I had was flying my Wing Chun Sifu Ng Wah Sum to the U.S. from Hong Kong for a seminar for all my students and their students. He inspired me not only with his Wing Chun, but also with his quality personality—which is most important. He is strong, but warm-hearted; smart, but humble.

h ow is the chi-sao aspect of training related to the practical application of the Wing Chun techniques used in the three empty-hand forms?

Chi-sao is used in close range. Others ranges that need to be covered and practitioners need to train in other ranges. Look what happens to the UFC fighters—a grappler who can't punch gets knocked out, and a striker who can't grapple gets choked out.

is there anything lacking in the way martial arts are taught today, compared to how they were in your beginnings?

I would say that time is the issue in today's martial arts. In the old days, we trained five to six days a week; therefore, the sifu was very personal to us. Today, students train two days a week, on average. Everybody rushes in and rushes out. It is hard for sifu and his students to spend time together.

Kung fu actually means "a skill from practicing." During the practice, you would have many hardships, but you should keep going rather than giving up too soon. To me, kung fu means a lot—including building my personality and values along with it. You also can use them to influence other people's lives, and I did it many times. There is no finish line for any knowledge. My Wing Chun is unlimited by chi-sao. Basically, there are

Wing Chun Masters

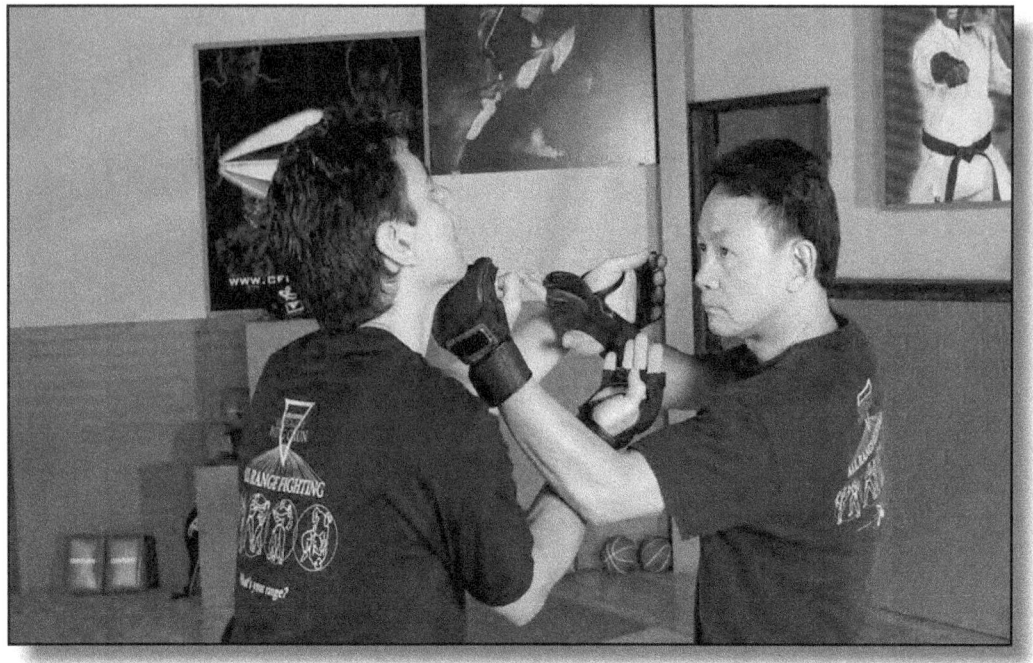

"As a Wing Chun sifu myself, I am looking for a student who is a good listener and good at managing his/her own time."

four ranges of fighting—long range, close range, takedown range, and ground range. Wing Chun is great in close range. I've expanded the Wing Chun range to other ranges, but there is still more to learn and to train in. That is why I named my Wing Chun as *Integrative* Wing Chun, not *Integrated* Wing Chun.

Could i ask you what you consider to be the most important qualities of a successful kung fu practitioner?

Someone capable of genuinely passing on his/her knowledge to the students, without putting on a facade. As a Wing Chun sifu myself, I am looking for a student who is a good listener and good at managing his/her own time.

What advice would you give to students on the question of supplementary training (running, weights, et cetera)?

There is no doubt that supplementary training improves your conditioning. Just remember—a good runner can't fight, but a good fighter can run. A weight lifter can't fight, but a good fighter can lift.

"I think the trend will be more and more mixed kung fu styles, including Wing Chun."

Why is it, in your opinion, that a lot of students start falling away after two or three years of training?

There are uncontrollable reasons and controllable reasons. Uncontrollable reasons are relocating, schedule conflicts, injuries, and finances. Controllable reasons are the students' lack of interest and sense of achievement. As a sifu or an owner of a school, one should have more communication with his/her students. Then, find a way to improve the student's interest.

have there been times when you felt fear in your kung fu training?

I don't think any kung fu practitioners should have fear in training. I think the closest thing is injury. I have been injured many times; I am afraid of getting injured and injuring others, but am not preoccupied by this fear.

What are your thoughts on the future of the art?

I think the trend will be more and more mixed kung fu styles, including Wing Chun. Bruce Lee already knew the trend when he was alive.

IP CHUN

Straight from the Source

Ip Chun began studying Wing Chun with his father when he was seven years old. In 1949, after the Communists established the People's Republic of China on the mainland, Ip's father left for Hong Kong and Ip, then 24, remained in Foshan to continue his studies in university. Ip studied Chinese history, philosophy, poetry, traditional music, and Buddhism.

By 1950, Ip Chun had completed his studies and he chose teaching as a profession. In addition to teaching Chinese history, music and science, Ip also helped the Chinese Foshan Entertainment Department organize opera plays. During that time, he was awarded "The Person with the Most Potential in Chinese Art" award for his research in music. However in 1962, due to the Cultural Revolution, Ip Chun and his younger brother, Ip Ching, were forced to leave Foshan and move to Hong Kong to join their father.

In Hong Kong, he worked as an accountant and newspaper reporter in the day and practiced Wing Chun in the evening under his father's tutelage. In accordance with his father's wishes, in 1965, he participated in the affairs of the "Wing Chun Athletic Association" (WCAA) and became one of its founding members when it was formally established in 1968. During the first three years in the association, Ip Chun took on the role of treasurer and was later appointed as chairman.

In 1967, he began teaching Wing Chun in Hong Kong and some of his first students, such as Ho Po-kai and Leung Chung-wai, still train with him at present. Between 1970 and 1971, Ip and Lau Hon-lam taught a class of about 20 students in Ho Man Tin. Ip's father died in December 1972. Ip Chun inherited his father's legacy and continued teaching Wing Chun.

He currently teaches at the "Wing Chun Athletic Association", as well as teaching a class in Sha Tin once a week. Between 1985 and 2001, Ip traveled abroad to promote and conduct seminars on Wing Chun, before semi-retiring in 2001 to concentrate on teaching in Hong Kong. In 1992, Ip set up the "Ip Chun Wing Chun Kuen Martial Arts Association" (www.ipchun.org) to certify and authenticate those among his senior students, who have attained instructor qualification under his tutelage, to teach Wing Chun to students from around the world.

Wing Chun Masters

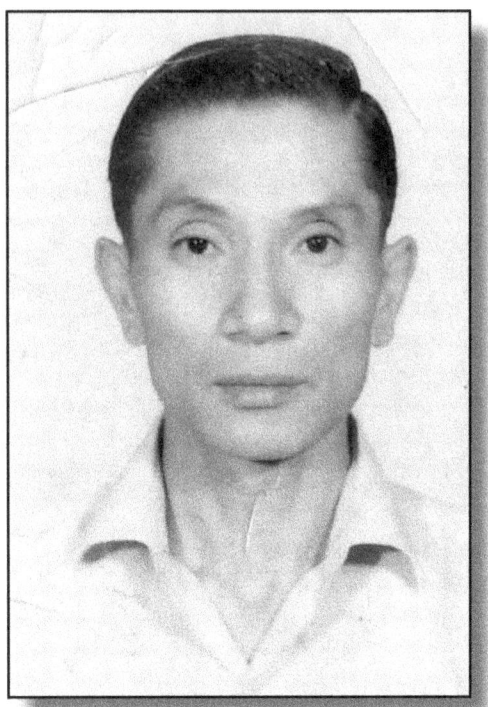

"I respect all methods and believe they all have some benefit, but my personal studies have been limited to Wing Chun."

how long have you been practicing the martial arts and who were your first teachers?

I began training as a child under my father in Foshan, China. My brother and I began training in Wing Chun at a very early age and continued our training when we joined our father in Hong Kong in 1961.

how many styles of Kung Fu have you trained in?

Just Wing Chun. I respect all methods and believe they all have some benefit, but my personal studies have been limited to Wing Chun. I am not sure if studying several systems of martial arts is something positive or negative. I think that maybe it depends of the individual. For me, being the son of Ip Man…Wing Chun is enough.

What are the main principles intrinsic to the three empty hand forms of the system and how they do interrelate with each other?

"Siu Lim Tao" is the starting gate for all Wing Chun skill. It teaches the relaxation of the body and the best physical structure of the defensive and attacking movements of the system. In Siu Lim Tao the student is also introduced to elbow energy. This teaches how Wing Chun generates power in movement.

"Chum Kiu" begins teaching the coordination of the hands learned in the Siu Lim Tao, with the horse stance and stepping introduced at this phase of training. Chum Kiu teaches directional changes along with shifting and stepping. Also, this form introduces kicking.

The "Biu Jee" form teaches about recovery from mistakes made in a fight, and also how to deal with angles that have not been covered in the first two forms. Relaxation is emphasized in this form to produce a soft energy. Trained together, these forms help the student develop into a more safe and secure individual.

how did you find the Westerners respond to traditional Chinese training?

Western students seem to take to the Chinese culture, including Wing Chun, with enthusiasm. When students visit Hong Kong they seem to be ready to be totally immersed in all things Chinese, and all things Kung Fu. They not only enjoy the training, but excel. I have had many Western students over the years who have become very good teachers of Wing Chun, and are now passing the system to their own students. This brings me a great deal of happiness.

Were you a 'natural' at Kung Fu – did the movements come easily to you?

I believe the health benefits of Kung Fu are just as important as the martial aspects. From the beginning I enjoyed Kung Fu, but have concentrated more on health than fighting. I never looked for fights and I think the true spirit of the Martial Arts is to avoid fights not to start them.

how has your personal Kung Fu has developed over the years?

As with anything we do, my understanding of Wing Chun has grown over the many years I have practiced, and grown in my understanding of how to apply the system. I have learned more about how to blend with and not physically contend with others to overcome them. This non-contention is the key to Wing Chun.

What are the most important points in your teaching methods? And what are the most important qualities for a student to become proficient in the Wing Chun style?

The important points to teaching Wing Chun is to get the student to trust the structure of the technique, and not depend too much on muscular strength to overcome the opponent. We must also teach students to be patient. Everything in nature has its timing. When we plant a seed, we water it, nurture it, give it sunlight. Eventually it begins to grow. If when we see the plant growing, if we begin pulling on it, in order to help it grow, we will only kill it. The same is true of Kung Fu. It takes time for skill to develop. We simply can not rush the process. We must let the natural learning process take place.

With all the technical changes during the last 30 years, do you think there are still 'pure' styles of Kung Fu?

If by pure, you mean unchanged from what was taught by the founder hundreds of years ago, no. Everyone who learns and then passes a system on to a new generation of students, brings some personal flavor to the system. We all have different physical builds, and different backgrounds and experiences. These factors have some impact on how each of us understand and perform the system.

Do you think different 'styles' are truly important in the art of Kung Fu?

People have very different physical body sizes and weights. Some are stronger than others. Some are taller…some are shorter. So different methods may appeal to different people.

What is opinion of Full Contact Kung Fu tournaments?

There is nothing wrong with sport Kung Fu. People just need to understand that there is a difference between sport and Martial art. In sport, there are limitations and rules. This is not true of a real self-defense encounter. So, while sport is good, people must be made to understand that being good at sport does not mean being skilled at self-defense.

h ow different from other Kung Fu styles do you see the principles and concepts of Wing Chun?

I see other methods that are more strength based or hard styles. Wing Chun is not a method that requires one to be stronger that the other but uses angle and sensitivity to gain advantage.

Do you think that Kung Fu in the West has 'caught up' with the technical level in China?

I have some very skillful Western students. Foreign students have been traveling to Hong Kong for many years, and have been training hard. Wing Chun has spread to the West through some very dedicated and knowledgeable practitioners. One of the big problems with Wing Chun as spread in the West, is instructors teaching incomplete or made up Wing Chun, due to instructors establishing classes, who never completed training in the system. This has been a problem in the West.

Do you feel that there are any fundamental differences in approach or physical capabilities of Chinese Kung Fu practitioner in comparison to European or American practitioners?

The biggest problem is getting Western students not to try to use too much muscle in the application of Wing Chun. Also, the Chinese have a better understanding of some of the ideas Wing Chun is based on, such as some cultural philosophy.

Kung Fu is nowadays often referred to as a sport (wu shu)... would you agree with this definition?

There is a difference between training for self-defense and sport. So to describes all Kung Fu as sport is not accurate. In the application of any method of Kung Fu in self-defense, you must get the idea of the limitations created by rules of a sport out of mind. There are no limited targets or methods of striking in a real self-defense situation.

Do you feel that you still have further to go in your studies of the art of Wing Chun?

As long as one is alive, there is always room for improvement. That is the wonderful thing about training Kung Fu, there is always something you can improve by training.

ho w do you see Wing Chun Kung Fu in the world at the present time?

With the movies which have come out about my father, Wing Chun is growing very popular around the world. I believe this is good because people are seeing good Wing Chun portrayed in the movies along with some idea of the history of how the art has reached the present age. Also, people are seeing Wing Chun portrayed as an effective method of defending oneself against aggressive assault.

"As long as one is alive, there is always room for improvement."

Does the weaponry aspect of Wing Chun [long pole and butterfly knives] enhance the student's empty hands ability or are those two completely non-related skills?

The weapons introduce some footwork not found elsewhere in Wing Chun, which does help the empty hand method. The pole also teaches a lot about generating power through total body coordination. So I believe the skills developed by weapons training is important to today's students.

Wing Chun Masters

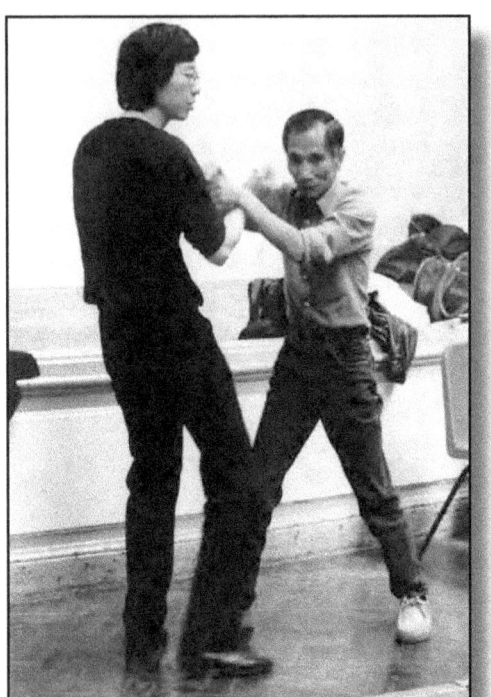

"I am healthy, despite my age, which I believe is credited to my training in Wing Chun."

ho w does the Wing Chun style differ from other Kung Fu methods when applying the techniques in a real self-defense situation?

I can only speak of my experience in Wing Chun. I believe Wing Chun is good for self-defense because it is direct and does not use fancy movements. Wing Chun is very practical because it is meant to be used I close to the attacker, and that is where most real self-defense situations take place is at close distance.

When teaching the art of Kung Fu – what is the most important element; self-defense, health or tradition?

While all are important, without health, you will be unable to use Kung Fu in self-defense. It is good to understand the culture and tradition, but this again is not as important as ones health. I have benefited greatly from training in Kung Fu. I am healthy, despite my age, which I believe is credited to my training in Wing Chun.

Forms and Chi sao...what's the proper ratio in training?

Forms build technique and structure. Chi Sao trains the use of technique, structure and sensitivity. I believe both are equally important to ones training. For the beginning student, form is very important. Technique must be developed before it can be used. Once forms have been trained long enough to develop proper understanding of technique, then Chi Sao will become very important.

Do you have any general advice you would care to pass on to the practitioners in general?

Research well before choosing an instructor to learn from. Be patient in training, don't try to rush the learning process. Work and train hard, be diligent in their studies. Once you find a good teacher, allow him to guide your training and progress. Be patient, skill takes time to develop.

some people think going to China to train is highly necessary, do you share this point of view?

It is good to experience the country, culture and people of the systems origin, but it is not necessary. There are good teachers to be found all around the world, and one can learn the system without ever coming to China.

What do you consider to be the major changes in the art since you began training?

The ability to record training on video is a great advantage for the students nowadays. Years ago this was not possible, so we had to rely on our memory. Today, everyone has a video camera, so they have accurate record of what is taught and help them to review when they need to.

What would you say to someone who is interested in starting to learn Wing Chun Kung Fu?

Choose a good teacher with a reliable background in learning the art from a legitimate lineage. This is most important. Once you find that teacher, follow his instruction. Today, there is a lot of information available on video and the Internet. Most of what is seen in these is not very good. So, don't rush your training by trying to learn faster by going to outside sources. Listen to your teacher, and allow him to guide your progress.

What is it that keeps you motivated after all these years?

Seeing new generations of students, excited about learning and spreading Wing Chun around the world. Wing Chun has a lot to offer in improving health and giving one skills of self-defense.

Do you think it is necessary to engage in free-fighting to achieve good self-defense skills in the street?

Students must train in a way to develop not only technique, but the ability to apply technique. In Wing Chun, we use Chi Sao for much of this training. With Chi Sao, skill can be developed with less chance of injury than in free-fighting.

What is-was your philosophical basis for your Kung Fu training?

The Confucian text "Doctrine of the Mean" holds a lot of meaning and kinship to Wing Chun. The "Mean" is the middle, or center. Wing Chun is a method based on maintaining the center, and not overreacting one way or the other. I have found great meaning and kinship between Wing Chun and the "Doctrine of the Mean"

Do you have a particularly memorable Kung Fu experience that has remained as an inspiration for your training?

Watching my father, the way he taught. The concern he had for the development of his students. I try to carry on that attitude in my teaching, and pass on that attitude to my students.

After all these years of training and experience, could you explain the meaning of the practice of Kung Fu?

I believe each individual has their own meaning of Kung Fu. Some place more importance on health, some on self-defense, some on competition. I believe your approach can bring out what you want from Kung Fu. It is very versatile, it can become what you want it to, depending on your approach in your practice.

h ow are Chi s ao aspects of training related to the practical application of the Wing Chun techniques used in the three empty hands forms?

Chi Sao is the glue that binds the forms to the application in fighting. Chi Sao teaches the student when and how to use energy, and how to overcome the opponents force with the proper use of angles. The forms give the student structure in technique, but Chi Sao teaches the student to apply the technique in application against an opponent.

is there anything lacking in the way martial arts are taught today compared to how they were in your beginnings?

Patience. Today everyone wants everything NOW. In the old days, a student learned at the pace set by their teacher. Today people are in too much of a hurry, and try to rush their training.

Could i ask you what you consider to be the most important qualities of a successful Kung Fu practitioner?

Integrity, respect, and good character. Kung Fu must follow the path of virtue. A Kung Fu man without virtue is dangerous to his fellow man. Kung Fu should be taught only to those who have the character to use it only for the good of society.

What advice would you give to students on the question of supplementary training (running, weights, et cetera)?

Anything the student does to increase their health will help in their Kung Fu training. As far as weight training, I do not believe it is necessary to good Kung Fu, because real Kung Fu is not dependant on physical

"I believe the future of Wing Chun is very bright. The series of movies on my father have brought worldwide attention to Wing Chun."

strength, but on proper technique to work, especially Wing Chun. But ones health is of utmost importance.

Why is it, in your opinion, that a lot of students start falling away after two-three years of training?

Today, many people seem not to have the patience to learn properly. Everyone is in a rush. Also, after a few years people have developed some useful skills, and sometimes feel they have become good enough.

What are your thoughts on the future of the art?

I believe the future of Wing Chun is very bright. The series of movies on my father have brought worldwide attention to Wing Chun. We now have instructors all over the world who are spreading the Wing Chun method. So I believe we will see Wing Chun flourish throughout many generations to come.

AUGUSTINE FONG

The Personal Truth

Augustine Fong was born on the island of Macao, off the coast of Southern China. In 1960, he was fortunate enough to begin training in a traditional Kung Fu style. His instructor was the honorable Wing Chun master, Ho Kam Ming. Master Ho, a top student of the late grand master Yip Man, had, at that time, introduced the style to the Macao area. Augustine Fong, without a second thought, became one of his first students. By 1964, Master Ho's school had grown considerably. The school had gained such a good reputation that to help with the increasing number of students, Fong was asked to assist Master Ho in teaching. This was quite an honor for the young Fong.

During this period, Sifu Fong began studying under the Chinese herbalist, Sifu Wong Bing Gong. Sifu Wong taught Fong how to use "Dit Da" massage to heal broken bones and to treat bruises, strains, and sprains. Sifu Wong also taught him how to prepare herbs, and their medicinal remedies, all of which was valuable knowledge for a practitioner of the martial art.

In 1967, due to civil disturbances in Macao, Augustine Fong moved to Kowloon, Hong Kong. There, his instructor, Master Ho, opened a Wing Chun school, where Fong practiced and taught for two years. Then, in 1969, following his father's footsteps, Sifu Fong immigrated to America. Moving to Nogales, Arizona, and then settling in Tucson, Sifu Fong soon began to teach and promote the Wing Chun style. Today, with over five decades of experience in the art, Sifu Augustine Fong is considered to be among the top Wing Chun masters in the world.

sifu, what can you tell us about your teacher Master h o Kam Ming?

My Sifu Ho Kam Ming spent all his life training and studying the art of Wing Chun. He was one of the very few who actually finished the Wing Chun training under the supervision of the legendary Yip Man. He was a second-generation Yip Man' student.

Sifu Ho Kam Ming used to take Yip Man to the Hospital and stay with him. Grandmaster Yip Man gave him the responsibility of teaching private students when he couldn't do it for any reason. Sifu Ho Kam Ming had two schools, one in Macao and another in Hong Kong. He was always a true example of what a true Kung Fu teacher and master should be.

Wing Chun Masters

"I was introduced to Sifu Ho Kam Ming by another school friend of mine. He stopped training a short time after I started. Sifu Ho Kam Ming was my first and only teacher."

how was your training in Macao and hong Kong?

I started training when I was 11 and against the wishes of my mother who was not very happy with the idea of me learning and training in Kung Fu. In fact, she didn't find out until the time I decided to move to the USA! It is not that she was against the Kung Fu teaching but mostly she was afraid I would start using my fighting techniques to get in trouble in the streets of Hong Kong like many other young guys.

I was introduced to Sifu Ho Kam Ming by another school friend of mine. He stopped training a short time after I started. Sifu Ho Kam Ming was my first and only teacher.

Training at the time was very hard. The teachers were very traditional and you have to prove your dedication and loyalty or you were going to learn nothing at all. They demanded a lot from the students but once you got to actually learn, the experience was incomparable. They were a very special generation of teachers that unfortunately doesn't exist nowadays.

Did you actually meet grandmaster yip Man?

Yes, I did meet the Grandmaster Yip Man although I never trained with him. Yip Man didn't believe in teaching kids, women or poor people. He thought that you had to work hard to make a decent living first, and then study Wing Chun so if you had no money...he was not going to teach you. My Sifu Ho Kam Ming was rich so he had all the time in the world to be with Yip Man, train and to go places with him. He was very fortunate.

you were one of the first instructors teaching Wing Chun in America, correct?

Yes, that is correct. I was one of the first Chinese in teaching Wing Chun in the US. Bruce Lee did it first in Seattle and Oakland before he developed Jeet Kune Do. The reason why I started teaching is because right before leaving Hong Kong I went to visit my Sifu and he told me that I should find someone to teach so I could practice my Chi Sao. So the main purpose was so I could just keep up my training. I was not looking for students or to make money from it. "Teaching is the best way to improve learning!" Sifu Ho Kam Ming told me. And so I did. I do teach the same Wing Chun system that was taught to me by my Sifu.

Please, tell us a little bit about the Wing Chun system.
Wing Chun is a very sophisticated system of self-defense. It originated from Shaolin master Ng Mui. Ng Mui combined the best from Shaolin with her own experiences and understanding to create the style of Wing Chun. Ng Mui then taught Yim Wing Chun who improved it further, arriving at its present form as we have it today. So, although it retains similarities with an older traditional method, it is one step improved. One might say the style has been modernized also because time has passed and people have added new ways of looking at the art and its applications. It has only three empty hand forms, a wooden dummy form and two weapon forms (Butterfly Knives and 6 ½ point long staff) but it is very practical since it is based on practical application of the movements and not on fancy forms or visual attraction. It also includes eight kicking principles, although the system uses mostly hand techniques, and a very specific training method called "Chi Sao' that translates as 'sticky hands'.

h ow important is it to know and to understand the three empty hand forms?
The three forms of Wing Chun have a very specific purpose in the martial art education of the student. Practicing a form might involve training a hundred things at once, both internal and external. To achieve the same results without the form, one would have to break all these things down and practice them individually. This would be less efficient. Siu Lim Tao is the most important form in the system. It develops Chi Kung, your Chi, and your physical power all at once and in one single form. You can learn the movements in one single day but to really understand and digest the true principles and applications of the concepts intrinsic to the form, takes a very long time. The forms develop important fundamentals and principles and like a time capsule, they preserve the knowledge and technique of the system. The three hand forms can be practiced individually or as one continuous form. Each form represents a different level of training. The three forms and techniques represent different fighting distances one must master. Siu Lim Tau generally contains outside fighting techniques.

These motions are based on direct attack, economy and practical simplicity. Many people don't see the important points and training of the form and they rush into the second form as soon as possible. Chum Kiu, focus on techniques applied at a closer distance--with the opponent at elbow's length. This form teaches the student how to use body unity and torque in order to generate power. The third form, Biu Jee, provides techniques for dealing with emergency situations. Such techniques can be applied at a very close range. Biu Jee set contains some larger motions. These theories relate to use of circular techniques from outside the line, redirection of power, protection and recovery of the centerline.

It is important to understand that all of the Wing Chun forms contain principles that can be used at varying distances. For example, Biu Jee's emergency techniques can be combined with Siu Lim Tau principles to deal with situations involving greater distance and time.

What about Chum Kiu?

Chum Kiu teaches you body unity. It shows how to use the hands and the body as a sole unit. The body is the foundation of the hand movement. With a strong body foundation all the hand techniques are much better and powerful. The body is like a hammer, and the hands are like a nail. If you have a hammer behind a nail, then it is easy to nail the technique in.

Some people mistake two principles in this form; 'searching bridge' and 'sinking bridge'. And that is very confusing when the students learn. The name of the form is "Searching Bridge", but the name of the hand technique is "sinking the bridge" and sometimes it may be interpreted as "sinking the elbow" too. They are two different words in Chinese but they are pronounced the same. Depending on the level of the teacher this can bring a lot of confusion to the students.

And Biu Jee?

Biu Jee is the last empty hand form. One of the myths is that 'Biu Jee does not go out the door". This doesn't mean that it is a secret form or anything. What happens is after years of training some people decided that they know enough Wing Chun and eventually leave and stop training. Therefore they never reach the technical level to learn Biu Jee. The problem is that if you don't know Biu Jee you can't really know and understand the second part of the wooden dummy form. This one of the reasons why there are so many different wooden dummy forms around!

Biu jee is based on the first two forms, Siu Lim Tao and Chum Kiu. The first form develops your steady power and balance. Chum Kiu controls that steady power in movement and Biu Jee combines both concepts. It is called "an emergency" form because it teaches you how to handle extreme situations using a different set of principles. The techniques are there from the first two forms but the principle of application is different. People think that because of the name you have to attack with the fingers when using Biu jee but there is no need to use fingers to attack an opponent's eyes when he can be blinded by a single punch. The eyes are a small target and missing with a finger strike can result in the fingers being damaged. The meaning of Biu Jee is not to use fingers to poke the opponent's eyes, but to employ shooting or thrusting techniques in emergency situations, to deflect and penetrate an attack. Finger techniques, however, can be used sometimes to attack the throat, eyes and other soft areas of the body.

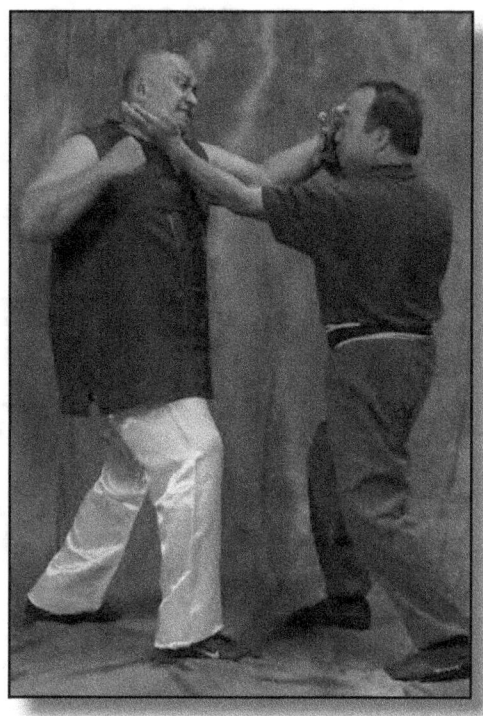

"The Muk Jong or wooden dummy is used to find the correct line in the execution of the movement and incorporates techniques from the three empty hand forms."

What is the role of the Wooden Dummy training in the Wing Chun system?

The Muk Jong or wooden dummy is used to find the correct line in the execution of the movement and incorporates techniques from the three empty hand forms. It teaches you the principle of the centerline, triangle, gates, timing, etc. It is the next best thing to a live training partner in the Wing Chun system. Students who are not familiar with the full form can practice individual techniques, just to get the feel of it. It is important to remember that techniques from Muk Jong further assist one in applying the hand forms.

Also, you don't have to hit the dummy hard at all. It is not a conditioning tool where you blast your arms! You energy is not based on brute force. Later on, you can do your techniques with a little force for more power but this is not the goal of the wooden dummy training.

Try to stick closely to the Wooden Dummy because this will develop economy of technique. Also, try to flow from one complete motion to another and not stopping between motions because this will disrupt the flow and retards the development of body mechanics.

Wing Chun Masters

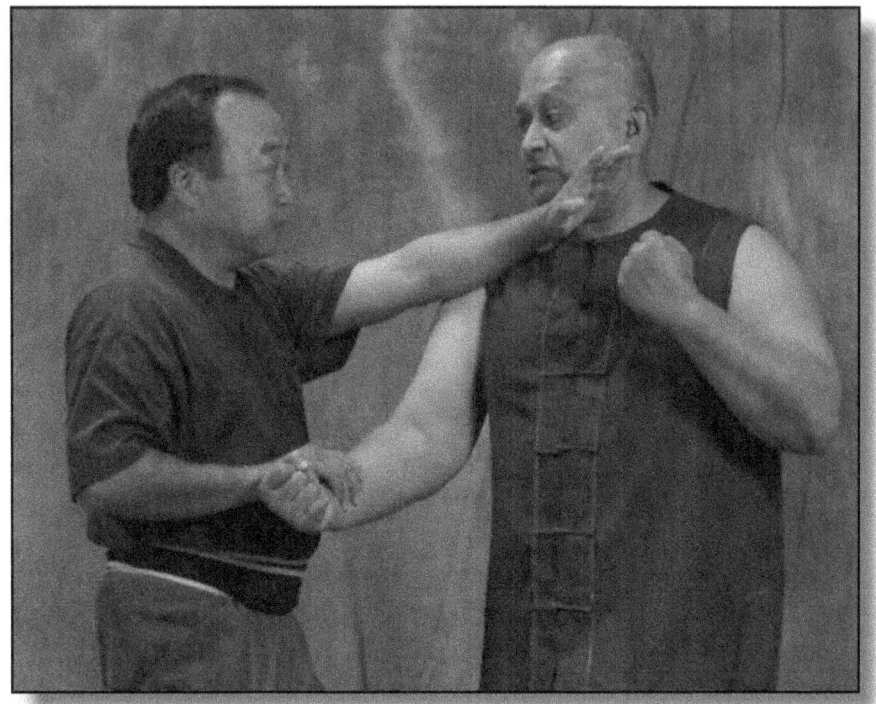
"Some people mentioned to me that my Muk Jong form is different than others wooden dummy forms."

The Wooden Dummy is a special training device that develops a variety of skills--skills that cannot easily be developed by practicing with a partner. For example, among other things, Wooden Dummy practice refines power, encourages proper use of the centerline, and also correct footwork to control the opponent's position.

Some people mentioned to me that my Muk Jong form is different than others wooden dummy forms. I can't say anything else but that I teach the same form taught to me by my Sifu Ho Kam Ming and the progression is the same; the first two empty hand forms, the first half of the wooden dummy form; then Biu Jee and then the last half of the dummy form. Then, the "Look Dim Boon Gwan" (long pole) and finally the Butterfly Knives or "Bart Jam Dao".

how important is the knowledge of the weapons within the complete format of the style?
Originally the Long Pole techniques were taught separately and it was

up to the student to put these techniques together in a form for training. It is not about the order of the set of techniques in the form at all…but about the use of these techniques. The sequence doesn't really matter at all as long as you have all the techniques and the understanding of the applications.

The term "six and a half" doesn't mean the amount of techniques like many people think! It refers to the way you hit the target. If you bring the right force to the tip of the pole, the right vibration will cause the tip of the pole to leave a six and a half mark on the target.

Something similar happens with the Butterfly Knives. They are not necessarily eight directions in the movements. It refers to the lines the butterfly knives describe in motion. The number eight looks like the two lines coming down to a point…similar to the chopping motion of the knives. It is about the mark that is made by the knives when you slash with them.

is Chi sao really the 'key' to the Wing Chun method?
Chi Sao helps to develop the 13 principles of combat; posture, position, timing, distance, power, reaction, guts, the way, aggressiveness, controlling, decision, reserve and adjustment. The Chi Sao motions are what make the forms. Forms are the textbooks as far as the right and correct way of doing the movement but Chi Sao will tell you how to apply them. Like a laboratory for the techniques you have learned in the three empty hand forms.

I teach eight types of energy in Chi Sau; 1. Bau Ja ging or "Explode Power". Ging is your internal power that is executed outwardly. This is when they can see Ging externally; 2. Chi Ging or "Sticking Power". In Wing Chun, we stick to every incoming attack so that we make our opponent's energy our energy. Therefore, we control him by using his force that is now our force; 3. Keng Ging or "listening Power". Listening means feeling your opponents energy and body talk ,so you trap him by counter moving before him; 4. Juun Ging or "Drilling Power". Drilling Power is the force that goes forward, like a circle, every straight line in Wing Chun has a circle. This does mean that the straight line is drilling like a spiral. Just like a bullet as it turns, as it goes through the air; 5. Jek Jip Ging or "Direct Power. This means I use the power to go from point to point by bouncing off the first point and going straight to the second point; 6. Yaan Ging or "Guiding Power". Guiding force is the one you use when your opponent's incoming force is on its way. You just turn the force a way to the side and carry on in a circle back to the starting point of the attack, just like a wheel; 7. Lin Jip Ging or "Connecting Power". Connecting Power is like

Direct Power from one motion move to the next motion without stopping. Like if you do a Pak Sau use the same hand to do Tan Sau or a Punch straight away without stopping and 8. Choung Ging or "Aggressive Power". This Aggressive Power is used outwardly, you must be very mentally calm. However, you must not be out of control. If you do not train this in the right way you will be out of control.

In Wing Chun everything comes naturally through Chi Sao training. Since there are almost no prearranged combinations in Chi Sao, the student applies the techniques as he or she pleases. This teaches him to react spontaneously - whether training at the "kwoon' or on the street. Sticky Hands practice helps to develop sensitivity, which in turn helps to develop reactions. Without good reactions, one cannot fight. Through sensitivity one can more easily develop essential skills like timing, accuracy, reaction and speed.

In Wing Chun there really isn't a direct relationship between the way you do the forms and how you apply the movements in Chi Sao. The real application of the moves found in the forms will be determined by the opponent and the amount of force and type energy he gives you.

In my classes I teach first how to make the right structure for each one of the Chi Sao moves. Then, the correct point of contact. After that how to control that 'point of contact' between the motion of Chi Sao and finally how to make yourself a strong structure so when the opponent pushes, you just maintain you structure without pushing back or allowing your technical structure to collapse.

Why is the principle of the centerline so important in Wing Chun?
Because a good centerline development and usage, promotes good structure. Correct structure in turn promotes good technique, energy flow and internal development. They are all related. In its simplest form, the centerline can be defined as the line (or plane) extending from the vertical axis-line of the body and representing the shortest distance between oneself and the opponent. It is important to remember that the centerline is an imaginary line between two subjects and usually indicates the closest line of attack. For instance, only when attacking or blocking can one talk of a real line.

Do you advocate weight training in order to improve in Wing Chun?
I don't think weight training is necessary but definitely will increase one's potential power. The problem is that many people cannot effectively use the power they already possess and they decide to get into weight

training before they learn how to use what they already have! Beginners need to learn how to use their natural power first and then when they reach an advanced level, increase it with resistance training.

In this style, there is no emphasis on weight training because the system does not rely on brute force but on what we call 'explosive power'.

This explosive power is based on what is called "Bone Joint Power." Once the initial motion of a strike has been started, snapping the joints at the moment of impact, and then relaxing, will cause the power to be completely released. Without relaxation and some degree of flexibility it is difficult to produce explosive power. Too much muscle prevents this important action. Wing Chun favors a more relaxed and natural punching method. This facilitates the development of this type of explosive power. From the Wing Chun point of view, punching with excessive strength results in a great deal of power remaining in the arm. This inhibits the instantaneous release of power.

"In this style, there is no emphasis on weight training because the system does not rely on brute force but on what we call 'explosive power'."

Sifu, you always mention the importance of the right timing when you teach, would you please elaborate on that?

Timing is a very tricky part of the Wing Chun system. There are many different types of timing and you need to know when to use them. Regular timing involves an attack between two motions - one strikes at the end of the opponent's motion, before he can start his next. Creating timing is used to initiate an attack; if a punch is coming, blocking and then countering simultaneously. Breaking timing involves attacking the opponent before he can complete his motion or intercepting. To use this timing one must be always quicker than the opponent. Double timing consists of two

Wing Chun Masters

"Timing is really the foundation of speed. If the timing is right, the speed is right."

consecutive attacks or timings. In this category we also have what we call "delayed" timing. Timing is really the foundation of speed. If the timing is right, the speed is right. The converse, however, is not always true, you can be very fast but if your timing is off…

Why is it that Wing Chun practitioners do not kick to the head like in other Martial Arts styles?

Well, kicking to the head has the same logic as punching to the feet! The distance is very long and in a self-defense situation you simply don't want to take any chances with high kicks. In Wing Chung we use kicks to supplement and back up the hand techniques. They are also generally directed below the belt level and are well-timed and executed in close association with the upper body movements. This makes it difficult for the opponent to tell when they are coming. Because of this, it is sometimes said that Wing Chun has "invisible kicks".

Do you agree with the idea of mixing styles?

You can mix styles but I recommend focusing on one style in the beginning. Otherwise you can simply get a superficial knowledge of the art and never understand it fully to reach higher levels of development. Mixing styles or methods is a very personal thing and definitely what may work for you may not work for anybody else. You simply have to be careful.

Would you please explain the concepts of 'classical' and 'non-classical' in the art of Wing Chun?

For me these two concepts are simply a level of development of the student and not only in Wing Chun but in every martial art style. You need to develop a strong foundation and base with a traditional training. Years of dedication to fully master the principles of the art are necessary.

"Don't look or be worried by other people's progress. Focus on your own development."

The non-classical concept can be fully realized only after years of practicing the fundamentals. At this level, the fighter becomes more independent, developing his own fighting style, and his own ideas. It becomes the 'master' of the art and its principles. The practitioner 'is' the style.

Any final advice for the readers?

Don't look or be worried by other people's progress. Focus on your own development. Also don't forget that a good teacher never holds knowledge back from the student, but the student must show respect and dedication. When the student is ready, the teacher will share more and more information. The Wing Chun principles and Chinese code of ethics were created and developed by a long line of traditional teachers, these may differ in the way they are expressed depending on the teacher but all must have the true philosophy of the Kung Fu art and spirit. Conquering the physical art of the art heightens your own personal internal growth. Find the universal law of personal truth and kindness through the art of Wing Chun.

FRANCIS FONG

Roads of Destiny

SIFU FRANCIS FONG IS CONSIDERED BY MANY TO BE ONE OF THE FINEST WING CHUN INSTRUCTORS IN THE U.S.A. BEGINNING HIS STUDY UNDER SIFU JIU WAN IN HONG KONG BACK IN 1965, HE DECIDED LATER TO SHARE HIS KNOWLEDGE AND PASSION FOR TRAINING IN THE ARTS BY MOVING TO THE UNITED STATES. IN 1973, HE TRAVELED TO NEW YORK, RELOCATING TWO YEARS LATER TO ATLANTA, GEORGIA. IT WAS AT THIS TIME THAT HE OPENED THE FRANCIS FONG MARTIAL ARTS ACADEMY.

SIFU FONG ALSO IS WELL KNOWN FOR HIS KNOWLEDGE IN EASTERN HEALING TECHNIQUES. AS A HEALER, HE APPLIES VARIOUS MANIPULATIVE TECHNIQUES, USING SENSITIVITY, STRENGTH, AND BALANCE TO PROMOTE AND DIRECT THE QI (CHI/ENERGY) THROUGHOUT THE BODY'S QI CHANNELS. THE MANY ROADS SIFU FONG DECIDED TO TAKE IN HIS MARTIAL ARTS JOURNEY ALWAYS LED HIM TO FIND AND "DISCOVER MORE ABOUT HIMSELF," AS HE DESCRIBES. WHILE SHARING KNOWLEDGE AROUND THE WORLD THROUGH CLASSES AND SEMINARS, THAT JOURNEY OF SELF-DISCOVERY MAY BE WHAT HIS DESTINY IS ALL ABOUT.

h ow long have you been practicing the martial arts – Wing Chun – and who was your teacher?

When I was 12 years old, I got involved in both Judo and Tae Kwon Do in two separate academies. The YMCA in Hong Kong offered Judo classes taught by Sensei Riki Hashimoto. I also joined a TKD school. I studied both Judo and TKD for three years. At that time, my friend Jason Lau brought me to his Wing Chun classes. He introduced me to Sifu Jiu Wan's school in Hong Kong. It was a closed school; you had to know a student there in order to be accepted as a member. I joined right away and began training there. Most of the time,we would come in and train with the Si Hings (senior students). If Sifu was not there, we would practice.

I got involved in a lot of different martial arts. I studied Wushu with my cousin in the U.S. and I studied Kali/Escrima and JKD Concepts under Guro Dan Inosanto, Muay Thai under Ajarn Chi Sirisute, Brazilian Jiu-Jitsu with the Machado brothers, Pentjak Silat, Savate, Shooto, and Tai Chi.

My love for the arts came naturally to me. I was very passionate about Wing Chun, so practicing was never a chore. I played soccer, and was very active outdoors as a teenager. So, I don't know if I was a "natural" or not. As long as you love what you are doing and put time into it, you will

Wing Chun Masters

"I never feel fear because kung fu helps me to get stronger and helps me to feel young and good about myself."

see results. The more you do it, the more you will see results... with anything.

have there been times when you felt fear in your kung fu training?
I never feel fear because kung fu helps me to get stronger and helps me to feel young and good about myself. It gives me positive energy.

What are the differences of the Wing Chun branch you teach compared to yip Man's?
I haven't studied the Yip Man branch of Wing Chun, but I believe that there would be a lot of similarities in the systems, especially with the concepts and principles. It depends on the individual instructor. My instructor emphasized a lot of sparring and practical application of the techniques in combat.

Kung Fu nowadays often is referred to as a sport. Would you agree with this definition?

I always understood Kung Fu to mean "achievement through great effort," or simply "virtue." Originally, to practice "kung fu" did not just mean to practice Chinese martial arts. It referred to the process of one's strengthening of the body and mind, through learning, training, and perfecting skills – rather than what actually was being trained. I use it to mean excellence achieved through long practice of any endeavor. You could say that a person's kung fu is good in cooking, or painting, or whatever area he or she has have worked hard to develop.

What are the main principles intrinsic to the three empty hand forms, and do they interrelate with each other?

Siu Lim Tao means "a little idea." The primary purpose of the first form is to focus on fundamentals – basic structure, energy, position, and understanding of the centerline theory. Controlling the *Dan Tin* trains the chi. Using toes to grip the ground maintains balance. Releasing chi from the Dan Tin enables proper release of power. Students learn to drop their shoulders and sink their elbows. The primary purpose of the second form, Chum Kiu, is understanding movement. Chum Kiu trains the stance and the waist, using footwork and rotation. The entire body moves as one unit. Students learn eye coordination, as well as loosening up the muscles and relaxing the mind. The third form, Biu Jee, focuses on speed, iron fingers for long range strikes, and elbow strikes for close range strikes. Students learn to intercept the line, recover the line, and create the line. All of the forms absolutely relate to each other. The first form is crucial for fundamentals. In the second form, the entire body moves as a unit. Without the first and second form, the third form would not be effective. Most of the dummy forms come from the first and second forms. A few movements in the dummy set come from the third form.

Would you tell us some interesting stories of your early days in kung fu?

When I was young, my brother Danny and I got into an argument, and I challenged him to a fight. I thought that there was no way that he was going to win, since I was the one who had all of the martial art experience. But he kicked me in the groin and took me down with one shot. I remember curling into a ball under the bed. It taught me a lesson – never to underestimate your opponent.

In the kung fu classroom, six of the students held down one of the students who was nicknamed "Giant." They asked me to pull down his pants, and I did it since I was the youngest. Then, the Si Hings asked me to throw Giant's pants out the window, so I hung them on the outside clothesline. As I looked outside, I noticed that our Sifu was coming back, so I warned everyone, and we all started practicing Chi Sao. Giant was very angry, and he came up behind me and used the palm shot on my kidney. I felt like I had just been shot. Just then, the door opened and Sifu came in. When Sifu saw my face, he asked what happened, and the Si Hings told him. Sifu told me to go the bathroom and drink cold water right away. Then I lost consciousness. Afterwards, I was so weak I couldn't move. Sifu yelled at Giant, but it was too late. Later on, Giant apologized to me for reacting in anger. I was unable to train for three months because of breathing problems. Sifu sent me to a Chinese herbal doctor. I couldn't go to the hospital, because they would have thought that it was from gang fighting, and I didn't want my parents to find out. So I was given herbal medicine. That made me realize not to play around.

how did you find the Westerners respond to traditional Chinese training when you started teaching the art of Wing Chun?

In 1973, there were not many people in the early days. Wing Chun really was new to the West. Karate was popular. Some people loved Wing Chun and saw the value in its concepts. A lot of people found the art difficult. Wing Chun really is simple, but it's not easy. Also, you need to have more patience and discipline. Not many people are willing to put the time into it, especially beginners. Wing Chun is not really fancy. You have to work on coordination and emphasize energy. So, it is not easy for Westerners to accept, because they don't grow up with the same cultural approach.

how has your personal approach to Martial Arts changed and developed over the years?

Kung Fu is a term; it can be anything. It can mean anything that people put time into. In 1981, I met Guro Dan Inosanto. I always liked to try and do different things. I learned from many friends, associates, and different people. But after I met Guro Dan working on the movie "Sharky's Machine", I incorporated Filipino Martial Arts and JKD Concepts. In 1983, with Ajarn Chai Sirisute, I began to practice Muay Thai. Wing Chun is the foundation and tool to help me to discover my own potential. Learning Wing Chun helped me to recognize body mechanics and structure, which I then adapted into different martial arts. At my Academy, I emphasize the benefits of cross-training to my students. The concepts of Wing Chun can be related in other martial arts and, as a result, help to improve your over-

"Keep learning and keep growing. Keep giving and sharing your knowledge with others."

all abilities. As with all martial arts, Wing Chun is all about self-development. I always learn and my students give me that opportunity. I learn from my associates, my friends, my students… everybody. Without them, I would never grow.

What are the most important points in your teaching methods? And what are the most important qualities for a student to become proficient in the Wing Chun style?
I tell my students that the most important thing is to keep an open mind. Keep learning and keep growing. Keep giving and sharing your knowledge with others. Give to people, and it will come back to you. Some people really have potential, but even if they are not outwardly talented, it doesn't mean that they cannot master themselves. Wing Chun should be used as a tool, not just a style. If you don't open your mind, you cannot learn. The most important thing is what you really want, and how you establish what you are looking for. In order to succeed at anything in life, you have to love what you are doing, have compassion for yourself and others, and the conviction to put in the time and effort to achieve your goal.

Some students excel faster than others because they are talented. Others

Wing Chun Masters

"It is very important to have positive energy. Attitude will determine your behavior."

do better because they put more time into it, and they are passionate about what they are doing. They are excited about practicing the art; they have positive energy, determination and a good attitude. Talent is not everything. If people have negative energy and a negative attitude, they never will succeed, no matter what they do in life. They blame other people for their failures, or blame it on something instead of taking responsibility for their actions. Your enemy is your own self. Control your temper, selfishness, attitude, and discipline. Martial arts will help to ground you and understand who you are. You have to keep your balance.

It is very important to have positive energy. Attitude will determine your behavior. I always tell my students, "Try doesn't work." "Try" never works, because when people try, their mind is set on trying and not doing. When you try, you don't put 100 percent effort into what you do. When someone asks you if you can do a job, do you say you'll "try your best" or you will "do your best"?

With all the technical changes during the last 30 years, do you think there still are "pure" styles of kung fu?

In my opinion, there is no such thing as a pure style. What is pure? That's really old fashioned. We have to be adaptable, because the world is changing. People need to change to adapt with society and cultures. If we stay with "pure," then we're never growing. I think that tradition has value, but I educate students to open their minds to be creative and dynamic, instead of being just a copy. I don't think in terms of styles. If it's a "style," then there is a limitation. I think that it's important to focus on the individual and what he/she is capable of, and one's development. Everybody is comfortable to do what they love to do. All styles have their own concepts and theories. Each system is different; they have their own beliefs. For me, Wing Chun is logical, and mathematically/physically it made sense to me. I was able to relate to it. I don't want to put down any other styles – it's just what works best for you as an individual. It helps me to learn each day.

Cross-training can help you to understand yourself better. You have to discover what is suitable for you, as well as for a particular situation. Focus on yourself. When you understand yourself, you then can begin to understand others. I would like to train with anyone who has integrity, loyalty, dedication, compassion, and passion for martial arts.

What is your opinion of full contact kung fu tournaments?
The participants deserve respect and credit for trying. They do whatever they think is right – it's not for me to judge or criticize. For myself, I never really watch them or know who does it. Tournament is still sport. In a street survival situation – that's totally different. Tournaments have rules. Full contact – it's still a game. So I'm not judging anything; I don't feel qualified to say whether it's good or bad. The street game is totally different. I used to train full contact fighters before. I focus more on teaching survival now.

Do you think that kung fu in the West has "caught up" with the technical level in China and h ong Kong?
Western culture is different. However, this country has a lot of opportunity. Many instructors have brought the knowledge to this country. I don't want to compare, because I am more focused on what people can learn. It's very difficult to compare, when you try to say who is better, then you are getting into negative energy. And it's not fair. I just want to focus on the people who want to learn, who want to teach. I never really think about who is better. I believe that everybody has something to offer.

It's not really the location; it has to do with the individual's instructor and what he/she emphasizes. Everyone is different. People have an opportunity and freedom to do whatever they choose.

Does the weaponry aspect of Wing Chun enhance the student's empty hands ability, or are those two completely non-related skills?
Everything is related. The weapons are an extension of the body. The same concepts hold for the empty hand forms, because it all comes from

Wing Chun Masters

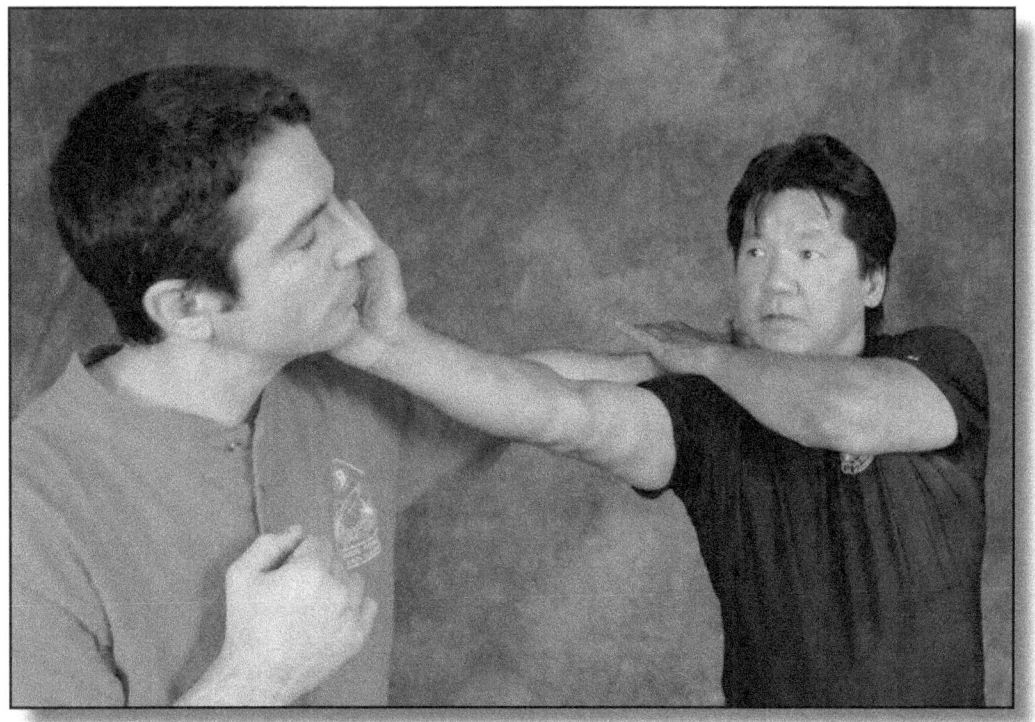

"I just want to focus on the people who want to learn, who want to teach. I never really think about who is better."

yourself. The weapon helps your empty hand, and vice versa. The 6" point staff helps conditioning.

how does the Wing Chun style differ from other kung fu methods when applying the techniques in a self-defense situation?

Wing Chun has good fundamentals, and I believe that it can help individuals grow mentally, physically, and spiritually. It definitely has helped me. Wing Chun focuses on reflex training and sensitivity – your timing, your response to the situation. You know even before your opponent moves; you sense it and feel it. You learn how to make the connection. It's just like playing chess; you know ahead of time.

When teaching the art of kung fu, what is the most important element: self defense, health, or tradition?

I don't just emphasize one thing. It's complete, whole. Just like Ying/

Yang. Balance is the key. It's not one or another. The most important things are motivation, self-discipline, and timing. You should love what you are doing, care about what you are doing, and have compassion for yourself and for others.

Forms and Chi sao: what's the proper ratio in training?

In the beginning, you have to work on form. It's important to focus on foundation and basics... form, drill, and application. Form is structure and sequence. Drilling provides repetition of technique. Application is understanding when to execute the technique. I start by teaching the student Siu Nim Tau. If you don't get the basics down, you can't go any further. It's just like learning English... first you learn letters and syllables. In Wing Chun, learn the basics – learn proper position and understand structure. You cannot just do it; you have to understand it. Chi Sao emphasizes energy, structure, body mechanics, timing, relaxation, response, understanding range and centerline concepts.

some people think going to China or Taiwan to train is highly necessary. Do you share this point of view?

In my opinion, there is a lot of opportunity in this country, and a lot of well-qualified instructors here who came from overseas. It depends on the instructor and how much he/she loves the art and is dedicated to what he/she is doing. How long has the instructor been training? You need consistency. It depends on how much time you put into it.

What do you consider to be the major changes in the art since you began training?

I emphasize a lot of different systems, just like going to a university, and that way people will get what they need. My students learn other martial art systems in addition to Wing Chun, to become well-rounded. In my opinion, I believe that the more you learn, the more well-rounded you are. If someone in a university learns three or four languages, he or she can communicate better. It depends on the individual's goals.

What would you say to someone who is interested in starting to learn Wing Chun kung fu?

Wing Chun is not easy because you need a lot of patience, even as an adult. It is never too late to begin. Age doesn't matter. What does matter is what you think. It doesn't matter what other people say. It matters how you feel. There are no excuses. Today, a lot of people are going back to college later in life. Some people are in their 60s, and they are studying for the

Wing Chun Masters

"Wing Chun has good fundamentals, and I believe that it can help individuals grow mentally, physically, and spiritually."

first time in many years. Don't let your dream die with an excuse. You can do whatever you set your mind to. If you want something badly enough, and you put your heart into it, you can achieve it.

What is it that keeps you motivated after all these years?

Motivation is internal. I love what I am doing. I learn different things every day I teach, especially from my students, my associates, and my family.

Do you think it is necessary to engage in free-fighting to achieve good self-defense skills?

Free fighting gives you good experience. You have to train. You have to have confidence. It helps, but it doesn't mean that the individual will be a survivor on the street. There is a Chinese saying, "You have to have guts (heart), you have to have strength (conditioning), you have to have skill." Skill is not necessarily the most important factor.

Do you have a particularly memorable kung fu experience that has remained an inspiration for your training?

Sifu Dan Inosanto is a true inspiration. He is always training, every day. He attends Master Chai Sirisute's Oregon Thai Camp every year, and he continues to learn. I have respect and admiration for Sifu Dan Inosanto – his dedication and discipline are truly inspirational. In addition, I admire Master Chai Sirisute's focus on discipline with his students.

is there anything lacking in the way martial arts are taught today when compared to how they were in your beginnings?

Some people are self-promoting and focus too much on titles and politics. Worrying about politics gets in the way of self-improvement, which is the main goal in your training.

Could i ask you what you consider to be the most important qualities of a successful kung fu practitioner?

What is really being successful? That is a very subjective matter. Just be happy with what you are doing, and enjoy each day. Success means different things to each individual.

What advice would you give to students on the question of supplementary training?

Do whatever you feel is right. You should be able to motivate yourself to do whatever you need to do to be healthy. Try to improve yourself so you can enjoy what you are doing, and then to give back to help the next generation.

"Students sometimes stop training because they have no internal motivation."

What do you see as the most important attributes of a student?

Honesty, respect, discipline, loyalty, open-mindedness, dedication, and appreciation for every day of life. Students sometimes stop training because they have no internal motivation. They have no discipline. And they have and find a lot of excuses, too.

What are your thoughts on the future of the art?

The future will take care of itself because everything constantly changes. Traditional values always should be there because they represent our roots and education. Practitioners should be responsible not only for their own actions and words but for the future of the arts too. Martial arts are an invaluable tool for use in real life. We must never forget this.

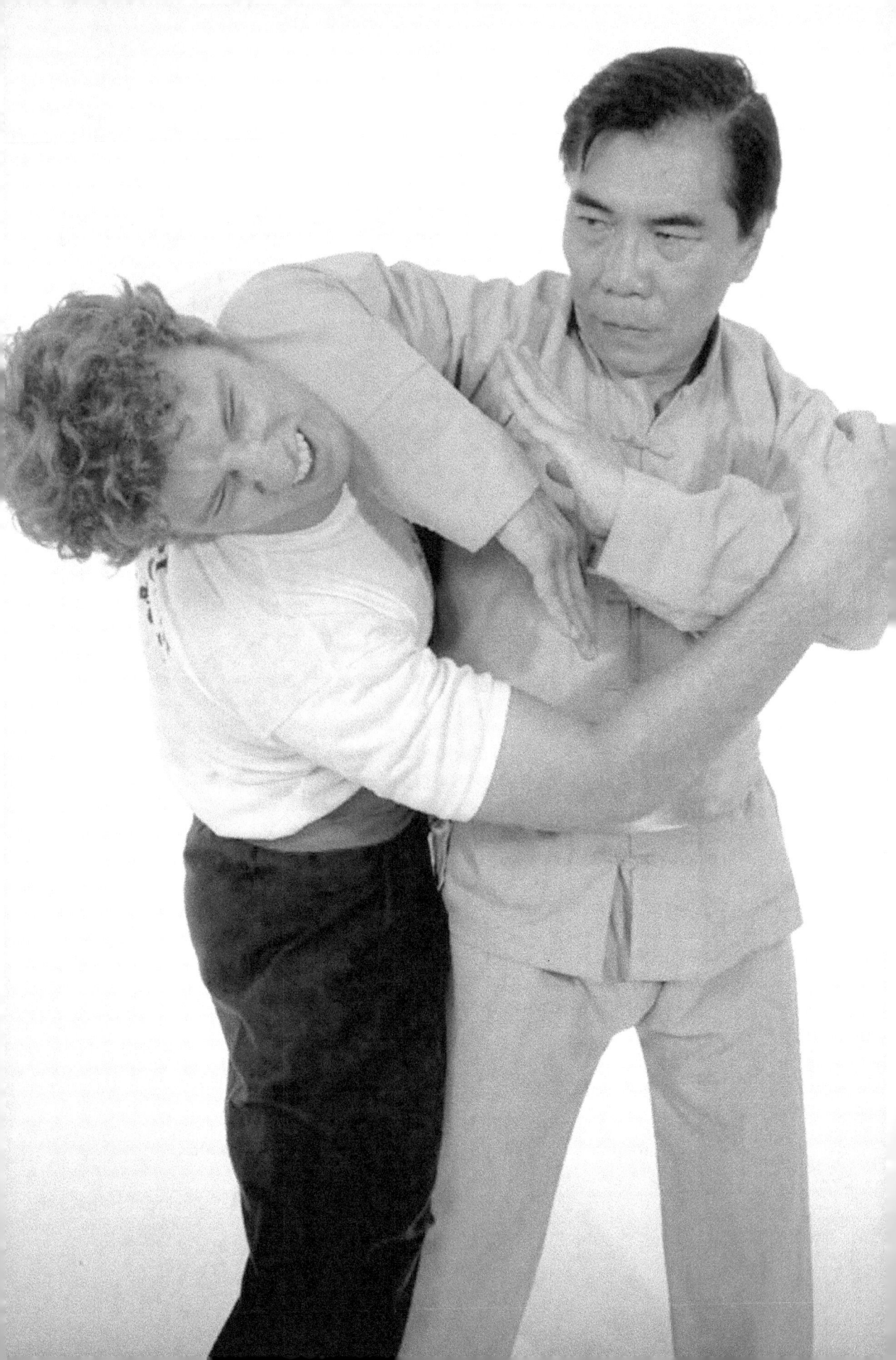

JIM FUNG

The Balance of Wing Chun

Grandmaster (Sigung) Jim Fung was one of the world's leading practitioners of Wing Chun kung fu. He trained under his master, Tsui Seung Tin, starting 1960. Great Grandmaster Tsui, chairman of the esteemed "Hong Kong Ving Tsun Sports Association," was one of the three closed-door students of the legendary Yip Man.

Sifu Fung's International Wing Chun Academy opened in South Australia in 1973 and in 1989, it became the first Martial Arts school to receive official Australian Government recognition for its two-year full-time Certificate Course in Wing Chun Instruction. The course attracted interest worldwide because of Sifu Fung's reputation and its standing as the first course anywhere to raise Martial Arts to the tertiary level.

Sifu Fung believed his business success was in part due to the universal appeal of the art: because it doesn't rely on brute strength, anybody, regardless of age, sex or physique can learn. "Wing Chun is a science which mixes physics, math, logic and biology all into one," he says. "It takes skill, speed and positioning to overcome your opponent." His dedication to preserving genuine Wing Chun through quality teaching and his own remarkable prowess were undoubtedly other important factors.

Conferred the title Grandmaster (Sigung) by Great Grandmaster (Si Tai Gung) Tsui in 1999, he was the author of two books, "Wing Chun Kung Fu" and "Wing Chun Weapons", and produced a teaching video, Wing Chun, in 1985.

Sifu Fung was chosen to represent Chinese kung fu at the "International Grandmasters' Martial Arts Exhibition" in Adelaide, Australia, in 1989, and received many accolades for his contribution to Martial Arts and the community. However, he said that the greatest honor was having his Academy officially recognized by the Chinese Government and world ruling body for Chinese Martial Arts in the All Chinese Martial Arts Register published in 1998. That recognition was afforded to only two other Martial Arts schools from outside China.

Sifu Fung died on March 18, 2007, at age 62.

Wing Chun Masters

"The more I learned about other systems, the more impressed I became with the Wing Chun system as taught by my master."

how long have you been practicing Wing Chun and who was your teacher?

I have been practicing Martial Arts for more than 40 years. My master is Sigung Tsui Sheung Tin, who was one of Yip Man's three closed-door students (the others being Leung Sheung and Lok Yiu), and is now the highest regarded Wing Chun master in the world. Sigung Tsui is chairman of the esteemed "Hong Kong Ving Tsun Sports Association."

how many styles have you trained in?

When I was 12 years old, I learned Tai Chi for about a year under Master Ng Gung Yee's son, Ng Dai Kwai. Master Ng was at the time a very famous Tai Chi master in Hong Kong.

After a while, I realized that the Tai Chi I was taught was more a style for relaxation and concentration than fighting, and you need to spend many years learning it before it can be used for fighting. At that stage, I did not have the time to wait as I was planning to go overseas to study after high school, and thought it would be useful to learn self-defense. With two friends who were very good fighters, I learned Wing Chun fighting techniques casually on and off for a few years before commencing private classes seriously with Sigung Tsui. At the time, Sigung Tsui was conducting most of Yip Man's classes.

As a student, I trained and compared fighting styles for many years with fellow students skilled in various styles of Martial Arts, some of who had already reached senior level. The more I learned about other systems, the more impressed I became with the Wing Chun system as taught by my master. On principle, Wing Chun beat them all. It was practical, scientific, and efficient. and did not require brute strength.

What are the main principles intrinsic to the main Wing Chun forms? Are they interrelated?

There are three Wing Chun forms: Sil Lum Tao, Chum Kiu and Bil Tse.

Sil Lum Tao is the most important because it forms the foundation of the whole Wing Chun system. Unless you are very good at Sil Lum Tao, you are wasting your time trying to learn the other forms. My master once likened the three forms to the components of a motor vehicle, with Sil Lum Tao as the chassis or framework, Chum Kiu the engine and Bil Tse the turbo-charger. He reasoned that if the vehicle structure is weak, it cannot withstand any impact.

In Wing Chun, your basic structure is composed of your stance, your bong sau, tan sau, and fook sau. These have to be really strong to prevent the body being knocked off balance when in contact with an opponent's arms in combat. Yip Man named Sigung Tsui the "King of Sil Lum Tao" and I believe the strong foundation he developed is the reason why he became so highly skilled in Wing Chun.

Sil Lum Tao in its advanced stages helps the practitioner develop thought force (nim lik), which gives you enormous power and strengthens your whole body structure. Acquiring thought force requires a teacher who knows how to do it properly, and perseverance and dedication on the part of the student. Unfortunately, this is an area where many people do not do well. Most only manage to copy and not learn the nitty-gritty of how each movement should be done. Doing it wrong is just a waste of time.

Chum Kiu utilizes the mobility taught by Sil Lum Tao by adding extra power. It teaches how to coordinate body and arm movements, utilizing multi-vectors of force to deflect and attack with maximum power. Without a good grounding in Sil Lum Tao, the practitioner is unable to harmonize his movements and maximize force to the target.

Bil Tse adds extra power through physical acceleration of the body. For example, when pivoting in Wing Chun, the top and bottom sections of the body move together. Bil Tse trains the student how to move the top section of the body further, giving greater and faster reach in striking. Bil Tse is the most devastating form of all three, but to be good at it, you have to have perfect balance and good coordination and be very skilled at Chum Kiu. Students trained in Bil Tse can have really destructive power and can amass their whole body weight to the point of striking.

Would you tell us some interesting stories of your early days in kung fu and the training under your master?

When I first began training with my master, he lived in a room on the top level of a private hotel in Sham Shui Po and he used to take my friend, Tony, and I out onto the balcony to do the form. We soon realized he was a very serious person and totally devoted to the art. However, he was very patient, giving us lots of individual attention, and we soon became hooked on the simplicity and utter common sense of the system.

When Tony left Hong Kong to study in England, I continued training privately with Sigung Tsui. These lessons were often preceded by meetings at restaurants for yum cha where we would talk and talk for hours about Wing Chun. A normal two-hour lesson became a four or five-hour one as he described the intricacies of the system, always enthusiastic, and never growing tired of my constant questions. His answers were always scientific and logical, not just in theory but in practice.

In my early days training, like a lot of students practicing Wing Chun, I found it difficult to relax when practicing the form. Sigung's advice was simple: "don't use brute force." He told me that when he began doing Chi Sao, he found himself pushed around by bigger students. But Yip Man taught him that it was vital that he not retaliate with brute force, to persevere and that one day he would be more powerful than the others (which of course he later became).

Another thing Sigung taught me was that the Wing Chun system is like a chain, and for that chain to be strong, it cannot have any weak links. The system is very articulate. To be really good at it, you must build up every joint and muscle, working body and mind in harmony.

I'll never forget the first time Sigung demonstrated to me the thought force (nim lik) of Wing Chun. I could see the movement of his muscles expanding down his forearms, making him so powerful, he couldn't be moved. He was like a 10-ton deadweight. Today, he is even better. He is around 5-foot-11" and 66kg, slightly built, but even when he is standing on one leg, four big guys pushing with all their might cannot overbalance him.

Many years ago, a seventh dan karate master from Japan interrupted one of Sigung's classes to challenge the Wing Chun punch. He threw a strike at Sigung. Sigung just lifted his arm to deflect the punch, then reached in to quickly catch him as he fell. The Japanese master was astonished and asked Sifu what technique he had used. Sigung answered, "no technique – I just raised my arm."

I have so much respect for Sigung Tsui, not just as my master but as a person as well. He is very private and humble – he never boasts about his ability – and I have learned a lot from his philosophy of life, his way of dealing with people. He always listens, is very patient, and never gets upset.

Once, while we were training in his apartment in Hong Kong, a guy walked in and began making a nuisance of himself, lampooning us by performing fancy movements. I asked Sigung if he wanted me to throw this person out. Sigung just said "leave him" and we continued training, ignoring him. After a while, our visitor left and no more was said of it.

Sigung refuses to take issue with politics in Martial Arts, preferring to focus solely on Wing Chun as a true preacher, a true master, would.

how did you find the Westerners respond to traditional Chinese training?
Most students, be they Westerners or Asians, want to learn a Martial Art quickly so they can apply the techniques straight away. They don't have the patience to practice forms like Sil Lum Tao for months on end. So what we do at my school is to give them a taste of the efficiency of the system and work backwards. After a few months training, most are able to fight successfully against much larger attackers.

"Wing Chun appealed because I found I could learn it quickly and apply it straight away."

From junior level to grade four, which normally takes about two years, we teach all the techniques. Then from level one, when we get into analyzing the form, students are then able to understand and appreciate what we are doing and why we need to spend more time doing it.

how has your personal kung fu has developed over the years?
In the beginning, my main emphasis was on self-defense. Wing Chun appealed because I found I could learn it quickly and apply it straight away. Later in my training, as I learned more about the system and how its principles comply with the basics of science, mathematics, and logic, my focus changed. Now, I regard it more as an art, and as with any true art, there is no limit to your learning.

With the help of my master, my skills continue to improve as I discover more things about the art. You could say Wing Chun to me is like a "hid-

Wing Chun Masters

"You need to realize that Wing Chun is like mathematics: you can improve or expand the formula but you can't change the fact that one plus one equals two."

den treasure." It is not just about effective self-defense techniques; it is more like enlightenment as understanding increases. Basically, it is a way of life.

What are the most important points in your teaching methods? And what are the most important qualities for a student to become proficient in the Wing Chun style?

The most important quality is understanding how the system works. I have devised a training program that teaches students from the first day step by step the logic and scientific reasoning of each technique. Understanding what and why they are learning makes training more entertaining, whereas rote learning inhibits a student's learning progress.

You need to realize that Wing Chun is like mathematics: you can improve or expand the formula but you can't change the fact that one plus one equals two. Students must understand the foundation and be willing to listen and practice the way I teach, which is a proven method passed down from Yip Man through my master. Students must also be prepared to put time into their training and realize that while they are able to learn techniques quickly, mastery only comes with years of practice. Teaching other students is also an excellent means of sharpening techniques and keeping the mind open to different aspects of theory. Naturally, commitment is very important if you want to succeed in learning.

With all the technical changes during the last 30 years, do you think there are still "pure" styles of kung fu?

In the late 1940s, when the Communists banned Martial Arts in China, some masters took their skills overseas. Most of those masters are now dead and it is arguable that the "pure styles" died with them. Also, in modern times, people don't have the patience to practice the many different forms of traditional kung fu so it was inevitable that these become simplified over the years. It is possible that along the way, the gist or main ingredient of some styles has altered. While I cannot comment on how many pure styles of kung fu are around today, it would be great pity to see them die off in years to come.

Yip Man was one of those masters who escaped from China to Hong Kong and my master helped him to teach for many years. The reason I have continued to learn from Sigung Tsui is to ensure that the purity of Wing Chun is retained so I can pass it on to my own students. However, because of the scientific nature of Wing Chun, I can see that while the basics have not changed, the style will always be progressive.

What is your opinion of Full Contact kung fu tournaments?

If their aim is simply to entertain, these tournaments have my support because they offer spectators the closest thing to real fighting. But they do not offer a conclusive argument as to what is the superior fighting style. Once you introduce rules, fighting becomes artificial to a certain extent. Again, even without rules, it does not necessarily mean that the winning contestant's kung fu school is superior to that of the loser.

In most tournaments, be they full- or semi-contact, many contestants seem to forget the techniques they have been taught in their kung fu schools and fail to apply them. Those who are able to apply what they have learned make a tournament more meaningful rather than something that has deteriorated into a wild, senseless brawl.

Do you feel that there are any fundamental differences in approach or physical capabilities of Chinese kung fu practitioner in comparison to European or American practitioners?

I believe most Westerners generally place a lot more emphasis on the fitness aspect while most traditional Chinese kung fu practitioners treat it more as an art. The Chinese place more importance on the correctness of the movements - perhaps partly due to their comparatively smaller stature. Eventually, though, serious students (whether Chinese or Western) gravitate towards this direction. Many of my dedicated senior students, who have been training 10 to 20 years or more, are Westerners.

Kung fu nowadays is often referred to as a sport (wu shu). Would you agree with this definition?

"Wu shu" means Martial Art. In the 1980s, the Chinese Government allowed Martial Artists to resume practice, but banned the deadly blows of the kung fu system. It amalgamated all the kung fu styles into something called "wu shu," which placed more emphasis on fitness and gymnastics. Therefore, when people think of wu shu, they see it more as a sport rather than a Martial Art. To that extent, I would agree with the general perception.

Do you feel that you still have further to go in your studies of the art of Wing Chun?

Although I have spent more than 40 years training in Wing Chun, I have found that like any other art, there is no limit to my learning development. My master has been around for a long time and continues to help me to improve my knowledge and skill. Up until now, I am still discovering new things about the system. It is very challenging and skills orientated. Had I stopped learning 30 or more years ago, my skills would have deteriorated to nothing. So I consider myself very lucky.

Does the weaponry aspect of Wing Chun [long pole and butterfly knives] enhance the student's empty hands ability or are those two completely non-related skills?

The weapons of Wing Chun are the butterfly knives (Bart Jarm Do, or "Eight Chopping Knives") and long pole (Lok Dim Boon meaning "Six and a Half Point Pole"). The butterfly knives are used as an extension of the arm, and some movements are very similar to empty hand movements like bong dau or bong sau. Chung do (piercing) is similar to punching.

While they may be viewed as a traditional or classical weapon, the butterfly knives have a lot of contemporary relevance and many realistic applications. If a person is well trained in using the butterfly knives, any similar type of object can become a lethal and effective weapon in his/her hands. Even a blunt object can be used, because the damage done by the butterfly knives does not rely solely on the sharpness of the blades. The force delivered to the target relies on the coordination of force through the whole body, the elbow and the wrist. This is achieved by serious training in the Sil Lum Tao and Chum Kiu forms.

Unlike what you see in kung fu movie stunts, there are no leaping or jumping movements involved in training with the butterfly knives. Such movements would take too long to complete and you would be cut to pieces by your opponent.

The pole was not part of the original Wing Chun system, having been introduced by a Buddhist monk, Chi Tsin Sim See, some years after its founding by Ng Mei. Training in the long pole includes many aspects of Wing Chun theory including directness, focus and deflection. It develops power in attacking and defending and this can be applied with any substitute weapon. It also teaches you how to economize all movements, which means you don't have to take a wide swing to fight, giving you a much better chance in any fighting situation. However, the stance for long pole is totally different from that of traditional Wing Chun training, involving a very low, half squat. You must be really good at Chum Kiu and Bil Tse to perform the movements because they involve a lot of turning or twisting of the upper half of the body. Thus said, the pole doesn't actually enhance the empty hand movements but like the butterfly knives, requires a really strong foundation to execute correctly. My students are only taught the pole when their training in the basic empty hand techniques is complete.

how does the Wing Chun style differ from other kung fu methods when applying the techniques in a real situation?

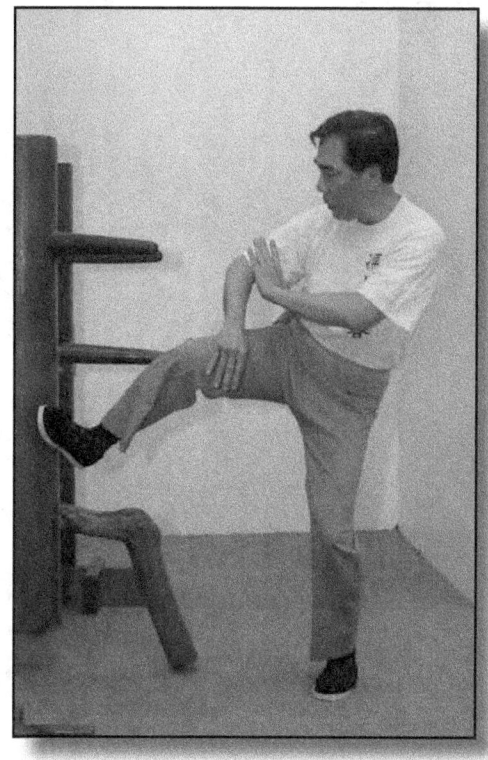

"My students are only taught the pole when their training in the basic empty hand techniques is complete."

Many Martial Artists tend to block, dodge, or deflect and hit back, which requires two movements. They begin on the defensive, letting their opponent throw the first punch. In Wing Chun, we counterattack rather than wait for the opportunity to hit back.

Most fights start close in after an argument and Wing Chun trains for close combat. We use fast, low kicks and powerful punches delivered from a short distance. This definitely gives Wing Chun students an advantage over their attackers as most people do not know how to do this. Also, Wing Chun does not involve any kicks above waist height. Kicks this high can be caught by an opponent and higher kicks cause the exponent to lose power. Our movements can be executed easily regardless of our clothing or footwear at the time.

Wing Chun Masters

"If you are serious about learning a genuine Martial Art, you have to find the right master to teach you."

With the forms Chi sao and Muk yan Jong, what is the proper ratio in training?

Chi Sao and Muk Yan Jong are different stages in learning. As mentioned earlier, Wing Chun trains your structure and power and therefore must be practiced every day. Chi Sao is like an application of techniques or movements that a student learns from the form. It should also be practiced daily. I also encourage my students to practice punching and kicking on a three-sectional wall bag.

Muk Yan Jong (wooden dummy) takes the place of a sparring partner, and is taught at the end of empty hand training, because most of the wooden dummy techniques arise from the three empty hand forms. Many Wing Chun students mistakenly believe that Muk Yan Jong is for toughening the arms and legs. In fact, this form actually teaches them how to move around an attacker effectively in a real combat situation, counter-attacking with ease and full body force without fear of "hurting" the dummy.

I would strongly recommend a student spending the majority of his/her training time on the three empty hand forms then moving on to Chi Sao, wall bag and Muk Yan Jong in that order. While it is difficult to determine a hard and fast ratio in training, a Wing Chun student should spend 60–70% of his/her training time on the three forms, 20–30% on Chi Sao and the rest on wall bag and Muk Yan Jong. I believe a student should practice whatever he/she feels like practicing at that moment. Sticking to a training program religiously might sometimes become a disincentive for training.

some people think going to hong Kong, China, or Taiwan to train is highly necessary. Do you share this point of view?

If you are serious about learning a genuine Martial Art, you have to find the right master to teach you, regardless of whether he lives in Hong Kong, China, Taiwan or wherever. Irrespective of where the teacher lives, the most important points a student must check out are, firstly that he is a genuine master (perhaps through his genealogy or family tree) and secondly, if he is truly interested in teaching. If he satisfies these criteria, it would not matter if he lives outside Asia.

Who would you like to have trained with that you have not?

While I consider myself the luckiest Martial Artist to have Sigung Tsui teaching me all these years, out of curiosity, I would have to say Ng Mei. To be able to train with a Martial Arts genius like her would be a real treat. The word "science" was never heard of more than 200 years ago when she founded Wing Chun. Imagine how one person could have devised the scientific principles such a long time ago, applying the multi-vectors of force of the Chum Kiu, Bil Tse and Butterfly Knives forms? It is incredible how all the Wing Chun principles of leverage and power generation can be proven by modern day science. I would love to see how the art has evolved since then.

What would you say to someone who is interested in starting to learn Wing Chun kung fu?

Wing Chun is a very useful self-defense system but while it is easy to learn, it is very hard to master. Like learning anything, you must be committed and open-minded. At the same time, you should not hesitate to ask questions about why you are taught certain movements because Wing Chun is based on a set of scientific principles and logic. This will help you to understand and build a strong foundation. It also makes the lesson a lot more interesting.

Do you have a particularly memorable kung fu experience that has remained as an inspiration for your training?

In the early 1980s, I was giving a demonstration in a hall in Sydney when a member of the audience asked me to demonstrate the one-inch punch. The floor was very slippery and to make matters worse, the volunteer for the demo was a huge guy – over 6 feet tall and weighing more than 250lbs. I didn't think I could do much in the circumstances. Well I focused my force on the phone book he was holding against his chest, not knowing what the outcome would be. Then, to everyone's surprise, including my own, I threw this guy several meters away and he landed in a heap on the floor. He must have been one of the heaviest people I have shifted, so it really inspired me. It showed me my training was on the right track and reinforced my belief from fights I had in the early days.

Wing Chun Masters

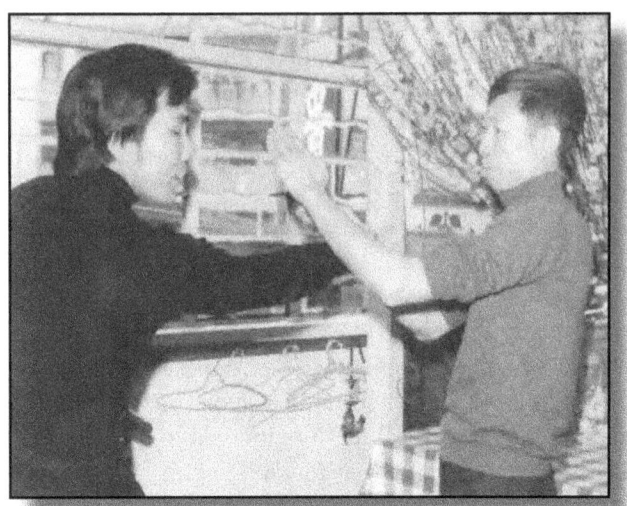

"Practicing the forms is like practicing scales in music and Chi Sao is likened to playing the actual music."

Another memorable experience was our Academy's 30th anniversary celebration in Sydney in September, 2003, attended by thousands of people. In our demonstration, I had to propel an "attacker" weighing more than 200lbs who was pushing against my forearms (as in a double tan sau position), which were outstretched in front of my body. By focusing my mind power, I was able to use my forearms to send this person flying backwards about four meters, knocking down the four students holding a training mat behind him.

how are the Chi sao aspects of training related to the practical application of the Wing Chun techniques used in the three empty hands forms?

Normally, you don't do Chi Sao until you have learned Sil Lum Tao because you need to have good stability and a strong structure, bong sau and fook sau. You commence with single sticking hands (Chi Sao) then both. Later, as you learn Chum Kiu, you discover how to coordinate your movements and move your weight around while doing Chi Sao. Chi Sao is like a summary of all the Wing Chun empty hand movements. It teaches you how to react spontaneously, search for openings and trap your opponent's hands while freeing one of your own hands for attack.

Once you have a good foundation from training with the three empty hand forms, you will find the practical application in Chi Sao is relatively easy. This is because the techniques and movements are the same. Practicing the forms is like practicing scales in music and Chi Sao is likened to playing the actual music. Unless you have a good basis in the three empty hand forms, you cannot practice Chi Sao successfully.

is there anything lacking in the way Martial Arts are taught today compared to how they were in your beginnings?

Judging from the limited number of schools I have seen, it appears to me there should be a lot more respect, and more time should be spent learning rather than concentrating on winning tournaments. Irrespective of the effectiveness of the style, all Martial Arts are beneficial and unique in their own way. Hence, students or followers do their best to preserve their own styles.

It is, however, inevitable that as the old masters have died off, their styles have become diluted because their students are not trained well enough. Also, not many people are able to make a comfortable living out of teaching Martial Arts, so there are few full-time professional teachers dedicated to preserving their particular styles. On the other side of the coin, students do not seem as dedicated as in the past mainly due to people's busy lifestyles today.

What do you consider to be the most important qualities of a successful kung fu practitioner?
First, patience and commitment. Then, respect for your master and instructors; willingness to meet the challenge; don't give up too easily; understanding what you have been taught; monitoring of skills and finally compare what you can do today with what you did yesterday, rather than looking for examples in other students because once you have reached their skill level, you will stop trying.. This way, you will continue to improve.

h ave there been times when you felt fear in your kung fu training?
My master has always treated me well and I have never seen him lose his temper. He is always friendly and laughing and never threatening. Even sparring or in Chi Sao training, he has never missed and hit me. I have full confidence in his skills so have never felt fear or intimidation.

What are your thoughts on the future of the art?
Wing Chun is easy to learn and apply, suits people of all ages and does not require brute strength or acrobatic skills. Its logic and scientific principles appeal to people who are more skeptical nowadays about what they are learning. For these reasons, I believe more and more people will take up Wing Chun in future. The rate of growth will depend greatly on the number of properly qualified Wing Chun instructors throughout the world teaching the art. These instructors must be willing to put aside their egos to seek further instruction from genuine Wing Chun masters or grandmasters to improve their knowledge and skills further. This will no doubt help the Wing Chun art to perpetuate.

VICTOR KAN

The King of Chi Sao

VICTOR KAN BEGAN LEARNING VING TSUN KUNG FU WITH THE LATE GRANDMASTER YIP MAN IN 1954, WHEN HE WAS 13 YEARS OLD IN HONG KONG.

HE WAS WITH YIP MAN FOR 7 YEARS AND IN THAT TIME DURING WHICH HE BECAME KNOWN AS THE 'KING OF CHI SAO' OR 'THE UNTOUCHABLE'. VING TSUN WAS VICTOR KAN'S ONLY INTEREST AND HOBBY AS A TEENAGER. WITH HIS EXCELLENT PHYSICAL AND MIND CONDITION, AND HIS PARENTS' SUPPORT, A FEW YEARS LATER HE BECAME ONE OF YIP MAN'S TOP STUDENTS. IN THE LATE 1950'S, HE BECAME YIP MAN'S ASSISTANT CHIEF INSTRUCTOR UNTIL HE LEFT HONG KONG FOR EUROPE IN 1961. CURRENTLY HE IS BASED IN LONDON, ENGLAND WHERE HE HAS BEEN TEACHING SINCE 1975. THE WALLS OF VICTOR KAN'S SCHOOL ARE ADORNED WITH PHOTOGRAPHS THAT MAKE UP A "WHO'S WHO OF VING TSUN", AND VICTOR HIMSELF IS IN MOST OF THEM. SOLID AND STRONG AT HIS AGE, VICTOR TAKES GREAT PRIDE IN HIS LINEAGE AND THE FACT THAT HE IS A DIRECT STUDENT OF YIP MAN. HE IS NOW THE ONLY STUDENT OF YIP MAN TEACHING IN EUROPE AND HAS BRANCHES IN ITALY, BELGIUM, LUXEMBURG AND HONG KONG. HE KEEPS THE HIGHEST STANDARDS OF AUTHENTICITY AND INSISTS ON TEACHING VING TSUN IN THE CLASSICAL WAY JUST AS YIP MAN TAUGHT HIM. HE ACCEPTS THE FACT THAT CHANGING ATTITUDES OF MODERN GENERATIONS HAVE LED TO MODIFICATION OF THE ART BUT IS ADAMANT THAT WHAT YOU LEARN FROM HIM WILL ALWAYS BE THE ORIGINAL ARTICLE, SIMPLE TO LEARN BUT HARD TO MASTER.

sifu Kan, tell me about your training under yip Man in the 50's.

When I was young, street fighting, violence and crime were common in Hong Kong. As I grew up in such a troubled society I felt that I needed to learn some form of martial art to protect myself and my family. In 1954, one of my friends took me to the Kowloon Catering Union headquarters in the Sham Shui Po area. This was to be my first experience with the Ving Tsun system. Upon entering I saw that many people were punching. kicking and grappling each other. After the class my friend took me to see a middle-aged bald gentleman who was teaching at the school. I remember that he was wearing the traditional Chinese long dress. He looked at me and said "You are rather big and well-built for your age. I will call you Big Boy." Everybody laughed at his remarks. I later found out that Grandmaster Yip Man always liked to address his students by their nicknames. After this encounter, with my parent's permission I joined the school at Lay Dah

Wing Chun Masters

street the following year. I continued to train under Grandmaster Yip Man until I travelled to London in the 1960's to further my studies.

Do you advertise your system as 'classical' Ving Tsun? Why do you use the term "classical"?

The Classical Ving Tsun meaning passed from one Sifu to another, from generation to generation without changing or modifying any of the movements, techniques and the way which time takes to learn. Like 'Classical Ballet', a good ballerina has to spend a lot of time and hard work learning from a good teacher in a reputable school, so that they can perform the 'Classical Swan Lake'. This has been going on for generations and will last forever - whilst the modern version of Swan Lake had appeared on just a few occasions and disappeared forever.

There are many modified versions of Wing Chun in the world nowadays. Those instructors go around saying that "in the 21st century everything needs to be modified". A 1950's Mercedes just cannot run faster and better than a 2000 Ford. It's true, we are in a hi-tech world - we all know that.

"The old way of learning and training is the best way."

A handgun can do a better job than any martial art weapon, but in Kung Fu bare hand fighting is the other way around. The old way of learning and training is the best way. Simply because that in the 'old days', people relied completely on their Kung Fu skill to defend themselves and stop other people killing them! This meant that they had to find a good Sifu and spend a lot of time practicing very hard. Classical Ving Tsun is the superior system.

The late kung fu star Bruce Lee also trained with yip Man at that time. Did you train with him?

Six months after I started training, the late Bruce Lee joined the school. As a Si-hing I was told to help Bruce with his basic training. In fact I spent a lot of time with him on the first form Sil Lim Tao, the little ideas. Bruce was talented and picked up things fast. Unfortunately, he could only train from time to time as his film work kept him busy - he was filming the old Cantonese film "The Orphan".

What was yip Man's influence on Bruce Lee?
In the mid 1950's Bruce was a very active teenager. He learned a bit here and a bit there in several different styles of martial arts. Until one day when he practiced some Ving Tsun, he was so impressed that he looked for the best instructor and he went to Yip Man to learn. His influence on Bruce Lee was so deep that later in his life he used what he had learned from Yip Man as the base for Jeet Kune Do.

in the 50's who were the most dedicated and loyal students that you can recall?
Leung Sheung who was the Chef of the Kowloon Catering Union was the earliest student. He was the one who invited Yip Man to instruct the fellow workers in the Union Canteen. Then Lok Yiu, Chu Shen Tin, William Cheung, Wong Shun Leung and myself became the top five students at that time. Bruce Lee was only a junior member then.

h ow did g randmaster yip Man become popular among the local people?
In the mid 50's, Yip Man was not very happy. He had a lot of personal problems. Two of his sons were still inside mainland China and he had a lot of financial burdens. The latter incidents virtually forced him to move his school into a very rough area of Hong Kong called Sab Gik in May 1957. I and only a few other loyal students were constantly at his side, helping out teaching and repelling many 'cross-hand' callers. These were very valuable experiences for me and I learned to apply my skills in all kinds of situations. I remember one particular occasion when I went to train and found a large crowd was gathered a few streets away from the school. I made my way up to the front and saw a woman was lying on the street pavement crying. There was blood all over her head. I also witnessed a stocky man who appeared to be her husband abusing her. Suddenly a small, slim figure appeared and confronted the bully, telling him to stop beating his wife. To my surprise I saw that this was my own Sifu. The bully told Yip Man to mind his own business but Sifu Yip replied, "It is wrong to beat up a weaker person. This is my neighborhood hence it is my business". The man then suddenly started to throw punches at Sifu Yip who responded with a right Lap Sau punch and a left Pak Sau punch. Within seconds the dispute was over and the man ran away holding his head with his hands. Sifu Yip then helped the woman back to her feet and

saw her safely home. After this public display of courage and skill people came to study Ving Tsun from all over the place. The school became so crowded that we had to train Chi Sao out in the street! I virtually became his assistant helping with new members. From then on Sifu Yip never looked back.

What is the real meaning of the term "Kung Fu"?

Kung Fu means time and energy expended on work. We can use Kung Fu as an adjective to describe the ability of a professional man. For example; if someone saying that the Chef of cuisine has not enough Kung Fu, it means that the Chef is not very good. Nowadays it is translated as 'Chinese martial art'.

When did you start teaching Ving Tsun in England?

I came to study in the early 1960's but I did not teach publicly until 1974. In the 1970's Bruce Lee did much to boost the Ving Tsun system worldwide. At that time there were not many qualified Ving Tsun teachers around. The system became a victim of its own publicity. Virtually anyone could become a Ving Tsun master overnight. Unfortunately, this ridiculous and sad situation still prevails today.

Nowadays people don't have as much patience as they had in the old days. In London or Hong Kong it is the same, it is normal because we are living in a fast world. I must say that I have gotten some good students in my school who understand the traditional way in which I teach them. Most of the young people in Hong Kong are more interested in finance rather than martial arts, and those that do practice martial arts want to finish the system in one year! Even though they have a better culture and understanding background - it is just impossible, they can never be good.

Today people take up martial arts as a past-time, for health reasons, exercise, to impress their friends or for self-defense, but they don't seem to want to spend too much time and effort on it. This means that the modern instructors have to please them as a customer, not as a student.

Many Ving Tsun practitioners are now also training with weights. Would the modern day followers of our time tend to train against the principles of the original Ving Tsun style?

I personally do not train with weights but some of my students do. I believe that such a method of bodybuilding can complement the Ving Tsun system. One of my instructors, who is a European weight lifting champion feels comfortable with the style. Isn't this a good example of combined training? Ultimately if one has a good teacher to guide him/her then one can achieve good results.

Towards the later part of Bruce Lee's training history he had changed not only the name of his system but also his fighting theories. What is your opinion on the subject?

Although I was the one who actually started Bruce in his first form training I did not train with him much because his attendances were very irregular. Nevertheless, in the early 60's although Lee did emigrate to the U.S. he did come back to Hong Kong to further his study in the Ving Tsun system seriously for two years. As far as a superior standard of kung fu was concerned I would say that it was for sure the Ving Tsun system that enlightened Bruce and took him on to the levels beyond. Lee was an intelligent and ambitious young man who realized that the only way that others would acknowledge his own talents and achievements was to break away from tradition and establish himself as a figurehead of his own right. Hence he took a big gamble and founded his own version of martial art: Jeet Kune Do.

"I personally think that Lee's work has given the Ving Tsun style more credit than any past Ving Tsun practitioners could have done."

Many Ving Tsun teachers of today have modified the traditional style one way or another - the consequences are there for us to see. Do you think that the work of the late Bruce Lee contributed more merit to the Ving Tsun system or not?

I personally think that Lee's work has given the Ving Tsun style more credit than any past Ving Tsun practitioners could have done. In his book about Jeet Kune Do, he mentioned that his JKD was mainly based on the Ving Tsun system. I respect Bruce to the point that although he had established his own status, he never failed to acknowledge his 'family tree' within the Ving Tsun style.

Wing Chun Masters

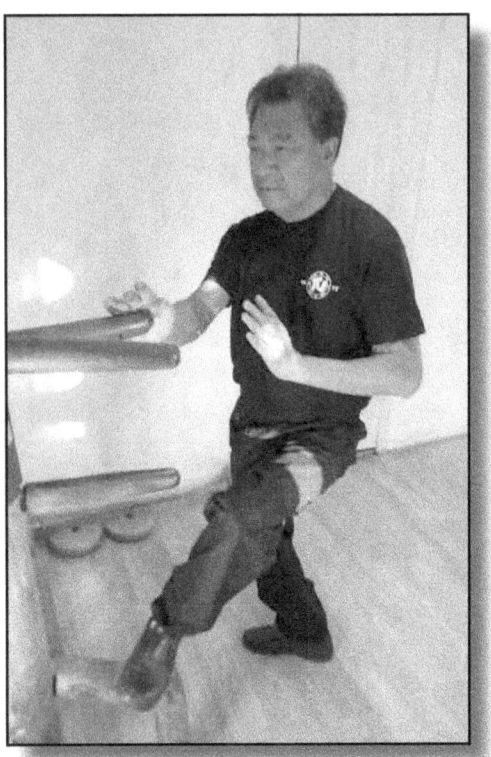

"I could say that the Ving Tsun style will flourish and attract more followers."

Can you tell us about the funeral of your sifu yip Man in hong Kong in 1972?

Near the end of 1972, I was told by my kung fu brothers, that Sifu Yip Man was very pale and thin and he could hardly talk. Yet he was quite pleased to see me rushing back to pay my respect to him. He tried so hard to comfort me, he even tried to put on a little smile. Yet the more I saw him suffering, the more I felt the sadness. I just broke down and cried. I stayed with him as long as I could until he passed away two days later. He was 72 years old. Since Grandmaster Yip had many friends, his funeral became one of the biggest events within the Chinese martial arts community of that time. Many other masters came to pay their respects. However, there was one prominent figure who was missing amongst the mourning crowd - Bruce Lee. The worst part was that Bruce was actually in Hong Kong at that particular time. It was interesting to see that Bruce acted so passionately, loyal to the dead teacher in his film 'Fist of Fury', yet when his real Sifu died he did not even bother to show his face at the funeral. When the rest of the martial arts community found out that he was so disrespectful to his own Sifu they planned to boycott all his films. It was not until Raymond Chow, the managing director of Golden Harvest Films put out a full front page apology in three top newspapers that the situation eased down. Whatever the reasons could have been, Lee should have been there with us paying his last respects to our beloved Master.

sifu Kan, since you are the highest authority of the Ving Tsun style in Europe, how do you see the future development of this popular style worldwide?

I could say that the Ving Tsun style will flourish and attract more followers. However, since there are many political differences among the leading figures of the style I cannot see any chance of witnessing a reconciliation and unification of the system internationally. I can predict that there will be more branches and sub-branches beginning to emerge all over the world. Each teacher will teach his own version like myself, the Victor Kan version. Maybe this trend is the only peaceful acceptance and honorable future development among the Ving Tsun system.

Sifu Kan, tell us about your own teaching methods and syllabus.

Some people criticize me for being too fussy. In reply I say to these people would they want the Sifu to guide them correctly though slowly or do they want some messy version? Any style of kung fu needs good foundation work without which the students will be unable to reach the higher levels of training. The speed of progress actually rests on how much the students are willing to put themselves into the training. A teacher can only show them the way to enlightenment which guarantees future success. This is similar to the English saying; "More haste, less speed". On the other hand only a responsible teacher will press for the perfection of techniques, the quality of the student is what counts, not quantity. As far as my syllabus is concerned, I will teach all that I learned from my Sifu Yip Man. Obviously they have to show their own dedication and loyalty before they earn their status among us. With my past twenty years of teaching experience I have devised my own grading system. There are ten grades of progressive syllabus with each having its own training methods.

Please tell us about the characteristics of the Ving Tsun system.

The main characteristics of what became known as the Ving Tsun system are its economy of movement, directness of action, its vertical straight fist, its sticking hands and its use of the center-line theory. This theory is based on the fact that the shortest distance between two points is a straight line, so techniques move from the centerline of the body. Ving Tsun uses no wide, flowing or circular techniques so each attack involves the minimum of movement. Therefore energy is conserved and distances are shortened. Ving Tsun also combines blocking with striking and has refined this skill to a high level. Ving Tsun practitioners consider it initially more important to develop skill with hand techniques because they are immediately useful for self-defense.

What about the three forms?

There are only three forms in Ving Tsun. The first is Siu Nim Tao, which means 'little idea'. The second is called Chun Kiu ('searching arms') and the third is Bill Tze ('thrusting fingers'). Siu Nim Tao is an important form because it contains most of Ving Tsun's hand techniques. It also trains students in stance work and helps them develop their chi. Students should spend at least 15 minutes practicing Siu Nim Tao.

The value of Siu Nim Tao in developing internal energy is illustrated by the following example. When I was 45 years of age, I decided to practice the form while on holiday in the ski resort of Val d'Isere. Despite a temperature of -15 degrees, I stripped off my jacket and prepared to practice. At first my toes went numb, so I couldn't feel them. Then an icicle formed on the end of my nose! Gathering my concentration I began the form and within minutes I could feel warm blood circulating through my body as my chi began flowing. The icicle melted, I could feel my toes again and I was wreathed in steam! It was a tremendous feeling!

how important is Chi sao?

After practicing Sil Nim Tao, the student should move on to sticking hands or chi sao. First the student uses just one hand ('dan chi'), then he goes on to use both hands ('sern chi'). Embodied within this unique form of training is the core Ving Tsun principle of using the opponent's strength against them. Unlike many other styles, Ving Tsun does not oppose the opponent's force with force because in that case the stronger person will nearly always win. Instead through sticking hands practice, students learn to develop sensitivity in their arms and wrists. This allows them to predict what an opponent is going to do, so they can respond at a very early stage. Sticking hands practice develops timing as well as reflexes.

Once the student has become proficient with sern chi, he should next learn how to use sticking hands to both attack and defend against the partner. This is known as 'qor sao' and it eventually develops into a full-blown fighting format. In class all techniques are used with restraint. However it is no problem to use them at peak force when circumstances require it.

how did you get the reputation as 'The King of Chi sao'?

At the same time (1957-58) I was more or less Yip Man's assistant. Yip Man was very old. That was what I call his 'blue period', and financially it was not very good. I was only sixteen or seventeen but I was big and strong for a Chinese person and I trained seven days a week, four or five hours each day. Yip Man was not physically at his best, so when students came I was the one they did the chi sao with. I would do chi sao non-stop with ten or twenty of them at one time and around thirty to forty people a day. It was never a problem, that's why they called me 'The King of Chi Sao'.

"Ving Tsun's two basic foot techniques are a front kick and a side kick. Both are delivered through the centerline of the body and strike home with the heel."

When do you introduce the second form?

Right after qor sao, the student moves on to learn Chum Kiu. This is basically a defensive form, teaching students how to turn and simultaneously block in response to attacks and then immediately counter them. Two blocks that are used extensively with this form are 'bong sao' and 'woo sao'.

What can you tell us about the kicking in Ving Tsun?

Ving Tsun's two basic foot techniques are a front kick and a side kick. Both are delivered through the centerline of the body and strike home with the heel. Neither kick is delivered above waist level because low kicks are the quickest to perform and the most practical in a true fighting situation. Typical targets are the groin, shin and knee. Ving Tsun's kicks are mainly used in addition to the hand techniques.

Wing Chun Masters

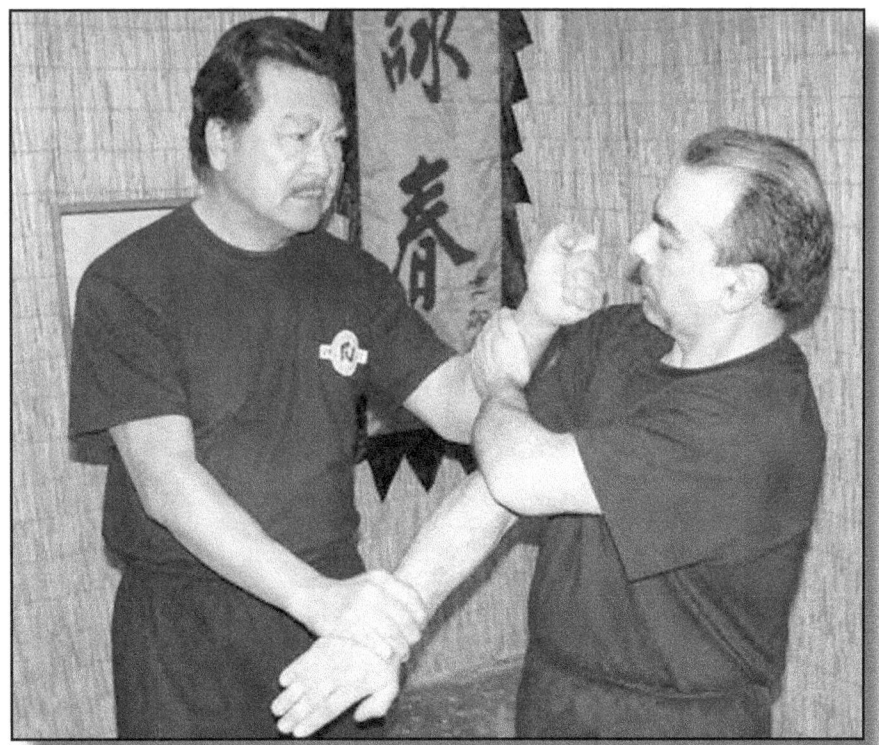

"Techniques used against the dummy are taken from Ving Tsun's forms. They were selected because they are highly effective and practical techniques."

And the Muk yan Chong?

The wooden dummy is intended to resemble a human opponent. It is used by more advanced students to develop their ability to fight with control. Proper use of the dummy involves an understanding of and skill in the Ving Tsun principles mentioned earlier. Novices do not know enough about Ving Tsun theory, footwork and stance to be able to use the dummy and must wait until they have more skill. Techniques used against the dummy are taken from Ving Tsun's forms. They were selected because they are highly effective and practical techniques.

The final Ving Tsun empty hand form is the Bill Tze form. Unlike Chum Kiu, Bill Tze is mainly an attacking form.

And the weaponry system?

The complete Ving Tsun system uses two weapons which are the butterfly knives and the long pole. The long pole was used in a large space against multiple opponents while the butterfly knives are short-range weapons. Nowadays neither weapon has any practical value as such, though the movements used in their deployment are important to Ving Tsun practice. Additionally, Ving Tsun is a traditional system and one cannot claim to know it without having knowledge of its weapons.

so the Chi sao is the 'key'?

Students come to my club for more advanced training. They say they know and understand all the forms but when they participate in real chi sao, their shallow knowledge shows itself. Their hand positions are wrong, they lack sensitivity and respond too slowly, and they can't block their opponent's strikes. This is the basis of the old saying that one minute's chi sao allows you to determine who is the better performer.

What do you think students are more attracted to these days?

Nowadays, students frequently ask to be taught more advanced forms before they have learned the first. They seem to think that the more forms they learn in a short time, the better they will become. This is of course nonsense! It is essential that students learn and understand the first form before progressing, otherwise their depth of knowledge will be shallow and they will develop bad habits. An old Chinese saying is that 'it is pointless having many knives in one's pocket if none of them cut".

how do you see the Wing Chun situation in the world today?

It is more or less the same story everywhere. A person wants to learn Wing Chun, so he picks an instructor from an advertisement. If this instructor has learned the modified or imitation Wing Chun from his Sifu, and his Sifu learned that from his so-called Master, then this person obviously learned the modified or imitation version. Years later, even though they found out that what they have learned and taught was not correct or genuine they are too deeply involved and have no choice but to carry on teaching that version and glorify each other - some even twist their story in order to keep their students. The result is that the authenticity is lost and the newcomers get confused and are unsure which or who is the genuine article.

To see whether the student has this attitude, the good sifu will test him and look for humbleness, desire to learn and perseverance. Those without these characteristics never develop real skill in the system. Remember, one thousand hours of training for one minute's use.

KEITH R. KERNSPECHT

The Kaiser of Wing Tsun

KEITH R. KERNSPECHT HAS AUTHORED ABOUT A DOZEN BOOKS ON MARTIAL ARTS, MOST OF THEM ON WING TSUN, BUT ALSO THAI MARTIAL ARTS AND ESCRIMA. HE STARTED AS A WRESTLER (CATCH-AS-CATCH-CAN) IN THE 1950, PRACTICED ALL MARTIAL ARTS AVAILABLE, FOUND WING CHUN IN ABOUT 1970 (LINEAGE: LEE SING/JOSEPH CHENG), CHANGED TO LEUNG TING IN 1976, INTRODUCED ESCRIMA TO GERMANY IN 1977 AND OPENED ONE OF THE FIRST MUAY THAI AND LING LOM CLASSES IN GERMANY IN 1978 (SANTHUS SUPASTURPONG). IN 1979, HE WENT TO SEATTLE TO WORK WITH BRUCE LEE'S FIRST STUDENTS JESSE GLOVER AND ED HART, WHO HE LATER INVITED TO GERMANY, AUSTRIA AND SWITZERLAND TO TEACH.

DURING THE LAST YEARS HE INVESTIGATED AND STUDIED 5 INTERNAL SYSTEMS, AMONG THEM TAI CHI, PAKUA AND HSING-I. BUT HIS FORTE AND LOVE ALWAYS REMAINS WING TSUN AND HIS ONLY SI-FU GRANDMASTER LEUNG TING.

PROFESSOR KERNSPECHT IS THE FOUNDER AND LIFE PRESIDENT OF THE LARGEST WING TSUN ORGANIZATION OF THE WORLD, THE EWTO ("EUROPEAN WING TSUN ORGANIZATION"), WHICH IS AFFILIATED TO GRANDMASTER LEUNG TING'S IWTA, HONG KONG.

What are you currently engaged in?
Fundamentally resolving the same problem that has preoccupied me since the end of the 1950s: how can I defend myself with as few movements as possible? Or rather, by the very nature of my movements.

And you needed more than 55 years to find this out?
Yes, as there was no style that could or wanted to teach it. As you know I practiced wrestling, Judo, Ju-Jitsu, Karate, Aikido, Kempo, Hapkido, Taekwondo, Escrima, Wing Chun, Ving Tsun, Wing Tsun. But none of these styles teaches pure self-defense. Shotokan Karate teaches Shotokan Karate, Ju-Jitsu teaches Ju-Jitsu, Wing Chun teaches Wing Chun.

Do you mean that each style sits in its ivory tower without looking out into the street to see what actually happens? And what about the modern Mixed Martial Arts?
They don't look out into the street either, only at the ring or octagon. I

Wing Chun Masters

"As Bruce Lee rightly said, "they all only do something that is "vaguely related" to self-defense.""

like MMA as a sport! There are now a few reality video clips available showing how frighteningly naive and un-streetsmart some MMA sportsmen can be in the world outside.

Do you mean that they too do not practice self-defense?

As Bruce Lee rightly said, "they all only do something that is "vaguely related" to self-defense."

Let me use a play on words to put my point: in all the 55 years of my incessant learning and studying, I have never had the impression that the aim was to teach me. They all only wanted to teach their style.

Yet every style, even the best, like Wing Tsun, only gives us part of the truth. Everything appears logical from its own point of view, but other styles also see themselves as logical. When I look at the very few really effective Asian martial arts styles, the opposite view of a given set of teachings often makes just as much sense! Nonetheless, their adherents have an almost religious belief in the partial truths that have been instilled in them.

so what are the styles that actually work?

Styles that look at function. Where function comes first, and then the form. Form follows function! Unfortunately most styles start everything with the form (Kata). And usually that's where they also end. In the meantime there are usually highly inventive explanations of the movements in the form based on zero street experience, plus far-fetched applications (Bunkai).

The new student wants to learn how to defend himself, and all he gets is forms. isn't the situation similar in Wing Tsun?

Traditionally that is probably true. But as my Wing Tsun Sifu Leung Ting once wrote, tradition means "Nothing has been improved!"

Wing Tsun begins with the "Siu Nim Tau" form, though its primary purpose may not be learning mere techniques, but rather mental training or unifying oneself. Training our attentiveness and power of imagination, while in an apparently motionless stance. Although very few actually say it or still know it, it is all about developing the mysterious Jin force, about creating links between the parts of the body, and about developing harmonious psycho/physical unity which includes breathing, something we do not really talk about in Wing Tsun at this stage because it adapts itself automatically.

But there are also movements to be learned in the first form (siu n in Tao).
Yes of course, but these are secondary. Try explaining that to a student! What do you think would happen if I left him standing in the special SNT stance (IRAS) for 30 minutes without moving?

Then you would not have the 60,000 or so students you have now!
Quite so, and perhaps that was the reason why the masters before us added arm movements. This makes it more interesting for beginners, for beginners in particular always look at the arms. This is where they expect movements, and we need to meet this expectation if we are to avoid standing in a school with no students. It is the standing, or standing meditation if you like, that is important, and the arm movements are the sugar coating that makes the bitter pill (standing still and pressing your knees together) bearable. This standing exercise is the first indication that Wing Tsun, which was originally a northern system according to Grandmaster Yip Man, is conceived as what we might call an internal style.

An internal style like Tai Chi, Pakua, h sing-i?
Yes, you can already see it from the structure: pole standing, few movements, a form of Chi Sao training, fighting based on situational awareness and tactile/kinesthetic training, use of sophisticated rather than primitive forces and clearly defined principles. Starting with relaxation. And the power comes from the legs and torso, and is transferred to the opponent via the arms.

But in the siu n imTau you don't notice this (yet), as only the arms move.
Wanting to avoid mistakes like good Confucians, it starts with the smallest details and the extremities that are furthest away from the central axis. With the 2nd form (Cham Kiu) it gets closer and closer to the central axis as the source of power and moves on to the 3rd form, which I consider to be the true Wing Tsun. If Ng Mui and Yim Wing Tsun had studied sports and movement science with Prof. Tiwald, they would have put the horse

before the cart! And they would have had the courage to let their students make mistakes, as you learn faster and retain more that way.

you clearly feel a need to bring new impulses into the teaching method.
I feel an obligation to bring about a rethink while I still can. That can only be a slow process. I find myself in the curious situation of contradicting some things that I parroted without critical examination in the 1980s. However you spell it, the Wing Tsun (Wing Chun, Ving Tsun) now practiced in most European countries (maybe with the exception of Great Britain) comes from what I taught at the time. Now that I know better and am presenting things differently, I am attacked using my own pronouncements from long ago. Clearly some people do not believe, after so many years and having been the first student of my Chinese Master Leung Ting to be awarded the 10th grandmaster level 13 years ago, that I am capable of learning more and being an independent thinker.

But perhaps some people don't want to learn more themselves, and prefer to close the door.
Very possibly. After all, it must be awful for someone who received his master certificate from me years ago, and only needed a few more sets of the knife form to round it all off, as he thought, to be asked to look at things again in a different light. A Sifu such as myself, who reinvents Wing Tsun each day, and who builds everything on the principles and explains everything by them, must be more of a curse than a blessing for some. I'm sorry about that, but I can do no other.

This is why I chose a team of successors: a 9th (Giuseppe Schembri, M.A., Switzerland), an 8th (Dr. Oliver Koenig, Austria) and a 7th degree (Andreas Gross, M.A., Heidelberg, Germany) Master to control me and protect the traditional Chinese Wing Tsun from my scientific desire to improve the teaching methods.

you constantly strive to learn more. To understand Wing Tsun even better, you even went back to u niversity.
And I dragged my students and martial arts colleagues along with me. Many of them have now obtained their Bachelor, Master degrees, and a few a doctorate.

I have been working together with several Bulgarian universities since the 1990s. My friend Prof. Dr. Margaritov, the former Minister of Sport and Vice Rector of Plovdiv State University, gives me wonderful support.

In a similar way we are working together with the University of Derby in

Buxton, England. At present we are conducting a semi correspondence course with 2 weeks of mandatory attendance with them on the subject of "Theory & Practice of the Martial Arts". And with the Bulgarians on "Theory & Practice of Wing Tsun". The English course of study requires no high school certificate, but a preparatory coaching course, while the Bulgarian course requires a Bachelor degree or similar. There will soon be more coaching courses for new students wanting to take part in the prestigious English course of study.

is it true that you learned the so-called internal styles of Pakua, h sing-i, Tai Chi Chuan for the university studies?

"Learned" would be too much to say, as I have so far only had time for five intensive weeks. But I have "studied" them, and feel that I have understood them and their principles to a good extent. Old, experienced northern Chinese masters (most of them University professors) helped me in the process, without any secretiveness. The relationship was eye-to-eye. We were colleagues and compared principles and their applications.

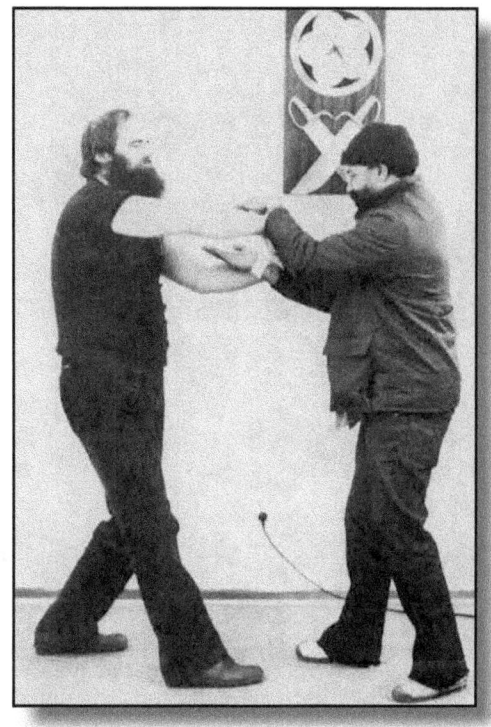

"Old, experienced northern Chinese masters (most of them University professors) helped me in the process, without any secretiveness."

ho w did you get this idea, and how did you make these contacts?

It was all on the initiative of my (late) mentor Prof. Dr. Horst Tiwald. I owe more to this man than I can express.

What do you actually want to change in Wing Tsun?

Strictly speaking, nothing. And nothing at all about our Wing Tsun techniques, or in the forms. But quite a bit about the traditional teaching method! The fact that our Chinese predecessors were able to develop as ingenious a "fighting system" as Wing Tsun does not necessarily mean, as I have often heard, that they also developed a correspondingly ingenious "teaching method".

Wing Chun Masters

"What also disturbs me, and delays learning progress in the individual, is the cessation of movement at the end of a technique."

When we look at how most masters teach we find out that their method is based on learning by rote, on the drill-like instilling of habits by repetition. This is entirely out of kilter with Chan-Buddhism, which is about presence of mind and also spontaneity.

What also disturbs me, and delays learning progress in the individual, is the cessation of movement at the end of a technique. This too is in contradiction with Chan-Buddhist thinking as I understand it. We must allow the student to let his movement flow, even at the risk of him making mistakes.

We must depart from the many details and don'ts, and go back to the two fundamental forms of movement, receiving and giving back. That is what it is all about. Otherwise the student will not see the wood for the trees.

in this case the wood is the principles, and the trees are the many techniques?

Precisely. The techniques are only examples with which we confront the student in the solo forms, and also in the partner forms conceived by my

Sifu, so that he understands and absorbs the principles involved. When he becomes a master himself, he really does not need them anymore – for himself that is.

Is that what you meant when you wrote this in "Essence – beyond techniques and thinking in applications": "The student should not learn the exercises, but learn by the exercises?"

Bravo! In the end the Wing Tsun master as I imagine him should not be distinguishable by specific movements, but by a way of moving that is "unspecific" – a term I did not invent but which I consider to be apt.

you said that for over 50 years, you have always been looking for "a self-defense system that solves all possible problems with as few movements as possible."

You are referring to what I termed "unspecific" movements. After studying with Prof. Tiwald I would now prefer to call it unspecific "moving", as we are not talking about specific techniques against something in particular, but about a "general way of moving".

In the belief that I had seen something similar from the Korean master Masutatsu Oyama, it seemed to me as a teenager that one could defend against and possibly counter all manner of punches with arm movements "resembling the blades of a fan".

The more I became immersed in Karate, the more I forgot this idea, as I was allowing myself to be overloaded with movements (techniques). The means were overrunning the purpose.

you no longer saw the wood for the trees?

I had forgotten why I started learning this. I was now learning Karate. But what I wanted to learn was "how to defend myself".

They did not teach you to defend yourself ...,

... instead they taught me their Karate style.

They did not teach you ...,

... but rather Karate! I am pleased to see that my use of language has fallen on fertile ground.

h ow do you see Karate now? you even hold the 3rd Dan, do you not?

For ten years I first taught Kempo, then Karate in the "Budo-Zirkel Kiel". I now remember that the Kempo style I learned from a Belgian or Dutchman had precisely such "fan blade-like movements" in which the opponent's attack was bound to become entangled. And I now also know that Master Oyama had learned Kempo, i.e. original Chinese Kung Fu, without confessing it.

i am certain that you have also found the original Chinese style.

You know me well. I also studied it in detail. Later it led me to Wing Chun, which I learned in London's Chinatown from Sifu Joseph Cheng, a student of Grandmaster Lee Sing, in the early 1970s. In 1975 Joseph "referred" me to Grandmaster Leung Ting, from whom I learned Wing Tsun to the 10th grandmaster level and beyond.

you were his first disciple who he gave the 10th degree to.

This is true. That was in the year 2000. Since then I have taken the liberty of becoming an independent thinker. But I owe a lot to my Sifu and value his knowledge and skill highly. He is the best Wing Tsun man I ever met in my life! And believe me I met more than a dozen original students of Yip Man, when they were still alive.

Did you find your unspecific movements in Wing Tsun?

Yes, but here too, I was distracted from the actual purpose by the overwhelming and detailed techniques e.g. in the partner forms. It is like being in a restaurant, when the waiter asks me how I found the steak. My answer: "Hidden beneath the sauce that was drowning it, and beneath the accompaniments that were there to fill me up!"

And where is "the unspecific" hidden in our Wing Tsun?

In my book "Essence of Wing Tsun – beyond techniques and thinking in applications" I assert that "Everything important is already taught in the first lesson."

For the beginner this applies to the unmoving stance during the Siu Nim Tau form. And for the advanced student it applies to the very first Chi Sao exercise, the "rolling arms" (Poon Sao).

As in a nucleus, this "rolling of the arms" already contains everything in combination with the three levels and the idea of "sticking" and deceptively adapting oneself, of taking the lead and then suddenly descending on the prey like a raptor at the right moment.

in your first bestseller and conceptual book "o n s ingle Combat" from the 1980s you quote the classic adage: "i fear the reader of only one book!"

Yes, in a sense this underestimated Poon Sao, which is probably also practiced with the wrong attitude, is this one book which contains everything needed.

really everything?

No, of course not. It is still missing the right energy. Striking power. Footwork. What I call "The Big Seven".

your Big seven according to you are Attentiveness, Adroitness, Balance, Body unity, interaction of the senses, Timing and sense of distance, Fighting spirit. These are the indispensable capabilities that a fighter must possess to defend himself?

To defend himself using "our Wing Tsun"! If he wants to defend himself with e.g. Kickboxing, he needs quite different capabilities such as strength, speed of movement, endurance, the ability to take punishment etc.

And how or where does the student develop these seven capabilities?

In the classical view, by practicing the solo forms. My Chinese Sifu Grand Master Leung Ting has added to these with his partner forms, i.e. application forms.

And you? What do you think of this?

I am now experimenting with exercises that develop these capabilities specifically, simply and without detours. Without the forms or the need to memorize, i.e. taking a direct route.

Many are concerned that you intend to abolish the classic Wing Tsun forms.

That would be nonsense! They give us structure and identity. After all, we only have four short weaponless boxing forms. I neither want to abolish them nor change them a bit. I teach them like my master taught me.

so what is your criticism of the forms?

They must not be the main teaching method. Partner training under guidance that directly addresses the Big Seven is at least as important.

"I am now experimenting with exercises that develop these capabilities specifically, simply and without detours."

Wing Chun Masters

"Leaving the 3rd form and perhaps the Wooden Dummy form aside, I think there is not enough flow when practicing the forms."

And otherwise?

Leaving the 3rd form and perhaps the Wooden Dummy form aside, I think there is not enough flow when practicing the forms. Constantly stopping and pausing in the final positions is counter-productive with respect to the aims of Wing Tsun as a fighting system.

What is to blame for this?

Maybe an incorrect understanding of the motto "Dim dim ching" (Every point clear). The student is constantly unsure whether he is performing the technique correctly, checks his final position in the mirror or waits for the ok of his teacher before continuing. The student therefore develops "the bad habit of pausing in final positions", and fails to develop the "flow".

But isn't this more of a teaching problem?

Yes, the teacher needs to be enlightened in this respect. There is nothing fundamentally wrong in Wing Tsun! But it must remain allowed to examine the teaching method critically from a scientific point of view. We must not shy away from this out of sheer piety. Wing Tsun Grandmaster Leung Ting said: "Traditional means that nothing is improved."

But to do this we need to be aware of the goals we want to achieve with Wing Tsun, the principles etc.

One goal is the develop the capability of defending oneself. Another is to develop attentiveness. Another is to maintain or restore good health.

But the desire for personal safety was probably first and foremost. should we now speak about your teaching method "BlitzDefense"?

Anybody who has practiced Wing Tsun for many years should have developed sufficient means of self-defense. Things are quite different for those who have perhaps only been training for a few months. Yet it is precisely those who have a need for security. The same is true of security personnel, police officers etc., who are allowed only a few hours of training. It is for those persons that I created "BlitzDefense".

Before the creation of "BlitzDefense", clients such as these were obliged to fire off salvos of chain-punches at anybody who stood in their path, is that right?

Right, and they can continue to fall back on this "straight blast" if, against expectation, the more reasonable means offered by BlitzDefense should fail to do the trick. I developed BlitzDefense at the end of the 1990s. It is made up of body language, verbal communication, automatic responses and an appropriate forward defense which proceeds responsibly and more commensurately, and in the ideal case consists of a single knockout blow should all attempts at de-escalation prove unsuccessful.

What was the problem with the chain-punches?

The frequently lacking proportionality that Western courts of law expect. Somebody who has overwhelmed another with 30 chain-punches just because he had the "impression" that he was about to be attacked will find little understanding in front of a judge.

I know the answer, but will ask anyway for the benefit of laymen: why do we have to strike anyway? Is it not better just to take avoiding action and apply a lock to calm the other party down ?

That would certainly be more humane. However this capability is only achieved after several years. An innocent party who has not provoked an attack cannot be expected to take such a risk. Moreover, we have found that a beginner has the best chances if he launches his own surprise attack.

how can the beginner bring himself from the correct decision – that he has to attack to have a chance – to the action of delivering a blow that eliminates the threat?

For example by using the "trigger-word", an idea for which I am grateful to my friend Geoff Thompson in England. It takes you from the decision to decisive action.

"BlitzDefense" has been around for quite a while now. how effective has it proved to be?

We can look back on 13 years of experience in private and official use in many countries of the world. It has more than proved its worth. In the roughest cities and in crisis areas. Corresponding reports and expressions of thanks have confirmed our expectations.

We have continuously developed it further on the basis of experience gained, by which I mean we have simplified it.

o n what is "BlitzDefense" based in technical terms?

On a disguised, non-provocative safety position, applied psychology, attentiveness, determination, distraction and a punch behind which the bodyweight is concentrated.

Did you develop it all yourself?

I wish that were so. But I was able to fall back on the findings of many experts. For example Jesse Glover, Bruce Lee's 1st student and assistant instructor. Geoff Thompson, Europe's most famous doorman, Escrima Grandmaster Bill Newman, who needs no more introduction from me than my Sifu Leung Ting.

To what does the "BlitzDefense" user respond?

To a few visual patterns.

h ow many techniques must be learned for this?

You know I am not in favor of so-called dead, i.e. fixed or pre-arranged techniques. I have managed to get by with fewer than six moves (combinations). Any further movement would be one too many to learn. There is also a division of tasks: our dominant (stronger) hand delivers the knockout, the weaker controls the opponent. I adopted this from weapon system thinking.

Can we really call this "true Wing Tsun"? i mean Wing Tsun as you understand it. After all, you teach a Wing Tsun that emphasizes Chan Buddhist attentiveness and is not based on habit or automatic responses.

The 6 movements used are fundamentally from Wing Tsun, as are the functional principles behind them. It is self-evident that BlitzDefense for beginners cannot be the high art of a philosophical, spontaneous and creative Wing Tsun that uses presence of mind to create "instant concepts", as Prof. Tiwald calls them, and realizes "movements of the moment". But neither are the blindly aggressive salvos of chain-punches of yesteryear the real Wing Tsun, where the preceding punch is the reason for the next and the function is overlooked. BlitzDefense is primarily about self-protection. A simplified Wing Tsun that meets the beginner's need for rapid security.

is it primarily security that the new student is looking for when he comes to an EWTo school?

I think this is the prevailing motive for starting to learn Wing Tsun. When this justified need is satisfied, there are other reasons to continue practicing Wing Tsun.

"Over and above pure self-defense, Wing Tsun offers so many attractive possibilities."

What would these reasons be?

To learn an Asian movement art, a philosophy in motion, to express oneself and realize one's potential. Over and above pure self-defense, Wing Tsun offers so many attractive possibilities.

Could one say that the "real" Wing Tsun only begins after "BlitzDefense"?

Just as one might talk about the art of eating well, of enjoying and being a gourmet when it is no longer a matter of preventing starvation? Yes, perhaps.

BlitzDefense is only an exercise and wants to be no more and no less than an "applied, simplified Wing Tsun for the beginner" who seeks a fast route to self-defense.

you often distinguish between the Wing Tsun or Wing Chun that we know and that which we do not know, the one that is already a reality for you as a visionary and developer, and with which you experiment, but which for the vast majority of your students – who are not in day-to-day contact with you – still remains remote and just a promise for the future.

That's right. I concern myself with the perfect Wing Tsun, how it could

Wing Chun Masters

"The conventional Wing Tsun (Wing Chun, Ving Tsun) is something external, or in the best case something half external and half internal."

be. A Wing Tsun that has Yin & Yang, and excludes nothing. I know that this confuses many and overtaxes others.

Could you perhaps give us an overview of how you personally distinguish between the two Wing Tsuns? Perhaps first the conventional Wing Tsun, the Wing Tsun we know?

The conventional Wing Tsun (Wing Chun, Ving Tsun) is something external, or in the best case something half external and half internal.

Students learn the traditional solo "forms" to acquire the movements (techniques) contained in them, absorb them through constant, rhythmical repetition and make them 2nd nature.

They learn the "applications" for each individual movement and practice them as "drills" until they become "fixed techniques". The appropriate counter-movement is "produced" in response to a certain move by the opponent.

The "attack" takes precedence over defense. The most effective attacking technique is the so-called "chain-punches", where one punch follows another. The 2nd punch follows because you have performed the 1st, and the 3rd because you have performed the 2nd etc.

The whole thing is aggressive and pretty headlong, without listening to the relevant argument (question) of the opponent.

As for the defenses, they only become necessary if one's punch fails to have the expected result. If the opponent is able to defend against the attack of the "external" Wing Tsun fighter, the latter will give way slightly with his arms/shoulders.

He then adopts an angled final position (Bong Sao, Tan Sao), the upper body is tensioned, especially the shoulder-blades, so that he can direct the incoming force through the abdominal muscles, knees and feet to the ground. In this way he can allow the opponent's pressure to turn him away by 45 degrees.

This the Wing Tsun that is generally known: It is arm-biased, mainly linear, bases itself on a "wedge" and works with what some American scientists call "automatisms".

And the Wing Tsun that is not known, Wing Tsun as a possibility?
For the sake of argument I will call it the "internal" Wing Tsun here, but I don't believe there is a dichotomy.

Here the student also learns the traditional solo forms, but not so as to instill the movements contained in them as techniques which he wants to "apply" in a fight at all costs.

In internal Wing Tsun we do not want to learn the exercises (form techniques), but rather learn "with the help" of the exercises (form techniques). As exercises the solo forms help us to unite ourselves into a "wedge" and a "ball".

In internal Wing Tsun it is fundamentally important not to execute specific movements by intent, but rather to explore the environment with movement and attentiveness to perceive current "arguments".

This is primarily a matter of imagining this environment (Yi), i.e. using an image (Yi) to attentively go out into this environment.

When it comes to "real combat", we have learned to extend our "attentiveness" towards the opponent, where we can perceive the current "arguments". So it is not a matter of realizing prefabricated movements or instilled habits that are a characteristic of rhythmical movement.

The perception of current "arguments" from the environment gives rise to a very specific form of movement which is particularly influenced by the interaction between the facets in the entire "linkage" ("muscle sense"). It is all about "Jin-power".

This is the Wing Tsun that is unknown:

It is torso-led, involves the entire body, is linear and round, spherical, is inspired by the "wedge" and the "ball". It maintains its structure when appropriate, but surprisingly gives it up for another. It is relaxed/tensed without being limpid or strained, but will also willingly give way like a willow branch ridding itself of snow. It follows Chan-Buddhism, and is not based on automatisms, conditioned reflexes and habits!

SAMUEL KWOK

In the Steps of Yip Man

SAMUEL KWOK WAS BORN IN HONG KONG IN 1948, THE SON OF A CHURCH MINISTER. HIS INTEREST IN THE MARTIAL ARTS STARTED AT AN EARLY AGE, AND HIS FIRST EXPERIENCE WAS IN WHITE CRANE KUNG FU, UNDER THE GUIDANCE OF HIS UNCLE, LUK CHI FU. SAMUEL KWOK'S WING CHUN TRAINING STARTED IN 1967 UNDER CHAN WAI LING IN HONG KONG. HE IS A MASTER OF WING CHUN KUNG FU IN THE TRADITION OF THE SYSTEM'S GREAT WARRIORS. HE HAS ESTABLISHED HIMSELF AS ONE OF THE MOST KNOWLEDGEABLE WING CHUN INSTRUCTORS OF OUR TIME. HIS BACKGROUND IN THE SYSTEM SPANS SOME FOUR DECADES, IN WHICH TIME HE HAS HAD THE OPPORTUNITY TO TRAIN WITH THE WORLD'S BEST. GRANDMASTER KWOK HAS BEEN A SENIOR REPRESENTATIVE OF THE IP MAN METHOD SINCE THE EARLY 1980S. HE HAS THE DISTINCTION OF BEING TRAINED AND BEING THE SENIOR REPRESENTATIVE OF BOTH OF IP MAN'S SONS, GRANDMASTERS IP CHUN AND IP CHING. HIS PERFORMANCE AT THE FIRST WORLD WING CHUN CONFERENCE IN 1999 IS LEGENDARY, AS IS HIS DEMONSTRATION AT THE GRAND OPENING OF THE IP MAN MUSEUM IN FOSHAN, CHINA. IN ADDITION TO HIS EXTENSIVE TRAINING UNDER IP CHUN AND IP CHING, HE ALSO HAS HAD THE OPPORTUNITY TO TRAIN UNDER SUCH FIRST GENERATION MASTERS AS LEE SING, CHU SEUNG TIEN, AND WONG SHUN LEUNG.

IN HONG KONG, AS WELL AS IN FOSHAN, HE IS TREATED WITH THE GREATEST RESPECT DUE TO HIS VAST CONTRIBUTIONS TO THE WING CHUN SYSTEM.

how long have you been practicing the martial arts and who were your first teachers?

Since I was nine years old, I watched kung fu movies on television until I was about fifteen or sixteen years. At that age, I started going to bazaars (refugees came from mainland China and sold a range of Chinese herbal remedies; for example, Dit Da Jow, where the people demonstrated their kung fu skills in order to sell their wares). I learned a lot from watching these demonstrations. I was introduced to the Wing Chun White Crane Fuijien Style. Master Cheng Man Lung—he was the full contact fighting champion in Canton (during the 1980s)—was very powerful because of his Dim Mak skill, and he trained with a bucket full of granite rocks. His fingers were very short and thick because of years of striking his hands into the bucket. My interest in Wing Chun continued in 1968 when a guy who played basketball showed me the Sim Lao Tao form; however, I was not very impressed at his demonstration of the form. I came to England in

Wing Chun Masters

"I have spent many years training under the guidance of the two sons of the great Grandmaster Ip Man"

1972 and started learning Wing Chun from Lee Sing, who was a student of Grandmaster Ip Man. Lee Sing was my first Wing Chun teacher, and it was he who introduced me to Grandmaster Ip Chun in 1978. I furthered my studies with Grandmaster Ip Chun, who taught me the Wooden Dummy form and all the other Wing Chun forms in great detail. I have invited Grandmaster Ip Chun over to the UK on numerous occasions to conduct seminars. Incidentally, Grandmaster Ip Chun is the most skilful practitioner of Chi Sao that I have ever seen. In 1992, I brought his brother, Grandmaster Ip Ching, to the UK to conduct seminars, and in 1995, I brought both of them to Chicago to conduct joint seminars. In 1994, I continued my training in Wing Chun under Grandmaster Ip Ching. I have spent many years training under the guidance of the two sons of the great Grandmaster IP Man and promoting them in the UK, USA, and Europe.

how many styles (kung fu or other methods) have you trained in?

I have trained in White Crane Kung Fu with my uncle, Luk Chi Fu, and his son. Luk Chi Fu also was one of the greatest Lion Dancing teachers in Hong Kong. He is a Grandmaster of the White Crane style. I trained with my cousin, sifu Luk Chung Mau, when he was teaching in London from 1976–1978 and continued my lion dancing studies with him. I chose to teach the Ip Man family Wing Chun. However, I also have come across a range of martial arts. I think it is important to have an open mind when it comes to your quest for knowledge of martial arts. For example, various martial artists who came to study with me exchanged their knowledge of their own arts. I have had people train with me from Karate and Tae kwon do, who were 4th Dans. In addition, I became friends with various Masters of Thai Boxing, Master Toddy (who is now teaching in Las Vegas), Master Win (we sparred together), Master Woody, and Master Krin. I have remained good friends with them all.

What are the main principles intrinsic to the three Wing Chun empty hand forms? Do they interrelate with each other?

The first form, Siu Lim Tao, is the most important—it has the basic positions and stance. For example, tan sau, fok sau and the centerline theory. This form focuses on how to train for power and energy; for example, focusing on the thumb while performing tan sau and the wrist when performing fok sau. In addition, the first form focuses on how to develop the correct use of elbow energy. The second part of the form teaches you how to use the energy correctly, i.e., the use of last moment energy. The transition from one movement to the other is in a totally relaxed state.

Chum Kiu is the next stage in the development of the Wing Chun style. This form is important in that it focuses on the turning and using Yu Ma—turning the legs and hips to generate the energy (as a whirlpool of the spinning top)—to redirect energy away from your centerline. It also teaches you how to "borrow" the energy from your opponent, who is attacking you. This form helps you concentrate on your "defense" and includes the use of the bong sau movement—using this movement to defend your centerline. In Chum Kiu you start to move; you use the "big bow" (provide an illustration of this concept) and "bridge the gap" (provide an illustration of this concept) with the use of footwork and "seeking the bridge." (provide an illustration of this concept) You also train to defend at various angles, for example, defending against 180 degree attacks from different directions. These movements are to enable you to cover your centerline when your hands are away from the centerline by using two-hand techniques simultaneously.

Bil Jee is very important in that it trains you how to recover your centerline in an "emergency" situation (provide an illustration of this concept). You train to use two energies going in different directions, in that you borrow the energy of your opponent and use many elbow techniques. The "emergency" techniques are used if an opponent is trying to control your elbow. In addition, you utilize your Yu Ma turning stance to increase your power for the application of your energy in two directions, for example, double larp sao (check spelling of term). All three Wing Chun forms are related to each other but have their own meaning and purpose. The Siu Lim Tao form teaches you all the basic techniques that are then used in combination in Chum Kiu and Biu Jee. The three forms all are to prepare us for Chi Sao, which prepares us for fighting.

Would you tell us some interesting stories of your early days in kung fu?

When I was watching the people in the bazaars, Ma Fei Lung (one of the many Masters who performed their kung fu skills)—this guy always impressed me—used rocks; he'd place one on top of the other and would break them with his bare hands. One day, my friend and I were watching the demonstrations and we changed the rocks in his basket—for some reason, he was unable to break the rocks that we had placed in his basket. Years later, Grandmaster Ip Chun introduced me to this Master and he said, "You changed my rocks!" This master inspired me to train in my early days as I practiced the techniques I observed at the bazaar and from the books on martial arts I obtained from the library. I eventually started training to hit small stones that I placed in a bag. The reason I taught myself was that I was bullied in school. After training in the techniques observed in the bazaar and my books, I overcame the guys who bullied me at school and was left in peace from then on.

h ow did you find the Westerners respond to traditional Chinese training?

When they come to the first lesson, most of the people I have come across ask the same question: "How long till I get a black sash/belt?" Most of them are more interested in getting a belt than learning the art itself. Some of my students are very dedicated, but I have found that a lot of people don't want to train hard—they want it too fast; they want the forms very quickly (as always, there are some individual exceptions). There are so many "keys" to learn, which take time to understand and develop, and then be able to apply naturally. Those who wan to learn quickly are going away with a framework but have nothing inside the framework (it's like the skin on an orange: it can look good but how good can it be if the inside is not as good as the outside looks).

Were you a "natural" at kung fu? Did the movements come easily to you?

Actually I am not very good at memorizing lots of movements and many forms. That's why I found Wing Chun a better style of kung fu for me to learn, but it takes many years to master. I happen to have the "renovated" 8mm film of Great Grandmaster Ip Man demonstrating SLT, CK, and the Wooden Dummy forms. I have been watching and studying this footage for many years; I can relate to the correct positioning of hands and feet. Of course, in 1981, I went to Hong Kong to train with Grandmaster Ip Chun.

ho w has your personal kung fu developed over the years?

I think it changed when I studied with Grandmaster Ip Chun, especially when I traveled around with him over a period of many years. He is only 5-foot-4 and of small stature; however, I have never seen anyone get through his defense in Chi Sao over the years (no matter what size physique the other person has).

"I have developed the ability to identify and communicate the "keys" of the core principles of the Wing Chun."

What are the most important points in your teaching methods? And what are the most important qualities for a student to become proficient in the Wing Chun style?

I teach the student to have dedication, i.e., don't train one day and leave it for several days. Train often and hard. Use your head—Wing Chun is a thinking art. You need to get the students to use their brains to find out why a technique works, to understand the principles and theories, to understand the "keys." It is 50 percent from the sifu and 50 percent from the student. You must remember that everyone's build/stature is different; you have to adapt your teaching method and the focus of your student. For example, a smaller person has to use more footwork and borrow the other person's energy. In addition, I tell my students that it is always good to observe other styles of martial arts, so that you can see the techniques and think how you will be able to "feel" these techniques if applied against

Wing Chun Masters

"Wing Chun Kung Fu can be very difficult to learn properly at the beginning."

you (for example, in a competition). It also is important to emphasize to students to avoid injuries, because if they become injured, they need to take the necessary recovery time. I have developed the ability to identify and communicate the "keys" of the core principles of the Wing Chun Style. I also tailor my communication of these "keys" to the capability of each student, who, as we know, have their own learning style and cultural background. I encourage all my students to analyze what they have learned from me, reflect upon their analyses, and return to the next training session with a list of questions that will enhance their understanding. In addition, I, myself, analyze my teaching sessions, reflect upon the problems that a few students may encounter during the training sessions, and design strategies to facilitate a deeper understanding for these students.

In regard to the second part of your question, it is important to encourage a student, especially in Chi Sao, to attack after they have a good defense. Again, it is important to encourage students to ask relevant questions, in order that they understand the "keys" and transfer that knowledge into their daily training. The use of mirrors is very important; mirrors aid your ability to check the positions. And always go to back to your teacher for corrections and advice. Wing Chun Kung Fu can be very difficult to learn properly at the beginning—the teacher has a responsibility to teach his students diligently. Students should be open-minded, receptive, analytical, and diligent, in a constant (search seek) of knowledge, and loyal and respectful to their sifu. In addition, they should be willing to pass on the true teachings of the Ip Man Style.

With all the technical changes during the last 30 years, do you think there are still "pure" styles of kung fu?

Talking about Wing Chun, I try to stick to the "traditional" style. It was my goal to learn as much as I could about the style as Ip Man had practiced it. I wanted the "real" Wing Chun. I did exhaustive research, studying with as many of Ip Man's senior level students as I could. I have had the good fortune to have Li Wai Chi, Chan Wai Hong, Chu Sheung Tien, and Wong Shun Leung, among others, share their knowledge with me. I have also studied the 8 mm film that Ip Man made for his sons just days before his death. It speaks volumes that Grandmaster Ip Man thought it so important to document his Wing Chun that he filmed it when he was so sick and close to death. In 1978, I went back to Hong Kong to further my studies of Wing Chun. I was blessed with the opportunity to study with the two sons of Great Grandmaster Ip Man, Grandmasters Ip Chun and Ip Ching. Grandmaster Ip Ching studied with his father (Great Grandmaster Ip Man in his younger days, and then from 1962, when he came to Hong Kong to live with his father. At that time, he had no permanent employment and he studied daily with his father until he unfortunately passed away in 1972. Grandmaster Ip Ching is one of the few Wing Chun practitioners who have learned the complete Ip Man Family Wing Chun system, including the advanced knives form.

Do you think different "styles" are truly important in the art of kung fu?

There is the history of different styles—each style has something to offer and all the styles have some similarities; for example, both the "internal" and "external" styles. Some styles are excellent for health benefits, e.g., Chi Kung and Tai Chi. Every style has its own specialties.

You cannot really compare styles; it depends on a range of factors. For example, it depends on how the style is taught, who actually teaches it, and how often and the quality of practice by the student. It must be remembered that, in the beginning, the majority of the Chinese martial art styles originated from the Shaolin Temple.

Different styles may suit different individuals. Some styles are more energetic, focus on relaxation, or focus on the street scenario applications. It also depends on the stature, age, and goal of the student (more athletic, more health-oriented, self-defense related). The Wing Chun style of Kung Fu is very good for practical self-defense. Some styles have too many forms and too many movements in each form—they are too complicated. This is not the case with the Ip Man Family Wing Chun Kung Fu style.

What is your opinion of Full Contact kung fu tournaments?

If a tournament is properly organized it can be very beneficial for the student and it is essential that there a correct set of rules that will minimize any injuries happening to the participants, for example, proper gloves with matching the protective padding. If no gloves were allowed, there would be the risk of severe injuries to the participants. I heard a story that one participant was killed in a tournament in Hong Kong, however, I cannot guarantee that this is a fact as I did not personally attend this tournament.

how different from other kung fu styles do you see the principles and concepts of Wing Chun?

For me, the Wing Chun style is very different, as it is based upon the "centerline" theory (the shortest distance between two points is a straight line). Wing Chun does not incorporate any 'flowery' techniques. Then, we have Chi Sao, which is an excellent exercise for training for sensitivity and reflexes, which is essential in defeating an opponent in a competition or a street fight. Chi Sao training helps the person to react without thinking. Due to the sensitivity training, the person learns to redirect any energy that is oncoming and use the Fan Sao technique in conjunction with the footwork of the style. In my opinion, the Ip Man Family Wing Chun Kung Fu style is unique, due to its inclusion of very fast techniques that can be applied in close-in fighting situations, e.g., attacks in a street environment. The principles and concepts are totally different from many other styles; for example, we have the centerline theory, simplicity and economy of motion (fixed-elbow position), and the concept of energy transmission at the last moment the fa jing.

Do you think that kung fu in the West has "caught up" with the technical level in China?

I think the standard is high, according to my Masters Ip Chun and Ip Ching; however, Hong Kong remains the highest standard. The grandmasters are based in Hong Kong. The problem, as I see it, is that while there are some instructors in the West teaching a good standard of Wing Chun, many are not. There are instructors who trained with Ip Man for only a short period of time and had to leave Hong Kong before completing their Wing Chun training. Some have gone on to establish themselves as instructors and teach an incomplete and adlibbed version of Wing Chun. There also are instructors who have trained in a seminar or two with Grandmasters Ip Chun and/or Ip Ching, and now claim their lineage as being through them. They mislead students as to their lineage and their depth of knowledge. This should not be. Bruce Lee was a great martial artist who learned from Grandmaster Ip Man. He always gave credit to Ip Man and Wing Chun for his accomplishments. He taught a method that was heavily Wing Chun-based, but since he didn't teach the traditional

"In my opinion, the Ip Man Family Wing Chun Kung Fu style is unique."

system, he didn't call it Wing Chun. He had the integrity to call what he taught by another name, rather than mislead people. If someone is claiming to teach "Ip Man Wing Chun," the system they teach should be recognizable as what Ip Man taught. If for example an instructor is teaching kicks and footwork within the first form, then it has been changed pretty dramatically from what Ip Man taught. If the system is changed to where it no longer is of the standard Ip Man taught, it shouldn't be called Ip Man Wing Chun. We intend to help correct this by educating the public as to the standard of the Ip Man system as passed to me through the sons of the Grandmaster. I have established the Traditional Ip Man Wing Chun Association in the United States. We are producing a series of instructional videos on the keys to the Ip Man Wing Chun system, as well as a book I have cowritten with my senior U.S. disciple.

Kung fu nowadays often is referred to as a sport. Would you agree with this definition?

Certainly not. In China, there has been a lot of research into the traditional styles. They have realized the importance of the traditional styles,

Wing Chun Masters

"Wing Chun is a very popular style around the world currently; it can be easy to learn."

and many people who have conducted the research have requested that the "old masters" come into the "limelight." However, many of them have refused to do so. There is an ongoing process of "re-tidying" the traditional systems. Kung fu should always be regarded as a martial art and a way of life, the main purpose of which is self-protection. Competitions are effective training tools, but it should always be remembered that they have rules. In a true life-threatening situation, there are no rules. That is why Chi Sau is so important.

Do you feel that you still have further to go in your studies of the art of Wing Chun?

I, personally, have a long way to go—the more I learn Wing Chun, the more I feel I have a responsibility to promote the style as Great Grandmaster Ip Man taught it. I also try to help my students apply the style more effectively. This has to be done with a "hands-on" approach. Some of my students have studied other styles for a lengthy period of time before commencing training with me. I have found this useful in explaining the correct application of Wing Chun techniques to aid my students' abilities to protect themselves.

I would like to add that I learn from my students who ask "searching" questions. This allows me to explain the theoretical underpinnings of the Wing Chun style in more depth. The most important point is to understand and be able to apply the correct use of the "appropriate energy"—for example, after a block, you should relax immediately, in order that you can "feel" and react instantaneously. In addition, it is essential to learn how to switch "on" and "off" the appropriate energy. This, in my opinion, is the highest level of training. Fa Jing training is learning how to develop and use energy correctly—"the last moment" energy. It is important to develop the style but not to "break" the underlying principles of the style.

ho w do you see Wing Chun kung fu in the world at the present time?

Wing Chun is a very popular style around the world currently; it can be easy to learn. It is a very scientific and effective style—that is why people are attracted to it. It is a very practical style for street self-protection, and Wing Chun is becoming as popular as Tai Chi.

Does the weaponry aspect of Wing Chun [long pole and butterfly knives] enhance the student's empty hands ability, or are those two completely non-related skills?

Wing Chun has only two weapons. The knives form is related to the hand forms; it is an extension of the hand techniques. The long pole is actually from a Shaolin style and became part of the system when name and name exchanged ideas. Grandmaster Ip Ching stated that the long pole form is very important for developing "wrist energy"; for example, it aids in controlling the other person during Chi Sao. In the original pole form, the stances were very low. Many people today train and perform the pole form with stances that are too high. The "spear" movement in the form is an excellent exercise for developing power for punching. The knives form is excellent for developing good wrist energy and for developing your footwork for fighting situations. The weaponry forms are extensions of the empty hand forms, utilizing the same basic principles, movements, and muscles, so they are just as important and any other part of the system.

h ow does the Wing Chun style differ from other kung fu methods when applying the techniques in a self-defense situation?

The difference is that the Wing Chun practitioner always should aim to control the other person's two hands with only one of his/her own hands. This creates the situation in which it is very difficult (if not near impossible) to be counterattacked. A Wing Chun practitioner should never lose the "initial contact" with the opponent. In addition, the Bil Jee form teaches you to improve your speed for attacking (feeling when there is an opening in your opponent's defense). This ability makes it more difficult for your opponent to defend against you. Wing Chun has the advantage of training you for close-range fighting, which is the case in a street environment.

When teaching the art of kung fu, what is the most important element: self-defense, health, or tradition?

They are all important aspects of the Wing Chun Ip Man family style; all are interrelated. Some people say that Wing Chun is only for health, but Wing Chun can be very aggressive if utilized by an experienced practitioner.

Forms and Chi sao, what's the proper ratio in training?

It all depends, because the forms can be practiced alone. You must have a partner to practice Chi Sao. In my opinion, Chi Sao is most important; you need to be able to perform the "turning" movement developed in Chum Kiu properly, and have someone "hands-on" to help you refine your sensitivity and movements, in order to increase your skill level. Chi Sao is the closest exercise to fighting and it is important to Chi Sao, on a regular basis. And have your teacher advise you why you have left "openings" in your defense. Forms should be regarded as an opportunity to refine your technique and position and Chi Sao as an opportunity to develop and use those techniques in a fluid and responsive manner. The two are intertwined, and one should not be practiced to the exclusion of the other. Grandmaster Ip Man was of the opinion that Chi Sao was the most important part of Wing Chun, that Chi Sao was its intelligence, its genius. He would therefore focus on this in a student's learning process, and it would make up almost 90 percent of the program—and I believe the same.

Do you have any general advice that you would care to pass on to the practitioners in general?

Personally, I spent two years learning and understanding the movement of SLT, as the basics are very important. I would advise anyone not to be hasty or greedy, in that you should get your basics correct and make sure you understand the theory that is the underpinning of the movement. Develop your "energy" and, again, it is most important to understand the theory—do not follow "blindly";, ask your teacher "why" are we doing this movement. These questions will aid your understanding.

Choose the right teacher; this will save you years in your training. Find a teacher who not only will allow you to ask questions, but will encourage you to do so. Your teacher should require himself to have the patience to listen to you (the student). You should find and remain with a teacher who will help you become a better person in life in general. You should be humble and avoid having an "ego."

Some people think going to China or Taiwan to train is highly necessary. Do you share this point of view?

Again, it all depends. We have been traveling to Hong King and China to train on an annual basis. In China, we visited (Grand Master Ip Ching accompanied us on this trip) two schools in Foshan and exchanged ideas. For example, both parties demonstrated the forms and we "played" Chi

Sao with each other. I was quite disappointed in the way that Wing Chun was being taught in China. I suppose it all depends on how much the sifu has learned from the Great Grandmaster Ip Man. There are a lot of good teachers in China; many Masters do not "come out" and demonstrate their skills or teach the general public. It is important to travel to Hong Kong. I go there to train with my Masters, and my students come to see and train with my Masters. My students see that I am teaching them, the same way my Masters taught me. The most important thing is to find a master who is willing to share his depth of knowledge and who is willing to communicate the "keys" of Wing Chun to the student.

What do you consider to be the major changes in the art since you began training?

If by art you mean Wing Chun, then all I can say is that a lot of people put themselves forward to teach the art without having the proper knowledge and qualifications. When I started, there were very few teachers. I think the standard of teaching has fallen; hence, that is why I continue teaching. My goal is to pass on the traditional Ip Man Family Wing Chun Style and make sure my students have the same develop the same skills.

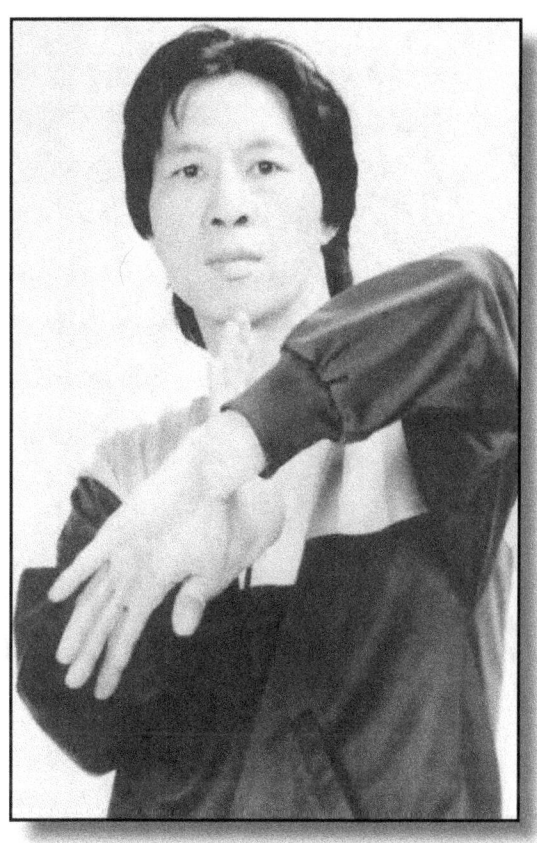

"My goal is to pass on the traditional Ip Man Family Wing Chun Style and make sure my students have the same develop the same skills."

Who would you like to have trained with that you have not?

I would have loved to train with the Great Grandmaster Ip Man, if only I could turn the clock back. I am sure his standard of teaching was superb. However, I am more than happy with the teaching I have received from Grandmasters Ip Chun and Ip Ching.

Wing Chun Masters

"By studying other styles, you can really appreciate the simplicity and directness of the Wing Chun style."

What would you say to someone who is interested in starting to learn Wing Chun kung fu?

I suggest you find the right teacher, learn the basics in depth, learn the theory, and understand it and the core principles. Ask questions that will aid your understanding and train diligently, especially in Chi Sao.

What is it that keeps you motivated after all these years?

I think my students keep me motivated—those you really want to learn and be able to pass on the art, those who love the art of Wing Chun. I don't want the art to be diluted or to be lost.

Do you think it is necessary to engage in free-fighting to achieve good self-defense skills in the street?

If you mean sparring in the class, I like to train people to create a situation (which mirrors a street environment situation) and then apply a relevant Wing Chun technique to defend themselves. I also encourage this type of training to include defense against a weapon; for example, against someone attacking with a knife. We try to make the situation as realistic as possible, taking into account that it is not a "live" situation.

What is your opinion about mixing kung fu styles? Does the practice of one nullify the effectiveness of the other, or can it be beneficial to the student?

By studying other styles, you can really appreciate the simplicity and directness of the Wing Chun style. This is what I have been told by students who have studied other styles and have chosen to follow with Wing Chun path now.

What is your philosophical basis for your kung fu training?

I think that if you learn the "mental" side of Wing Chun kung fu, this helps you on other areas of your life.

Do you have a particularly memorable kung fu experience that has remained as an inspiration for your training?

As previously mentioned, I enjoyed watching the various Masters demonstrate their skills at the bazaars in Hong Kong. Also, I get tremendous pleasure and enjoyment traveling around the world accompanying both Grandmasters Ip Chun and Ip Ching, conducting seminars for practitioners of the Wing Chun style, and helping to introduce the Wing Chun style to people who have studied other martial arts.

After all these years of training and experience, could you explain the meaning of the practice of kung fu?

With regards to Wing Chun Kung Fu, it is a way of life, I think it teaches you to work hard and achieve your goals, not to give up easily and to do a lot of thinking—to use your cognitive abilities during your Wing Chun training and in everyday life.

h ow are the Chi s ao aspects of training related to the practical application of the Wing Chun techniques used in the three empty hands forms?

Chi Sao applies the techniques of the three forms and the turning movements of Chum Kiu. In addition, it teaches you four things: a) the correct way to use energy; b) how to develop good sensitivity (i.e., not using strength against strength); c) to use the other person's energy against him/her); d) to develop good positioning of both the hands and feet which can be applied in any situation.

Chi Sao, if done properly, teaches you how to react automatically. Chi Sao is a special technique and training method used in Wing Chun. To the ill informed, it often is confused with the "pushing hand" techniques of Tai Chi. A familiar term for Chi Sao that is often used is "sticking hands.". It must be remembered that Chi Sao is not a method of fighting; it is a method of developing sensitivity of the arms, so that you can feel your opponent's intentions and moves. Chi Sao, teaches you correct elbow positions. Mastery of elbow control and positioning is Chi Sao's mystery ingredient. The exercise teaches you how to use the right type of energy and feeling for an opponent's emptiness, and defending with the minimum motion or effort.

The relationship of Chi Sao with the practical application of Wing Chun is best answered as follows: "To learn Wing Chun through the Chi Sao exercise, one can begin to understand the forms, and also realize what specialty of strength is needed, or indeed. ot needed, in the distinct and subtle changes of each move".

Wing Chun Masters

"Chi Sao, if done properly, teaches you how to react automatically."

Correct application of Chi Sao can control the movements of your opponent and cut down his angles of attack. In fighting, a student cannot only control both hands of the opponent, but also can make it hard for the opponent to get away once in contact. I feel that whatever level a student is training at, he should and must be able to understand the importance and usage of Chi Sao in Wing Chun. Chi Sa is compulsory in the Wing Chun system because it is the bridge between the forms and the fighting techniques. The student cannot go straight to the sparring techniques after learning the three forms without first having a good basic knowledge of Chi Sao.

I am in total agreement with Ip Man's statement that "The distance of fighting or sparring is the distance of Chi Sao." In fighting or sparring, reflex and sensitivity is the major advantage that enables the Wing Chun practitioner to win.

Chi Sao is the practical application of the techniques learned in the forms. Chi Sao teaches the Wing Chun practitioners to use their techniques in a way that is not static or constrained, with no fixed pattern. It is still training and should be used as an opportunity to enhance your skills. It is not fighting, but rather a way of applying your techniques to improve your fighting ability.

is there anything lacking in the way martial arts are taught today, compared to how they were when you began?

I think you will find it more intense. Today, people focus on the physical side rather than the technical side—the "energy" side of the art.

Could i ask you what you consider to be the most important qualities of a successful kung fu practitioner?

Dedication and the ability to ask pertinent questions of your teacher. You should develop the correct attitude and understand the theoretical drivers of the Ip Man Wing Chun system.

What advice would you give to students on the question of supplementary training (running, weights, et cetera)?

Running is very good for aerobic and anaerobic training for full-contact fighting, and weights can be useful, depending on the type of training; for example, training the biceps and triceps muscles. Be careful and avoid "bulking up" the upper body muscles. Training should focus on your forms and Chi Sao. These are the most important elements in the Ip Man Family Wing Chun system

What do you see as the most important attributes of a student?

It does not matter how hard you train: the person has to be talented to some extent. For example, the person should be intelligent, diligent, respectful, honorable, humble, and open to new experiences—to have an open mind. He or she must be able to understand the theoretical drivers of the system, to look at the theories of other styles, and be able to identify the differences in the styles.

Why is it, in your opinion, that a lot of students start falling away after two-three years of training?

I think it is because of personal problems; for example, there may be too many distractions in life. The most important point is that people do not treat their training as a hobby; their training in the Wing Chun system should become part of daily life.

h ave there been times when you felt fear in your kung fu training?

Of course there is fear; all my teachers live far away. However, I visit my Masters every year and I speak to them on a weekly basis. In some cases, you can "hit a brick wall" in your training; you get stuck on an aspect of your training; you need to speak to or visit a more senior person to ask for assistance. In my case, I always asked my teachers, Grandmasters Ip Chun and Ip Ching.

What are your thoughts on the future of the art?

I want the art (Ip Man Family Wing Chun Kung Fu System) to flourish and be passed on the correct way of the Great Ancestors of the Wing Chun system. This was the purpose of establishing the "Traditional Ip Man Wing Chun Association".

ALAN LAMB

A Great Journey

SIFU ALAN LAMB IS ONE OF THE MOST INFLUENTIAL TEACHERS OF MARTIAL ARTS IN THE WESTERN WORLD. THE FIRST NON-ASIAN MASTER TO BE CERTIFIED IN HONG KONG, SIFU LAMB'S LIST OF WING CHUN STUDENTS READS LIKE A WHO'S WHO IN THE MARTIAL ARTS. ALTHOUGH VIRTUALLY A HOUSEHOLD NAME IN ENGLAND AND EUROPE WHERE HE TAUGHT FOR MANY YEARS, SIFU LAMB IS NOT NEARLY AS WELL KNOWN IN THE UNITED STATES, SPECIFICALLY, SOUTHERN CALIFORNIA, WHERE HE NOW RESIDES. THIS IS BECAUSE, AT THE HEIGHT OF HIS CAREER, LAMB WAS FORCED INTO SEMI-RETIREMENT AFTER CONTRACTING SEVERAL SERIOUS TROPICAL ILLNESSES WHILE TEACHING AND FILMMAKING IN THE COLOMBIAN ANDES.

BORN IN THE MINING TOWN OF NEWCASTLE-UPON-TYNE, ENGLAND, SIFU LAMB ORIGINALLY DREAMED OF BECOMING A COMMERCIAL ARTIST. LATER, INFLUENCED BY UP AND COMING MUSICIANS OF THE TIME SUCH AS ERIC CLAPTON, PETER GREEN AND STEVE WINWOOD, LAMB BECAME ENAMORED WITH THE BLUES GUITAR AND SPENT TWO YEARS AS A PROFESSIONAL GUITAR PLAYER IN A BLUES BAND. AFTER VIEWING A WING CHUN DEMONSTRATION GIVEN BY SIFU PAUL LAM IN LONDON, HE BECAME COMPLETELY SOLD ON THE ART. AFTER SEVERAL YEARS OF STUDY WITH SIFU LAM, LAMB MOVED TO HONG KONG IN 1973, WHERE HE LIVED WHILE STUDYING UNDER SIFU KOO SANG, WHO LATER CERTIFIED LAMB AS THE FIRST NON-ASIAN MASTER OF WING CHUN KUNG-FU.

PRESENTLY, HE TEACHES PRIVATELY TO A SELECT GROUP OF TEACHERS AND CELEBRITIES IN SOUTHERN CALIFORNIA. HE ALSO TRAVELS TO OTHER STATES, GIVING WING CHUN SEMINARS. LAMB CONSIDERS HIMSELF TO BE A KIND OF FINISHING SCHOOL FOR WING CHUN MASTERS, TEACHING THEM THE ADVANCED ASPECTS OF WING CHUN, INCLUDING THE WOODEN DUMMY, LONG POLE, AND BUTTERFLY KNIVES, FORMS LONG HELD TO BE SECRET BY OTHER WING CHUN MASTERS.

h ow did you first become interested in the martial arts?

When I was growing up in England, I saw an episode of The Avengers where the character Steed was trapped in a room. Suddenly, a gloved fist smashed through the door and Steed said, "Let's get out of here. They know karate!" I'd never even heard of karate. Wow! I thought. I really want to learn that!

Wing Chun Masters

"The injury level was quite high from sparring."

What happened next?

Well I found a guy called Bob Wilkinson who was teaching a combination of shotokan karate and jiu-jitsu. Bob was somewhat of a maniac so he did not have a lot of students! I enjoyed training with him but it still wasn't what I was looking for because I was looking for pure karate.

Were you eventually able to find the type of school you were looking for?

Yes. Eventually I found Sensei Danny Chaganis. He was teaching the wado-ryu style of karate and had studied under Sensei Tatsuo Suzuki, the highest-graded wado teacher in the world. Suzuki was a student of Hironori Ohtsuka, the founder of wado ryu. Chaganis opened his school in South Shields, a small fishing town known for its tough, working class people.

how hard was your training under sensei Chaganis?

Very hard! Danny was not in the business of readily giving out belts as some commercial schools are here. You had to work your butt off and often you had to test two or three times for a particular grade. Danny would fail you for the slightest mistake, and he would actually demote those students who did not attend class on a regular basis, or those who allowed their skill level to drop.

Did sensei Chaganis concentrate more on forms or sparring?

Both! The injury level was quite high from sparring, but nothing serious - the usual things you get from a contact sport like sprained fingers, ankles, and toes.

Did you suffer many hardships to attend Chaganis's class?

Yes. Winters can be brutal in the north of England and there was no heating in the school. Many times, there would be a thick coating of ice on the mat. Even so, we were required to do the class barefoot, which was pretty tough. In fact, our feet would still be numb even a couple of hours after class ended. Then once or twice a month, Danny would hold a marathon training session which would consist of four hours of punching, followed by four hours of kicking. Our limbs would be literally shaking for hours after one of those grueling sessions.

how did you go from wado to wing chun?

I had some Chinese friends who were always advocating kung-fu over karate. One day they showed me an article about Sifu Paul Lam, the first Chinese teacher to open a school for non-Asians in London. Since I had already read about Bruce Lee and his connection to wing chun, I decided to take a train to London and check it out.

What was your first impression of wing chun?

As soon as I saw wing chun I knew it was the art I had been looking for. What really sold me was meeting three old Chinese guys at Paul's school. Although they were masters of more traditional styles, they were studying with Paul. So I asked them, if they already knew martial arts, why were they studying wing chun? Their unanimous response was "Because we think it's better!" Their confidence in and enthusiasm for wing chun really impressed me.

"As soon as I saw wing chun I knew it was the art I had been looking for."

Was it easy for you to enroll in sifu Lam's class?

No. He required personal references from my Chinese friends, and, because London is a four to five hour drive from Newcastle, I had to relocate to London.

how did your training with sifu Lam differ from your training with sensei Chaganis?

Paul was also a very strict teacher. He would only accept students who were seriously committed. Also, because his was the first school to teach non-Asians, he had to contend with other Chinese kung-fu teachers who were angry at him for teaching foreigners. Those teachers would send in some of their best students to fight with us because they wanted to discredit Paul and close him down.

i would assume then that your training with Paul involved a lot of sparring?
Yes. We would often leave class sporting bloody noses and busted lips. We had to be constantly on our guard against people coming in to fight us. Consequently, our sparring sessions were very intense. In fact, one night some of us went out for a beer after class and our lips were so badly swollen that we had to drink our beer through a straw. We all had a good laugh about that later.

h ow did your wing chun training compare to your karate training?
Physically it was just as tough, but the emphasis was more on stance work and hand techniques. In addition, wing chun required a higher level of concentration because the art is more strategically oriented.

Conceptually, how did wing chun differ from karate?
Surprisingly, there are a lot of similarities between wing chun and wado ryu. Ohtsuka Sensei was a master of jiu-jitsu, which was actually developed from the Chinese Southern Eagle Claw system. So the wing chun concept of block and simultaneous strike exists in wado, only you don't start practicing it until you are brown or black belt level. However, in wing chun, simultaneous blocks and strikes are taught from the very beginning.

What prompted you to move to h ong Kong?
Sifu Lam had a small livestock business which he was working on expanding and eventually, he no longer had time to teach. I really wanted to finish learning the system so I wrote to the Hong Kong Martial Arts Association and they put me in touch with Sifu Koo Sang who agreed to accept me as a student. In fact, he was the only teacher who would agree to accept a foreigner at that time. It took me about a year to save up the money to move there.

Did you continue to practice wing chun during that time?
Yes, Sifu Joseph Cheng was running a class in London's Chinatown and I practiced at his school for a year before leaving for Hong Kong.

"During chi sau practice, they would constantly throw me fresh guys to practice with in an effort to physically break me down."

Was sifu Cheng's wing chun different from sifu Lam's?

Yes. Joseph was a disciple of Sifu Lee Sing, who had also studied with Yip Man, and they were teaching a mainland version of wing chun. It was interesting to experience a different form of wing chun. Joseph was a terrific martial artist and one heck of an athlete as well. Studying mainland style wing chun definitely helped to make the form of wing chun that I now teach more complete.

ho w did the mainland style differ from the hong K ong style?

There are actually several mainland versions of wing chun. Briefly, Joseph focused more on forty-five degree fighting stances and diagonal footwork. Also, he emphasized wing chun as more of a "hard" style.

Wing Chun Masters

"Koo Sang's chi sau was a lot softer, and he emphasized more counter-fighting techniques."

i would like to turn now to your training under Koo sang. h ow did you like h ong Kong?

It was different from anything I had experienced at that time. I enjoyed experiencing the culture, which was very intriguing to me. The people were polite but it took a while to get to know them. I agreed to help some of the high school kids in Koo Sang's class with their English, and they in turn invited me into their homes to meet their families. It was a great experience.

What was your training with Koo sang like?

Really tough! I was constantly being tested by both Koo Sang and the students. During chi sau practice, they would constantly throw me fresh guys to practice with in an effort to physically break me down. The other students would practice for a while and then quit when tired. However, I would have to work for hours with student after student. Of course, I knew that to give up would have been a sign of weakness so I had to push myself harder than normal. At night I would fall asleep with my arms cramping and locked into weird positions, only to wake up exhausted and unable to move. But after a few months my body adapted to the grueling pace of the class.

Did any of the students resent you being there?

Hell yes! Most of the guys were alright. They eventually accepted me. However, there were a couple of students who were gang members and they hated foreigners. They would try and attack me full power, and often sparring sessions would erupt into real fights. I was warned by some of the decent guys in the class not to rough up these characters because they would wait outside the school and try to get even. However, I continued to give them as much as they chose to dish out but nothing serious ever came of it.

What was your relationship with Koo sang like?

Good. In retrospect, I wish I could have learned Chinese before I went because the language barrier kept us from developing a closer relationship. A few times I screwed up because I did not fully understand what he was saying. Once I was supposed to go with him to the cemetery to sweep Yip Man's grave as a sign of respect. However, I misunderstood what time we were supposed to meet at the school, and when I got there he was already gone. After that I always asked the senior students to translate any instructions he left me so there would be no similar misunderstandings.

how did Koo sang's wing chun compare with sifu Lam's?

Paul Lam's Chi Sau was more physical, with a heavy emphasis on push-pull techniques. Koo Sang's chi sau was a lot softer, and he emphasized more counter-fighting techniques. Working with both of them made me realize that wing chun can truly be classified as a hard-soft system.

i understand that while you were in hong Kong you also trained with a Buddhist monk from the shaolin Temple, sifu Wong. What was that like?

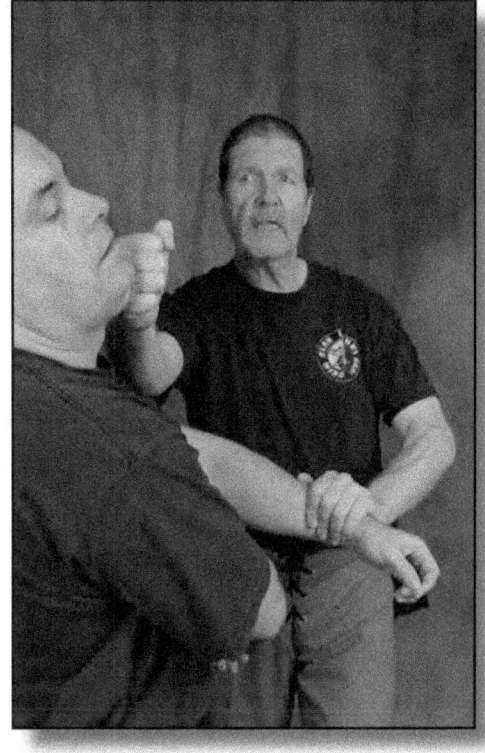

"I believe that wing chun is tailor-made for women because it relies on technique rather than strength."

Very enlightening. Wong's style of kung-fu, siu lum-ji, was the parent system of wing chun. He had been a friend of Yip Man, and they had exchanged many ideas with each other. Wong was incredible. He knew everything about kung-fu. Many of the top teachers in Hong Kong studied with him because he knew the classic eighteen siu lum-ji weapons, and he specialized in iron palm techniques. He was also a renowned healer in the Chinese community.

What did you learn from him?

He taught me many aspects of chin-na, self-defense techniques, and weapons. However, before he would consent to teach me, he looked deeply into my eyes to read what kind of person I was. I really respected him for the high value he placed on honor and character.

While we are on the subject of the shaolin Temple, i would like to turn to the most famous legend that surrounds the origins of wing chun. Do you believe that the art was developed by the Buddhist nun, n g Mui?

Although the exact truth as to how wing chun developed may be obscure, I like to believe in the legend that subscribes to the belief in Ng Mui as the creator. What I can say with certainty is that when I have taught women who were really motivated to learn, they learned the art and adapted to it much quicker than men. Somehow the art just seems to naturally fit a woman's frame better than a man's. Also, I believe that wing chun is tailor-made for women because it relies on technique rather than strength.

Do you really believe that women who learn wing chun can protect themselves against men, especially ones who are larger and stronger?

Absolutely. I truly believe that wing chun is the best self-defense art that a woman can study and use effectively.

Why then do you think there are so few women interested in wing chun, or, for that matter, in true martial arts, as opposed to kick aerobics, executive boxing, or similar exercise programs?

That is a good question. When I was teaching in England, I had lots of women who studied with me who were really good fighters. However, it seems as though the majority of women in the U.S. like to keep in shape by practicing forms of exercise that resemble martial arts, which is fine, but those systems you mentioned will not do you a whole lot of good in a real fight, or if you are suddenly attacked on the street, although they will keep you in great shape. Now, those women who study real kickboxing, which involves sparring, will be able to protect themselves.

Do you think that one of the reasons that women don't study wing chun is because it is not a flashy system, with the high kicks that women seem to like?

Possibly. But in terms of keeping in shape, which seems to be the main motivator for women, wing chun is great. People who have never tried wing chun cannot immediately recognize its exercise value. However, once they start training, they realize what a good workout wing chun is because it combines resistance training, aerobics, and chi kung. And, of course, in terms of being able to protect yourself, wing chun is outstanding. I would like to see more women studying wing chun, especially in view of the recent increase in violent crimes against women, especially sexual assault. I think women definitely need to learn something.

have you ever had to use your martial arts in a fight?

Yes. Several times. Hong Kong, London, New York, and Bogota are all pretty tough cities, and I've been both challenged and attacked, especially after appearing in magazines and on television.

What was your most serious fight?

The scariest one was in Colombia when I was attacked by three robbers. They attacked me simultaneously. I had one hanging on my back trying to choke me, one wrapped around my leg trying to drag me down, and another rushing at me from the side who was trying to cut me with a knife.

Were you badly hurt?

No. I wrestled the knife away and rolled down the mountainside to get them off me. They took off when I started to fight back, but my jacket was pretty badly hacked up. Knowing martial arts definitely saved my life in that situation.

"I think that Keith is the most organized and best wing chun teacher in Europe."

i would like to turn to your career as a teacher. you have taught so many famous martial artists, i don't know who to ask about first. Let's start with one of Britain's top fighters, Terry o'neill.

Terry is one of the best martial artists in the world let alone Britain. He is a hell of a kicker and a great athlete to boot. He picked up on the wing chun techniques very quickly. In fact, he's one of those individuals who can adapt to any martial art. His background is in shotokan, but he has a natural fighting style and spirit. He is definitely one of the toughest individuals I've ever worked with.

one of your most famous students, sifu Keith Kernspecht, has sometimes been called the "Kaiser of Kung-Fu." Why is he called that?

Because he is so well organized and he actually lives in a castle in Germany.

Wing Chun Masters

"I've never had the gall to call myself a grandmaster."

What did sifu Kernspecht learn from you?
Basically, I taught him the wooden dummy, long pole, and butterfly knives which were taught to me by Koo Sang.

What kind of a student was he?
You cannot use the term "student" in the literal sense and apply it to Keith. He was a master martial artist, and he had already established quite a few kempo karate schools in Germany before he began his wing chun training.

What was unique about Keith compared to others who have studied with you?
I think that Keith is the most organized and best wing chun teacher in Europe. He has so much knowledge about the martial arts in general, as well as knowledge about highly scientific methods for building up body strength, technique, and special conditioning exercises specifically for martial artists. In addition, Keith is always taking classes and refining his knowledge. Some of the other teachers he has studied with are Jesse Glover and Escrima Master Rene Latosa.

i would like to turn to your time in n ew york and your training with Professor Vee. ho w did that come about?
Well I had a small school on the West Side and one morning Professor Vee walked in. We had already met briefly at Madison Square Garden where I had done an exhibition show.

What type of person was he?
A real gentleman. At that time he was working on a blocking system he called the "human makiwara," and he wanted to know how much I would charge him to learn the wing chun wooden dummy. I was completely flabbergasted. I explained that I had way too much respect for him as a martial arts teacher to charge him anything. However, he said his pride would not allow him to accept training for free.

so what happened?
Well at that time I was also very interested in studying the Filipino martial arts so we struck up a deal. I would teach him the wing chun and he would teach me the escrima. He was a great teacher and a wonderful human being. We were friends for a long time, and I was deeply saddened to hear of his death. He was a bright light in the martial arts arena and he will be sorely missed.

i understand r andy Williams also studied with you for a short time.
Yes. I believe that Randy's main teacher was Walter Wong, but he studied with me briefly. Unfortunately, Randy studied with me during the period when I wasn't doing much hands on training with my students because I was still suffering from the illnesses that had I contracted while I was teaching in Colombia. Randy eventually moved on to Sifu Augustine Fong, an excellent teacher.

Can you name a few other martial artists who you have taught?
Yes. Paul Maslak and Rex Kimball. They studied with me in the early '80s. Rex is a wonderful martial artist with a strong karate, taekwondo and jeet kune do background. He was a natural for wing chun. Paul also had an eclectic martial arts background and was very analytical in his approach to training.

you have an incredible teaching record and are very well-respected in your field, yet, throughout your years of teaching, you have remained somewhat distant from the martial arts associations in Europe and the u.s. Why have you never affiliated yourself with any of the wing chun organizations?
I have never wanted to tie myself to a specific organization because there are so many politics involved. After all, I graduated from Koo Sang in Hong Kong during the '70s, long before the current crop of wing chun teachers here in the U.S. I believe that one of my greatest values as a teacher is that I have no political agenda, nor do I have any affiliation with any of the big wing chun groups who are promoting themselves throughout the U.S. When people study with me they get exactly what they pay for - pure instruction and pure wing chun. They do not have to join or contribute to any organizations in order to study with me, and that makes me unique in the field of wing chun.

Do you consider yourself a grandmaster?
Hell no! I've never had the gall to call myself a grandmaster. To me, that title is reserved for the founder of a system or his legitimate heir.

I would like to talk briefly about the time period beginning with your return from teaching in Colombia, which marked the beginning of your now past health problems. How did your illness affect your career?

It had a great impact on my career. I was devastated and extremely depressed. My weight dropped from 240 pounds to 120. The problem was that I had so many things wrong with me that the doctors could not get a handle on my condition.

Do you feel you lost opportunities because of your health?

Very definitely. Nobody wants a teacher who is unwell. The lowest point came when I had to back out of a movie deal. I had written a script for Jim Kelly and myself, and I was able to get funding for the movie, but I was just too ill to follow through.

Do you still speak to Jim Kelly?

Yes, on occasion, but I feel badly about the way things turned out. Nobody knew how sick I was at the time. Its something that no one can understand unless they've been through it. Later, I was told by several doctors that, given the kinds of tropical diseases I had - malaria, giardiasis, and filariasis - I should have been dead! Just having one of those diseases is enough to kill you.

Do you think that your martial arts training played a role in your recovery?

Yes. The doctors told me that if I hadn't been training for all those years, my body would have been too weak to survive.

When did you start teaching wing chun full time again?

Just within the last couple of years, really. But even during the time I was ill, I was still practicing wing chun, and I never stopped exchanging ideas with other teachers.

Can you name some wing chun teachers who you enjoy working with?

Bob Stevenson in Canada, is an excellent wing chun guy. He was Paul Lam's assistant instructor when I was studying in London. Also, Joy Chaudhuri of Arizona, who studied with Augustine Fong for many years. He is a man with a wonderful intellect and a lot of practical fighting experience. Both Joy and Bob have a lot of knowledge about wing chun and are incredibly gifted practitioners of the art. It is a pleasure to work with them, not only because they possess such high skill levels, but because they both place a high value on honor and integrity. Currently, I am working with Sifu Steve Cottrell, an excellent martial arts teacher who resides in Fort Worth, Texas.

"The doctors told me that if I hadn't been training for all those years, my body would have been too weak to survive."

Anyone else?

Yes, many, but recently I met Robert Chu, who is an excellent wing chun teacher. He also spent some time with Koo Sang in Hong Kong. He has a lot of experience and his wing chun technique is very strong. Also, I enjoy working with Eric Lee, who is one of the most incredible martial artists in America today.

What are your plans for the future now that you have recovered from your health problems?

I still have many goals and dreams that I was never able to realize. Mainly, I want to open up people's minds to the value of wing chun. I really feel that it has a lot to offer people of all ages.

Wing Chun Masters

"Avoid the "jack of all trades" approach to the martial arts. It is best to study one or two arts at the most and try to become expert at them."

so you feel that wing chun be learned at any age?

Yes. wing chun can be learned by anybody, respective of age because you don't have to be super flexible or particularly acrobatic to do it. It is a very practical system. In addition, it is truly a thinking person's art because it emphasizes technique and strategy over brute force.

What do you like most about teaching the martial arts?

I enjoy watching people learn and grow. I get a big charge when I can see that someone has benefited from martial arts training, both physically and mentally. I would like to see more people take advantage of the positive benefits that martial arts can offer. People living in America don't realize how lucky they are. They have such a variety of martial arts knowledge available to them. Everything from chi kung to karate to kung-fu is taught openly here. When I began studying martial arts, there were very few legitimate teachers who were practicing openly. It was all a big secret, and when they did consent to teach, they would charge their students an arm and a leg to learn the most basic of techniques.

What advice can you give to potential students of wing chun about how to avoid bogus teachers?

Just like any other style of martial arts, there are people who's backgrounds are questionable. I know of a couple of people who claim to be masters of wing chun, Jun Fan, tai chi, and kickboxing, but their credentials don't check out. I would say, in general, students should be wary of people who claim to be masters of every style. It's not possible! Avoid the "jack of all trades" approach to the martial arts. It is best to study one or two arts at the most and try to become expert at them.

name some other positi ve benefits of learning martial arts.

A good martial arts training program will improve a person's self-image and heighten self-confidence. But to me, being able to protect yourself is one of the most important benefits. Many of my students can attest to the fact that wing chun has saved their lives. One doctor who was studying with me privately was doing it just to keep in shape. He never dreamed he would have to use it. One day he was attacked in a hospital elevator by a crazed white supremacist who was about forty pounds heavier than him. The doctor was not only able to block and deflect the bombs the guy was trying to land on him, but he knocked his assailant cold with elbow strikes to the head. To this day, the doctor is convinced that the attacker was hell-bent on trying to kill him and that his martial arts training saved his life. I feel good when I hear stories like that.

What do you dislike most about the martial arts?
The punk mentality and lack of respect for others that I have been seeing more and more within the last few years. I believe that this is only a reflection of what is going on in society in general today. However, I feel that it is the responsibility of martial arts teachers to be positive role models and to set a good example for their students.

What do you think are the biggest misconceptions that people who practice other styles of martial arts have about wing chun?
That it is strictly a "centerline" system that only uses "chain punching," that there are no circular techniques. This is not true. There are lots of circular techniques in advanced wing chun. Other misconceptions are that wing chun is not mobile enough, and that wing chun practitioners are weak kickers. The footwork for advanced wing chun makes it highly mobile. Concerning wing chun kicks, this is simply a matter of how hard a person is willing to work. I have seen many wing chun practitioners with great kicks. Lastly, critics of wing chun contend that it doesn't have grappling techniques. Wing chun does contain basic grappling techniques, but the main emphasis is on neutralizing such techniques. Overall, wing chun stresses counter-fighting techniques, the emphasis being on neutralization. Most misconceptions arise from people who have never studied wing chun or those who have only studied a portion of the wing chun system, and whose knowledge is incomplete. Practicing wing chun correctly requires finesse, and the incorporation of the Chinese principles of the Tao. Wing chun is truly based on yin and yang. It is the perfect balance between two opposing forces.

GARY LAM

The True Spirit

Throughout the years, Gary Lam has remained true to the teaching and philosophy he learned from the great Wing Chun master, Wong Shun Leung, his instructor. With an always friendly and humble attitude, this Wing Chun master's goal is to preserve the true spirit of the art in modern society. Sifu Lam is unique, both in his profound knowledge of kung fu and Chinese philosophy and in his innovative spirit. His virtues make him one of the most remarkable instructors of Wing Chun kung fu in the world.

how long have you been practicing the martial arts and who was your teacher?

I have been practicing martial arts since I was 15. It has been a great journey. I have had special interest in fighting and kung fu from an early age. I practiced two years with Sifu Lok Yiu and later with Sifu Wong Shun Leung for more than two decades. I consider myself very fortunate to have trained under the legendary Wong Shun Lung. Besides his fighting and Wing Chun skills, my Sifu Wong Shun Leung also was very open, kind-hearted, and had a great sense of humor. After training, we spent a lot of times hanging out, playing Mahjong, and eating out. I also trained in muay Thai boxing.

I always will remember one particular event in Hong Kong in which a challenge was presented to us by a group of Choy Li Fut practitioners. Our school picked four students to represent Wing Chun, and I was one of the participants. We went with our Sifu to meet the Choy Li Fut group at a park and were shocked to find they had brought about fifty students there. Thankfully, it was a one-on-one match. I'm proud to say we won three out of four matches.

What are the main principles intrinsic to the three forms of Wing Chun?

Siu Nin Tao covers the basics and foundation of Wing Chun, like the alphabet: A, B, C, D. The second form, Cham Kiu, teaches you the functions of each action and how to utilize them in the right manner, such as hitting and defending against moving targets. Biu Jee opens our eyes to emergency and abnormal situations. Each form is very useful and interrelated.

Wing Chun Masters

"I learned not to be stubborn and used more common sense in training, fighting and teaching."

how did you the Westerners respond to traditional Chinese training?

My first experience dealing with Westerners was when I was teaching at my Sifu, Wong Shun Leung's school. There, I had firsthand opportunities to instruct many students from different countries. My Sifu advised me to be more "gentle" with them. It made me aware that different countries have different cultures and we always have to take that into consideration. Based on my personal experiences teaching thousands of students from many different countries, I think that American students in general put more emphasis on creativity, Chinese students on traditional values, and the Europeans on discipline.

how has your personal kung fu changed and developed over the years?

Although I believe the basics and foundation of Wing Chun remain the same, it definitely has evolved for the better as I gained more experience. I learned not to be stubborn and used more common sense in training, fighting and teaching.

What are the most important points in your teaching methods and what are the most important qualities for a student to become proficient in the Wing Chun style?

I only like to teach what works in the real world, and the students need to understand the logic behind every move. Wing Chun is a very scientific art, not based on any animals, myths, or fancy moves. Other than training hard, having patience, and maintaining a strong interest, the most important quality for a student to become proficient in Wing Chun is "understanding." By that, I mean a student has to totally understand what he or she is doing. If you practice a particular move for ten years without knowing the functions, logic, and reasons behind that move, then you're just wasting your time. Students also need to set realistic goals. Bruce Lee did not become the best fighter overnight.

Do you think different "styles" truly are important in the art of kung fu?

Yes, I think different styles are good for kung fu in general. It allows people with different backgrounds to choose and compare which styles suit them better.

What is your opinion of a Full Contact kung fu tournament?

I think it's good. Besides having technical skills and heart, you need strength, speed, conditioning, and experience in order to show that what you have been practicing will work in the tournament.

how different from other kung fu styles do you see the principles and concepts of Wing Chun?

In my opinion, most kung fu styles rely on physical strength and condition. They make their fist, palm, and even the head tougher by subjecting them to rigorous training. Wing Chun, on the other hand, is based on directness, logic, and centerline. Smaller guys like Sigung Yip Man and Sifu Wong Shun Leung easily could overpower

"Kung fu definitely is not Wushu. We have so many different kinds of arts under kung fu."

guys almost twice their size. Wing Chun is quite popular at present as we have practitioners from all over the world, but it should become more popular because it's an art that's very scientific, effective, and long-lasting. Once people start to see the effectiveness of Wing Chun, the market will grow. Wing Chun is an advanced art that continues to grow with the practitioner. I'll continue to learn for as long as I shall live. Kung fu definitely is not Wushu. We have so many different kinds of arts under kung fu. Wushu is a fixed system in which different arts are put together for demonstration, sport, or competition purposes.

Does the weaponry aspect of Wing Chun enhance the student's empty hands ability, or are those two completely non-related skills?

The weaponry aspects definitely help. The long pole helps the coordination of hand, leg, and body, sitting power, movements, and accuracy, while the butterfly knives teach us to change under different conditions,

Wing Chun Masters

"Wing Chun is a deadly art built to incapacitate an opponent in the shortest possible time."

understand the "chance" aspect in fighting, help build guts, and improve speed.

how does the Wing Chun style differ from other kung fu methods when applying the techniques in a real situation?

Wing Chun is a deadly art built to incapacitate an opponent in the shortest possible time. It's designed for a real situation, not for the ring or sport. Try to understand what you are learning and have patience in Wing Chun. When you fully understand the moves, things will make more sense and start to come together.

Self-defense, health, and tradition all are important, but I'd say Wing Chun is more focused on self-defense. From a technical point of view, forms and chi-sao are very important, but I think we should focus 30 percent on forms and 70 percent on chi-sao. However, it's important to fully understand why you're doing certain moves when performing the forms.

You could be doing the forms thousands of times but they'd still be useless if you don't understand what you're doing. Chi-sao helps practitioners develop the "feeling," "changes," and "control."

Some people think going to China or Taiwan to train is highly necessary to get quality instruction. Do you share the point of view?
No. It all depends on the teachers and their teaching systems. It does not matter which countries you go to. The most important thing is to find a teacher with a good system; otherwise, it's difficult to learn and improve, no matter where you are.

What do you consider the major changes in the art since you began training?
The art of Wing Chun remains more or less the same. In the past, (Yip Man's era), Wing Chun wasn't open to non-Chinese, but now it's different. To be fast, strong, and powerful was my philosophy at the early stage. Now, the focus is more on skills, control, feeling, and explosive power.

Who would you like to have trained with that you have not?
Again, I consider myself very lucky to train under the legendary Wong Shun Leung. To me, that's more than I could ever ask for. He was the best Wing Chun master/teacher/fighter I have ever seen.

Do you think it is necessary to engage in free-fighting to achieve good self-defense skills in the street?
Engaging in free sparring is important as it helps build self-confidence. I had the opportunity to test my Wing Chun skills against various martial artists and I had to adapt to different opponents. They all inspired me to train harder in Wing Chun. Wing Chun is the most advanced, direct, and scientific art that has been proven to work in real situations.

What is your opinion about mixing kung fu styles? Does the practice of one nullify the effectiveness of the other, or can it be beneficial to the student?
I don't think it's a good idea to mix different kung fu styles as most of them are different in structure, philosophy, and approach. Wing Chun is such a high level art that it's like a chess game. It's a very deep art and there are different approaches to each situation. There's a counter to every move, and this makes the art interesting.

Wing Chun Masters

"I don't recommend that any of my students develop big muscles, as Wing Chun is not based on brute force."

Do you have a particularly memorable kung fu experience that has remained as an inspiration for your training?

Watching my Sifu Wong Shun Leung used his Wing Chun against masters of other different arts also gave me long-lasting inspiration for my personal training. Training in kung fu has a deeper meaning. Not only does it help boost one's self confidence, it also promotes coordination, heightens awareness, increases positive energy, and controls stress. Kung fu also could teach one to handle many difficult situations in life and make solving problems simpler.

how is the chi-sao aspect of training related to the practical application of the Wing Chun techniques used in the empty hands forms?

They all are interrelated. Again, Siu Nin Tao is the alphabet, Chum Kiu and Biu Jee are the words. In chi-sao practice, you learn to put them together and make sentences.

is anything lacking in the way martial arts are taught today compared to how they were in your beginnings?

The major drawbacks these days are lack of patience and not setting realistic goals. Wing Chun is not an art that can be mastered overnight because it's so in-depth.

What advice would you give to students on the question of supplementary training?

I don't recommend that any of my students develop big muscles, as Wing Chun is not based on brute force. The other sports I'd probably recommend are running and swimming. Running helps develop speed and stamina. Swimming improves one's sense of balance and patience. Students who try to understand the true meaning, respect and enjoy the art of Wing Chun and are willing to work hard and set realistic goal for themselves. To me, a successful kung fu practitioner is someone who's able or always tries to find his/her own weaknesses, correct the problems, and fully understands each and every move he or she practices. Once people start to realize the true effectiveness of Wing Chun, the art will grow, as it's an art that's very scientific. Everything is geared toward directness, logic. and practical street application.

Why do you think a lot of students start falling away after two-three years of training?

I believe the Internet has changed many things these days. Students learn for two or three years and start comparing their skills to other arts on the Internet. Some also want to follow trends. What they fail to understand is that Wing Chun is not an art that can be learned overnight because it continues to grow with the practitioners. I taught muay Thai as well and can tell you that I can produce quality muay Thai fighters in very short period of time. But the same can't be said about Wing Chun, as it takes time. However, the growth potential of a Wing Chun practitioner is higher and more durable.

"There's nothing to fear when you have full understanding of what you're practicing."

ha ve there been times when you felt fear in your kung fu training?

There's nothing to fear when you have full understanding of what you're practicing.

JIM LAU

The Intelligence of Wing Chun

JIM LAU'S OPINIONS ARE SUPPORTED BY LONG YEARS OF EXPERIENCE AND BY CONSIDERABLE THOUGHT. A FORMER COLUMNIST ON THE ART OF WING CHUN FOR SEVERAL KUNG FU MAGAZINES, LAU'S WRITINGS WERE CONSIDERED TO BE AMONG THE MOST THOROUGH TO EVER APPEAR IN A MARTIAL ARTS PERIODICAL. HE HAS APPEARED ON THE COVER OF SEVERAL MAGAZINES, AND HIS TEACHING METHODS HAVE BEEN THE SUBJECT OF ARTICLES FOR MORE THAN THREE DECADES. HE BEGAN HIS STUDY IN HONG KONG, WHERE HE WAS BORN AND RAISED, AND HE HAS BEEN LIVING AND TEACHING IN THE UNITED STATES FOR MORE THAN 40 YEARS. JIM LAU IS AN APPEALING COMBINATION OF CALM EASTERN PHILOSOPHY AND EFFICIENT WESTERN PRAGMATISM, EXEMPLIFYING THE LOGIC AND PHILOSOPHY OF THE ART THAT, AS A CHILD, HE CHOSE TO PRACTICE IN HONG KONG. "THAT CITY IS AN VERY SPECIAL PLACE TO GROW UP," LAU RECALLS. "LEARNING MARTIAL ARTS IN HONG KONG IS LIKE LEARNING BASEBALL IN THE UNITED STATES, EVERYBODY PICKS UP SOMETHING, SO IT IS NO BIG DEAL. THE PEOPLE THERE CAN BE A VERY TRICKY AND YOU DEFINITELY NEED TO KNOW YOUR WAY AROUND TO SURVIVE!" SIFU LAU IS ONE OF THOSE RARE AND TALENTED PEOPLE WHO FOUND THEIR WAY IN THE "TRICKY" STREETS OF HONG HONG, AND WHO HAS NOW BECOME ONE OF THE MOST SOUGHT-AFTER WING CHUN EXPERTS IN THE WORLD.

h ow did you get involved in wing chun?

I began when I was 11 years old with the study of various styles of kung-fu. At 14, I started my study of the wing chun system. Like most other boys of that age, I did not understand the significance of such an experience. The seeds of my appreciation for wing chun as an intelligent and practical art were, however, planted. During this period I also made what eventually turned into a close friendship, as well as an ongoing learning relationship, with one of master Yip Man's first and most capable students, Sifu Wong Shun Leung.

At the age of 20 I immigrated to the U.S. to join my family. Settling in Los Angeles, I attended Pasadena City College where I began teaching wing chun as a means of arousing local interest and perfecting my own talents. It was after I moved to America that I began to feel the true strength and intensity of my desire to explore the potential of the art, and I studied and practiced over the ensuing years with uninterrupted intensity. The value placed on directness and efficiency in America provided me

Wing Chun Masters

"I believe that only through teaching can one practice and reach the highest goals of martial arts understanding."

with an unusual appreciation for those characteristics as exemplified in the wing chun system of kung-fu. The physical separation from my homeland left a void which developed into an insatiable appetite for Chinese literature. Those factors have provided me with the basis for a unique, personal method of analysis which utilizes the simple, economical, direct, and complete characteristics of the wing chun system, complemented by numerous organizational concepts found in Chinese literature.

After my graduation from college, I devoted a lot of my time and effort into professional teaching, training, researching, and promoting the true value of this ancient art. I believe that only through teaching can one practice and reach the highest goals of martial arts understanding. Today, I still live by the ancient Chinese proverb that says, "The person who teaches will learn himself, and the person who learns will always be the teacher of himself."

After all these years, I don't like to speak of any achievements other than those which are more personal in nature. Certainly, the friendships I have made along the way are the most important to me. My travels and years of study and teaching have led to a number of close friendships which are particularly special.

Another personally satisfying achievement has been the growth of my abilities to communicate verbally, and in written form, both in Chinese and English. As my desire to progress in wing chun grew, my need to develop precision in both forms of communication had to be expanded. Communication is a form of influence, and the ability to properly influence someone without having to use physical capabilities is an art within martial arts. I also have grown to know myself more intimately than I would have thought possible. In order to really study kung-fu, you must study what it means to be a human being. This entails a great deal of personal introspection and it is certainly not a simple or painless process, but for me, it has been a major personal achievement up to this point in my life.

What are the main principles of the art?

Wing chun is essentially an art of maneuvers, specifically those designed to deal with practical fighting situations. Hence, formal bowing, artistic forms of dancing, symbolic imitations of animals and showy movements of any kind are not a part of this art. In theory, wing chun stresses simplicity, directness, economy and completeness. These terms are almost self-explanatory. Simplicity means that movements and techniques should be clean and uncomplicated. Directness implies immediate effectiveness. Economy is the conservation of energy and effort. And completeness signifies the use of all possible body tools like hands, arms, feet, legs, body, et cetera.

At the core of wing chun maneuvers is the concept of the centerline, the imaginary vertical line running down the center of the body-in front and back. A wing chun practitioner must preserve and protect his own centerline while, at the same time, breaking and invading the opponent's centerline. This maxim of combat is accomplished by constantly pushing forward, controlling the opponent's arms, and narrowing the distance between you and him.

Once contact is made with the opponent's arms, he can be effectively maneuvered by adhering to the wing chun motto: "When hands approach, withhold. When hands withdraw, follow. And when hands slip from control, strike." With this motto in mind, the wing chun practitioner must put his whole body to work, systematically executing maneuvers and attacks. The techniques for maneuver and attack fall into four categories: strikes, kicks, throws and holds.

The wing chun system has a very precise method for preparing a student for combat. This training method includes three empty-hand forms, a set of 108 wooden dummy techniques, Muk Yan Jong, a long pole form, Luk Dim Bun Gwun, and a short knives form, Bot Jeom Do. But the real trademark and focus of wing chun training centers on sticking-hands practice, Chi Sao, which is exclusive to this art.

Are the wing chun forms flashy?

In contrast to other styles of kung-fu, wing chun forms are not always graceful or entertaining. The reason is that wing chun forms are designed to practice maneuvers. The three empty-hand forms of wing chun are Sil Lum Tao, "The Little Idea," Chum Kil, "Searching for the Bridge," and Bil Jee, "Thrusting Fingers." These three maneuver forms are relatively simple and short, yet refined and sufficient. Each form has its own specific purpose, theory, and techniques. At the same time, each one represents a specific level of learning. In order to learn the forms efficiently, practitioners are advised to master each one individually, in the proper sequence of sophistication. Theoretically, wing chun forms serve as a reference guide which articulates all the basic movements and fighting techniques within the context of the centerline. Learning the forms properly, practicing them diligently, and understanding them thoroughly are the three essential steps towards a successful wing chun experience.

Do you have a personal training program?

I do not subscribe to the theory that each individual quantity of labor or effort produces a directly proportional quality of result. For maximum result one must put forth maximum quality of effort. Quality cannot be measured in raw terms such as the number of hours in which routine physical labor is performed.

The art of wing chun, particularly through its three empty-hand and, one wooden dummy, and two weapons forms can represent an essentially complete overview of human kinesiology. Regardless of the style, individual practice should be based upon personal motivation, desired result and precise physical and mental work to achieve that result. Because of this, I do not follow a personal training regimen which prescribes specific physical exercises to be completed over a determined length of time each day. Such training would produce mental and therefore, physical rigidity. And this is not what I am looking for. I vary my training to fit my own desired results. Regardless of the type of exercise, I always have a precise concept of the desired result when I train. This is not to say that some individuals do not need the type of discipline found in a more materialistic kind of training structure particularly in the early stages. Such training throughout one's lifetime, however, produces a rather static and labor-oriented individual in my opinion.

Do you follow a particular diet?

One of the elements of wing chun centerline theory is moderation. Much like one uses a compass to check his direction, if one knows moderation it is safer to deviate and still find your way back. I do not consider my normal diet to be special. I eat food just like most people, hopefully of reasonably good quality. When I find my diet beginning to vary towards an extreme, for instance junk food, I am simply aware that this represents a deviation that may not produce satisfactory results if continued in excess over long periods of time.

Do you consider yourself a traditionalist or a modernist in your expression of the art?

I believe that the type of thinking which allows for either/or answers truly limits our ability to progress. The more educated and pragmatic students of today care only very briefly about the names of one's instructors, conflicting claims concerning who is a master or successor of a style, or other such irrelevancies. They generally seek instruction from those with obvious personal ability who can communicate as well as actualize that ability. This modern attitude can be productive for the student if properly channeled.

The current non-traditionalist trend was actually fostered by the rigidity of some of the so-called traditionalists. In fact, everyone follows an established tradition. In spite of learning from the same teacher, practitioners of many different traditional martial arts disagree about what is authentic. Such insistence often leads to retrogression and failure to explore the potential of the art's original concepts. What turns out

"The current non-traditionalist trend was actually fostered by the rigidity of some of the so-called traditionalists."

to be practiced and preserved is merely their interpretation of their teacher's interpretation of the art-an honorable achievement but certainly not a guarantee of authenticity or a benefit to the art. In their attempt to escape the obvious limitations of such a myopic perspective on a truly dynamic human condition, many people simply end-up confused. Certainly a number of kung-fu styles offer the basic framework by which one may achieve far greater understanding of these dynamics. This requires one to pursue his study far beyond the simple repetition of the physical mechanics in fond hope of some mysterious personal transformation. A teacher can only guide you. He cannot work or think for you. Guidance, however, should not be underestimated. Without truly comprehensive study, which entails far more than casual study of a multitude of styles over a period of years, the non-traditionalist goal of attaining sophisticated analytical abilities is simply a myth.

"Each individual merely expresses to the best of their ability their own understanding of a style."

What is your attitude towards full-contact Kung Fu Tournaments and the uFC?

Although it is referred to as "full-contact," in a true sense it is certainly not. It is actually a protective, though admittedly rough, contact sport which permits one to employ only a limited number of specialized fighting methods in a controlled environment. Because it allows for the general safety of the participants I believe it has a legitimate place in our modern society much like boxing, football or other contact sports.

h ave you made any innovations in your style?

Innovation implies "new" and if one seriously studies the past he will find that we are generally rediscovering our potential. Realization and understanding of our commonality rather than searching for the unusual provides the greatest insight.

i'm not sure. What are the special strengths of the wing chun system?

I prefer not to make comparisons between styles. Each individual merely expresses to the best of their ability their own understanding of a style. It is somehow inappropriate to make public comparisons since they are of such a purely personal nature. I believe it is sufficient to say that my style is wing chun and I enjoy practicing it.

ho w many years of training are necessary to reach instructor level?

There is no formal ranking in wing chun kung-fu. Teaching is part of any complete learning process and as a result a few of my more advanced students assist with instruction. As I mentioned earlier, given quantities of individual time and labor don't automatically produce proper results. I assess students by the quality of their output not the quantity of their inputs. My students are taught to assess their own abilities in the same manner.

Chi sao is considered the key factor in the art of wing chun; how do you describe this aspect of training and how important is it to the overall structure of the style?

Chi sao, or sticking hands practice, is the final wing chun training method. This drill is used to sharpen and condition one's instinctive fighting responses. There are two forms of chi sao practice. Single chi sao, in which one sticks to only one hand at a time, prepares the novice for double chi sao. And double chi sao, where one sticks to both hands simultaneously, is the preliminary to actual combat.

If the forms are the textbooks of wing chun, then chi sao is probably best described as a "living laboratory." Within the laboratory, practitioners of this style of kung-fu may experiment and analyze all the technical movements previously learned in the empty-hand or the wooden dummy forms. Because chi sao is practiced at close range, practitioners gradually build confidence and fearlessness in confronting an attack. They also become acquainted with combat situations, and develop a calm presence of mind and relaxation of body under stressful situations.

During chi sao practice, the three pivotal hand techniques of wing chun are ingeniously interlinked through the theory of the yin and the yang. Since the hand techniques of bong say and tan sao produce one another, through a twist of the arm, they represent the yin principle. But fook sao, which opposes them, represents the yang principle. From this peculiar relationship which exists between these techniques during chi sao, hundreds of other patterns, positions, and mutations of hand techniques are generated. Through the lin sil die dar principle, simultaneous attack and defense, a punch or finger jab could be used for blocking and neutralizing. The latter principle is best expressed by the motto: "A striking hand is a neutralizing hand, and a neutralizing hand is a striking hand."

Once chi sao is mastered, all that remains to prepare a student for combat is an adjustment in the basic stance. In wing chun, there is a technical distinction between the fighting stance and the training stance. The training stance is governed by learning demands, and tends to be more open to the opponent. However, both the training stance and the fighting stance are designed to enhance the qualities of stability and mobility.

Actually, chi sao serves many purposes. During the initial training period, chi sao provides a lot of different benefits. It develops a certain sensitivity and a certain kind of muscle tone. Before most people train, their arms are not flexible-and so through chi sao they develop flexibility. So those are some of the basic training functions of chi sao, but of course there are many more. During the practice of chi sao a person is gradually getting used to the feel of the range. When you fight you have to get in close-if you can't touch, you can't hit. And if you can't hit, you can't finish. The overall idea is just really getting used to something. Like trained race car drivers-they have no fear. They see a curve and they turn; they see a slope and they go up. A normal person cannot achieve that simply because they are not trained. There's no secret or magic to it. If you train your hands, you know they can do something for you, and you are confident enough to relax. You see that street-fighters are always very calm and relaxed. That is because they've fought many times and been in a lot of situations like that. In wing chun, the training is also that way-you practice getting used to confrontation so you no longer have fear.

We have another term for free sparring-we call it *lut sao*. This is a situation where there will be a defender and an attacker, and the attacker will attempt to keep the defender near his range, while the defender will make every attempt to keep him away. In other words, one will practice how to get away, and the other will practice learning how to pursue their prey.

h ow does it apply to real fighting?

When you talk about fighting, your eyes, your ears, your nose are not as important as your sense of touch. You could say that chi sao is a very limited kind of sparring, as opposed to free sparring, which would be unlimited. But the difference is that in an unlimited situation, you cannot go back to pick up what you did wrong. With chi sao, it's more productive in a sense. You get hit if you don't do it right, and right away you know if your elbow is off center. Wing chun is constantly hitting, and where there is an empty gap, you hit. The saying in wing chun that, "when the hand slips off, straight lunge." Chi sao helps you build hand sensitivity-and that's basically the idea, to develop that instantaneous reflex to reach without thinking, because when you talk about movement, your eyes cannot be as fast as your mind. So you have to be able to let things happen by themselves. I think some people get confused nowadays; they cannot differentiate what is for training and what is for actual application. This is something that a lot of people don't understand about wing chun. A lot of wing chun students think that to develop the chi sao ability is the highest expression of combat. They think that if you can do chi sao, you can fight. This is not true. The competence at self-defense is only partly a product of chi sao practice. Also necessary for development of real fighting ability is training in footwork, free sparring, and in strategy or tactics. The time spent practicing on the wooden wing chun dummy is very much related to development of self-defense ability.

is it correct to say that chi sao is the common thread for all wing chun techniques?

To a certain extent. The practice of chi sao remains one of wing chun's trademark training methods. And like I said before, there are enough variations on the exercise to make it appropriate for both beginners and advanced students. Other variations include pak sao, "slapping hand," and lop sao, grabbing hand. In these versions of the exercise, the students learn open-hand and grabbing techniques. Proper chi sao, the two-handed pushing exercise, is usually the final step before a student spars live. Chi sao is like learning a song. You learn the notes and lyrics, and then you put the song together. Also, when you practice in a school, there are always people of different sizes and different characters, and you get to practice with each one. Some are artistic, some are chicken, and you get used to the feel of each one. So after a while, chi sao becomes a way to study characters.

"The practice of chi sao remains one of wing chun's trademark training methods."

some people are trying to create a formal chi sao competition. Do you agree with this?

A:I honestly don't believe in chi sao competition, because I think the martial arts should be something more than that. There are good things, of course, in the sticking hands, but the sad fact is that some people have the tendency to think that they have reached the highest goal when they win a sportive championship of some kind. There is more to the art than just chi sao.

ho w is a typical wing chun class structured?

It depends of the instructor but typically my students spend an equal amount of time on the dummy and at chi sao. If they practice chi sao for 15 minutes, then they work on the dummy for another 15 minutes to get balance. The dummy has special qualities-consistent drilling in the dummy allows a practitioner to correct the alignment of his hand positions and to go full blast with the hand and foot techniques. Human partners sometimes get hurt, or tired, or overcompensate for their sparring partner.

Wing Chun Masters

"Practice of the 108 movements on the dummy is a good workout and develops a certain amount of toughness as well."

But the dummy never changes, can't be hurt and never tires. Practice of the 108 movements on the dummy is a good workout and develops a certain amount of toughness as well.

speaking of the muk yan jong, what can you tell us about training with this piece of equipment?

The muk yan jong is a training device. Translated literally, muk yan jong means "wooden man pile," but is better known in English as the wooden dummy. The muk yan jong is made from a tree trunk and has two wooden arms and a wooden leg, attached to resemble a man. This "hypothetical opponent" is probably the most advanced apparatus in existence for kung-fu training.

Since the wooden dummy cannot be physically injured, one may actually practice techniques with full strength, and thus feel the power of one's internal energy. At the same time, the wooden dummy allows one to practice striking and kicking techniques individually, or simultaneously, in a manner which builds power. There are a total of 108 movements in the wing chun wooden dummy form. These movements are considered to be techniques of the higher levels of learning. This ingenious device also comes in handy whenever a real sparring partner is absent.

What is the importance of footwork in the wing chun system?

It's a very important part of the whole package. The role of footwork in wing chun is the reason why there are few, if any, blocks in the system. The footwork is our way of blocking. Blocks are unnecessary when your opponent can't touch you.

so do you think that realistic self-defense depends upon awareness of a given situation?

You have to have sensitivity, when you know what your attacker wants, then you can decide what to feed him. For example, a person who is only trying to steal your wallet would be treated differently from a person who has decided to beat you up because he doesn't like you. Different kinds of motivations require different responses. Drunks are usually just evaded. Muggers, bullies, or persons who are just in a bad mood are other types of attackers who would require different responses. The one general rule is to stay calm and be reasonable. Always try to reason with your aggressor, even though you may be dealing with someone who is not quite rational. I think the most important thing is studying the motivation of the aggressor, to find out why he's doing what he is doing. If you can focus on that, then your response will come naturally, and you can choose the right tool for the job."

"Too many people want to be the chief and nobody wants to be an Indian. I'm still an Indian."

What is the essence of wing chun training?

Although wing chun emphasizes individuality as the ultimate ideal, it is impossible to learn the art by oneself, or through a book. Just as a child needs guidance in learning to walk, so too does the novice need instruction in learning to fight. Only after years of practice can one comprehend the theories and practice of wing chun. And only with a proper foundation can one venture out on their own to discover new dimensions in the art by themselves.

What is your opinion on the growing number of unqualified wing chun instructors?

It's funny, but is seems that as soon as anything becomes popular it becomes corrupted. Too many people want to be the chief and nobody wants to be an Indian. I'm still an Indian.

ALAN LEE

Moment by Moment

IT'S QUITE AN ACCOMPLISHMENT TO DELVE DEEP INTO THE MYSTERIES OF WING CHUN KUNG FU. FEW PRACTITIONERS HAVE THE PATIENCE, LET ALONE THE SELF-DISCIPLINE, TO MASTER THE ART'S INTRICATE SKILLS. BUT IT'S A DISTINCT HONOR TO HAVE TRAINED WITH THE LATE YIP MAN, WHO IS LAUDED WORLDWIDE AS WING CHUN'S MOST CELEBRATED INSTRUCTOR. ALAN LEE IS AMONG THE HANDFUL OF ELITE MARTIAL ARTISTS WHO TRAINED DIRECTLY UNDER YIP MAN.

A FORMER PRIVATE DISCIPLE OF THE RENOWNED INSTRUCTOR, LEE POSSESSES PANORAMIC INSIGHTS INTO WING CHUN (AND MANY OTHER FIGHTING SYSTEMS) MATCHED BY FEW OF THE MOST SEASONED MARTIAL ARTS. A PROTÉGÉ OF SEVERAL TOP-NOTCH TEACHERS BESIDES YIP MAN, LEE'S WING CHUN RESUME IS SIMPLY FLAWLESS.

DURING AN EXCLUSIVE INTERVIEW WITH MASTERS MAGAZINE, LEE SHARED A TREASURE CHEST OF INTIMATE EXPERIENCES HE HAD WITH HIS LEGENDARY MENTOR. LEE ALSO REVEALED MANY LITTLE-KNOWN FACTS ABOUT HIS BELOVED ART. THESE INCLUDE COMMON MISTAKES IN TRAINING, HOW WING CHUN DIFFERS IN THE EASTERN AND WESTERN WORLDS, AND HOW THE ANCIENT ART CAN BE LEARNED MOST EFFECTIVELY TODAY.

how long have you been practicing Wing Chun, and who was your teacher?

I learned Wing Chun in Hong Kong from Sifu Lok Yiu from 1967 until 1971, and I served as an assistant instructor at one of Sifu Lok Yiu's schools. Later, Yip Man selected me as a private disciple, and I trained under him for approximately two years. I learned from Sifu Yip Man during the late years of his life. After I immigrated to the United States, I met Sifu Duncan Leung in 1975. Sifu Duncan Leung also was a private disciple of Sifu Yip Man; he helped me with further training, and together we taught Wing Chun at a school on Great Jones Street in New York's Greenwich Village. I consider all of these instructors my sifus, especially Sifu Duncan Leung, who gave me deeper insight into Wing Chun, and I am grateful to all of them for their guidance and instruction.

When I was around four years old and still in mainland China, my father sent me to learn Char Keun Hop Kar and Tai. But what I learned was very basic, and I was introduced only to the styles. During high school, I practiced boxing, but this also was only at a basic level. I did not become seri-

Wing Chun Masters

"Our Wing Chun forefathers designed the form to illustrate specific ideas."

ous about my martial arts training until 1967, when I first began learning Wing Chun.

What are the main principles intrinsic to the major Wing Chun forms? Are they interrelated?

In Wing Chun, there are only three empty-hand forms: Siu Nim Tao, Chum Kiu, and Bil Gee. None is more advanced or deadly than the other. The movements in the three forms contain some of Wing Chun's basic elements and ideas. In the beginning, because Wing Chun uses power in a scientific way, students must concentrate on the form to learn basics, such as how to generate the right kind of power, train body mechanics, use body structure, understand coverage, and understand the reasons for each movement. Each movement in the form stands for a certain meaning or idea, but you cannot fight with the movements in the form. It is helpful to think of the movements as similar to letters of the alphabet. For instance, the letters "a," "f" and "h" do not mean anything by themselves, but if you put together letters—"a-p-p-l-e"—you now create a word with meaning.

Similarly, the movements in the form by themselves are not used in fighting, but you can combine them or use them a little differently than the way they are practiced in the form to create a technique to encounter a situation. Here, it's important to explain that there is a correct way to play the forms. I believe it is critical that the form be played as perfectly as possible. Our Wing Chun forefathers designed the form to illustrate specific ideas. Many of these ideas are totally beyond one's imagination if one were simply to see the form played. But once I explain the idea to you, you will be able to understand it. A sifu should not think he is too smart and invent his own way to play the form and the techniques. Doing this will misguide students from correctly understanding Wing Chun's basic ideas, and will water down the style's effectiveness. Later, we have the Wooden Dummy Form and the Tri-Pole Kicking Form. As students progress, I explain to them the deeper ideas of the forms and how to break down the forms for fighting applications.

All of the above forms are interrelated. They are different expressions of the basic ideas of Wing Chun, although each form has a different emphasis.

Would you tell us some interesting stories of your early days in kung fu and the training under your legendary g randmaster?
Many people have heard of Sifu Yip Man's incredible physical prowess and martial arts knowledge. However, very few people got the opportunity to experience his teaching skills outside of class. For instance, when Sifu found out that my father knew someone who bred champion dogs for pit fighting, he wanted to see the matches. When I went with him, Sifu noticed many details about the dogs' fighting strategies that few others could understand or appreciate. Specifically, he told me how the dogs exchanged footwork to attack, fake, and defend, and he explained how this strategy applied in Wing Chun.

My sifu and I spent a lot of time together, and many of our close personal times were marked by humorous memories. Sifu and I constantly played practical jokes on each other. He had the habit of removing his Chinese shoes when he put his foot on the bench in a restaurant, so one time I put a hot pork bun inside his shoes when he was distracted. The look he gave me meant payback was coming. So on another occasion, Sifu and I were strolling along a farm within the Hong Kong New Territory, and suddenly a vicious dog began chasing us. Sifu dashed off toward the car first and locked himself inside. He had a good laugh watching me run around and over the car like a monkey to escape the dog.

After we trained, we frequently enjoyed good conversation and food at Lung Fung Tea House in the Mong Kok area, listened to Chinese opera at Yul Nam Tea House, or played mah jong at Sifu Lok Yiu's school or at my home in Kowloon City. In summertime, Sifu told me to drive him around the New Territory to enjoy the fresh air away from the grime and congestion of Hong Kong, and we often ended up having a late supper, such as fresh chicken congee, in the Sar Tin area. In fact, I owe my Hong Kong driver's license to sifu's influence, because after I explained I didn't have a license, he asked one of his students who worked in the government to help expedite my license approval. Together we drove many places to have fun and relax.

When I spent time with sifu after class, he often shared his wisdom by asking me many questions and guiding me toward the solution. Sifu had an incredibly analytical mind, was well versed in Chinese philosophy, and stressed a scientific approach to Wing Chun. Importantly, sifu didn't want me to do something simply because he said it should be done that way. He often told me not to blindly believe what he said. Instead, he told me to think about it, test it out, and then, if it worked and was practical, to believe him. Looking back, I cherish those close times with Sifu Yip Man. He did his best to ensure that I developed a practical approach not just to Wing Chun, but to all problem solving. I am lucky to have learned from someone with such a truly remarkable mind and gift for teaching.

in your experience, how did Westerners respond to traditional Chinese training?

To tell you the truth, I have found little difference between Easterners and Westerners when it comes to training. Right at the beginning, all find the serious training to be torturous, tiring, and painful. Often, it is not until the student has had an actual fighting experience that he can understand why traditional training is so important, because the training teaches you how to respond to an attacker who may attack suddenly in any area, and may be looking to kill you in the conflict.

Were you a natural at kung fu? Did the movements come easily to you?

Most Wing Chun movements have come easily to me. Of course, I still have had to practice extremely hard so I can make each movement completely natural and respond to an opponent's attack by reflex and instinct. But actually, the movements of Wing Chun were designed to fit the human body's natural movements, and all of the art's ideas and movements can be explained in a scientific way.

how has your personal approach to Wing Chun changed over the years?

Sifu Yip Man taught me that learning Wing Chun was for self-defense, to be able to beat someone up and to learn confidence, patience, a hardworking attitude, never to give up, always to aim higher, to solve problems with better methods and procedures, to be a better person, to have good conduct and morals, and many other things. These are all things I have continued to develop over time.

Also, teaching Wing Chun has changed tremendously from the old times. For instance, in the beginning, a student would have to sit in the horse, play the form, and work only on basics for many, many months, and do little else. This was to help the student completely learn the foundation. Nowadays, students will not learn like this because they will consider this too boring and leave the school. Also, I remember when we played the form and sat in the horse, my sifu would burn me with a cigarette if my hand was off, or he would set a bowl of rice on my head. When we did sandbag training and the skin came off our fists, we were not allowed to stop. We went through all sorts of hard training like this because we had no choice. But today, because many students do no listen and obey the way we used to, you cannot teach like this. You will be sued. Or your school will be empty. The reason for the change is that the student-teacher relationship is so different now. The student-teacher relationship used to be like a father-son relationship. But now the student is more like a customer the teacher has to please.

"The student-teacher relationship used to be like a father-son relationship. But now the student is more like a customer the teacher has to please."

What are the most important points in your teaching methods? And what are the most important qualities for a student to become proficient in Wing Chun?

Regardless of style, I believe all schools should have a refined curriculum that teaches students to understand the ideas and theories behind

Wing Chun Masters

"In a real fight, you will not have time to think."

their techniques, analyze what is correct, improve their techniques, and make their techniques more efficient. Understand it, analyze it, and earn it.

There are two main points in my teaching methods. First, I emphasize the practical application of the style, and for this there are a lot of different kinds of training (you can see some on our Web site). I want my students to apply what they have learned, try it out with various opponents, analyze the results, and find out whether it works. I don't want my students to believe blindly what I tell them. Just because I can make a technique work for me doesn't mean the technique really works or is that good. Perhaps the technique works only because I am strong or fast, or I rely on my own special physical attributes. But what if you are not strong or fast? Is there a better way to do the technique that relies less on using power against power, or speed against speed? In Wing Chun, we assume that we are weaker, smaller, and slower than our opponents; therefore, we must have a clever way to overcome a more powerful adversary. But you must try the techniques with people who are really punching or kicking at you to learn the technique and make it work. Of course, in the beginning, students start with slow attacks so they can learn correctly, but as students progress, they must take more pressure and learn to respond without thinking. In a real fight, you will not have time to think. Your opponent will not tell you if he will hit high, low, or whatever, so you must train like this to gain this ability.

The second main point of my teaching method is that students must analyze for themselves how and why things work (or do not work). I cannot be with my students for their whole lives. When I am in my grave, a student cannot knock on my grave and ask me, "Sifu, is this technique correct?" There is a reason for every detail in Wing Chun. I want my students to understand why we do each technique, why certain positions and movements work better (or why something is worse), and how to correct and improve themselves. To use a simple analogy, you can cut a piece of metal with a handsaw, buzz saw, sword, or an ax. Which tool works better for your purpose and why? How can you find the most efficient way to use it? This constant questioning will give you a better understanding of the tools and their applications. Similarly, if you look around in Wing Chun, you will see many different ways to do a bong sau. Are they equally effective? Why does one bong sau work better than another? A student should be able to answer this because everything in Wing Chun can be explained scientifically, using basic principles of physics and biology. When Yip Man taught me, he emphasized this scientific nature of Wing Chun and how there was a scientific reason for all of Wing Chun's details. He guided me to reach an understanding of these things, but he expected me to earn this knowledge through careful study and research. I want to pass this knowledge, approach, and attitude on to my students, too.

The most important qualities for students to become proficient in Wing Chun are serious and consistent dedication to hard training, use of common sense to understand what you are learning, and the willingness to try what you have learned to determine whether it really works.

With all the technical changes during the last 30 years, do you think there are still pure styles of kung fu?

Without a doubt, every style progresses, especially as people see and experience more from different styles. There must be some modifications to certain styles or techniques to deal with other fighting methods. But I also am sure that there remain pure styles of kung fu. The question is whether you can find such a school, whether you dedicate yourself seriously to your training, and whether the sifu will teach you wholeheartedly.

Why do you think different styles are truly important in kung fu?

Each style of martial arts has a unique approach to fighting, so when these styles compete against each other, the practitioners adapt, learn, and improve their knowledge. It is just like "nature's savage garden," where competition results in survival of the fittest. Martial arts continue to improve as each generation competes against other styles. Without such interaction, you are stuck doing only your own games. You need to encounter other fighting methods to improve and evolve more effectively.

What is your opinion of full-contact kung fu tournaments?

Each style has its own specialty and method of dealing with opponents. So, if a full-contact tournament has rules or restrictions prohibiting certain types of attacks, inevitably some styles will be disadvantaged. Others will be unaffected. For instance, Eagle Claw practitioners won't be allowed to break joints. Nonetheless, such tournaments are useful experiences because they teach about other fighting methods and test whether their kung fu is practical. However, it is important to remember that such a tournament is just a competition and not a life-or-death fight.

how different from other kung fu styles do you see the principles and concepts of Wing Chun?

Wing Chun, unlike some other styles, is designed for fighting only. The most important principle in Wing Chun is simultaneous offense and defense; that is, defense is offense and offense is defense.

Do you think kung fu in the West has caught up with the technical level in China?

After Bruce Lee demonstrated his lightning-quick hand movements and magnificent techniques in the movies and at the Long Beach, California, tournament, he brought kung fu to America, making it one of the most popular activities in the United States. With the emigration to America of many kung fu masters, the serious training of many students, numerous martial arts competitions, and the assistance of modern technology, I believe the Western technical level has totally caught up. It's also important to remember that China's and Hong Kong's progress were delayed by many factors, including the "Opium War" and the addiction of many to opium, the Confucian philosophy that prioritizes scholarly pursuits over martial arts, the many years of civil war in China that caused tremendous upheaval, and the Communist ban on many martial arts in mainland China.

Do you believe there are fundamental differences in approach or physical capabilities of Chinese kung fu practitioners compared to European or American practitioners?

Chinese kung fu is an ancient art with a history dating back thousands of years. Some foreigners may first believe kung fu is mysterious or even strange, but if a sifu can properly explain the art to a student, there should be no real difficulty. After all, kung fu is just a type of physical training, philosophy, and body of knowledge about an art. All students who devote themselves with determination and fighting spirit can achieve the art.

Kung fu is currently referred to as a sport (wu shu). Do you agree with this definition?

Kung fu is an art that requires serious dedication to perfection.

Unfortunately, most people treat it like a hobby and practice it only part-time. Too many students are occupied with other activities and do not concentrate diligently on their training. Worse, some con artists tell practitioners they can learn part-time, anytime they want, and will guarantee them a black belt or some other certificate after a certain time. Can people go to college, attend class, or study whenever they want, and truly learn their subjects properly? No. Also, in China, the government prohibited people from using wu shu for fighting, so the movements became like gymnastics. Some practitioners do not care about the practical application of what they do, and this is why wu shu is referred to as a sport.

"You need to encounter other fighting methods to improve and evolve more effectively."

Do you think you still have further to go in your Wing Chun studies?

The learning in Wing Chun never ends. Your knowledge in the art depends on how much research you do to understand the application of the style to different situations and fighting methods. For me, I definitely feel there is more to learn about Wing Chun.

ho w do you see the present status of Wing Chun in the world?

The sifu-disciple relationship no longer exists. Kung fu has been commercialized, and the sifu has to accommodate the students. If there are no students (customers), there is no school, which is a reversal of older times. In addition, most people today approach Wing Chun as a hobby rather than genuinely trying to apply it. Many just do forms, sticky hands, and believe they have completed the Wing Chun curriculum. This is laughable because the forms and sticky hands are only the beginning of the whole syllabus. Nobody will do forms or sticky hands with you in a street fight. If a practitioner never actually applies what he has learned from the art, what you have is just a "fighting hero talking behind the desk."

Wing Chun Masters

"Kung fu is an art that requires serious dedication to perfection."

Do the weapons of Wing Chun enhance a student's empty-hand ability, or are those two completely unrelated skills?

In Wing Chun, the weapons are an extension of the arms, but they are more harmful and can take someone's life in a conflict. Or you might lose your own life in a conflict against someone else's weapons. The learning of weapons requires absolute dedication and seriousness. The ideas behind weapons training come from the empty-hand techniques, but they are modified to fit fights with weapons and add a lot more gung lek training. Students who learn the weapons properly gain increased understanding of the empty-hand techniques in a different or more skillful way. However, without a solid foundation of empty-hands ability, it would be extremely difficult to achieve mastery of Wing Chun weapons.

ho w does Wing Chun differ from other kung fu styles when applying the techniques in a self-defense or real situation?

As mentioned before, I did not train much in other martial arts styles, so it's difficult to make a definitive comparison. But through many years of exchanging knowledge and sparring with practitioners of other martial arts styles, I believe Wing Chun differs in certain important ways. First, Wing Chun relies on simultaneous offense and defense. The time that I defend is the same time that I attack or injure an opponent. The time that I attack is the same time I defend through coverage. Also, Wing Chun training emphasizes response to situations by reflex and feeling, rather than with one specific technique against another technique, which is what you find with many other kung fu styles. We train this way because, in reality, you will not know how suddenly your opponent will attack, where he will attack, or whether the attack will be fake or true.

What's the proper ratio in training for the forms chi sao and muk yan chong?

To apply Wing Chun and fight, the forms chi sao and muk yan chong are not enough. These are just the basics to help you understand the ideas of Wing Chun. Nobody fights in the form. Nobody on the street will do sticky hands with you. And the wooden dummy will never move or fight back, however many times you hit it. Beginners should start by learning the forms and doing sticky hands to get the basic ideas of Wing Chun. Then you need to train how to break down the wooden dummy form with technique training, and by having people attack you in a certain way. With technique training, you also train in circle fighting. Although technique training and circle fighting are useful to learn the application of Wing Chun, this is still not fighting. After you become proficient with techniques and circle fighting, your response to attacks will come naturally, and then you can add sparring and advance to real fighting.

Do you have any general advice for practitioners?

If you work hard, are serious and consistent with your training, have an open mind, and have a sifu who will wholeheartedly teach you, you will succeed.

some people believe going to h ong Kong, China, or Taiwan to train is highly necessary. Do you share this point of view?

Who I am is not important. Who I learned from is not important. The most important thing is whether what I have learned is practical. Hong Kong, China, and Taiwan have a lot of con artists too. If I can learn stuff that works, I don't care where in the world it is. I will go for it.

What do you consider the major changes in the art since you began training?

Ever since I learned from my sifus, I have seen a lot of so-called "Wing Chun" around the world reputed to be the only real, traditional Wing Chun. Worse, many confuse Wing Chun with other martial arts without understanding Wing Chun's ideas, and they create a kind of chop suey. I don't blame other martial artists who laugh at Wing Chun. Over the years, the style has become diluted with many teachers who don't seem to understand the ideas behind Wing Chun, and who don't really understand how to apply it.

Who would you like to have trained with but never got the opportunity?

Before I learned Wing Chun, I heard about many Wing Chun fighters, including Bruce Lee, William Cheung, Pan Kam Fat, Wong Shun Leung,

Hawkins Cheung, Din Ma, Hong Jai (this was Sifu Duncan Leung, though I didn't know it at the time) and Lok Yiu. These fighters made names for themselves because they successfully fought many other martial artists and made Wing Chun famous. For instance, I remember one story about Lok Yiu, who was challenged by a White Eyebrow fighter in a marketplace. Lok Yiu used gum sao and a punch against the fighter. There was such a loud cracking sound when Lok Yiu hit him in the head that the whole crowd wondered about this style, which was Wing Chun. Of course, at that time, there also were Bruce Lee's amazing movies, and I idolized him for his lightning-fast movements and physical ability. These fighters inspired me to train hard so I also could be a Wing Chun fighter, able to defeat challengers from other styles. Unfortunately, by the time I learned Wing Chun, I did not have the chance to train with these fighters (except Lok Yiu and Hong Jai and Sifu Duncan Leung) because they were too old, some had passed away, or the timing didn't work.

Also, when I learned privately from Sifu Yip Man, he told me he had five other private disciples that he taught basically everything. Because I trained with Yip Man late in his life, he said it was too difficult for him to show me certain things, so he wanted me to find these five disciples and complete my training. Eventually, I met Sifu Duncan Leung in New York, though this was by coincidence, and we trained together extensively. I met only one other of the five private disciples. I wish I could have trained with those three other private disciples.

What would you say to someone interested in starting to learn Wing Chun?
I want serious students only. I tell people interested in learning Wing Chun to look at other schools first to make sure they see what's available and not commit to something without doing more research. If people are serious about learning, I would advise them to arrange their lives to make sure nothing will disturb their serious, consistent training, and to have their finances arranged so they can support themselves. If you start to learn, but then must quit or interrupt your training, you are wasting your time—and mine.

What keeps you motivated after all these years?
To me, Wing Chun is like a treasure. I am so lucky my sifus have shared their knowledge with me; through them and through training in this Wing Chun, I have learned much about the art of fighting, physical training, Chinese philosophy, and how to live life. I believe it is my duty to pass on the legend and dignity of Wing Chun properly.

"The ideas behind weapons training come from the empty-hand techniques, but they are modified to fit fights with weapons and add a lot more *gung lek* training."

Do you think it is necessary to engage in free fighting to achieve good self-defense skills on the street?

We have no intention to create monsters or those who would abuse their Wing Chun fighting knowledge. This is against Wing Chun rules. In my school, I teach students to apply Wing Chun techniques in practical situations. This requires that attackers go for real (though in the beginning, they can begin light and slow), because if you cannot handle it in the classroom, you cannot handle it in the street. We have training called dar wai, which is fighting in a circle, and other more advanced sparring training. This type of training allows students to become proficient in free fighting so they can handle street fights.

What is your opinion about mixing kung fu styles? Does the practice of one style nullify the effectiveness of the other, or can this mixing benefit students?

No martial art is perfect. Each has a specialty or different approach to fighting. Though it is important to understand how practitioners of other

Wing Chun Masters

"No martial art is perfect. Each has a specialty or different approach to fighting."

styles fight, I think it is unwise to mix different styles because students can become easily confused and apply techniques incorrectly. It is better to learn one art first, until you fully understand its ideas and how to apply it practically. Once a student has finished learning one style, he can get involved with another. Without a total understanding of at least one style, a student might just end up with chop suey.

What is or was your philosophical basis for kung fu training?

Go for real; experience it; try it to find out what is true. This is what we call applied Wing Chun.

Do you have a particularly memorable kung fu experience that has remained as an inspiration for your training?

Sifu Yip Man once told me to attack him using a long sword against his long pole. When I attacked, I found there was no chance for me to get near him, and he totally defeated me. He then showed me the accuracy and speed of his long pole. He stood three white pieces of chalk on a table and shot the long pole to break each piece, one by one, into three pieces: the middle section, where the pole hit; the top section; and the bottom section. However, because he had struck them so quickly and precisely, the bottom of each piece of chalk remained undisturbed on the table. I was completely in awe of what he showed me that day. His skill, which came from years and years of hard practice, inspired me for life.

After all these years of training and experience, could you explain the meaning of the practice of Wing Chun?

Self-respect; self-confidence; self-defense; always aim high; never give up; be more humble; always work hard; be a better person in conduct and morals; carry on the knowledge of Wing Chun with dignity.

how are the chi sao (sticky hands) aspects of training related to the practical application of the Wing Chun techniques used in the three empty-hand forms?

In a nutshell, the three empty hand forms are only the basic hand movements of Wing Chun, like the letters of the alphabet. Nobody can fight in the form. Sticky hands (chi sao) is just a way of training to use some of the hand movements correctly, combine the different hand movements together, coverage, reflex, and improve your techniques and combinations. It also enhances your nonstop movement with a practice partner in short range, simultaneous coordination of hands, legs and entire body, and how to react by feeling without thinking (instead of thinking "this" technique against "that" technique). Sticky hands is one part of the syllabus learned before training how to fight. Unfortunately, some people erroneously think if they practice sticky hands long enough, they can fight using sticky hands. Yes, some ideas in sticky hands can be used in fighting situations, but sticky hands is merely a drill to help students sharpen their skills. It should not be practiced by students who are trying to beat each other up, who are endeavoring to show who has more power, reach, or speed, or who are striving to prove who can take more punishment. Training like this will simply lead to students exchanging hits during sticky hands, which is against one of Wing Chun's premises. Actually, the forms and sticky hands are only the beginning in the Wing Chun curriculum. There is a lot of other specific training necessary in order to achieve the art of fighting in Wing Chun.

is there anything lacking in the way martial arts are taught today compared to how they were taught when you began?

In old times, we trained almost 365 days a year at least six hours daily. We were totally dedicated and serious about our training and practiced dog hard. However, nowadays, too many people train only part time, treating martial arts like a hobby. Students get involved with too many activities and give all kinds of excuses for not attending every class, so the quality of Wing Chun is diminishing. Also affecting Wing Chun is that so many sifus invent their own stuff or add inappropriate things to Wing Chun. Some sifus even have offered diplomas to people for attending their seminars or workshops, and these diploma holders suddenly become "qualified" to teach Wing Chun. This is a joke. Actually, in Wing Chun, even if you study full-time, you will need at least five or six years to finish learning the art.

Wing Chun Masters

"Sticky hands (chi sao) is just a way of training to use some of the hand movements correctly."

What do you believe are the most important qualities of a successful kung fu practitioner?

A successful student must have a hardworking attitude, determination and dedication to train diligently and consistently, common sense to analyze how to improve his kung fu, and open-mindedness to accept other ideas. A student must not isolate himself and think his techniques and ideas are the only and the best way. I also want to emphasize the mental strength and dedication needed to succeed. There is an ancient Chinese story about a dumb old man who wanted to move a mountain. People laughed at him because they thought it would be impossible. But the old man said that even if he could not move the mountain, his sons would continue to work on moving the mountain, and if his sons couldn't finish, then the old man's grandsons or great-grandsons would finish. This is the Chinese philosophy behind our martial arts training and our belief that you must consistently dedicate yourself to achieve mastery.

What advice would you give to students about supplementary training (running, weight training, etc.)?

Wing Chun has a full curriculum for training students regarding power, speed, endurance, timing, reflex, and precision. Together, this training is gung lek training and forms all the supplementary training a Wing Chun student will need to master the style.

What do you see as the most important attributes of a student?
Respect, humility, dedication, diligence, open-mindedness, consistency in training, good conduct, and morals.

Why do you believe so many students start falling away after two or three years of training?
In my school, students who have stayed for two years usually do not leave but, rather, seek further intensive training in Wing Chun. This is because the two-year level is when they see what they can do and how much more there is to learn. Actually, our experience is that more students leave before they reach the first year level because they find the training too difficult to maintain. From what I've seen in other schools, many students leave after two or three years because they concentrate on the forms and sticky hands and perhaps think they have nothing left to learn. So these students go on to learn mixed martial arts or something else to give them variety. If I have students who are dedicated to learn, they can pursue at least five more years of intensive training.

h ave there been times when you felt fear in your kung fu training?
After Sifu Yip Man said that he had taught me as much as he could because it was late in his life, he was going to introduce me to his five private disciples who he said could show me all the gung lek training needed to complete the art. Years later, after Sifu Yip Man passed away, I finally met Sifu Duncan Leung, one of the five private disciples that Yip Man mentioned to me, in the United States. Together we had a school in New York City, and during that time we had numerous opportunities to spar. That's when I was introduced to fear. Sifu Duncan Leung's Wing Chun is outstanding. He has incredible fighting prowess and unbelievable power. During one of our sparring sessions, I thought I could get him, but in reality he skillfully set me up, and I fell into his trap. Suddenly, a bil jee technique came out of nowhere that was unstoppable. Even though he held his power, I felt the effect of his strike for days. I knew that if he didn't hold back, he could have killed me.

What are your thoughts on the future of the art?
I consider Wing Chun to be the best martial arts style. However, I believe most practitioners of our style are too proud. Too many fail to have an open mind, and too many blindly accept what they have without testing its validity and practicality. I feel these attitudes will continue to splinter our family, dilute Wing Chun, and may even lead to the style's demise.

GORDEN LU

The Legacy

SIFU GORDEN LU IS THE SON OF THE LEGENDARY MASTER LO MAN KAM WHO WAS YIP MAN'S NEPHEW AND STUDENT. HE WAS BORN IN TAIWAN IN 1971 AND BEGAN HIS WING CHUN TRAINING AT THE AGE OF 15 UNDER THE TUTELAGE OF HIS FATHER. HE SOON REALIZED THAT THE ART OF WING CHUN WAS HIS CALLING AND STARTED TRAINING DILIGENTLY. AFTER COMPLETING STUDY OF THE SYSTEM UNDER HIS FATHER, SIFU GORDEN TRAVELED TO AMERICA TO CONTINUE HIS TRAINING UNDER THE GUIDANCE OF ANOTHER WING CHUN MASTER, THE VENERABLE SIFU DUNCAN LEUNG.

SIFU GORDEN STARTED TEACHING IN THE U.S., USING A FRESH PERSPECTIVE AND YOUTHFUL ENTHUSIASM TO GUIDE HIS STUDENTS. HE MAINTAINS THE CLASSICAL METHODS HANDED DOWN FROM HIS FATHER AND KUNG FU UNCLE, BUT AT THE SAME TIME COMBINES MODERN TRAINING WITH THE TRADITIONAL ASPECTS. SIFU LU' STUDENTS ARE TRAINED TO INTEGRATE MODERN TEACHING METHODS WITH THE FUNDAMENTAL PRINCIPLES AND TECHNIQUES OF THE WING CHUN STYLE.

BECAUSE OF SIFU LO MAN KAM'S INTERNATIONAL REPUTATION, WING CHUN SCHOOLS AROUND THE WORLD SEEK OUT SIFU GORDEN LU TO SPEAK AT SEMINARS AND DEMONSTRATIONS. HE HAS FOLLOWED IN HIS FATHER'S FOOTSTEPS TO SHARE THE ART OF WING CHUN IN HIS SCHOOL AT VIRGINIA BEACH – WHERE HE RESIDES – AND ALSO BY TEACHING SEMINARS IN THE UNITED STATES AND OTHER COUNTRIES.

how long have you been practicing Wing Chun and who was your teacher?

I started to learn Wing Chun when I was 15 years old. I learned Wing Chun from my father, Master Lo Man Kam, who is Wing Chun grandmaster Ip Man's nephew. I studied Wing Chun not only because I like the art, but also as a personal mission for me, to keep Wing Chun instruction direct from the family and to follow the family tradition. Since the early 80s, there had some exchange training between my father's school students and Sifu Duncan Leung's school. In 1994 summer, I followed my father's instruction and traveled to the U.S. to study another style of Wing Chun from his junior Kung Fu brother Sifu Duncan Leung, the disciple of the grandmaster. So I really had two major instructors, both my father Master Lo Man Kam and Sifu Duncan Leung.

how many styles of Kung Fu or other methods have you trained in?

Wing Chun is the style I really concentrated on. Due to the influence of my father, I also spent some time on training special techniques for practi-

Wing Chun Masters

"There are many details and ideas in each Wing Chun form."

cal application that can be easily used in the military and law enforcement. I learned some basics of Judo, hands grabbling and joint lock skills, under my father and had some training at the Taiwanese Police College.

In addition, Wing Chun has two fighting styles – the short bridge and the long bridge. The "short bridge" method is close range fighting, tight and nail on the opponent, and emphasizes quick response and continuous follow-up with various combinations of control techniques, strikes, and kicks.

The "long bridge" is more distance-fighting – move in fast and get out fast. It emphasizes good body structure with crash in power and flexibility to provide different combination strikes and kicks. Long bridge also is done by the timing, break-in to the center and distance control. There is one thing a lot of people do not know is that the famous Wing Chun one-inch punch is long bridge style. Master Lo Man Kam is expert on short bridge and Sifu Duncan is expert on long bridge.

What are the main principles intrinsic to the three Wing Chun forms? Do they interrelate with each other?

There are many details and ideas in each Wing Chun form, but there always are a few key things that represent each form that the practitioner needs to pay more attention to.

Siu Lim Tao is most important form of whole system. The form doesn't just teach the hand movements and structures. The most important is to let practitioners know the idea behind each move. There are some main ideas I want to point out here: the idea of how to generate elbow power, center line concept, straight line theory, and the idea of covering the upper body center area are in the first section of the form. The fighting range and speed are in the second section, and the last section teaches how to generate power in a short distance, relaxation power, pull and push power idea.

Chum Kiu emphasizes footwork, kicks, mobility and hand leg coordination. Chum Kiu also uses a lot of principles and the movements from Siu Lim Tao (for example: center line, pull and push power, idea of protection, etc.). Chum Kiu also expands the ideas of using the movements from the first form to be a technique or a way of application in a close-range fighting. Chum Kiu in English is "seeking the bridge." That is why this form has a lot of movements with idea of "intercepting." Intercepting your opponent's hand technique will build a bridge. Bil Jee is unique form and a lot different from the first two forms. The first form (Siu Lim Tao) teaches how to generate the power from the elbow. The third form (Bil Jee) teaches how to generate and extend the power from the shoulder. The third form also combined the first two forms' ideas, hand movements, and footwork, and emphasizes open and longer fighting distance applications. Fa-sao in the third form can very effective by covering a wider area; the elbow exercise not only trains you to know how to extend the shoulder but also is a powerful strike and cover technique. Shooting the fingers to the opponent's soft point is the trademark. This technique requires accuracy, speed, extension, and penetration.

The first form is more abstract and needs a lot of understanding and imagination. Most movements are teaching the position, structure, and the ideas behind the move. The second and third form have more applications techniques involved. The second form contains a lot of controlling techniques. It provides close fighting range concept, generating the pressure power by stepping in, turning the horse and fighting direction. The third form also emphasizes covering a wider range, pull and push power and distance control, and concentrating on accuracy of finger and elbow strikes techniques.

Would you tell us some interesting stories of your early days in Kung Fu?
I don't have too much very interesting stories to tell, but there was one that I find very interesting. I remember that after I learned Wing Chun (it was about the time I studied Chi-sao [Sticky Hands]), I was involuntarily swinging my hand a lot, doing lap-sao, pak-sao, or some other Chi-sao techniques while I was walking on the street, waiting for someone, or just when I had nothing to do. Every time I was doing those hands movements and people passed by, they'd give me a look and probably thought I was crazy.

h ow did you find that Westerners respond to traditional Chinese training?
I have taught Wing Chun in many different countries and have noticed that westerners respond to traditional Chinese training in different ways. In

Wing Chun Masters

"Most Chinese people know learning Kung Fu is not an easy thing to do."

Europe, people more look into the spiritual, health and skills. In America, people are more interested in the fighting techniques, along with quick results and strength. Most Chinese people know learning Kung Fu is not an easy thing to do, and they also know it takes time, and tremendous patience. That is why in my school, all the students know that there is no "fast-food Kung Fu." In China, Taiwan or Hong Kong, if the Kung Fu class that teach a student an advance technique at first day, student(s) may feel they are missing something because they know they did not get the good fundamentals yet. In many schools, if the instructor to ask students only to stand on the horse position or just give one or two movements to let them repeatedly practice for the first week, they won't complain and just respect the art and the training. They know the training is testing their patience, will power and provide a strong basic.

Were you a 'natural' at Kung Fu – did the movements come easily to you?

I was always very athletic and consistently performed competitively in sports, from primary school through college so the Kung Fu moves were not physically challenging. In addition, I had grown up literally watching my father teaching and his students practicing the techniques, so I was exposed to everything at a very young age which helped me to become skilled when I entered my formal education in Wing Chun. I think it was very natural for me, because I lived in that environment all my life.

how has your personal Kung Fu has developed over the years?

I learned from my father who is an expert on the short bridge Wing Chun, I also learned from my Kung Fu uncle sifu Duncan Leung and who is an expert on long bridge Wing Chun. I was in Taiwanese army Martial Arts and sports team. I worked for the Taiwanese police force as defensive tactics instructor. During those years of learning, practicing, training and developing I did develop my personal style in the system. So when I use and teach the art, I have a broader experience and background than other people. I utilize Wing Chun system short and long bridge fighting techniques in a more complete way and bring these other areas of experience to the table as well, so my students gain access to this more flexible approach. In addition to the short and long bridge styles, I also learned how to teach these two styles by following Ip Man's teaching curriculum and that is the biggest difference to most people who teach in the current time that they only emphasize one style. Finally, my experience with modern sports theory inspired me to adapt these types of approaches in training my students in Wing Chun. I try to use the sports theories in developing the supporting exercises to give my students an advantage in learning Wing Chun in the shortest period of time to reach the same high quality.

"I like to find where students' talents are and to teach students Wing Chun with their talents."

What are the most important points in your teaching methods?

The most important principle in my teaching is not just to teach my students Wing Chun. I like to find where students' talents are and to teach students Wing Chun with their talents. Wing Chun is very abstract and flexible. I want all my students to have their own Wing Chun style. They should not fight like me. They should fight like them but with a base on Wing Chun principles.

And what are the most important qualities for a student to become proficient in the Wing Chun style?

I know some people asked same question of Ip Man before. These days, Ip Man Wing Chun still is the same and I think my answer will also be the same as Ip Man said before. If you want your Wing Chun to be good, you need to meet 5 things: you need to have "time" to train whole day and not worry about go to work or go to school; you need to have a "chance" to meet a right teacher; you need to have "money" to pay someone for your full time training and your own cost of living; you need to have some "tal-

Wing Chun Masters

"In Wing Chun, some things don't really need to be original due to the personal experiences."

ent" on physically and mentally to do Wing Chun and finally you need to have some "guts" when you need to use your skills to fight. It's not easy.

With all the technical changes during the last 30 years, do you think there are still 'pure' styles of Kung Fu?

People's lifestyle differ, their backgrounds differ, as do their experiences, personality, talent, body size, etc. ... That's why a lot of people teach the same style but the techniques are different. In Wing Chun, some things don't really need to be original due to the personal experiences, but something should be the same: the basic principles. I do not know enough about other Kung Fu styles to comment, but for Wing Chun it is like that. I think that in any style of Martial Art, if they can keep and follow their principles and right teaching methods then they can continue to keep the purity of the style.

For example, Ip Man was a police detective prior to teaching Wing Chun; because of his job function, he improved his Martial Arts skills as related to what he was doing. That's why Ip Man styles of Wing Chun also have some joint lock and take down techniques. But when Ip Man was teaching Wing Chun, he still followed the same curriculums and Wing Chun principles as he learned.

From my experience, there are some reasons that Kung Fu purity may differ after being passed down generation to generation: a) Misunderstanding of the techniques/applications; b) Lack of real life experience or expertise in the arts as opposed to those who spend years in the study. In that case the person may have learned just enough to open the school, so he can only provide limited training and knowledge to the students. A lot of time when the person has not enough knowledge of that style he is teaching, he usually will create his own exercises and that may not match original principles or will mislead the students to the wrong training; c) The instructor never learned how to teach. Sometime it takes years to figure out the right teaching methods, but after a few years, students may already have bad habits; and d) not having an open mind.

Do you think different 'styles' are truly important in the art of Kung Fu?

Yes, in fact, in every style has a story and a reason to exist. Different styles of Kung Fu are here to represent a country or a region's culture, history and faith. In a broad sense, they are a guideline of disciplines, philosophy and spirituality. They represent a way of living, a life style, a life skill and more...along with sustaining health and creating a skill in self-defense. Different styles of Kung Fu are like different styles of painting. Different painting may tell you a different story, age, culture, the feeling, history, background, and emotional aspect of the artists.

What is your opinion of Full Contact Kung Fu tournaments?

I always encourage my students to participate different competitions in the tournaments. I want them to understand what type of tournament fit for them because this is very important. It is a good idea to participate any type of Martial Arts competition include the full contact because there always have something can learn for any participant. The thing you can learn is not just to the fight in the ring but also the training before the competition and review and corrections after the fight.

h ow different from other Kung Fu styles do you see the principles and concepts of Wing Chun?

Other Kung Fu teach how to fight from the form, copy the moves from the animals, religion ceremony ... imagination (like fire, water, earth, wood, and metal – five elements), etc.... In Wing Chun, we learn how to fight by the principle; we see scientific effects in the system and the movements that we practice use the natural reaction (such as dodge the ball, kick the ball, push a car, slam the door, draw the hand back fast when get burned by the cigarette, etc.) People are born with those basic skills, which mean you don't need to learn you already know and have muscle memory to react fast. In Wing Chun, we just use all those thing plus Wing Chun principles of movement to apply fighting techniques. That why people always say Wing Chun use a lot of use economy motion and it is very easy to learn.

Do you think that Kung Fu in the West is at the same the technical level as in China?

I am not sure about other styles of Kung Fu, but in Wing Chun most are not. There are few reasons: Geographically, most Ip Man students are not teaching in the West. There are some students of Ip Man and some people who may have good Wing Chun knowledge from Taiwan, Hong Kong or China who came to the West, but the amount is still small. The area of whole United States compared to the amount of people who have good knowledge of Wing Chun from the East that will take a lot of longer to develop this art to the same level over there.

Culturally, Taiwan, Hong Kong, and China still have many Kung Fu schools that are following the tradition. Most people and potential students know learning Martial Arts take years and not everyone can be good or a master. Traditionally, even after years of study, if your Sifu does not say you are good enough to teach or prove, you should not teach or open the school, the students will not disobey. This is also is how the students show loyalty and respect to the Sifu, school and the art. This also is the best way to maintain a good quality of Kung Fu and develop better skills and knowledge to pass down to next generation.

I have heard many stories and people talked about someone who learned Wing Chun for a year or two, or 10 months or less, and then opened a school in the West. Or some people may learn for a few years but never learn how to teach. Some people learn from DVD or go to a seminar for few hours then say they are good enough to teach those masters' Wing Chun, and use their names.

A lot of moves and techniques may be easy to copy but it is hard to be an expert. If you don't understand or if someone not tells you correctly the lesson behind the technique or exercise or you are not really focus on some details, and then you will have huge gaps. A little mistake you make now in the technique or principles after years of practice will be big mistake. This is like shooting a rifle. If your focusing on the center of target is just a little bit off the mark, but after 100 yards you will find out you missed the target by a lot.

Do you feel that there are any fundamental differences in approach or physical capabilities of Chinese Kung Fu practitioners in comparison to European or American practitioners?

As I mentioned before, there are some differences. We always teach the same in Europe and the U.S., but a lot of people react differently. I will say the European has better patience, emphasizes detail, and is in better shape. In the U.S., people look more for a fast pace, quick results, and more enjoyable workout than technique, and emphasize power and action.

Kung Fu is nowadays often referred to as a sport (wu shu). Would you agree with this definition?

No. I think people misunderstand it in the West. I believe most people in Taiwan, Hong Kong and China know Kung Fu is Kung Fu and wu shu is just wu shu. The common definition for most Chinese people, Kung Fu is a skill for fight and self-defense and wu shu is a type of demonstration or performance.

"Your creation is your study and your experience is the key for your creation."

Do you feel that you still have further to go in your studies of the art of Wing Chun?

Chinese people always say, "You always learn as you live longer." I also tell my students, Wing Chun is your life and your life is Wing Chun. We learn from our life and a lot of life experience can also reflect Wing Chun training. Wing Chun is very abstract. Wing Chun is art. Wing Chun is like painting, you can use different colors in the painting or you can just use one color to make the same painting. You can mix two or more colors to create a new color. Your creation is your study and your experience is the

Wing Chun Masters

"Wing Chun originally had no weapons."

key for your creation. As a Wing Chun Sifu I am not just teaching, I also learn from teaching. I have found similarities between teaching Wing Chun and my police job. There is always something new every day.

Chi-sao is the heart of Wing Chun and Ip Man used to say, "the older you are the better you will get on Chi-sao" – which means your Wing Chun study should never finish. Chi-sao requires a lot of feeling and understanding. Often, when you get older you will understand better due to your Martial Arts experiences and life experiences. Because of your understanding, you will relax more and be smoother when doing the Wing Chun exercises. Your contact feeling also will be easier to build up. Because of your good feeling, better understanding and experiences, all these main elements add to your power and increase your reaction speed, which can lead you to have better skills.

how do you see Wing Chun Kung Fu in the world at the present time?

Every time I travel to different countries to do seminars, I see more and more new students studying Wing Chun. I also notice a lot of people enjoying the study of Wing Chun, not because of the fighting techniques alone but also due to the art itself. Wing Chun has already been popular for years and many people are still interested in it for its emphasis on traditional training, not "fast-food Kung Fu." I think this is a good sign and I also have positive view on Wing Chun for the future.

Does the weaponry aspect of Wing Chun [long pole and butterfly knives] enhance the student's empty hands ability or are those two completely non-related skills?

There are many stories about Wing Chun weapons. Some people say the knives are arms' extensions; others say they are two different things. Wing Chun originally had no weapons. It does not matter which one is right or wrong; from what I know, the knives training can enhance empty hands' flexibility and strength because a lot of knife movements copy the hand techniques and Wing Chun principles.

The Wing Chun long pole is longer than most other Chinese Kung Fu styles' pole or stick, so the Wing Chun pole is also heavier. If students practice the long pole form a lot, that can easily stronger on their arms, footwork and structure. Long pole also has a lot of unique exercise along with. When we do those exercises, we can use an 11-foot-long pole to train to give better power training and those long pole exercises are very good to the horse (leg power), footwork, hip power and Wing Chun punch. All these power training can always benefit the empty hands.

h ow does the Wing Chun style differ from other Kung Fu methods when applying the techniques in self-defense and real situations?
I think there are two big differences. The first thing is that other styles fight "by technique" and Wing Chun teaches how to fight by theories such like shortest distance between two points or simultaneously cover and attack. In Wing Chun we don't learn how to hit. We learn how to not get hit. We always cover our opening and make sure we are safe and control the situation then hit back.

Second, we use a lot of natural reactions (something you born with and you don't need to learn or train), scientific effects (such like leverage: a lot of thing you may already have learned in 5th grade), etc. ... in fact, a lot of the things I point out here, people don't really need to learn from Wing Chun, because they already know those ideas, or can do those movements in their regular live. The main thing they don't know is how to put everything together to be a fighting technique. The Wing Chun system just provides this training, so people who learn Wing Chun may not need to spend a lot of time then they can easier hands on and apply to situation. That's why in Wing Chun we have a saying, "the best technique is no technique," which mean you just react to the situation without thinking about it.

In other styles, one may learn how to fight from the forms or katas, or emphasize punching the bag or kicking the bag a lot every day, or need to learn the movements from the animals which may not the natural for humans. Sometimes, to practice those movements may take longer time because those whole new movements our muscles are never experience before or very limited and may need to take longer time to be good and turn to natural reaction or muscle memory.

From my point of view, Wing Chun is like any other Martial Arts style; they all have something special and unique. The Wing Chun system is just

Wing Chun Masters

designed to make it easier for the practitioner to react and fit into the situation.

When teaching the art of Kung Fu, what is the most important element: self-defense, health, or tradition?

The Wing Chun system includes all three of these. I try to be balanced. Students also need to know how to keep up after they have learned, so they won't emphasize one thing too much. Sometimes, I will make a plan for students and lead them to the way they need to be more focus. For example, if a young lady comes to my school, I will teach her more self-defense. If the person is older, I will focus more on health than self-defense. If a student has a passion to be an instructor, I will let him know more about the tradition and teaching skills. Everybody who learns Wing Chun has a purpose, condition, talent, and background and they may always focus on something more than another. My way of teaching is to consolidate all the conditions of the individual and provide the best training plan to him or her.

"My way of teaching is to consolidate all the conditions of the individual and provide the best training plan to him or her."

"Learning how to teach" is very important. I also will emphasize to my students if they want to teach Wing Chun one day, because we are not just teaching people Wing Chun but also increasing the students' understanding of the art, helping them to develop their Wing Chun style, and letting them acquire this life skill.

Forms and chi-sao: What's the proper ratio in training?

Everybody who learns Wing Chun should know chi-sao is the heart of the art and the first form is the most important form of the system. Following the tradition of Ip Man's teaching and curriculums, in my classes, every student needs to do the first form before they start to do any other forms or exercises. If a Wing Chun practitioner only learns the fighting techniques or sparring, that person's Wing Chun skill may only be able to reach a certain level and he/she will have a hard time improving afterward. If the practitioner focuses on chi-sao and obtains some skills (such as reaction, timing, feeling, controlling, and follow-up), he or she can work on more fighting techniques. This can make it easier for the practitioner to reach a higher lever and master the techniques. For the beginner, the first form is the most important. Beginners need to understand the ideas behind each move and do it right. When students start to learn chi-sao then they need to more focus on that, but they still doing the form everyday just to reinforce and refine the skills.

some people think going to h ong Kong, China, or Taiwan to train is highly necessary; do you share this point of view?

Everyone has the purpose to learn Kung Fu. If they like the style and enjoy then, I think it doesn't really matter where they learn because they enjoy the style, not the location. Since I came from China and also teach in the U.S. and Europe, here are some good reasons from my experience why people really should go to Hong Kong, China, and Taiwan. First, people who want learn the system in a shorter time develop higher quality skills. So many things in Chinese Martial Arts are not really easy to explain in English or other languages. In Hong Kong, China, or Taiwan, they may find it easier to understand the style or get a better answer for their question on the style of Kung Fu they learn.

Second, for those who want to be an instructor, it is better to go there and learn more from an old master. In Martial Arts, there always are some tricks to refine the techniques or to get the techniques better in an easier way. Learning from an old master's experience can really save a lot of time compared to the individual trying to figure it out by himself.

Some other reasons for to people to train Kung Fu over there are that the practitioner can concentrate more on training in days and nights, helped by Kung Fu brothers, learning the original and obtaining first hand information. Another key point is that you need to pay a lot of money to go there, so you will really work harder than your hometown's school.

Who would you like to have trained with that you have not?

My granduncle, Ip Man.

What would you say to someone who is interested in starting to learn Wing Chun Kung Fu?

Wing Chun is simple, direct, easy to learn, and practical. People who want to learn Wing Chun only need to focus on three things: First, understand the basic Wing Chun theories; second, learn how to react with your natural reaction; and third, relax and enjoy.

Wing Chun Masters

What keeps you motivated after all these years?

I guess it is family tradition. My granduncle passed the art to his sons and his nephew, who is my father Master Lo Man Kam, and my father also passed the art to me. As a member of Ip Man's family, I feel this is my duty and responsibility to keep the tradition and spread the art and pass it to next generation and the people who love this art. Not only that, as I am the only younger person in the Ip Man's family teaching Wing Chun, I know I need to keep going. I love Wing Chun but I also love to teach, because I don't just teach people to fight … I am also helping all my students to build their life style and life skill.

Do you think it is necessary to engage in free-fighting to achieve good self-defense skills?

From my experience, if we just talk about self-defense skills in the street, we may not really need to engage in free-fighting to achieve good self-defense skills. Find a good teacher, learn the right techniques and a good training can provide the skills you may need to use in the street. A lot of time, that depends how good you want to be. If you only want to learn how to protect yourself when something happens, you really don't need to engage in free-fighting to achieve good self-defense skills.

What is your opinion about mixing Kung Fu styles? Does the practice of one nullify the effectiveness of the other or on the contrary, it can be beneficial to the student?

This is a matter of opinion, but for me, I would say that if you truly want to master Wing Chun, you should not mix styles because there are too many conflicts. For example, a lot of Chinese Kung Fu learn to fight from the form of the animals or imagination. We don't; Wing Chun is very abstract. We learn to fight from the theories. Other styles may emphasize hard power but Wing Chun can be hard or soft depending on the opponent and situation. From my teaching experience, students who learn different styles at the same often will miss focus in the classes, confuse themselves with different techniques, find a lot of conflict, and finally never master any style. Wing Chun is very flexible and sometimes is very easy to adapt to other styles. You may not need to really learn the style; you just need to learn the right techniques and you may open your mind and increase your skills both ways.

What is your philosophical basis for your Kung Fu training?

There have many philosophical bases for my Kung Fu training. Here is the one that I always have in my heart. The old saying goes: "Benevolence is the precious of all Martial Arts; master of skills is due to disciplined training."

Do you have a particularly memorable Kung Fu experience that has remained as an inspiration for your training?

I think a lot of Kung Fu experiences inspired me to train harder and better. I remember when I was young ... about 19 years old. I fought with a guy at school and he pulled a knife out and tried to stab me. I did not even think. I reacted quickly and sidestepped back with pak-sao (snap his hand) and knocked his knife off. I think this type of reaction (speed of reaction – do something without thinking of it) is the benefit from training Chi-sao. Also, many things have happened in my daily live. Sometimes, I have one hand holding something but it slipped and my other hand will automatically move to catch it. There have been more experiences related to fighting or just in the daily life, and all of them are because the unique training from Wing Chun Chi-sao did not just benefit me with good reaction or fighting techniques. It also made me more alert in my life.

"Kung Fu is not just doing the same move over and over."

After all these years of training and experience, could you explain the meaning of the practice of Kung Fu?

First of all, I want to say that the correct way of practice Kung Fu is not just doing the same move over and over. You should have a training plan, right tools, and a systematic and supporting exercises program. When you practice a subject, you need to use your heart, you need to feel the move, and you also need to feel that your body cells are practicing, too. You need to have a good understanding of the movement. You need to think, explain to yourself and teach yourself while you practice. Finally, you should achieve mastery through a comprehensive study of the subject.

Wing Chun Masters

"It is good to have this kind of training. However, it's better to have the supplementary training that benefits what your Martial Arts style needs. For example, in Wing Chun."

how is the Chi-sao aspects of training related to the practical application of the Wing Chun techniques used in the three empty hands forms?

This is very complex but let me put this way: the movements from the Wing Chun forms are like the English alphabet. Each move doesn't mean anything. Like letters A, B, C, etc. don't mean too much, but if you put different letters together, that can be a word and have meaning. If you put more words together, there is even more and deeper meaning, Wing Chun is just like that. Chi-sao is combining a lot of different movements from the form to be a special exercise of training. As Ip Man said, "Chi Sao is the heart of Wing Chun." However no one fights with Chi Sao. True Chi Sao teaches significant fighting techniques and also trains the students in the elements that we will use in combat like fighting distance, idea of cover the opening, reaction, timing, structure, contact feeling, strategies and a very important Wing Chun principle of "Fan-sao" (continuous follow-up with defense and offense techniques to control and strike the opponent.)

is anything lacking in the way Martial Arts are taught today compared to how they were in your beginnings?

Some Martial Arts schools today are too commercial. Schools should focus on benefitting the students. Some schools are missing the traditional spirit or give students wrong ideas of training Martial Arts with quick result lack fundamentals. I think the times are changing. People in old times were looking for less entertainment, more focus on training and training harder. People were more respectful to the arts, school, and appreciated the teacher. I think that I have more strong feeling of these because I lived and grew up in the Kung Fu school and I have seen many different people come and go. I also teach and live in the West now. I know the difference between two cultures.

Could i ask you what you consider to be the most important qualities of a successful Kung Fu practitioner?

There are some important things a student should have. A person needs passion for that chosen style, good moral character, benevolence and magnanimity, ability to make the mechanical movements of Kung Fu turn alive (smooth and fluently to apply the techniques), good contact feeling, and finally, the ability to create a good fighting plan and strategic and flexible on adapt to different situation.

What advice would you give to students on the question of supplementary training?

It is good to have this kind of training. However, it's better to have the supplementary training that benefits what your Martial Arts style needs. For example, in Wing Chun, a wall bag that can develop push straight power for the punch along with strengthening the knuckles and wrist; And a Wing Chun long pole which emphasizes power training and body structure. Some kick-punch-kick drills are very good on endurance, speed, and explosive power and some pad drills benefit a student with whole body workout along with reaction, speed, power, cardio, and endurance. I also use a weighted bar and medicine ball to train power, structure, and reaction.

I love to use supplementary training methods and I found that can always benefit my students on learning and using Wing Chun. In fact, one of the big differences of my Wing Chun teaching from others is that I use a lot of supplementary training methods and drills, which can speed up students' learning processes and also can lead to a good quality of Wing Chun.

Wing Chun Masters

"The Wing Chun system has been out there for years. The system does not changes much, but people change."

What do you see as the most important attributes of a student?

Patience first and foremost, because with patience you will not hurry and will spend the time to master the exercises and techniques. It is also important to understand why we are doing a technique; it is not just the technique but the theory behind it that is important. We need to understand why and how this works this way because eventually all the Wing Chun knowledge that you are exposed to will build your own personal Wing Chun style.

Why is it, in your opinion, that a lot of students start falling away after two-three years of training?

It's interesting when you look at students back in Asia; the average student is willing to stay far longer than the average Western student. The reason is that the Asian culture already tells the people that learning Martial Arts take years and also need a lot of hard work ... so they are willing to study far longer because they have that expectation. In the West, a lot of students are interested in learning mostly the new techniques as opposed to fundamentals. Many people learn Martial Arts because they watched some Martial Arts movies or heard people talking about the arts and stimulate their imagination and interest. When they come to the Martial Arts classes and do not find what they watched in the movie or have to face hard work, they lose interest. In the current society, we have too many things that can distract people – video games, new methods of workout programs in the fitness center, rock climbing in the summertime, and snowboarding in the winter season. People can be very busy on a lot of things. People can be very interested in something today and lose their interest the next day. People may have different life styles, change jobs frequently, move from one place to another every few years, get married, or have some other things or events happen to them and make them stop training. This life cycle, for me, is very normal. Not everybody can master everything or fit for everything. There's an old Chinese saying, "the art always passes to the people who have fate with that art." The Wing Chun system has been out there for years. The system does not changes much, but people change. That is why I say the most important attribute of a student to learn Wing Chun is patience.

h ave there been times when you felt fear in your Kung Fu training?

Never ... because when I learned Wing Chun, in the very beginning, my father taught me that the very first thing I would need to do to become a good martial artist is to conquer the fear. When I started training I knew that getting hurt and getting bruised would happen. That is part of the training process so I was mentally prepared.

What are your thoughts on the future of the art, and is there anything you would like to add?

I believe the future is great for Wing Chun. It has become increasingly popular and more well-known to a greater audience. This is very good as the system spreads and more people want to learn, want to experience and find out the truth of Wing Chun, its history and techniques.

On the other hand, as it gains in popularity, I worry about the Wing Chun instruction becoming so commercial that it ends up ruining both the name and quality of Wing Chun. There is always a worry as to authenticity and quality control ... firsthand instruction versus someone who learned from a video or a few seminars or someone who is not fully versed in the art. The very best instruction comes from people who live and breathe Wing Chun. Lineage, training, background, and many years of instruction in Wing Chun are the most important.

TONY MASSENGILL

Carrying the Heritage

TONY MASSENGILL IS A THIRD GENERATION MASTER IN THE IP FAMILY LINEAGE. HE IS THE SENIOR U.S. DISCIPLE OF MASTER SAMUEL KWOK, WHO IS THE TOP WORLD-WIDE MASTER UNDER BOTH OF IP MAN'S SONS, GRANDMASTERS IP CHUN AND IP CHING.

HE IS THE U.S. DIRECTOR OF THE TRADITIONAL IP MAN WING CHUN ASSOCIATION AND IS IN CHARGE OF DEVELOPING INSTRUCTORS AND TRAINING GROUP LEADERS IN THE UNITED STATES.

SIFU MASSENGILL, ALONG WITH SAMUEL KWOK, HAS COAUTHORED TWO BOOKS ON THE IP MAN WING CHUN SYSTEM, ONE OF WHICH WAS PLACED IN THE IP MAN MUSEUM IN FOSHAN, CHINA IN 2007, AND HAS APPEARED IN ALMOST A DOZEN INSTRUCTIONAL DVDS PRODUCED BY EM3 VIDEO.

MASSENGILL IS RETIRED FROM A 25-PLUS-YEAR CAREER IN PUBLIC SAFETY, WHERE HE WORKED AS A POLICE OFFICER, FIREFIGHTER, AND EMERGENCY MEDIC. HIS STREET EXPERIENCE COMBINED WITH 45 YEARS IN THE MARTIAL ARTS HAS GIVEN HIM A UNIQUE PERSPECTIVE ON THE "REAL WORLD" APPLICATION OF WING CHUN IN VIOLENT STREET ENCOUNTERS.

SIFU MASSENGILL TEACHES A SMALL GROUP OF STUDENTS IN YORKTOWN, VIRGINIA, AND SPENDS MOST OF HIS TIME TEACHING SEMINARS AND INSTRUCTOR DEVELOPMENT PROGRAMS ACROSS THE UNITED STATES.

how long have you been practicing the Martial Arts and who was your teacher?

I began training in the Martial Arts at the age of five. I earned Black Belt rank or Instructor certification in several Martial Art systems prior to seeing Wing Chun for the first time in 1979. I began training in Wing Chun at that time, getting my introduction into the system under the instruction of Shiu Hung (Duncan) Leung. I trained with him steadily until I began a career in the police department in 1982. I trained sporadically from that time until 1984.

Since that time, I have continued my training under many different instructors, some as a formal student, and some in seminars or in having the opportunity to just do short-term research, but not as a formal student. Eventually, I began training under the Ip Family method under the Ip Chun / Ip Ching / Samuel Kwok lineage, where I earned a Master Level certifica-

Wing Chun Masters

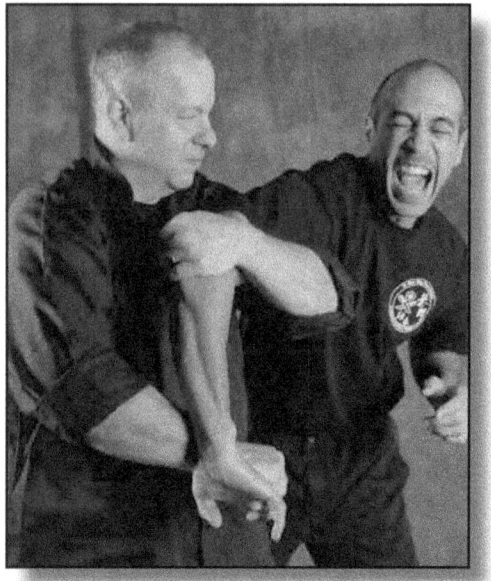

"My Sifu, Samuel Kwok is the only person to be ranked at a Master Level under both of Ip Man's sons."

tion in 2005. My Sifu, Samuel Kwok is the only person to be ranked at a Master Level under both of Ip Man's sons.

I had the good fortune to have the opportunity to training directly with Ip Chun and Ip Ching through travels to Hong Kong and Foshan, China with Samuel Kwok. I spent quite a bit of time with Ip Ching in researching the system during the time I was writing the book Mastering Wing Chun – The Keys to Ip Man's Kung Fu (Empire Media). I served for several years as the U.S. Director of the Traditional Ip Man Wing Chun Association. Upon leaving that post I formed the Ip Man Wing Chun Union which offers seminars, instructor training, and certification to those interested in the Ip Man FAMILY system. Info on these programs can be found at (www.IpManWingChun.com)

ho w many styles (kung fu or other methods) have you trained in?

In the 46 years I have been training in the Martial Arts, in addition to Wing Chun, I have earned Black Belt rank or Instructor certification in Tae Kwon Do, Tai Jutsu Kenpo, Kajukenbo, Chin-Na, Muay Thai, and Stick and Knife combatives.

What are the main principles intrinsic to the Wing Chun forms and do they interrelate with each other?

In late 2006 Master Samuel Kwok asked me to write the book "Mastering Wing Chun - The Keys to Ip Man's Kung Fu. It was produced as a co-written project with Master Kwok. I wrote the book and Master Kwok flew in for the photos. I am very grateful to Master Kwok for giving me the opportunity to write the book.

In "Mastering Wing Chun", I explained the forms in the following way:

Siu Lim Tao – building the weapon. This set and related training form the foundation of your weapon. Siu Lim Tao builds your structure. If you compared this to building a firearm, you would not be able to use the firearm as a weapon until it was fully built and operational. Until the firearm has a firing pin, a trigger, a hammer, and a barrel it is not a useful weapon in your defense. Wing Chun is much the same. In Siu Lim Tao level training, we must concentrate on how the movements and shapes in the defense and attacking techniques relate to our own body. This is what I call "self-structure." We must learn the boundary lines of our own body. We must come to understand how the body generates energy by the use of proper movement, not by the overuse of muscular strength, but by way of the body's natural structure. This is what is learned by way of training in the Siu Lim Tao.

Chum Kiu – Using the weapon. After we have built a functional weapon, we can begin to learn to use it against an opponent. In this level of training the student learns to apply their structure against another individual. I call this "applied structure." In Siu Lim Tao, once the basic stance is assumed, there is no more footwork. In Chum Kiu, the student begins to learn to apply the techniques learned in SLT with the use of shifting and stepping to add power to the technique.

Biu Gee – Emergency techniques. In the Biu Gee form, we learn to recover from mistakes we make in the application of our techniques, or if we are taken by surprise and caught off guard by an attack.

So, as you can see, the forms interrelate very well. The first builds the foundation for the second. The second is pretty much the way we want to apply our techniques under ideal conditions. And the third is to save our backside when things don't go according to plan – which, by the way is almost always the case. I believe it was General Eisenhower who said, "No plan survives first contact with the enemy." I believe he would have approved of a system that made preparation for recovery from such emergencies.

Would you tell us some interesting stories of your early days in kung fu?

When I first found a Wing Chun school, I had been training in the Martial Arts for many years. I had earned Black Belt rank in several systems, and did some kickboxing. I had always fared pretty well in fights. So, I didn't think this strange looking system would be much of a problem. I visited the school and had an opportunity to fight this 16-year-old Korean kid named Kwan, who had been training for less than a year. This kid beat me like a drum. I was accustomed to the "your turn, my turn" cadence of the average kickboxing fight. To my surprise, Wing Chun fighters didn't play well with others. They had not been taught the manners of taking turns. Every time I thought it was my turn, Kwan showed me it was "always his turn." I realized fast that Wing Chun was counter-offensive ... not defensive like my former training had conditioned me. It was extremely effective and sold me on Wing Chun from that day forward. I have not seen Kwan for many years, but if he reads this, I want him to know I owe him a debt of gratitude for the life changing lesson he gave me that evening.

Were you a "natural" at kung fu – did the movements come easily to you?

I have always been pretty good at learning physical movement. The most difficult thing in Wing Chun was the concept of relaxation during the act of defending against attack. I found Chi Sao training to be a great method of developing this attribute.

h ow has your personal kung fu developed over the years?

My personal Wing Chun is a synthesis of all I have learned from all of the instructors I have had over the years. I believe that Wing Chun is a living art. Not fixed, not stagnant, but continually developing. In the movie Ip Man – The Legend Is Born," my Sigung, Grandmaster Ip Chun, plays Ip Man's second teacher, Leung Bik. At one point in the movie, when Ip Man first meets him, there is a discussion in which Ip Man continually refers to what he has learned as "Authentic Wing Chun." Ip Chun's character responds by telling Ip Man that "the only person to have ever taught "authentic" Wing Chun was the founder." The inference is that everyone else has modified, improved, or personalized the system in some way. I believe there is a great lesson in this.

I consider myself a perpetual student. If I am not studying, learning, and researching how to be better, I am not happy.

What are the most important points in your teaching methods? And what are the most important qualities for a student to become proficient in the Wing Chun style?

Real world application. Training for realistic application under street conditions. I retired after a 25-plus-year career in public safety, where I worked as a police officer, firefighter, and emergency medic. I have been on the street. I know what a real fight is. The difference between sport and street application is as far away as east is from west.

My teaching methods focus on the practical application of Wing Chun in a violent street environment. Too many Martial Arts suffer from what I call "sport leakage" in their training. We have an old saying in law enforcement that "We don't rise to the occasion, we sink to our level of training." The meaning is that we react according to the way we train. If you are train for sport, you cannot expect to respond appropriately in a violent street encounter.

With all the technical changes during the last decades, do you think there are still "pure" styles of kung fu and more specifically Wing Chun?

If by "pure" you mean practiced and taught, unchanged, from the way it was practiced and taught centuries ago ... or even as Ip Man himself trained and taught as recently as the 1950s–1970s, my answer is, I certainly hope not.

Consider that in Hong Kong during Ip Man's teaching career, there were only a few dominant kung fu systems that his students were likely to have to face. Hung Gar and Choy Li Fut are two that come to mind.

Fast forward to 2012, in my home base of Yorktown, Virginia. To my knowledge, there is not a Hung Gar or Choi Li Fut academy within 200 miles of my school. So for me to teach with a focus on applying the tools of the Wing Chun system against those methods, as Ip Man needed to, would not make any practical sense.

"We are fortunate that Ip Man did film the first and second hand set and dummy set just before he passed away."

My students are much more likely to have to face an opponent schooled in wrestling, Tae Kwon Do, or Western boxing. So, while I still teach the "Wing Chun System," I'm sure I teach, by necessity, the application of those tools differently than Ip Man did.

Again, refer back to the movie "Ip Man – The Legend Is Born" and the statement by Ip Chun's character, Leung Bik: The only person who ever taught "a pure, authentic version of any system was the founder of that system; everyone else has changed it in some way, even if they didn't intend to make changes.

That being said, I believe that if one is teaching what they are calling "Ip Man Wing Chun," it should be in line with the structural foundation that Ip Man taught. For example, the Ip Man Wing Chun "system" is made up of the three hand forms, the wooden dummy set and the pole and knife sets. We are fortunate that Ip Man did film the first and second hand set and dummy set just before he passed away. So, we do know, without a

Wing Chun Masters

"It is wrong to attempt to get undue credibility by a false claim that it was taught by Ip Man."

doubt, his standard of those sets. Thus, if someone teaches the student to do a back kick in the middle of the Siu Lim Tao form, this would not be in line with the Ip Man standard. This has in fact been a problem according to Grandmaster Ip Chun. He states, "There are people who never completed their training under Ip Man, but established themselves as instructors of his method and have made up the missing parts of the system they never learned and teach their ad-libbed method as Ip Man Wing Chun. This should not be so."

The "system" is like the English alphabet. There are 26 letters, not 24 and not 30, but 26. While I may have a different "style" of writing than someone else, I will still be using the same 26 letters available to anyone else who writes in English. This is, in my opinion, the same principle as in Wing Chun.

If one is going to teach things they have developed, they need to be ethical enough to be honest about that fact and let it stand on its own merit. It is wrong to attempt to get undue credibility by a false claim that it was taught by Ip Man. If the method is practical, it will be respected, no matter the source, but be honest about what is being taught.

Do you think different "styles" are truly important in the art of kung fu?

I believe all systems have something to offer. Different people are drawn to different aspects of the arts. I do not think different styles are necessarily important other than for their appeal to the differing taste of the individual practitioner.

What is your opinion of Full Contact kung fu tournaments?

Anytime you turn a Martial Art into a martial sport, you diminish that art. I believe these and the current MMA craze give people a false idea of what will work in a real fight. I spent many years in public safety, as a police officer and street paramedic. I know what a real fight is, and have unfortunately been in my share. There are techniques that dominate in the ring, but will get you killed in the street. Ground and pound, for example, is a bad strategy when the ground is covered with broken glass and gravel, or has bottles and rocks that can be grabbed by the opponent and used as a weapon against you. Third parties often enter street fights. When you are on the ground, you can only deal with one opponent. So I feel that these events leave one ill prepared for a real world encounter.

how different from other kung fu styles do you see the principles and concepts of Wing Chun?

You're trying to get me in trouble with that question! First, let me say, I respect all Martial Arts from the perspective of the culture, and exercise of training. That said, I have a problem with methods that do not translate well from the training floor to the violent street encounter. There are a lot of things that work with a compliant training partner that won't come close to working against a violent street predator. I believe that, often, it is not the system itself as much as the way the system is trained that makes the difference. I have seen many instructors teach students unrealistic self-defense combinations that do not take anatomical reaction into consideration. For example, they will strike a target that would drive the opponent away from them, followed by a technique that requires reaching the opponents limb that would have just been driven out of reach if the technique had actually been delivered. These types of techniques leave the students ill prepared to apply their methods in a real encounter.

Do you think that kung fu in the West has "caught up" with the technical level in China-hong Kong?

I have had the opportunity to train in both Hong Kong and Foshan, China. I found that like America, some practitioners are good, and some not so good. A lot depends on the focus of the instructor. Some are very Chi Sao-oriented, others more into fighting applications, and still others into how good they look in forms. Some are Martial Artists while others are martial hobbyists.

I personally do not believe that race or ethnicity has anything to do with advancement in kung fu. I believe it all comes down to your teacher's ability to teach, and the student's desire to work, train and research what is taught.

It's funny, a Wing Chun instructor recently visited my school and after training with us, made a statement that he was very disappointed and felt that what he had learned from his instructor didn't measure up to what he had run into in our class, despite the fact that his instructor was supposedly a relative of the great Ip Man. I explained to the instructor that my medical training had taught me that there are many things that travel through a blood line, such as diabetes, high blood pressure, and heart disease. Unfortunately, knowledge and skill are not on the list. One must be in a classroom with an instructor who can, and will, impart the system, and then it takes hard work on the part of the student. Being related to a great master does not really count for much in and of itself.

Do you feel that there are any fundamental differences in approach or physical capabilities of Chinese kung fu practitioners in comparison to European or American practitioners?

Not that I have seen. I have trained in China and have trained with a lot of Europeans. I believe the only real differences I have seen are in attitude. The Chinese seem to be a little more into comparing Chi Sao, while I feel the Americans and Europeans tend to be a little more into application of technique in a fighting situation.

Kung fu nowadays often is referred to as a sport (Wu shu); would you agree with this definition?

Unfortunately, the Martial Arts in general seem to be dominated by a sporting mind-set. I believe this is bad for the Martial Arts. We are losing so much of the real art by focusing on sport. We train to develop conditioned reflex. If our training develops this reflex for sport, we will not be able to react differently under non-sporting conditions. As I pointed out before, "We do not rise to the occasion, we sink to our level of training." You cannot train for sport and have the "combat fairy" tap you on the head with his magic wand and make you react properly for the "real world."

Do you feel that you still have further to go in your studies of the art of Wing Chun?

I am always looking to learn. I am the perpetual student. I was certified at a Master level in the Ip Family method under the lineage of Ip Man, Ip Chun / Ip Ching through their senior student, Samuel Kwok. I have begun to research different branches of Wing Chun in order to understand why different instructors teach things that differ from the Ip Family method. My Sifu, Samuel Kwok, is a great researcher of Wing Chun and has influenced and inspired me to be and do the same. As a matter of fact, when I became Samuel Kwok's personal disciple, I was given the family name Kwok Ching Yin by my Sifu. Kwok is his family name, and Ching Yin translates to "studious researcher."

"Being related to a great master does not really count for much in and of itself."

ho w do you see Wing Chun kung fu in the world at the present time?

I believe that people are getting a little more open with sharing and working together. The politics is still pretty bad, but I believe it is getting better. There are still instructors who seem to just be in it for their ego, but I believe as a whole, the Wing Chun world is becoming a more pleasant place.

Does the weaponry aspect of Wing Chun enhance the student's empty hands ability or are those two completely non-related skills?

The knives add a lot to the student's empty hand skills. There are footwork and angles that do not exist elsewhere in the system. So I would say that the knives are a very important aspect of Wing Chun training. Since there are two knives in use, the knives relate well to the empty hand system. The pole also adds to the student's Wing Chun, but I believe to a much lesser degree. The pole is so different in structure from what we normally think of in empty hand Wing Chun that many people do not see the relationship. I see it as being very similar if you were to think of how you would fight from a Wing Chun perspective if you were hurt and could

Wing Chun Masters

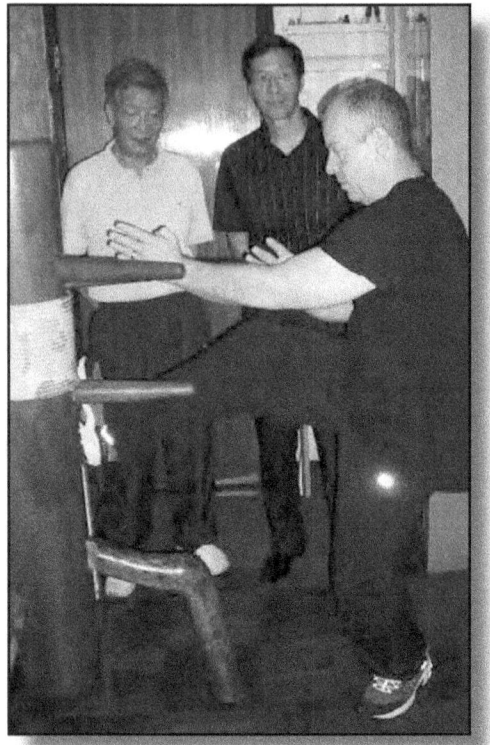

"I believe that people are getting a little more open with sharing and working together."

only use one arm to defend and attack. This will take some thought on the part of the student, but I believe if one looks at the pole form from that angle, he/she will see a relationship to empty hand application.

how does the Wing Chun style differ from other kung fu methods when applying the techniques in a self-defense situation?

First of all, Wing Chun tends to be a more upright fighting method with less low stances than other kung fu methods I have trained in. There are very few movements that could be called pretty or flowery. I often tell my students that Wing Chun is an ugly system in comparison to many other methods. But, in my opinion, you shouldn't try to be pretty during the fight ... it's more important to be pretty after the fight.

Wing Chun emphasizes simplicity of use, economy of motion, and practicality. These three should guide a student's training. If what you are practicing does not meet these three criteria, the method needs to be reevaluated.

When teaching the art of kung fu, what is the most important element: self-defense, health, or tradition?

In my opinion, it's self-protection. Tradition is good to know, but I think it falls short of being "most important." Health, of course, is important, but there are many things one can engage in if their focus is health. But self-protection: now that's what sets kung fu in general and Wing Chun specifically apart from other activities. I believe all three play important roles in the education of a Martial Artist, but in my opinion it's self-protection that is hands down the most important. This is what I focus on in both my regular classes and in the many seminars I conduct around the U.S.

Forms and Chi sao: what's the proper ratio in training?

Forms are important to teach and reinforce proper structure, alignment, angle, and Yiu Ma (waist energy) development. A student does not always have a training partner available, so forms and the wooden dummy become important components in training. Chi Sao, on the other hand, is very important in developing sensitivity, reaction, conditioned reflex, and relaxation in the midst of chaos. I do believe some people train Chi Sao improperly and allow it to become a competition. This is a mistake and robs the student of the true benefit of Chi Sao training. The other problem is that often Wing Chun people mistake Chi Sao skill for fighting skill. Chi Sao does develop attributes that can be added to your fighting ability that will make you more effective, but being good at a game of "Slap Sao" does not mean you will be a good fighter. Being a fighter is as much about attitude, courage, tenacity, and motivation as it is about skill. There are many times just plain "mean" will beat "skillful." And the motivation of protecting one's loved ones can turn a mild mannered person into a dangerous fighter. So, all of these must be taken into account when looking at what makes one an effective Martial Artist.

Do you have any general advice you would care to pass on the practitioners in general?
Concentrate on proper structure in technique. Practice dynamic footwork. Make sure that your footwork is supporting your hands. The Chinese speak of the trinity of motion, Body + Step + Hand. These three must be coordinated in order for your kung fu to have power. Also remember the saying "Slow is smooth and smooth is fast." Too many students sacrifice structure for speed and power. This is a mistake. Don't get into politics, just train hard and be the best you can be. Judge your kung fu by how practical it is, not on how pretty it looks.

Some people think going to China or Taiwan to train is necessary; do you share this point of view?
I think it is a great trip. It is very good to visit from a historical perspective. But I do not think it is necessary in order to learn good Wing Chun. I enjoy every time I go, and will continue to visit there as often as practical, but I do not think the average student needs to make the trip in order to be a good Martial Artist ... but I do encourage it.

What do you consider to be the major changes in the art since you began training?
As an instructor, I find I am working against YouTube and instructional videos. When I began in Wing Chun in 1979, we were totally reliant on our Sifu. Today, if the Sifu is not teaching the student at a pace that satisfies the student, then the student simply learns the next form or whatever from Sifu YouTube. This can be frustrating because as an instructor I try to

guide the students from skill to skill in a logical manner and at a pace that they can follow. When they try to move ahead on their own, they often develop bad habits and erroneous ideas that are hard to overcome in the classroom.

Who would you like to have trained with that you have not?
First of all, I have to say that I have been truly blessed. My Sifu, Samuel Kwok, is a really good Wing Chun instructor. And through my Sifu, I have had the opportunity to train with both of Ip Man's sons. So I have trained with several of the greatest living Wing Chun masters. But to answer your question, naturally the first on the list would be Grandmaster Ip Man himself. And just for kicks, next would be Bruce Lee. It would be nice to see just how good his Wing Chun was. He appeared to be very skillful. I have tremendous respect for David Peterson, and hope to one day get the opportunity of meeting and training with him. The same is true of his Kung Fu brother Gary Lam. And, although he is not a Wing Chun instructor, I hope to meet and train with Donnie Yen, who played Ip Man in the great movies on the Grandmaster's life.

What would you say to someone who is interested in starting to learn Wing Chun kung fu?
I have been involved in the Martial Arts for 46-plus years and Wing Chun is the best system I have found for my needs. I encourage students to search around. Look at several systems and judge them by one's own needs. I would say that if the student is interested in sport, Wing Chun is the wrong method. But if one's interest is in the area of practical self-protection, I believe he or she would be hard pressed to find a better system.

What is it that keeps you motivated after all these years?
I love to learn and train. I also see the state of the world and believe that martial skills will become more and more important as time marches forward. If you look at situations like Hurricane Katrina and the conditions faced by the residents in Louisiana, I think you can see the need for martial knowledge. There was no police protection for days, and there were desperate people who resorted to violence to meet their needs. With natural disasters and the possibility of terrorism, I believe the need to be prepared is more important today than at any time in our history.

Do you think it is necessary to engage in free-fighting to achieve good self-defense skills in the street?

Yes and no. It is important in order to develop timing and balance in motion, but it can also develop bad habits that you don't want to invade your ability to protect yourself in the street. It's like comparing sport and "real-world" application. Sport and real self-protection do not coexist. They are like "security" and "free access." The more you have of one, the less you have of the other. If a building is "totally secure," there is NO free access. If there is "free access," there is NO real security. Sport and self-protection work in much the same way.

We react the way we are trained. That is the reason for training, to develop reaction. It's called "conditioned reflex." That is the goal of Martial Art training. If you are training in a method that can be used in a legal sporting event, like a karate or Tae Kwon Do tournament or even the highly popular MMA events, then you are not learning the things you want to have "conditioned reflex" in the event that you are the target of a violent attack in the street.

"Tradition is good to know, but I think it falls short of being most important."

The problem with sport-oriented programs is that they teach the student to react in a manner other than the way they will need to react in order to protect themselves in a violent street encounter. In law enforcement training, we found that we had to change the way we were training in order to make the training more reality based. There were two specific situations that helped to change the law enforcement training paradigm.

One was in Canada, where a uniformed officer who was also a defensive tactics instructor had a gun pulled on him in the street. He performed a flawless gun disarm, and then automatically returned the gun to the bad guy, out of "conditioned reflex." The reason for this was that in training, the disarms were performed in such a way that immediately after the dis-

Wing Chun Masters

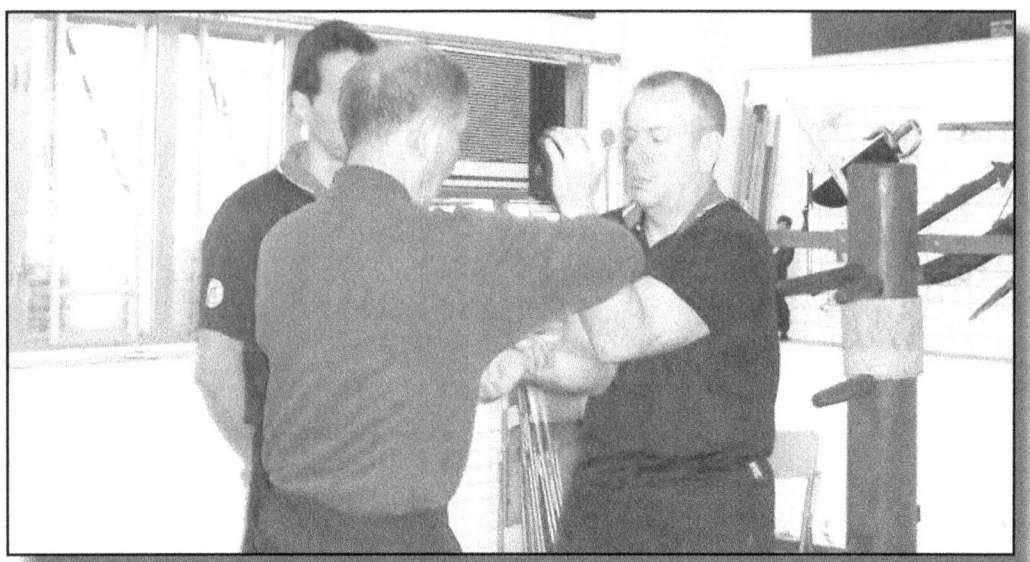

"We react the way we are trained. That is the reason for training, to develop reaction. It's called *conditioned reflex*."

arm, the officer would return the gun to the training partner so they could perform the next disarm. This built the return of the gun into the "conditioned reflex" of the officer, and under stress, the body performs what it has been trained to do.

In the second situation, there was a shoot-out between police and a group of bank robbers. During the shoot-out, several police officers were killed. In the post-incident investigation, one of the police officers was found with four empty shell casings in his hand. On the shooting range, the officers were required to pick up their own brass (empty shell casings). During the shoot-out, under stress, with his life on the line, the officer reverted to his trained "conditioned reflex" and was picking up his empty shell casings. This was what his body had been trained to do, so it (his body) did it.

These two "real-world" examples demonstrate the need of realistic training methods. Sport Martial Arts, like Modern Tae Kwon Do and many systems of karate, do not adequately develop "conditioned reflex" that can be counted on in a violent street encounter. The reason is that sport Martial Arts are based on rules that limit the target areas you can attack, and limit the natural body weapons you can use to attack those targets. Rules in sports are designed with two purposes in mind. One is to protect the competitors, so if your opponent misses his block and you hit him, you won't do too much damage. He won't be maimed or killed. The other purpose is to make the fight last longer in order to make it a spectator sport. Protecting the other guy from injury and making the fight last longer are not the things you want to happen in a fight on the street where your life is on the line.

What is your opinion about mixing kung fu styles? Does the practice of one nullify the effectiveness of the other or can it be beneficial to the student?

I do not see the necessity of doing this. You see a lot of people wanting to "Mix the BEST of each system" into one fighting method. But how do you know what the BEST of a system is until you have studied the system in depth. The student is not going to get the best of any system in a short period of time. The problem I see with the mixing of systems is that the student ends up being "a mile wide but only an inch deep" in his or her knowledge. I don't think being at a beginner level in a lot of systems makes you more proficient than having a depth of knowledge in a single system.

What is/was your philosophical basis for your kung fu training?

I personally don't look at the Martial Arts from a philosophical direction. I am Christian, so the Eastern religious background and philosophy hold no interest for me. I train the Martial Arts strictly from a practical application point of view. The moral or philosophical foundation for the way I live my life lies in my relationship with Jesus Christ.

Do you have a particularly memorable kung fu experience that has remained as an inspiration for your training?

My main inspiration is that I was in the Martial Arts since the age of five and thought I knew how to fight. Then I was schooled in the harsh realities of the street when I became a police officer. I learned very quickly that all of the "sport-based" tournament Martial Arts do not stand up to the realities of the street. From that point until today, I have been standing on my soapbox and preaching the importance of "reality-based" training in the Martial Arts.

After all these years of training and experience, could you explain the meaning of the practice of kung fu?

I believe Ronald Reagan summed it up best, "Peace through superior fire-power." In order to really live in peace, one must have the power to wage war effectively. This is as true in our personal security as it is in the world of national security.

I teach my students that the first two principles of self-defense are "Exit!" The first exit is yours: if you can avoid the fight, do so, even if that means running away. Avoidance is always the best option. If you do not have an exit, you need to give the opponent an exit. If he is talking trash to you, and you talk trash back, you have taken away his exit. He is already pushing for a fight. If you talk trash back to him, especially in front of his friends, he will have but two options. Fight you or lose face in front of his friends. You need to verbally de-escalate the situation in order to avoid the fight in this situation. If you do not, but choose to stand your ground, you will have taken his exit away.

No one ever wins a fight in the street. There is always a price to pay if you have to injure another human being. Even if you are totally in the right, you will likely have to hire an attorney to defend your actions in criminal and/or civil court. And if you ever have to really injure someone, it is not a good feeling to live with.

But, if you do not have an exit, and the bad guy refuses to take the exit you offer him, then you "must" have the ability to "win" the violent encounter.

how is the Chi sao aspect of training related to the practical application of the Wing Chun techniques used in the three empty hands forms?

Chi Sao is the bridge between the forms and application in fighting. Chi Sao teaches very important elements such as sensitivity, relaxation under stress, and proper structure in technique. It teaches how not to use force against force and how to gain control of the fight. Chi Sao is the one element of Wing Chun that I believe puts it head and shoulders above any other method I have ever been exposed to. When we come into contact with the opponent, our ocular senses are of very little use. The eye is too slow to recognize an action and pick a proper response fast enough to keep us from getting hurt at such a close distance. It works in much the same way as maintaining a safe following distance when driving. You need "reaction time." The sense of touch, and the development that takes place in Chi Sao of being able to translate the input we receive by way of our sensory nerves and develop an instant, conditioned response, is unparalleled in any other method.

is there anything lacking in the way Martial Arts are taught today compared to how they were in your beginnings?

Respect! Today's Martial Artists have lost the element of respect. There is too much emphasis on sport. The Martial Arts were originally about eliminating the ego. Today, however, they seem to be about the building of a massive "I'm the baddest man on the planet" ego. The MMA has brought the WWE mindset into the Martial Arts and I believe that is a tragic loss for the Martial Arts.

What you consider to be the most important qualities of a successful kung fu practitioner?

I believe it is important to be compassionate and respectful. Real kung fu is real power. It is the power to injure another human being. With power comes responsibility. Without compassion, one with these skills can do more harm than good. So when I am looking at a student, I look for that quality above all in determining just how far I am willing to go in his or her training. After that comes honesty and integrity. It is sad but I have personally seen so many people in Wing Chun attempt to play "lineage leapfrog." This is where the students decide that they are no longer happy with their Sifu, so they approach their Sigung and attempt to "leap-frog" over their Sifu and become a direct student of their Sigung. While that is shameful, what I believe is even worse is I have seen the Sigung accept the student, thus showing no loyalty to the original student. This kind of action shows a lack of integrity on the part of both the student and the Sigung.

So these are the qualities I consider important: loyalty, compassion, responsibility, honesty, and integrity.

What advice would you give to students on the question of supplementary training?

Anything that improves health and fitness is good. I just warn the students to consider their ultimate goal. Is it looking like Mr. or Mrs. America or being to apply their skills with flow, speed, power and accuracy. If their goal is the second, then I warn them against "heavy" weight training.

What do you see as the most important attributes of a student?

I believe the top attributes are dedication and intelligence. You can overcome a lot of learning problems with these two attributes. It is important to understand the desired outcome of a technique application. The learning process requires a lot of assessment and reassessment as skill improves. It is good to be a free thinker. Wing Chun is not meant to be a system that produces robots. There is a lot of freedom in the application of Wing Chun, but you have to have the analytical intelligence to see what may not be immediately obvious, or see the obvious (simple) we sometime overlook while looking for the complicated answer. This is what I call the simplicity at the far side of complexity.

Wing Chun Masters

"I train the Martial Arts strictly from a practical application point of view."

Why is it, in your opinion, that a lot of students start falling away after two-three years of training?

I believe they become comfortable with the skills they have developed and decide that further effort is not necessary. Also I believe that just tends to be the attention span of the average adult. They have become pretty good by the two-to-three-year mark and feel they are "good enough!" Remember the old saying, "Good is the enemy of Great."

have there been times when you felt fear in your kung fu training?

Well, I must say, the first time I crossed hands with my Sifu, Samuel Kwok, was pretty scary. Not that he hurt me, but he so totally controlled me and let me know just how easily he could have finished me if he chose to. This was scary and at the same time very exciting, because I had found an instructor who had a great deal of knowledge and skill that I did not have at the time. I was very fortunate that Master Kwok accepted me as his personal disciple and taught me so much in the many years that have now passed.

One other thing I have found scary is just how ill prepared most Martial Artist are for a "real-world" street encounter. Sport leakage into their ability to protect themselves in a Non-Sport environment has left them very vulnerable. I am trying to help in this area with my Reality-Based column, "Efficient Warrior" in Martial Arts Masters magazine, and with my seminars.

What are your thoughts on the future of the art?

I believe the future is uncertain. I see some great teachers out there, who are bringing detailed Wing Chun to the masses. But unfortunately I see some instructors – even some with big names and reputations – accepting students and traditional disciples without the development of a relationship, and issuing instructor certification to people with no depth of knowledge or skill, all in order to expand their associations. This hurts the future of Wing Chun. So which side will prevail? I think that's anyone's guess. I know I am rooting for the good guys.

"I just plan to train and teach the best Wing Chun I am capable of. I plan to continue my training and research in the art"

Could you tell us a little about your hopes for your future?

I just plan to train and teach the best Wing Chun I am capable of. I plan to continue my training and research in the art. I plan to continue running my class in the Yorktown, Virginia area, as well as doing seminars and instructor training. I am working on a couple of new books and video projects as well.

As director of the Ip Man Wing Chun Union I have developed an in-depth instructor training program and have developed a Training Group Leader program that will help prospective instructors develop training groups with the backing of the association. This will allow them to reinforce what they have learned by teaching others, and at the same time earn funds from their training to further their journey to full instructor status in the direct Ip Man Family lineage.

DAVID PETERSON

The Finger Pointing to the Moon

DAVID PETERSON BEGAN TRAINING IN THE MARTIAL ARTS BACK IN 1973. HE IS A DIRECT STUDENT OF THE LATE GREAT WING CHUN MASTER WONG SHUN LEUNG, A GRADUATE OF THE UNIVERSITY OF MELBOURNE, AUSTRALIA, WHERE HE MAJORED IN CHINESE STUDIES, AND A TEACHER OF THE CHINESE LANGUAGE FOR OVER TWENTY YEARS. HIS ACCOMPLISHMENTS AS A TEACHER AND WRITER ARE EQUALLY WELL-KNOWN. AS THE FOUNDER AND HEAD INSTRUCTOR OF THE MELBOURNE CHINESE MARTIAL ARTS CLUB, SIFU PETERSON CONTINUES TO SPREAD THE PHILOSOPHIES AND TEACHINGS OF WONG SHUN LEUNG AS A LASTING TRIBUTE TO HIS MENTOR.

HE ALSO HAS WRITTEN NUMEROUS ARTICLES ON WING CHUN KUNG FU AND WONG SHUN LEUNG'S METHODS AND AUTHORED THE BOOK "LOOK BEYOND THE POINTING FINGER: THE COMBAT PHILOSOPHY OF WONG SHUN LEUNG."

SIFU PETERSON IS ONE OF ONLY TWO QUALIFIED INSTRUCTORS OF WONG'S SYSTEM IN AUSTRALIA, AUTHORIZED BY SIFU WONG PERSONALLY BEFORE HIS DEATH, AND A FULLY ENDORSED MEMBER OF THE WORLDWIDE "WONG SHUN LEUNG VING TSUN MARTIAL ARTS ASSOCIATION" AND THE HONG KONG-BASED "VING TSUN ATHLETIC ASSOCIATION."

h ow long have you been practicing the Martial Arts and who was your teacher?

I began studying the Martial Arts in 1973, learning Shaolin Ch'uanfa under Sifu Serge Martich-Ostermann. By the end of 1974, he had stopped coming regularly to Melbourne to conduct the classes (he was from Sydney), and the numbers had fallen drastically, as had the enthusiasm of those remaining at the school, myself included. At that time, I became acquainted with a guy claiming to be a student of Wing Chun great Sifu Wong Shun Leung (as it turned out, this was to be a complete fabrication), and I eventually took up classes with him. That relationship lasted just on 10 years, with me running most of his schools/classes around Melbourne and generally being his "do-it-all" guy: I printed the T-shirts, answered the phone calls, stuck up the posters – you name it, I did it – all for virtually nothing apart from continuous excuses why he could not teach me more of the system. Truth be told, he hadn't even learned it himself, so there was no way I was ever going to get very far at that school. After speaking to members of the local Chinese community, as well as doing quite a lot of research of my own, especially in Hong Kong Martial Arts magazines

Wing Chun Masters

" I want to understand how all the other "engines" work, but I only drive the one car – WSLVT"

and the like, I soon realized that if I was going to really accomplish anything in Wing Chun, I would have to seek out Sifu Wong Shun Leung myself. So, toward the end of 1983, that's exactly what I did. The rest is, as they say in the classics ... history.

how many styles (Kung Fu or other methods) have you trained in?

Over the years, I have done quite a bit of training in Taijiquan (Chen & Yang systems) and also in the Hung Kuen system, as well as "dabbling" in Choi Lei Fat, some BJJ and Kali, amongst other things. I am intrigued by all forms of the Martial Arts, but my true passion is of course the 'Wong Shun Leung Method' of Wing Chun (Ving Tsun) which I have now been involved in and dedicated to for some 30 years, since that very first trip to Hong Kong. While I thoroughly enjoy cross-training and the experience of being a new learner again and again, not to mention the extended knowledge that it brings to my experience, for me it is WSLVT that answers all my questions and is what works best for me. I want to understand how all the other "engines" work, but I only drive the one car – WSLVT.

What are the main principles intrinsic to the three Wing Chun forms? Do they interrelate with each other?

The "Siu Nim Tau" and "Cham Kiu" forms encompass all the most essential skills and concepts of the Wing Chun system. They are the basis of everything that we do in combat. "Siu Nim Tau" provides the 'alphabet' of the system, while "Cham Kiu" teaches us the "grammar" and links it all together. "Siu Nim Tau" gives us the structures that form the foundation of all actions and concepts that we utilize; "Cham Kiu" combines these foundation skills into 'short words and phrases' that assist us in understanding how the system works and how to enhance what we know. Through the many drills inherent in the system, such as "Paak Sau," "Laap Sau" and of course "Chi Sau" (in its many variants), we then develop the means to "communicate" with our opponent in a language of combat that is simple, direct and efficient. The "Muk Yan Jong" (wooden dummy) form then provides us with ways of recovering from the kinds of typical errors that can occur in combat, as well as enhancing our ability to utilize the best distancing, timing and angles, while the "Biu Ji" form shows us ways of escaping relatively unharmed should all of the essential elements fail due to outstanding circumstances, such as being caught completely by surprise, overwhelmed by force and/or numbers, injured, or otherwise unable to apply the more basic skills. The entire system is cleverly linked and there are no loose ends.

Would you tell us some interesting stories of your early days in Kung Fu and the training under the legendary Wong shun Leung?

I have so many wonderful memories of training in with my Sifu over the years, but there are two that spring to mind immediately. The first took place in the early 80s, on the occasion of Sifu's first-ever trip to Australia to teach at my school in Melbourne. He had arrived after a long flight from Hong Kong and was feeling quite tired. As we had arranged for him to attend the class that very night, I suggested that he lie down and try to get some sleep for a while before leaving for the lesson. As the time approached to head off, I innocently entered the room where he was sleeping and tapped him on the shoulder to wake him. In that moment, I quite literally saw my life flash before my eyes and experienced the biggest adrenalin dump of my life! Sifu had awakened, in unfamiliar surroundings and feeling the effects of jet lag, so his reactions had gone into autopilot – his eyes opened with a ferocity I had never seen before and locked onto me, his body primed like a cat ready to pounce. I was stunned and froze on the spot for what seemed like an eternity, before gathering myself long enough to say, "Sifu, it's me, ...David!," – by which time he had obviously managed to gather his thoughts and realize where he was. He just grinned as I quickly backed out of the room, later telling me that when he had been in his younger years and testing his skills regularly in "beimo" (challenge matches), his mother had resorted to waking him by throwing rolled-up socks from the doorway, following a similar reaction where he almost struck her. I never tried to wake him with a tap on the shoulder again after that.

The second story took place in Hong Kong around Chinese New Year in the late 80s. We had all enjoyed a great, hard training session and a group of us had decided to take Sifu out to dinner in a nearby restaurant district. When we finally arrived at our destination and had sat down at a large round table, the conversation, food, and wine flowed freely, with everyone really having a fun time talking about Martial Arts and the "good old days" when Sifu studied under Ip Man. Someone turned the topic of conversation to the so-called "tricks" of certain teachers, including the breaking of chopsticks on the throat. On hearing the comment, Sifu immediately picked up a pair of chopsticks and started breaking them on his throat, explaining to us how it was easily done - no special talent required. With that, he invited us all to try and soon the restaurant owner was beside himself, frantically begging us to stop breaking chopsticks. This was, of course, my Sifu's way of constantly trying to expose the charlatans and remove the B.S. in the Martial Arts.

Do you teach Westerners? h ow do you find that Westerners respond to traditional Chinese training?

My classes have always involved both Western and Asian students, as did those of my Sifu. My attitude is quite naturally the same as his – so long as a student is prepared to train hard and brings honor to the system, we should train anyone who wishes to learn, no matter color, creed or race. As far as the training goes, I always incorporate a combination of traditional and modern teaching methods, so that the students are comfortable with both methods. Each way has merit and each way gets good results. Most Westerners expect to line up and be given guided training with clear instruction and encouragement. The traditional Chinese way is to show them a simple skill and expect them to go off and practice, motivating themselves, or working one-on-one with more senior classmates with only limited interaction with the teacher. I believe a healthy blend of the two provides the best method, so I incorporate both guided drills, as well as what we like to call "Hong Kong-style" training. As time goes by and skill levels increase, one tends to find the students enjoying the "Hong Kong-style" training more and more. Now that I am based in Malaysia, the proportion of Asian students is naturally higher, but I continue to get great results from utilizing the combination of formal (guided) and informal training.

Were you a "natural" at Kung Fu – did the movements come easily to you?

I have no special talents and had to work as hard as anybody to develop my skills. In fact, even after all these years, I am still working on them – the journey doesn't end until we die! What I did have that has held me in good stead over the years, is an extreme passion to learn and a keen eye, such that I could quickly grasp the essence of how something was done and then go away and work on it until it worked well for me. Another huge personal benefit was the fact that I was able to communicate with my Sifu in his mother tongue, with little or no need for any translation, thus I didn't miss out on the little details that someone without the language might fail to appreciate.

ho w has your personal Kung Fu has developed over the years?

I wouldn't say that my personal Kung Ku has changed over the years, but it has certainly developed in the sense that I am now finding more efficient ways to use the system. You could say that as I've gotten older, I have gotten a little wiser too. This is largely due to the fact that the body is not getting any younger, and that injuries have taken a toll that I've had to learn to compensate for, to "train smart" in order to overcome. As such, in many ways I think that I have reached an even better understanding of the system now than I ever had before, and that in many ways, I am a far better exponent of the system now than ever before. Teaching has certainly played a huge role in that regard because when you stand out the front and have to instruct, to answer the questions and provide individual solutions and coaching, your own level of understanding and expertise increases tremendously.

"The most important thing in both teaching and learning Wing Chun, in order for the student to become proficient, is the correct development of the foundations of the system."

What are the most important points in your teaching methods? And what are the most important qualities for a student to become proficient in the Wing Chun style?

The most important thing in both teaching and learning Wing Chun, in order for the student to become proficient, is the correct development of the foundations of the system. These are correct structure, correct footwork, the use of the elbow and waist, relaxation and using the Centerline. Unless these foundation skills and concepts are understood and trained consistently, progress in Wing Chun is slow and the chances of reaching a high level of proficiency, unlikely. As a matter of fact, I consistently tell my students that the most "advanced" skills that they will ever learn are all

Wing Chun Masters

"Technical changes do not make a system "un-pure," they merely help to make a system more effective."

covered in the very first lesson: the basic stance ("Yi Ji Kim Yeung Ma"), the basic punch ("Yat Ji Kuen"), forward stepping ("Saam Gok Bo"), defensive stepping ("Tui Ma") and the first section of the "Siu Nim Tau" form. These five things incorporate every single skill or concept that will ever be used or required in combat, no matter how simple or complex the situation, and are the keys to everything else that one will ever learn in Wing Chun.

With all the technical changes during the last 30 years, do you think there are still "pure" styles of Kung Fu and more specifically Wing Chun?

Yes, I do think that there are still "pure" styles of Kung Fu, including Wing Chun, so long as the core concepts of these systems has remained unchanged. Technical changes do not make a system "un-pure," they merely help to make a system more effective, both to train and to apply. Developments in sports science, particularly in strength & conditioning, healthier diet and safer ways to exercise, has provided us with the means to enhance what we do, but has not forced anyone to abandon the "purity" of the arts. Some individuals have done so, but I personally feel that it is like throwing the baby out with the bath water if one does abandon the ways of the past. Modifying them, on the other hand, is not at all a bad thing, so long as the modifications are done to enhance the system, rather than just dress it up. My own teacher often had debates with his Sifu, the late Wing Chun patriarch Ip Man, and made changes to the system in order to make it more combat efficient. He did so without abandoning any of the core concepts and in many ways, proved that the core concepts are still valid in the modern era.

Do you think different "styles" are truly important in the art of Kung Fu?

First of all, I see Wing Chun as a system, rather than a style, because it is a complete, scientifically developed method of combat that utilizes a complete program of skills and concepts that are adaptable and interlocking – styles do not have the cohesion that a system has, generally because they are simply one individual's view or interpretation of combat, rather than a systematic method of developing flexible attributes. As such, styles often only suit certain individuals who have certain athletic talents, but do not provide the "common man" with methods that can easily be applied. Systems, on the other hand, have a basic set of structures and concepts that link together and can be adapted by anyone – Wing Chun is one such system. Styles exist in the Martial Arts because people have an innate desire to express their individuality. We see this in art, we see this in cooking, we see this in fashion, so it shouldn't be a surprise that we see this in the Martial Arts as well. Everyone needs to find their own niche and for some it is Wing Chun, and for others it is something else again. Remember that these days, the majority of people do not study Martial Arts because their survival depends upon it, so this is why many people choose to study forms of the Martial Arts (perhaps better termed Martial Sports?) that appeal to their need to engage in physical exercise, but not really

"Styles exist in the Martial Arts because people have an innate desire to express their individuality."

have to engage in real combat training. Hence, many such styles have developed to cater for this shift in thinking. Wing Chun, at least as far as "WSLVT" is concerned, has only one goal – to develop truly effective personal combat skills – it is not a sporting, fitness, demonstration or meditative system.

What is your opinion of Full Contact Kung Fu tournaments?

From what I see in such tournaments (and in the past I have myself competed in them, as have a number of my students), most of the fighters involved totally abandon what they have trained and the matches become a slugfest that does not see systems expressed well. A lot of this has to do with the wearing of equipment and the need for rules to protect the fighters, but there are also a large number of people who do not know their chosen system well enough before they step into the ring. That's not to say that I expect to see "pure" skills being demonstrated – it's a fight, not a movie and I accept that – but you would hope to see at least an expression of the concepts of each system being displayed, rather than a brawl no better than two drunks on a Friday night can accomplish. Having said all that, I think that tournaments are an important test for any practitioner who wants to know how he or she will perform under real pressure, and it's a far safer option that the "good old days" in Hong Kong when they took their skills out into the streets and on rooftops to test their validity.

h ow different from other Kung Fu styles do you see the principles and concepts of Wing Chun?

The goal of any legitimate combat system is the incapacitation of the opponent, so overall it is fair to say that all good systems have that in common, even if the specific methods differ. However, on a specific concept level, Wing Chun is radically different in its approach compared to other fighting systems and I can summarize the differences in the following ways: in Wing Chun, we do not block the attack, we deflect it and simultaneously attack in one motion; we do not chase the limbs, but always attack the centre of mass, making sure that in every exchange, at least one of our limbs is attacking; we utilize a springy, flexible form of energy that enables us to read the opponent's energy once contact is made, thus allowing for rapid changes in attack and defense that is reflex driven, thus instantaneous and not requiring conscious thought; we "steal" the opponent's energy and return in through the effective use of a stance that channels strength up from the ground, rather than relying upon the upper body alone; and we always face the adversary front-on so as to reduce the available targets that we provide to them, while enabling us to use two, sometimes even three limbs, constantly for both attack and defense. Most importantly of all, in Wing Chun, we always attempt to attack an attack with aggressive, scientifically-based methods of counter-fighting – we do not fight defensively at any stage if it can be avoided. I often compare Wing Chun to a gunfight – when the enemy fires at you, you immediately present the smallest target possible and return fire – you don't try to block the bullets!

Do you think that Kung Fu in the West has 'caught up' with the technical level in China?

I cannot speak on behalf of all Kung Fu systems or styles, but I can say with a great deal of confidence that Wing Chun in the West has very much "caught up" with the technical level in China/Hong Kong in recent years.

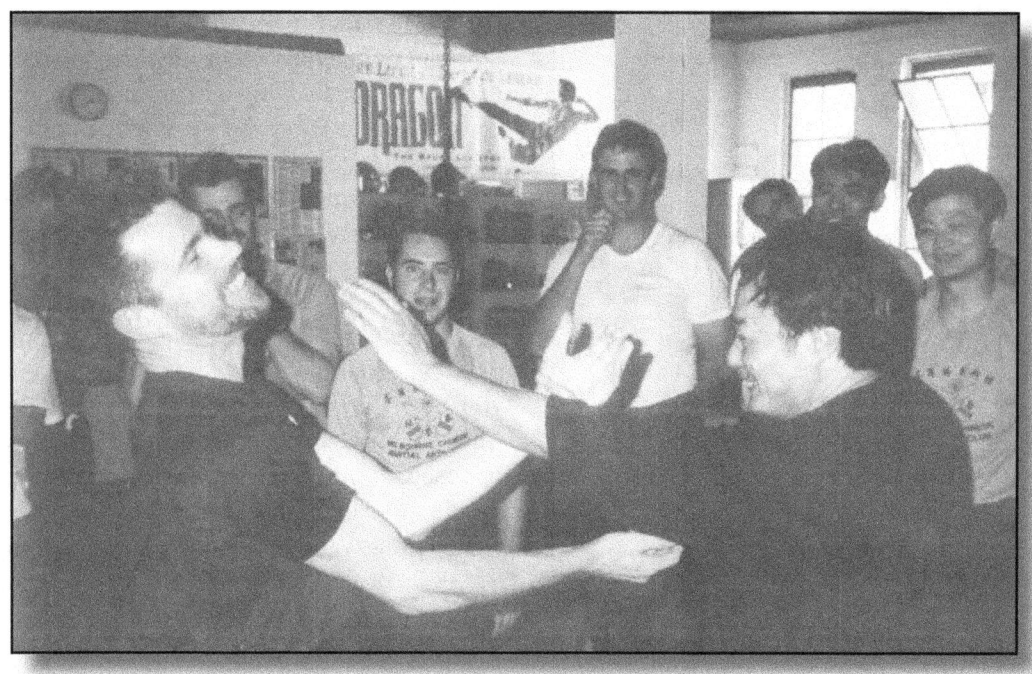

"My own teacher was barely five-foot seven-inches tall, and I witnessed him throwing six-foot nine-inch giants around like rag dolls!"

This is because in the West, the street-orientated aspects of Wing Chun have been very thoroughly explored and developed, whereas in Hong Kong, a lot of practitioners have gone into a "Sticky-hands Bubble" whereby they think that the practice of "Chi Sau" alone will be enough to enable them to deal with a violent street attack – sadly, they are very much mistaken on that score. While they are extremely skilled in the practice of "Chi Sau" and can still show many Westerners a thing or two in that area, they are not well equipped to deal with anything outside of that arena of expertise. The Wing Chun episode of the TV program "Fight Quest" that was shot in Hong Kong showed that weakness very clearly – even with just five days of training, the two non-Wing Chun fighters from the States gave the local Hong Kong Wing Chun guys a real lesson in what it's like to get into a real fight. The trouble is that if you only ever train against a fellow Wing Chun exponent, and not "pressure-test" your Wing Chun, your "Chi Sau" skills alone are just not enough.

Wing Chun Masters

"The word "Master" is one that is too easily bandied about in the modern era."

Do you feel that there are any fundamental differences in approach or physical capabilities of Chinese Kung Fu practitioner in comparison to European or American practitioners?

Overall, apart from the obvious difference in physical size between Western and Asian practitioners (and this is gradually changing due to diet and hygiene anyway), there is really little, if any, difference in the physical capabilities of either group. When you take into account the fact that Wing Chun, by and large, is concept-driven, as opposed to any definite physical attribute, the differences in physical ability are more or less nonexistent. It really comes down to the skills of the individual and I have seen first-hand great exponents on both sides of the divide, both large and small, Asian and Western. My own teacher was barely five-foot seven-inches tall, and I witnessed him throwing six-foot nine-inch giants around like rag dolls! As for differences in approach, well my previous answer pretty much sums that up, except in addition I would say that the learning in the West is far more guided, even regimented in some schools, than it is in the East, where the "Hong Kong-style" of instruction tends to prevail. As I said earlier, both methods work and perhaps a blending of the two works the best. It certainly always has done, ...and still does, ...for me.

Kung Fu is nowadays often referred to as a sport (Wushu). Would you agree with this definition?

The term "Wushu" in Mandarin Chinese does not mean "sport" – a direct translation is "martial skills" – however it is true to say that much of what is labeled "Wushu" these days (as a generic term for the organized practice of traditional Martial Arts in China) is indeed more sporting or demonstrative in nature, as opposed to being a true combat system. Having said that, it is also true that much of the Kung Fu (yet another generic term, more Cantonese in origin as a slang term for skill in ANY art and better represented in English as "Gongfu") practiced both in China and the West is very much not sporting in nature and retains its combat nature. People simply like to place things in baskets for ease of discussion, so "Kung Fu" and "Wushu" have become a victim of this trend to the extent that many people now believe that all Chinese Martial Arts are for sport and exercise, having no real combat merit – nothing could be further from the truth!

Do you feel that you still have further to go in your studies of the art of Wing Chun?

Yes! I have until the end of my life to go in my study of Wing Chun. I haven't "mastered" the system and I truly never will – I don't think anyone ever does! We are all constantly striving to improve both our physical and our mental abilities and it is a lifelong pursuit. The word "Master" is one that is too easily bandied about in the modern era, largely because of a mistranslation of the Eastern terms for teachers of the Martial Arts. We are teachers, coaches if you will, with skills and knowledge that, at least initially, is greater than that of our students. We should be going out of our way to improve both them and ourselves, not worrying about labels, titles or thinking that we have suddenly "arrived" and are now "masters" and beyond improvement. I am very happy to be called a coach, a sifu if you like (although even now it doesn't seem quite right as I still see my own teacher as sifu or teacher), so whenever I am asked, "What should I call you?" my reply is always the same: "Just call me David." I just hope that I can continue to improve myself, but more importantly, continue to impart the knowledge such that my students exceed my standard. That is the real goal.

h ow do you see Wing Chun Kung Fu in the world at the present time?

This is a particularly good time for Wing Chun in the world, following the enormous interest in the system that has been generated by the recent "Ip Man" movie franchise and other films and TV shows that have featured Wing Chun. As a result, more people have become aware of Wing Chun and many have taken up the practice of this system. Some schools that may have once struggled to get 10 students through the doors are now having to turn potential students away, such has been the effect of these films, and the Internet has also been a great source of information for people wanting to know more about Wing Chun. Many practitioners of quite different systems have been drawn to Wing Chun and have found that its direct approach and logical methods are very appealing, compared with what they have previously studied. Some estimates have suggested as many as 3–4 million people are now training in Wing Chun around the world today. That is an enormous figure when you stop to consider that when Ip Man first brought the system to Hong Kong in 1950, there were probably less than two dozen notable practitioners of Wing Chun over the previous 150 years!

Does the weaponry aspect of Wing Chun enhance the student's empty hands ability or are those two completely non-related skills?

The two weapons of the system, on the surface at least, would seem irrelevant in the modern world. After all, how often would one be carrying around a pole over nine feet long, or a pair of rather large meat cleavers? However, on further examination it is easy to see that there are definite benefits to the practice of both weapons, and a relevance that is far reaching. Most weapons fall into three main categories: long, short or flexible. In the case of Wing Chun, two of these, long and short, are dealt with in the system. The "Luk Dim Boon Gwan" ("six-and-a-half point pole") is an excellent way to develop and enhance the Wing Chun student's wrist, waist and stance strength. It also helps to improve the use of the elbow to generate power and improves the posture whilst at the same time teaching a realistic way to use any long weapon to attack and defend. Interestingly, in many respects, the long pole is even closer in nature to the concepts/actions of the empty-hand component of the system than the knife form is, which is one of the reasons why it is usually taught earlier than the knife form. The "Baat Jaam Do" ("eight-slash knives") not only teaches an effective means of utilizing a short weapon, either singularly or a pair, but it is also able to enhance the strength of the wrists and stance in a similar way to the pole form. Being a pair of knives, it also confirms the concept of "facing" that the system advocates, as well as instilling a completely different approach to footwork so as to deal with an adversary who is armed with a longer weapon. It is this point in particular that determines that the knives are usually taught much later because otherwise they can actually screw up the student's progress.

how does the Wing Chun style differ from other Kung Fu methods when applying the techniques in a self-defense/real situation?

As I've already indicated, in Wing Chun, the aim is always to counter an attack with an even more effective one, so the Wing Chun response is very offensive in nature. We do not follow the classical "first block, then counter attack" approach that is quite commonly used elsewhere in the Martial Arts, nor do we try to apply complicated routines and/or flamboyant actions. We do not employ high kicks and do not move about unnecessarily – Wing Chun is primarily a striking art and close-range combat is our true strength. Thus, we are very comfortable where most people are not, and can generate loads of power over very short distances, all while fighting with the aid of contact reflexes at the neural level, making our responses extremely fast and difficult to predict and counter. Our goal is the quick and total incapacitation of the enemy, reversing the roles of attacker and victim within the first one or two blows being thrown and making sure that we throw the majority of the rest, keeping the enemy off balance and under threat until they are unable to continue, or until a means of escape is found. It is simple, it is direct, it is intentionally brutal, but based on science, logic, geometry and physics all the way.

When teaching the art of Kung Fu, what is the most important element: self-defense, health, or tradition?

"The Wing Chun forms are cleverly designed to teach both techniques and concepts."

I would say that the most important element is reality. We must always strive to make the training reality-based and to ensure that we are honest about the way that we train. Health and exercise is not a priority (you do not need to be a super athlete to perform Wing Chun), nor is tradition, if what you mean by that to be bowing, fancy uniforms and rituals. We have a tradition to uphold, but it is one of training realistically and adhering to the core concepts, forms and drills of the system, as passed down to us from Sigung Ip Man and Sifu Wong Shun Leung. It would be more accurate to say that what we do is about personal protection concepts, or close-quarters combat, rather than the term self-defense which I personally do not like to use. We are not in the business of self-defense – it is an unrealistic expectation to think that one can merely defend oneself – we are in the business of learning to fight better than our opponent, so what we are doing is definitely not self-defense. Wing Chun is a combat skill designed for attack.

Wing Chun Masters

"Be honest with yourself and with your training partners."

Forms and Chi sau: what's the proper ratio in training?

There needs to be a balance in all aspects of training. Just training forms or just doing "Chi Sau" or just sparring ... none of those alone will make you a complete fighter. Each has a role to play in the overall development of the student, just as the other drills, wall-bag training, the "Muk Yan Jong" and weapons have a role to play. They are all like pieces in a jigsaw puzzle and we need them all to complete the picture. Many Wing Chun schools (and non-Wing Chun schools for that matter!) place too much emphasis on just one or two of these areas. As far as the forms are concerned, they need to be practiced regularly and not discarded early on in the training or rushed through occasionally. The Wing Chun forms are cleverly designed to teach both techniques and concepts, to strengthen attributes such as footwork and the use of the elbow, and to impart skills on a steadily increasing and overlapping level of complexity that ties in with other aspects of the learning curve. Whenever things are not working elsewhere in one's training, returning to the forms is generally the very best way to both identify and correct the problem. Like the forms, "Chi Sau" training imparts different levels of skill and allows for the development of both concepts and attributes that might otherwise go without improvement if not practiced in this way. "Chi Sau" provides a laboratory in which one can experiment on subtle skills and enhance reactions and reflexes that sparring or other combat-oriented drills cannot replicate. It is not a replacement for fighting, nor is it meant to be applied as practiced in actual combat. Instead, "Chi Sau" is again one of the many clever ways in which key attributes which MAY be required in a microsecond within the actual fight, can be loaded into the neural system and become a natural part of our arsenal of skills. Our aim is never to "Chi Sau" with our opponent, but should a situation occur where the limbs are trapped, jammed, grabbed, dragged or obstructed in any way, "Chi Sau" instills the necessary reflexes and reactions to deal with these issues and allow us to continue to attack whilst keeping our enemy in check.

Do you have any general advice you would care to pass on the practitioners in general?

Be honest with yourself and with your training partners. Don't "cheat" in drills because this takes away whatever benefits that they are designed to bring you. Train with reality at the forefront at all times, taking care of your partner's improvement and safety at all times. If your partner improves, you will too, so it is in your own interest to make sure that he or she is given all the best possible opportunities to develop. Take new ideas on board, train them, test them and only then question them if they fail to work. Chances are that you are using the system incorrectly, not that the system (or the individual skill) is faulty. Far too many Martial Arts practitioners blame the system that they are practicing for their failures, when what they should be doing is asking, "What did I do wrong?" If, after a reasonable amount of serious research and practice, you still cannot make something work, then consider modifying it so that it will work, or discarding it altogether for a method that does work for you. The first day I ever met my late Sifu, he said to me, "If you can show me a better way to fight than I am doing now, I want to learn from you!" That is the attitude that you must take if you want to improve both as a person and a practitioner.

some people think going to h ong Kong-China or Taiwan to train is highly necessary; do you share this point of view?

As someone who did travel to Hong Kong and China to explore the Martial Arts, I can honestly say that at the time that I began my training, that really was the only way to be sure of learning the "good oil" – good teachers in the West were rare and difficult to find. All that has changed now, and the standard of the Martial Arts in all its many forms has improved dramatically all over the world, so one may not have to venture beyond their own borders to find excellent instruction. However, there is something to be said for returning to the source as a means of inspiration, a kind of "completing of the circle" if you will. There is also the fact that things can get a little stale if training only with the same small circle of friends, so interacting with people with whom you are relatively unfamiliar, or whose training methods may deviate slightly from your own, brings out the adrenalin and opens the mind to new ideas that can definitely improve one's skills. This is why I always have, and always will, encourage my students to travel not only back to Hong Kong to seek training, but also to other countries around the world to meet up with other Wing Chun devotees and train with them. There is always more to be learnt and gained.

What do you consider to be the major changes in the art since you began training?

The most obvious major change is the fact that there are now so many more people training in Wing Chun. When I began my training in Hong Kong, there were only two or three non-Chinese guys training and it remained that way for the first few years. Now there are Wing Chun practitioners everywhere, including Hong Kong. The other thing that has changed is that in the early days, only one or two names were associated with Wing Chun, especially in the West where, I think it is fair to say, that some individuals created a myth that they were the most advanced guys, even the only guy in one case! ...who had learnt the system from Ip Man. With the advent of the World Wide Web, these guys were gradually revealed as liars and those who really had been great students of Ip Man were eventually brought to the attention of the Martial Arts community. With that exposure, people came to realize that there was more than one approach to Wing Chun, and that some methods on offer were a pale representation of the full potential of the system. Thankfully, my late teacher, who was a very humble and self-effacing man despite his achievements and skills, started to gain the recognition for what he had contributed to Wing Chun and his very modern, scientific approach was revealed as an outstanding and extremely practical version of the system. I am proud to be able to help to carry on his legacy and share it with Wing Chun devotees around the world now that he has passed on.

Who would you like to have trained with that you have not?

I would have loved to have been able to train with Sigung Ip Man and to have witnessed the beginnings of Wing Chun in Hong Kong in the middle of the last century. From all accounts he was a fascinating man whose skill level was extraordinary. One of his friends from Fatsaan (Foshan) in China and a great Wing Chun teacher and fighter in his own right, Yuen Kay San, is another person whom I would have loved to be able to meet and train under. Recent research suggests that he may well have been the real force behind the skills and methods of Ip Man, but that because he remained in China, his prowess and expertise was never appreciated outside of the mainland. Some even suggest that without his guidance, Ip Man would never have become the fighter that he was, but everyone knows of Ip Man and his "Hong Kong Wing Chun," while few have heard of "Yuen Kay San

Wing Chun". Hopefully, more of his life and achievements will gradually be revealed. My wish list is longer, but these two gentlemen are right at the top.

What would you say to someone who is interested in starting to learn Wing Chun Kung Fu?

Seek out a good teacher, train hard and concentrate on learning the basic skills very well. No point being in a hurry because without great basics, you've got nothing good anyway. Be patient, train honestly and always follow a path that demands realism and efficiency.

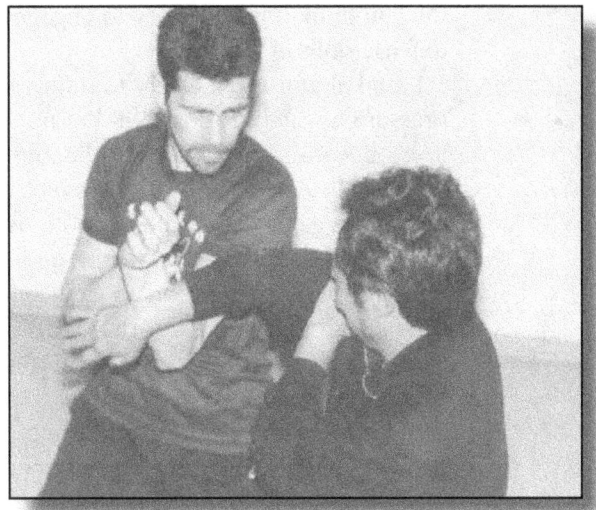

"A real fight on the street takes seconds, not minutes, and the aim of the game should be to end it as quickly as possible."

If you are not hitting something often, or working out with training partners often, then you are at the wrong school. Wing Chun is about interaction and about real combat skills – you don't get that from standing in the line throwing punches all the time or from ritualized sequences practiced on a compliant opponent.

What keeps you motivated after all these years?

I am simply very passionate about the system and love to share it and train it. It is so appealing to me because it is so logical and you cannot argue with the simplicity of its science. I also feel an enormous pride in having been accepted as a student by my late Sifu, and feel a strong need to honor him by continuing his legacy in any small way that I can. He shared with me something much more than just how to punch and kick – he taught me how to be a better person and to apply Wing Chun concepts in all aspects of my life. It is a privilege to be able to share his knowledge and experiences with others – that's what keeps me motivated, ...that and seeing the gleam in the eyes of a student when he or she finally grasps an idea or makes something work – that's cool!

Do you think it is necessary to engage in free-fighting to achieve good self-defense skills in the street?

I think that it is necessary to train with regularity and to drill skills under pressure as often as possible. I'm not so sure that sparring is the best way to go because it does tend to become a game of "tit-for-tat" if not monitored well. A real fight on the street takes seconds, not minutes, and the aim of the game should be to end it as quickly as possible. If it goes on for long, then the chances of getting badly injured are greatly increased. Free-fighting/sparring can tend to drag out and become more like a "game," obviously because of the protective equipment and any rules that may apply. I agree that it is a great way to raise the adrenalin level and learn to deal with both pressure and hits, but I personally think that more time should be spent on "pressure-testing" through what we like to call "open drills" whereby you have an opponent (who can wear protective equipment if desired) acting as the aggressor and the other person has mere split-seconds to deal with the attack in whatever form it may come. As "open drills" we can then change the level of pressure, aggression, style of attack, and so on, gradually reaching a point where anything goes, thus replicating more accurately what may occur on the street. Sparring in the ring cannot really do that as effectively.

What is your opinion about mixing Kung Fu styles? Does the practice of one nullify the effectiveness of the other or on the contrary, it can be beneficial to the student?

Styles or systems do not necessarily complement each other, with some being diametrically opposed to each other both physically and conceptually. Therefore, mixing styles is not guaranteed to produce better results – in fact, it may end up decreasing one's ability to fight well at all. I compare this to the idea of taking a few pieces from three or more jigsaw puzzles and expecting to produce a useful picture – it isn't going to happen! Systems have specific concepts or techniques that they use to attain their combat goals. If you try to combine such concepts or techniques with methods that are completely different, I cannot see much benefit being achieved. In fact, it is more likely to create confusion and cause a complete "mental logjam" in the fighter such that he cannot use any of his skills well and just gets himself into a worse predicament. Training in another system so as to form an understanding of and an appreciation for its methods is quite another kettle of fish. There is a lot to be gained from getting into the head of one's enemy so as to know how he or she might think and react. Knowing how their "engine" works not only gives you a better knowledge of how to beat them, it may well give you a better appreciation of your own system. Mixing the two, however, is less likely to be a successful venture.

What is your philosophical basis for your Kung Fu training?

My philosophy with regards to my own training is simple – keep an open mind, always seek knowledge, and never assume that you know everything. If I do that, and always seek to improve what I am doing, then I believe that I will continue to grow as a person and as a Martial Artist and teacher.

Do you have a particularly memorable Kung Fu experience that has remained as an inspiration for your training?

Every single day that I spent with my late teacher and my Sihing-dai (Kung Fu brothers) was an inspiration and I cannot really pick out any one thing that inspired me more than any other. I guess the whole Wing Chun experience has been, and continues to be an inspiration in my training.

After all these years of training and experience, could you explain the meaning of the practice of Kung Fu?

For me personally, the meaning of the practice of Kung Fu is self-fulfillment. It has enabled me to improve who I am and to give something of value to others through teaching the system and writing about it. It has made me aware of myself and others, enabling me to remain healthy, alert and, hopefully, to leave something of value behind when I'm gone. I cannot imagine what sort of person I would be, or what direction my life might have taken, had I not become involved in Wing Chun.

h ow is the Chi sau aspect of training related to the practical application of the Wing Chun techniques used in the three empty hands forms?

If "Siu Nim Tau" is the ABCs of Wing Chun, and "Cham Kiu" is the grammar and short phrases, what "Chi Sau" does is teach us to "converse" and to make use of this "language" in a very effective and individual way, rather than just being robots who repeat a pattern of sounds. Through "Chi Sau" we are taught how to "read" the opponent's intentions and to counter those intentions instantaneously with actions that control and hit the opponent. In "Chi Sau" we are given an opportunity to explore the infinite number of ways in which not only the techniques, but also the concepts of Wing Chun can be applied under constant forward pressure. We learn how to operate at the worst possible distance (extreme close-range) and under the worst possible circumstances (already jammed-up, restrained or

Wing Chun Masters

"We are training combat, not paper folding, so there has to be realism involved at all times."

grabbed), so as to learn how to effectively deal with such circumstances and still be able to fight effectively and with powerful counter-fighting skills. If things get totally screwed up, then there is also the possibility of utilizing concepts and strategies contained in the "Biu Ji" form to escape the predicament, while it goes without saying that the concepts in the "Muk Yan Jong" form can be explored as well, especially in terms of recovering from simple errors, improving footwork and managing distance.

Is there anything lacking in the way Martial Arts are taught today compared to how they were in your beginnings?

I think that some instructors water down the reality side of training in order to retain students and keep people happy. There is a perception in the public that one can miraculously defend oneself from real violence by simply taking a few classes here and there, gain a "black belt" and then you're safe for life. Most "black belts" that I meet haven't trained for years, or else they just do forms and break the occasional board, thinking that that somehow makes them great fighters. Sadly, in terms of real combat proficiency, they are deluding themselves. Either train your students in a fashion that prepares them for real combat, getting them to face the reality of what that entails, both physically and emotionally, or be honest and tell them that you are merely practicing a sport which does not guarantee any real fighting ability. I cannot remember a single day when I did not come home from training without a cut lip, blood nose or bruises somewhere on my body, ...and I still don't! We are training combat, not paper folding, so there has to be realism involved at all times. It's like saying that you'll teach someone to swim, but guarantee them that they won't get wet! That's what I feel is missing in many Martial Arts schools today.

What do you consider to be the most important qualities of a successful Kung Fu practitioner?

I think that to be a successful Kung Fu practitioner, one needs to remain humble and not presume that they are better than anyone else. We should be training to improve ourselves, not to belittle or overpower others. Sure, the goal of the system is to hit the opponent's nearest target with our closest weapon ... and hit them hard! ...but that doesn't mean being a bully in class or acting like you're someone special. Perseverance, hard work, humility, a positive attitude towards others – these are all qualities that will take us far in our journey along the Martial Road. Most of all, the willingness to help your training partner to improve as much as possible because – and I firmly believe this – if we do our best to help them improve, the result will be a great training partner who helps us to improve.

What advice would you give to students on the question of supplementary training (running, weights, et cetera)?

When I was younger I did a lot of running, especially long-distance running, and it kept me very fit and built up my stamina considerably. It especially helped me to learn how to breathe well, something that still comes in very handy when working out with the younger students. Unfortunately, I suffered knee damage and the running career came to an end for me, but I would still recommend it to anyone seeking all-round exercise and fitness. I have never really been into weight training and mostly stay fit by training my Wing Chun. A personal favorite method is to work through my forms as a circuit routine: start with "Cham Kiu" then "Siu Nim Tau" then "Cham Kiu" then "Biu Ji" then "Cham Kiu" then the "Jong" then "Cham Kiu" then reverse the sequence – you can mess with the pattern anyway that you like, but I like using "Cham Kiu" as the linking form as it keeps you moving through the most important combinations again and again. Other than that, it's just regular training, hitting the bags, and so on for me. I have no special diet as such, just a little of anything in moderation, and I don't drink or smoke. I think that I'm in pretty decent shape for my age. My only vice is chocolate...

What do you see as the most important attributes of a student?

Enthusiasm, but not obsession; healthy skepticism, but not arrogance; trust, but not blind faith; the ability to push yourself hard, but knowing when to take a break. Loyalty, honesty and sincerity go a long way in earning the respect of one's teacher too, not to mention the respect of one's peers. Most of all, don't take yourself too seriously and enjoy your training – it's okay to have fun when you train – no need to act like you're on a divine mission.

Wing Chun Masters

"It's the age in which we live, the generation of the quick fix. Nobody wants to work hard for anything; they want it all yesterday, at the cheapest price and without the effort."

Why is it, in your opinion, that a lot of students start falling away after two-three years of training?

It's the age in which we live, the generation of the quick fix. Nobody wants to work hard for anything; they want it all yesterday, at the cheapest price and without the effort. They want to be Bruce Lee, but don't appreciate that he worked hard for years to make it look so effortless. When I took up the Martial Arts, like most of my peers, I did it with the intention to make it my life's pursuit. These days, trends come and go and it's a consumer society where we buy it and then throw it away for a newer, flashier one. Thus, people enter the school all fired up to be the next Bruce Lee, only to realize that it going to take time and hard work to get there. Many simply don't have what it takes to stick it out. We also now lead even busier lives than ever before, with demands coming from every angle. It isn't easy to find the time to train once you get married, have a family, move into a demanding job, and so on. Most can't see any point in continuing to train when they are facing all that, plus many also think that once they've trained for a couple of years they already know all that they need to know. It is only a very rare breed of student that sticks it out for longer, but I'm happy to say that I have some guys who are still with me after 20+ years! I must be doing something right, although I suspect that it's the brilliance of Wing Chun theory that keeps them coming back rather than my bad jokes.

have there been times when you felt fear in your Kung Fu training?
I can't recall ever consciously feeling fear in training, at least not knee-shaking, teeth-chattering kind of fear, but I suppose there have been times when I've felt a surge of adrenalin because of a particular opponent or training partner, but you just deal with it and try to turn a negative situation into a positive one. I think that one usually only feels the fear after the event, when you've had time to think about it. In the moment, there simply isn't time for that to be allowed to get in the way. Besides, fear is such a great motivating factor that if it happens, it is can be a very good thing.

What are your thoughts on the future of the art?
I feel that the future of Wing Chun is looking very good, especially the WSLVT branch of the tree to which I belong. People are becoming increasingly aware that there are different approaches to this system and that not all branches of the tree are the same. In recent years I have seen a number of Wing Chun practitioners with dozens of years of experience coming across to seek out our training methods, having found that what they were doing just doesn't much up in terms of efficiency and practicality. The general Martial Arts public also is learning more about Wing Chun, especially since the "Ip Man" movies hit the screen, and they too are being drawn to the system, so things are definitely looking very good for the future of Wing Chun all over the world. It isn't to everyone's taste, and that is to be expected, but the person who appreciates logic and science is sure to find Wing Chun fascinating and may well be drawn to take up its practice. I will certainly continue to do what I can to preserve and disseminate the WSLVT legacy to future generations both here in Malaysia, and via my students scattered around the globe. That's the least that I can do to honor my amazing teacher.

SHAUN RAWCLIFFE

A Path to Simplicity

SIFU SHAUN RAWCLIFFE BEGAN STUDYING WING CHUN IN 1979, FOLLOWING SIX YEARS OF SHOTOKAN KARATE. HE STUDIED WING CHUN IN THE UK UNDER THREE CHINESE SIFU'S FOR ALMOST TEN YEARS, OPENING HIS FIRST SCHOOL IN THE HALL GREEN AREA OF BIRMINGHAM, WHERE HE STILL TEACHES TODAY.

IN JUNE 1985, GRANDMASTER IP CHUN, VISITED ENGLAND AND SIFU RAWCLIFFE WAS SO IMPRESSED WITH HIS DEPTH OF KNOWLEDGE AND OPENNESS THAT EVERY YEAR SINCE THEN IP CHUN HAS BEEN INVITED TO GIVE A SEMINAR AT SHAUN'S SCHOOL.

FOLLOWING ONE OF THESE SEMINARS IN 1989, IP CHUN GAVE SHAUN A PERSONAL INVITATION TO GO TO HONG KONG TO TRAIN WITH HIM, AN OPPORTUNITY THAT WAS NOT TO BE MISSED.

SHAUN'S FIRST VISIT TO HONG KONG IN MAY 1989, IT WAS SIX WEEKS OF INTENSIVE ONE-ON-ONE TRAINING AT THE HOME OF IP CHUN. HOWEVER, BEFORE SHAUN WAS ALLOWED TO BEGIN TRAINING AND WAS ACCEPTED AS ONE OF HIS STUDENTS, IP CHUN TOOK HIM TO FANLING IN HONG KONG'S NEW TERRITORIES TO VISIT YIP MAN'S GRAVE AND TO PAY HIS RESPECTS. AT THE END OF HIS STAY SIFU RAWCLIFFE WAS MADE A PERMANENT MEMBER OF BOTH THE "VING TSUN ATHLETIC ASSOCIATION" AND THE "YIP MAN MARTIAL ARTS ASSOCIATION". THE "VING TSUN ATHLETIC ASSOCIATION" ALSO PRESENTED HIM WITH AN INSTRUCTOR'S CERTIFICATE.

SINCE 1990 SHAUN HAS CONTINUED TO RETURN TO HONG KONG TO REFINE HIS SKILLS. SIFU RAWCLIFFE HAD THE OPPORTUNITY TO MEET AND DISCUSS WING CHUN WITH SEVERAL SIFU'S INCLUDING PANG NAM AND LUN KAI, AND VISITED THE FORMER HOMES OF LEUNG JAN AND IP MAN. WHILST IN FOSHAN, SHAUN AND IP CHUN GAVE A WING CHUN DEMONSTRATION AT THE "CHING WU ASSOCIATION" AS A PRELUDE TO IP CHUN STARTING A WING CHUN CLASS AT THE UNIVERSITY IN FOSHAN.

SHAUN CONTINUES TO TEACH WING CHUN IN THE SAME MANNER THAT HE WAS TAUGHT IN HONG KONG, TRADITIONALLY AND INFORMALLY. HE NOW HEADS AN INTERNATIONAL ASSOCIATION, BUT STILL REFUSES TO TEACH FOR A LIVING, BELIEVING THAT TEACHING WITHOUT THE NEED FOR PERSONAL FINANCIAL GAIN ENSURES THAT HE REMAINS FOCUSSED ON THE QUALITY OF HIS TEACHING, RATHER THAN THE QUANTITY OF STUDENTS.

how long have you been practicing the martial arts – Wing Chun - and who was your teacher?

I discovered Wing Chun in 1979 and for the first 10 years I predominately trained in the UK with several Wing Chun Sifus including; Stephen

Wing Chun Masters

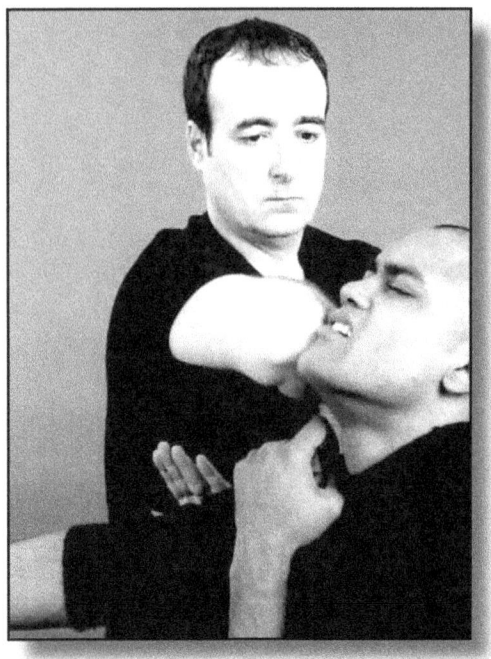

"I started Martial Arts with Judo when I was just 11 years old, which lasted a whole 6 weeks."

T K Chan, Simon Lau and Samuel Kwok. It was May 1989, following a seminar at my school by Sifu Ip Chun that I decided to accept his offer to train with him in Hong Kong. I have since made 36 training trips to Hong Kong to train intensively with Sifu.

ho w many styles have you trained in?

I started Martial Arts with Judo when I was just 11 years old, which lasted a whole 6 weeks. I then started training Shotokan Karate, which I studied until I was 18, earning my first Dan. It was then I came across Wing Chun (that was 1979).

What are the main principles of the three empty-hand forms and how they interrelate with each other?

Siu Nim Tao and Chum Kiu are very closely intertwined, Chum Kiu being a logical extension of Siu Nim Tao training; Siu Nim Tao is a static, solo, simple, single handed (when both hands are utilised, the left mirrors the right, either simultaneously or sequentially) personal development sequence.

Chum Kiu uses this sequence, the tools and the lessons learnt from developing Siu Nim Tao, as in multiple simultaneous awareness, Gung Lik, posture, stance, Fa Ging energy and muscular awareness's etc, and then builds on that, in a mobile, more complex, two handed spatial awareness sequence of movements and combinations.

Biu Tze is kind of set apart, Sifu told me that if your training, deployment and utilisation of Siu Nim Tao and Chum Kiu was perfect, then you would never need Biu Tze, since Biu Tze, (also known as 'Gow Gup Sao' - emergency hand) is to recover from mistakes. However as Sifu always points out: The reason for Biu Tze is because we are human and shit happens! (roughly translated)

Would you tell us some interesting stories of your early days in kung fu and the training under the ip Chun?

Well for a start I nearly didn't train with Ip Chun at all; on my first day in Hong Kong he took me to the Ving Tsun Athletic Association, where he and many Wing Chun Sifu's were holding a meeting about the forthcoming Ip Man Genealogy book. There I met many of SiGung's senior students including Wong Shun Leung, Lok Yiu, Tsui Sheung Tin, Leung Ting, Ip Ching, Law Bing, Siu Yuk Men, Wong Kiu and several others. As soon as the meeting finished however and despite the fact I had travelled 6000 miles to see him, Sifu Ip Chun left me there with the other Sifu's. I was very put out to be honest and very nearly accepted some of the offers I received to train with some of the Sifu's who remained, not realising this was Sifu's way of testing me. Thankfully I realized it was his way of saying you have travelled all this way .... Make your free choice... luckily for me I recognized this and knew whom I wanted to learn from.

Sifu also has a great sense of humour.... In 1995 I took a group of students with me to Hong Kong to train and experience what I had been fortunate enough to experience. Whilst there we went out for a meal with Sifu and his wife; I asked Sifu 'I call you Sifu and your wife SiMo, my students call you SiGung, how should they address your wife?' He looked at me and smiled and replied 'It doesn't matter she's mostly deaf!'

Do you teach Westerners? h ow do you find the Westerners respond to traditional Chinese training?

I teach everyone who earns their place in the school.

I don't teach for a living so I am in the privileged position where I can be very selective whom I teach; every potential student has to go through a 16 lesson probationary period so I can judge their character, dedication and suitability for Wing Chun. Every student is potentially one of the next generation of instructors, so it is important to get the right personalities. Not every westerner, nor Chinese or any other genre will take to traditional Chinese training, it is up to us instructors to find and nurture the right ones.

Were you a 'natural' at kung fu – did the movements come easily to you?

No, I was not and am not a natural at Wing Chun, I have had to, and still have to, work hard at developing and maintaining my skills. I was very fortunate that I found a martial art that worked for and suited me.

h ow has your personal kung fu has changed/developed over the years?

My Martial Art has matured and developed immensely, and my reason for training has also changed totally. I initially started Martial Arts as I was bullied at school and needed to build my self-confidence. At the age of 18 I started working in the close protection industry and my Wing Chun complemented my unarmed combat and close quarter battle training. Now however my motivation, though still self-protection based is to be a better instructor and produce higher quality instructors than myself.

What are the most important points in your teaching methods? And what are the most important qualities for a student to become proficient in the Wing Chun style?

For anyone to become proficient in Wing Chun, they must understand how their body works and how it can be used most efficiently and effectively. Wing Chun is a very scientific art based upon human anatomy, it requires a student to re-educate their mind and their muscle groups to a new and alternative way of moving and reacting; learning how to relax where necessary, learn the correct and most efficient skeletal alignment. They need to understand how to use their bodies mass and specific muscle groups to generate huge amounts of force offensively whilst controlling their body core and limbs to position them effectively defensively.

With all the technical changes during the last 30, do you think there are still 'pure' styles of kung fu and more specifically Wing Chun?

I find it hard to define what 'Pure' Wing Chun is. Wing Chun has so many flavours. The keys I believe are to maintain the core concepts of Wing Chun through the forms, the interpretation and applications will always be and should be unique to the individual. I visited Foshan with Sifu on several occasions as was able to meet, watch and practice a little with several of the Wing Chun Sifu's there including Pang Lam, Lung Gai and Gwok Fu. Their Wing Chun is different from 'Hong Kong' Wing Chun, placing more emphasis on internal energy and Ch'i. But even the Wing Chun Sifu's in Hong Kong differ from one another in their application and deployment of their Wing Chun tools. The simple reason being that Wing Chun is a systematic set of tools that you must learn to apply appropriately and accordingly yourself, to quote Sifu 'Wing Chun doesn't define you ..... you define your Wing Chun.'

Do you think different 'styles' are truly important in the art of kung fu?

I think there is a martial art out there to suit everyone, some styles which are very athletic and require a great deal of flexibility, others are hard and physically punishing. There are gentle soft styles, ones that mimic animals, competition styles and practical styles. The key is to find the one for you....

What is opinion of Full Contact kung fu tournaments?

I don't believe Wing Chun has any place in Full contact tournaments. I do respect and admire anyone who has the confidence to enter such competitions, however, I learnt Wing Chun for simple, practical self defence... no rules, no referees, no corner-man, no protection, no tapping out and no instant medical treatment available...it is supposed to be a no nonsense street self defence system, with no belts, no grades, no rules, just principles and concepts to guide the practitioner to improving their skills.

In the street you aren't trained to peak fitness for a fight you knew of months in advance; you aren't facing an opponent who is known to you and who you had studied their style from watching DVD/films of their previous fights. You will not be adhering to a set of rules that prevent eye strikes, groin attacks, weapons or multiple opponents, You probably will not be wearing highly practical clothing allowing huge freedom of movement, or in known surroundings; such as a flat slightly sprung floor, where there are no sharp objects, no hard surfaces, no furniture or opportunist weapons to be concerned about. For me Wing Chun tools and the training around it, is for practical use in the unknown.

"I don't believe Wing Chun has any place in Full contact tournaments."

how different from other kung fu styles do you see the principles and concepts of Wing Chun?

I find that hard to answer and it's unfair of me to make an uneducated judgment as I have very limited knowledge or awareness of other Kung Fu styles other than watching them being demonstrated.

Do you think that kung fu in the West has 'caught up' with the technical level in China?

I think now that Hong Kong and China have opened up, access is easy and flights relatively inexpensive. So access to a good teacher, either by

Wing Chun Masters

"Wing Chun was never meant to be a sport and learning rules etc dilutes the street skills in my humble opinion."

travelling to China/Hong Kong or the teachers/their students travelling to, even living in the west, means that good quality affordable tuition is now readily available. Therefore learning the details and nuances of Kung Fu is much easier, if someone is prepared to make the time and effort to study and learn diligently.

Do you feel that there are any fundamental differences in approach or physical capabilities of Chinese kung fu practitioner in comparison to European or American practitioners?

I think the only difference in approach is that westerners are less patient on the whole and want quick results; the Chinese tend to understand that Kung Fu means time and effort to achieve reward.

In regards to physical capabilities, well you can't beat the laws of Physics; particularly Newton's 2nd law of nature, $F=M \times A$. If two Wing Chun practitioners have equal skills etc, but one is much heavier than the other, then the force (for example their punching power) of the heavier will be the greater, and unfortunately westerners on the whole tend to be bigger and heavier than the Chinese. Of course that's purely hypothetical and for the most part irrelevant, but it's fun to quote to wind up my Hong Kong Kung Fu brothers!

Kung fu is nowadays often referred to as a sport (wu shu). Would you agree with this definition?

Not in the case of Wing Chun, Wing Chun was never meant to be a sport and learning rules etc dilutes the street skills in my humble opinion.

Do you feel that you still have further to go in your studies of the art of Wing Chun?

Absolutely, I don't believe I will ever stop learning or improving. My teaching skills alone have developed and improved over time considerably. And as I am now starting into my 50's its fair to say I keep re-evaluating my Wing Chun. The Gung Ho way I moved and reacted in my 20's is considerably different to how I now move and respond, maturity does that to you...although mentally I still feel and act in my 20's...

Throughout my years as a teacher, I have felt it necessary to keep up to date with teaching methodologies and perhaps more importantly, I have devised new ways to cater for the ever-changing needs of my students. In an attempt to provide explanations that suit the different learning styles of my students, I have differentiated my teaching, providing explanations through auditory, visual and kinaesthetic means. I have learned that one of the most effective tools for aiding students has been my illustrations, which I have been drawing for over fifteen years. I allowed my original hand drawn diagrams to be included in a published article entitled 'Grandmaster Yip Man Centenary Birth Book' (1993), along with several articles I had written about Wing Chun. From both this publication and my students' comments, I have received positive feedback regarding the value of these diagrammatical exemplifications and consequently, I decided to use them in and as the basis for my first book.

h ow do you see Wing Chun kung fu in the world at the present time?

I think Wing Chun is going through a huge evolution. On the one hand various 'new versions' of Wing Chun are emerging from little known and sometime tenuously linked families. On the other hand there are now so many schools all claiming to teach 'Ip Man Wing Chun', it's quite scary, I have no idea what they base that claim on as they have never met Ip Man, let alone know what he taught (which was different to each students according to Sifu).

My biggest concern is the growth in politics. Wing Chun should be one large family and it predominantly still is in Hong Kong, but as it grows and spreads there is a risk of any differences breeding an unhealthy competitiveness and criticisms.

Does the weaponry aspect of Wing Chun [long pole and butterfly knives] enhance the student's empty hands ability or are those two completely no-related skills?

Developed during a period when self-defence was literally a matter of life or death, the practice of the Baat Cham Dao form today is not learnt or practiced for street practical application, but to enhance the practitioners understanding of Wing Chun theory, footwork and energy usage. The Baat Cham Dao form consists of a systematic set of movements and techniques that utilize the essential footwork, positions and structures of the Wing Chun system. It combines the most advanced parts of all the empty hand forms of the system, though the Baat Cham Dao form does contain one unique knife technique that does not mirror any of the empty hand techniques.

Historically, the movements and the benefits of using the Pole as a weapon were to increase the fighting range and to benefit from increased angular momentum, and therefore power, when striking or blocking, which really has little direct or practical bearing on improving street combat skills. However, the training required to perform the pole form powerfully and accurately does bring with it several benefits, such as increased muscular training and strengthening of the body posture. The Pole form requires tremendous strength from the entire body and develops the back, shoulders, triceps, biceps, forearm, wrist and legs. The development of the tremendous forearm and wrist strength required by the Pole form benefits Wing Chun's punching power in addition to some of the basic hand techniques. Moreover, the practice of the pole form improves coordination, balance, control and accuracy

h ow the Wing Chun style differs from other kung fu methods when applying the techniques in a self-defence situation?

All martial arts are unique, though obviously there are a limited way the body's skeleton can move, but I see Wing Chun as the ugly runt of the litter; it's not aesthetically pleasing, not classy nor particularly elegant, but fights dirty and hard!

When teaching the art of kung fu – what is the most important element; self defence, health or tradition?

I believe if you teach the forms, drills and Chi Sao correctly, honestly and openly on a technical level, then those seeking self defence will find that and be able to use and steer their Wing Chun in that way. Those looking for health aspects of the art, will find that in those same movements and exercises and those looking for tradition will find that in the attitude and approach to the learning. Wing Chun training is different for each person, by not influencing or flavouring the training focus I hope to give each student the opportunity to take from it what they need.

Forms and Chi sao, what's the proper ratio in training?

I believe that Forms are 25% of the system and Chi Sao is a further 25% of the system. The other 50% being split equally between Drilling and self defence application....

Forms are a solo performance of a preset sequence of movements which

"Sticking hands should be practiced and played as a 'game', in the same way that Tiger cubs learn to 'kill' without using their claws during the learning process."

practice, refine and instil a set of structures, body mechanics, principles and techniques. There are no direct applications of these movements; the forms do not teach the student how to apply those techniques, as they are not the fluid interaction with another person whilst under threat, duress and stress that is self defence. It is possible, however, to train these positions and moves to 'perfection', as there is no one else involved.

Chi Sao is a unique training method, which develops sensitivity and contact reflexes in the arms, allowing the practitioner to assess the situation and to perceive and deflect the opponent's force as soon as they come into contact with their opponent's arms. Chi Sao also develops close distance co-ordination, mobility, balance, timing, accuracy and the correct use of energy. Sticking hands should be practiced and played as a 'game', in the same way that Tiger cubs learn to 'kill' without using their claws during the learning process.

Drilling involves taking a single position or technique and practising it over and over again. Any new skill involving co-ordination requires time

Wing Chun Masters

"The key to learning is to be patient, students have to learn to replace old habits with new learned skills and the transition between the two is difficult one."

and practice until the new combination of movements and muscle contractions required to execute that movement have been learned; only then can that movement be performed without concentration and conscious effort. This process is known as consolidation, which requires attention, repetition and associative ideas.

Applications, usually trained in the form of one attack/one defend, teaches how to apply the techniques that have been refined within the forms and structurally developed within drilling. Fighting application teaches the second and third stages of fighting: the second (through lots of practice) to recognise the form and direction of the attack and the third, to bridge the gap and make contact, simultaneously defending and striking.

Do you have any general advice you would care to pass on the practitioners in general?

The key to learning is to be patient, students have to learn to replace old habits with new learned skills and the transition between the two is difficult one. It is difficult to have the faith, trust and confidence to let go of those habits, which may have served you well in the past; it takes time and practice …. the essence of Kung Fu.

some people think going to China or Taiwan to train is highly necessary, do you share this point of view?

On a personal level, going to Hong Kong to train was essential for me. I learnt so much and gained a huge appreciation about Wing Chun, trained with some awesome people and learnt so much, but that was back in 1989 when Wing Chun was still hard to find and a good teacher even harder. Today Wing Chun is much more accessible so the need to travel is much less a necessity.

What do you consider to be the major changes in the art since you began training?

The biggest change since I started is the availability and awareness of Wing Chun as an art. When I started in 1979 most people thought Wing Chun came with rice on a Chinese menu!

Who would you like to have trained with that you have not?

I guess the obvious answer is SiGung Ip Man or even Bruce Lee, but the truth is I have been very fortunate to have met and even touched hands with some of Wing Chun's greatest Hong Kong trained Sifu's. Particularly in the early years when Sifu began teaching at the VTAA Sifu's such as Wong Shun Leung, Lok Yiu, Tsui Sheung Tin, Leung Ting, Ip Ching and Siu Yuk Men would come and visit and I would have ample opportunity to discuss Wing Chun with them and they were always willing to show me techniques, energies and applications. I was like a kid in a huge sweet-shop!

What would you say to someone who is interested in starting to learn Wing Chun kung fu?

The key to starting training in Wing Chun is to do your research; remember that web sites, "YouTube" videos and the equivalent that promote a martial art school are put up there by those doing the promoting, so are not necessarily honest or legitimate. My advice is be discerning, go watch a lesson or two, be respectful, but ask the questions that matter and see if you feel comfortable in that environment.

What is it that keeps you motivated after all these years?

My motivation hasn't really waivered, I learnt Wing Chun for me, to protect myself and those I love. I teach because I want to share what I have been privileged to learn whilst I am still capable of doing so and, on a purely selfish level, I want to get my students/instructors to the highest standard possible so I have some excellent hands to train and practice with between my trips to Hong Kong. Training, teaching and learning is a never-ending process of discovery, consolidation and reappraisal.

Do you think it is necessary to engage in free-fighting to achieve good self-defence skills in the street?

Yes and no, depending on your definition of free fighting. If you mean get in to street fights then no; that is a very painful and reckless way to learn. Full contact competition fighting is, as I discussed earlier, a false environment as it doesn't contain many of the essential ingredients of street self defence; however aggressive it is, it is still a controlled environment.

The best way to learn is to take the Wing Chun out of the class room and increase the variables and unknown s whilst still making it a training and learning experience. When I learnt hostage retrieval, we didn't use live rounds and live targets, but predominantly trained with wax bullets and cut out targets that could be made to represent a hostage or a threat. Yet that role play learning served me well and taught me all the real life skills I needed for my job and for when the sh*t hit the fan!

What is your opinion about mixing kung fu styles? Does the practice of one nullify the effectiveness of the other or on the contrary, it can be beneficial to the student?

I find that a difficult question to answer, mostly because I am not clever enough to learn more than one style to any reasonable level. However, I personally don't see the need to train more than one style as Wing Chun encourages the practitioner to take the simple tools and explore their own applications. The only limit is the limit of ones mind and understanding. For example I often hear people say that Wing Chun is limited as it has no ground fighting ... what a load of rubbish! Do they think the Chinese never fall over or get knocked over? Wing Chun punches, deflections and kicks can equally be deployed kneeling, standing, even lying on your back; it's only a matter of taking the tools and making them work freely.

What is your philosophical basis for your kung fu training?

To be honest and frank when I started Wing Chun, I had no appreciation of any philosophy or any interest in that side of the martial art. I was a professional bodyguard and wanted a fighting system that would work simply and practically at very close quarters; any opponent/threat further than arms reach would just get shot! Of course that was many years ago now and as I matured and developed my views changed, though to be honest the practical side is still one of my prime motivators. I have however read and researched more into the main three doctrines of Chinese martial Arts:

- Taoism (Lao Tzu, circa 604 BC) - a doctrine of naturalism based on the soft, yielding, ways of nature. This played a pivotal role in the development of the principles of Kung Fu through the introduction of the fundamental teaching that there is a harmony of Yin and Yang. Two opposite, equal, interacting forces working together to maintain harmony and balance. Understanding the concept of Yin and Yang is perhaps the most important aspect in the learning of the Kung Fu system.

- Confucianism (Confucius, circa 551 BC) - a doctrine of humanism based on the efficacy of ritual and conformity as the means to salvation. For me an essential read for all Martial artists is The Doctrine of the Mean (Chung Yung), which is both a doctrine of Confucianism and also the title of one of the Four Books of Confucian philosophy. In essence its goal is to give guidance to maintaining balance and harmony and to direct the mind to a state of constant equilibrium.
- Buddhism (Buddha, circa 506 BC) - promoted non-materialism, compassion based on the realisation that all is illusionary. Buddhism is the most important component of Chinese martial arts, in that the practice is necessary for self-defence and self-cultivation.

"The meaning of the practice of Kung Fu is that through focus, diligence, hard work and determination anyone can learn to do the seemingly impossible."

Do you have a particularly memorable kung fu experience that has remained as an inspiration for your training?

Watching Sifu practicing Chi Sao for the first time, making it all look so easy and effortless. When I held my first seminar for Sifu in the UK in 1985, I remember thinking if a 5 foot tall, skinny 62 years old can easily control and dominate much younger larger partners seemingly effortlessly, there was something I was missing and I needed to know what that was....

After all these years of training and experience, could you explain the meaning of the practice of kung fu?

The meaning of the practice of Kung Fu is that through focus, diligence, hard work and determination anyone can learn to do the seemingly impossible, develop skills that you didn't think possible and comfortably interact with others in a physical language with ease.

how the Chi sao aspect of training is related to the practical application of the Wing Chun techniques used in the three empty hands forms?

"As far as Chi Sao in relation to application and real combat, well there are only two guarantees in street self-defence; Contact and movement."

Well first of it is necessary to realize how important Chi Sao is outside of fighting and training. Alongside football (soccer) and Music, Chi Sao is like an international language. When I first went to Hong Kong, I spoke no Cantonese, Sifu spoke no English, nor did many of my Si-Hing's. Yet the moment we linked arms in Chi Sao we communicated on a physical level without the need for spoken words. I have been fortunate to have taught all over the world and even though I could not speak many of their languages, nor they speak mine, we 'chatted' through Chi Sao ...

As far as Chi Sao in relation to application and real combat, well there are only two guarantees in street self-defence; Contact and movement. It is those two elements that are the basis of Chi Sao. Chi Sao is a close quarter, contact oriented, continually moving training exercise, which enables the Wing Chun practitioner to develop the sensitivity and awareness to be able to feel and directly respond to an opponent's movement through contact. By gaining and maintaining contact with an opponent's arm or arms, it is possible to control their movements, restrict their ability to use force and to close down their attacks, whilst allowing the Wing Chun practitioner to deploy a counter attack based upon the weaknesses felt or created through that contact. However only once the basic techniques, functions, positions and associated energies have been developed and understood through the forms and associated drills, is it possible to apply freely, explore and react according to the fluid and unpredictable scenarios, responses and techniques faced within Chi Sao.

It is important to understand why Chi Sao is beneficial, where it fits into the training process and how it applies in self-defence.

A fight or attack situation escalates very quickly and is a very fluid and volatile situation. The time from reception to disengagement can be a matter of seconds and the consequences can be terrible, potentially deadly. In those few vital seconds, damage limitation is the key to survival. To achieve that at such close proximity and within such a short time frame, every movement must be an instinctive, automatic, subconscious and accurate response without any time for thought, consideration or indecision.

It is this close quarter proximity that Chi Sao practice aims to imitate, control and dominate. Through correct continuous practice and training, Chi Sao develops the skills and abilities to enable Wing Chun practitioners to respond quickly, accurately and precisely to the movements and even energy changes of the opponent. That enables the defender to control and dominate the situation and therefore the opponent.

is there anything lacking in the way martial arts are taught today compared to how they were in your beginnings?

I think there is an element for instructors catering to the market, less and less instructors seem willing to specialise in one art but seem to teach 4 or 5 styles, sometimes blending them or moving to MMA as it is the popular trend. I guess that's because more and more instructors teach martial arts as a commercial venture. I follow my Sifu's way which is quality, not quantity and having a full time job means my 30 year passion remains just that and I can be selective who I teach and remain true to what I was taught.

What you consider to be the most important qualities of a successful kung fu practitioner?

The most important qualities are a good personality, an open mind, a willingness to learn and dedication to put in the time and the practice required. With those ingredients an instructor can teach the Wing Chun skills knowing that they will be training and used correctly.

What advice would you give to students on the question of supplementary training?

I think health and general fitness is important to a healthy lifestyle; however it should not be a prerequisite to learning Wing Chun. As a street self defence system, it cannot work if you need to warm up, stretch etc in order to be able to perform the necessary moves, nor should it only work when you are at peak fitness. Though general fitness is no doubt beneficial, the best exercise to improve your punches; that uses all the muscle groups in exactly the right way is …. to punch. Supplementary exercises may develop muscle groups that are detrimental or antagonists the muscle group required to drive a powerful punch for example. Weight training can, if someone doesn't fully understand the result of their actions, be detrimental. I would never say do not weight train, join a gym or do other exercises, but I would get them to consider the pro's and con's of that training in regards to their Wing Chun development.

What do you see as the most important attributes of a student?

Over 30 years I have learnt that I can develop someone's skills, nurture their physical development, their understanding of the movements and techniques and even tease out their teaching skills. What I cannot do is stop a bully being a bully, a racist being racist and a sexist being sexist. So I look for someone with the right mental attitude and approach. I don't want to equip bullies and idiots with greater tools than they already have.

Why is it, in your opinion, that a lot of students start falling away after two-three years of training?

I think part of the reason is the lack of dedication of the student and frustration of not being a 'master' within a few years, part of it is the financial and time commitment that it puts on individuals. I think there is a psychological aspect to this where students who train through Siu Nim Tao get to the point where other students who haven't trained as long look up to them and ask their advice. Then when they move on to Chum Kiu, they feel like they are starting again, beginners in Siu Nim Tao are asking the advice of the senior Siu Nim Tao students and other Chum Kiu students ask the advice of the senior Chum students. I also feel instructors are partly to blame, not all students are as dedicated as they are, not everyone can learn as well or as quickly, yet some instructors instead of nurturing their students berate them for missing a lesson or two, even ring them up if they don't attend, that pressure is enough to put anyone off after, all students attend because they want to, not because they have to. And let's not even begin the conversation of instructors holding back information, charging more money for 'advanced techniques' and using one to one training as the only way to move forwards!

have been times when you felt fear in your kung fu training?

Absolutely, in order to develop Wing Chun skills within Chi Sao or in application training it is vital to train with, not on, your partner. All physical and mental tension must be discarded, the natural instinct to resist and tense, even lock the muscles under pressure must be trained out, as must the desire to use brute strength when applying techniques. Wing Chun practitioners must learn to relax, use energy only where necessary and appropriate and stick to and control the opponent's arms and attacks. Then it is possible to learn to redirect the opponent's force and momentum and use it against them. However on a few occasions I have practiced Chi Sao or explored applications with individuals who were excessively aggressive, had no self control or restraint and whose only aim was to beat you and prove they were better than you.

"I think Wing Chun is going through a huge change and I am as yet unsure how it will come out the other side."

What are your thoughts on the future of the art?

I think Wing Chun is going through a huge change and I am as yet unsure how it will come out the other side. The Ip Man films have been both a curse and a blessing. They have raised awareness of Wing Chun to new heights and it is growing exponentially, but it is also spreading so quickly that there is a danger of the quality degrading, particularly as there is no governing body to maintain any quality control.

WONG SHUN LEUNG

Master of Logic

ONE OF THE TOP WING CHUN FIGHTERS AT YIP MAN'S HONG KONG SCHOOL, SIFU LEUNG TAUGHT BRUCE LEE PRIVATELY FOR ONE-AND-A HALF-YEARS AND RECALLED "HIS KUNG-FU WAS NOT VERY GOOD, HE COULDN'T FIGHT." LEUNG'S OWN INTRODUCTION TO THE WING CHUN SYSTEM WAS LESS THAN STELLAR, HE CHALLENGED YIP MAN TO A TRIAL BY COMBAT, CONVINCED HE COULD DEFEAT HIM. WHEN MAN EASILY WON, LEUNG BECAME A LIFELONG BELIEVER AND DISCIPLE OF THE SYSTEM THAT BRUCE LEE WOULD EVENTUALLY TURN INTO THE MOST POPULAR KUNG-FU STYLE EVER TAUGHT. YIP MAN, SEEING MORE IN LEE THAN OTHERS, PREDICTED TO THE INCREDULOUS LEUNG THAT, "THIS LITTLE KID WILL MAKE WING CHUN FAMOUS."

A DEDICATED AND TALENTED STUDENT, LEUNG WENT ON TO BECAME YIP MAN'S PERSONAL ASSISTANT AND WAS PUT IN CHARGE OF PASSING ON THE ART TO THE SCHOOL'S "JUNIORS." LEUNG, DESPITE HIS INITIAL MISGIVINGS ABOUT THE WILD AND YOUTHFUL LEE, EVENTUALLY DEVELOPED A PERSONAL RELATIONSHIP WITH "THE LITTLE DRAGON" AS THEY BOTH MATURED. HE REFUSED, HOWEVER, TO APPEAR IN THE "GAME OF DEATH", LEE'S LAST UNFINISHED PROJECT, BECAUSE HE FELT THAT BEING DEFEATED IN A MOVIE WOULD REFLECT POORLY ON HIS TRUE SKILL. HIS RELATIONSHIP WITH BRUCE LEE WOULD LAST UNTIL THE END OF THE ACTOR'S LIFE.

WONG SHUN LEUNG WAS A CHARISMATIC TEACHER AND A DYNAMIC LEADER, WHICH IS WHY LEE RESPECTED HIM. LEUNG'S DEEP KNOWLEDGE OF WING CHUN MADE HIM ONE OF THE MOST SOUGHT-AFTER INSTRUCTORS OF HIS ERA. ANALYTICAL, INQUISITIVE, AND PERCEPTIVE, HE WAS SAID BY YIP MAN TO BE "THE LOGIC BEHIND WING CHUN."

When did you start training under yip Man?

My father had friends who practiced wing chun. One of them was a man named Chan Wah Sun. He would always tell me how good his teacher, Yip Man, was. I didn't believe him, so I decided to go to Yip Man's school and challenge him. He was around 50 years old and I was 17, strong, and in good shape. To make a long story short, he beat me up easily, which really surprised me. I just couldn't believe this little old man was so good.

you were considered one of wing chun's best fighters, right?

That's what they say, but I really don't like to talk about it very much. Many people, when they get old, start talking about how great they were

Wing Chun Masters

"Martial arts techniques can be adapted to be used with gloves."

when they were young and sometimes they say a lot of thing that are not true. If you were really good, then people will know already-you don't have to talk about it. If I tell stories about how I used to fight, it means that I can't fight anymore. If I can still fight today, I don't need to talk about my past. I don't see any point in proving to people how tough you are. Being a good fighter depends on how hard you practice, and how much time you put into it. Fighting abilities are based on perseverance, confidence, and physical power-not talk.

Did you ever consider competing in combat sports?

I have always liked boxing-I like anything about fighting, but my kind of fighting is not the sport version, it is real fighting where there are no rule, no restrictions, and your life is hanging in the balance. If you put on gloves then it becomes a matter of winning points, which is not total fighting. Martial arts techniques can be adapted to be used with gloves, but is not the same. However, it is true that contact training and sparring can be a very revealing experience for the student. Fighting with martial arts skills is partly a branch of learning, and partly an art. Perhaps Chinese martial arts should, taking into account the realistic social environment, formulate a set of competition regulations that would allow what I call the "trial of skills" to be brought into full play.

Why did you stop boxing?

I was sparring with my instructor and I hit him very hard. He got real mad and came at me very hard. I fought back with wing chun and he ended up bleeding. Boxing was over for me!

Do you look at wing chun as a philosophy or an art?

For me, wing chun is a skill. If you describe it as an art, there is no way to determine if it is effective or not. For example, you might like Picasso's work more than Monet's paintings, but it is purely subjective and just a matter of preference. In combat, the fighter left standing is the winner. It is not a matter of likes or dislikes-the skills can be proved. So I look at wing chun more as a skill than an art. Taken in that context, there nothing wrong with using your skills if you have to.

you were one yip Man's top assistants. Did you ever teach Bruce Lee?

I taught Bruce Lee privately and also watched him train under Yip Man at the school. William Cheung introduced Bruce Lee to the wing chun system. Bruce trained and studied wing chun from me for over one-and-a-half years.

Did you keep in touch with Bruce after he moved to the u nited s tates?

He used to write me telling me how he was doing and the direction his research was taking. Sometimes he would ask for clarification of a wing chun technique or principle. When he came back to Hong Hong to do movies, we would meet and talk about martial arts for hours. We had a very good relationship until the very end.

Did he ever explain jeet kune do to you?

Yes. Bruce was totally aware that jeet kune do is very hard to do because it depends on the student's capabilities. This can be really confusing for the students, especially if they lack a strong base and deep understanding. Jeet kune do was simply a personal format Bruce used to apply his knowledge and experiences. I told him most likely there was a missing link in his research and that he was trying to cover too much distance in too short a time. On other hand, there has been only one Bruce Lee and no one could play like him, some of the old rules didn't apply.

h ow did you see the evolution of Bruce Lee from wing chun to jeet kune do?

First of all, Bruce didn't get to see the best part of wing chun during his early days of training under Yip Man. He then came back to Hong Kong, and truly learned the foundation of what would eventually become his own style. He was a very naughty boy at times but also very smart. So once in the United States, he filled in the blanks in order to make things work for him.

In the later days of his life Bruce said to me, "If I could take back jeet kune do, I'd take it back." He realized that he could make the movements work, but that was because his style was designed for his own specific talents. His students, however, had problems making the techniques work under real situations. While jeet kune do was a significant art for Bruce, it has not been that way for other people who followed his method.

Bruce was a good fighter, but not as good as movies have portrayed him-almost invincible. People used to see Bruce Lee and have kung-fu dreams. They wanted to do the same things he did and duplicate his methods. Unfortunately, it seems nobody wants to wake up.

h ave you made any changes to the wing chun system?
Basically I teach the same method I learned from Yip Man-but I would say that I teach it in a more systematic way. At the same time, though, I'm still very intuitive in my teaching.

Most people associate you with the principle of lut sao jik chung. Why?
Because it is probably the most important concept in the whole wing chun system, perhaps the only exception being the bart cham dao techniques. As soon as the opponent offers an opening, the hand should attack instantaneously.

it is true that Bruce offered you a part in one of his movies?
Yes, he did. It was for "Game of Death", but I declined because I thought that the moves of wing chun style wouldn't look good on film. I think the wing chun method is ugly for movies but very good and very logical for real fighting.

h ave changed your overall view of the art since you were young?
Of course. When your are young you like to fight. As you grow, you look at fighting in a different way. You have a different point of view about physical confrontations. It is important to educate the students about this. Unfortunately, if a student wants to fight, there's really nothing you can do about it.

Are you a traditionalist?
I firmly believe that wing chun is something very logical. As long as it stays logical it doesn't matter what you call it or what you're actually doing. If it is logical, if it works, use it! Make the art your slave, and never allow the art be your master.

Why do you think wing chun is so popular around the world?
I think Bruce Lee contributed a lot to that! But if a martial art system is not logical, simple, and useful it will disappear. It's just a matter of time.

"Bruce was a good fighter, but not as good as movies have portrayed him-almost invincible."

Think about the many countries or political systems that don't exit anymore. If there is something lacking in meaning and purpose it will definitely fade away. Wing chun is growing all over the world-so that should tell you something.

When you teach in a different country, do you change your method?
I have to adapt my mentality to the country. Of course the Chinese customs are different from the American or European, but the wing chun system is taught the same. The approach can be different but the techniques are the same, and the philosophy as well. Anyone who learns martial arts must be combat-minded. If one learns martial arts' skills, but does not pay attention to fighting, then they are neglecting the essence to pursue trifles-since martial arts are not just physical exercises. To learn and to try skills are the two stages of martial arts training, and I think there's nothing wrong with that. One should be encouraged to test the skills as long the

Wing Chun Masters

"To learn and to try skills are the two stages of martial arts training, and I think there's nothing wrong with that."

purpose is to study and learn from others. But it is a pity that many people have distorted the meaning of the trials of skills, and take it as a way to show their power-or even to bully people around!

Do you feel that chi sao is an important part of wing chun?
Chi sao is very important in wing chun, but too much emphasis is placed on the idea of "sticking" to the hands-this causes the student to end up chasing the hands instead of punching and trapping. This mistake totally contradicts the wing chun basic principles. Wing chun theory is flawless if you can execute it perfectly. But a theory is just a theory. It means nothing if you can't put it to work. You might have a better fighting theory behind you system, but if your skill level is lower than your opponent's skill, you'll be easily defeated. All the theory in the world can't save you from losing.

Are you happy with the way wing chun is being taught?

Well, I have seen some instructors turn simple things into big mysteries, misleading their students. They not only deceive themselves but other innocent people, too. They'd do better teaching the students how to not make mistakes in real fighting.

Do you follow any particular diet?

If you have to fight in the street the kind of food you eat is not going to be that relevant so, I don't. But if you are a professional fighter or are you planning fighting in the ring, then the food will affect your energy and performance.

Do you have a martial arts philosophy?

There is an old Chinese saying that goes, "Courage first, strength second, and kung-fu third." To secure victory in a face-to-face fight with fist and kicks, one must be courageous. The courage comes from one's own self-cultivation and is one of the purposes of trials of skills. The second is strength and vigor. The kung-fu you see in real combat is only a few actions. What counts in real combat is determination, courage, and vigour. If you're superior in this aspects, then you can often knock down you opponent with two or three simple techniques. The prolonged fighting seen in martial arts movies is artificial. Bruce Lee was a master of kung-fu in his own right, but the kung-fu he actually mastered should not be confused with what you see in the movies. There are wing chun disciples whose achievements in martial arts are not even second to those of Bruce Lee. But they never made movies and got famous so no one knows them. Movie fans only know Bruce Lee because his movies are shown all over the world.

Do you think people respond well to your teaching methods?

I can only say that I try to share wing chun in an honest way. I teach in a logical manner because the art is very logical. I can't talk about what other people may do or say. I'm only responsible for my own acts.

LEUNG TING

The Soft Way

LEUNG TING STARTED HIS KUNG FU TRAINING UNDER THE GUIDANCE OF LEUNG SHEUNG, THE FIRST STUDENT OF GRANDMASTER YIP MAN IN HONG KONG. AFTER THE YEARS PASSED, LEUNG TING HAD A FALL-OUT WITH SIFU SHEUNG.

WHEN LEUNG TING COMMUNICATED TO HIS "UNCLE" SIFU KWOK KEUNG THAT HE WOULD LIKE TO BECOME A KUNG FU TEACHER BUT HIS TEACHER WON'T TEACH HIM THE ADVANCED PART OF THE SYSTEM, KWOK KEUNG DECIDED TO MENTION THIS TO YIP MAN WHO ALREADY HAD HEARD LEUNG TING'S NAME MENTIONED IN THE NEWSPAPERS BECAUSE LEUNG WAS THE FIRST PERSON WHO EVER ESTABLISHED A WING CHUN CLASS IN THE UNIVERSITY. GRANDMASTER PROMISED TO TEACH BOTH OF THEM AS "CLOSED-DOOR" STUDENTS AS SOON AS HE RECOVERED FROM A STOMACH OPERATION.

IN DECEMBER 1969, GRANDMASTER YIP MAN PASSED HIS CLASS AT THE "VING TSUN ATHLETIC ASSOCIATION" TO LEUNG TING. DUE TO POLITICS AT THE VTTA, LEUNG TING RESIGNED FROM HIS POSITION AS THE CHIEF INSTRUCTOR OF THE VTTA AND CHANGED THE NAME OF HIS METHOD TO "WING TSUN".

LEUNG TING GRADUATED FROM THE HONG KONG BAPTIST COLLEGE IN 1973 AND DEVOTED ALL OF HIS ENERGY TO DEVELOPING WING TSUN KUNG FU.

IN DECEMBER 1978, DR. LEUNG TING PUBLISHED HIS FIRST BOOK AND THE FIRST EDITION WAS SOLD OUT WITHIN FOUR MONTHS.

DR. LEUNG TING, IS THE PERMANENT PRESIDENT AND 10TH LEVEL MOC OF THE "INTERNATIONAL WING TSUN ASSOCIATION".

THE "INTERNATIONAL WING TSUN ASSOCIATION" HAS GROWN INTO A WORLD-WIDE KUNG FU ORGANIZATION WITH BRANCHES IN OVER 60 COUNTRIES AND IS REGARDED AS THE LARGEST PROFESSIONAL KUNG FU ORGANIZATION IN THE WORLD.

h ow was you training under g randmaster y ip Man?

My training under grandmaster Yip Man started when I already knew the basis and fundamentals of the Wing Chun method. When Grandmaster Yip Man accepted me as his "closed-door student" it was to teach me what we can call a more 'sophisticated' version of the art. He was at an advanced age and many of the applications that he taught and used in his young days were not effective for him anymore because of his age. He had modified the application of the Wing Chun method to use even less physical strength in the movements.

Wing Chun Masters

"Grandmaster Yip Man knew that what he was teaching at that stage was slightly different in application from what he taught in his early days."

how was the method that yip Man taught you?

Grandmaster Yip Man knew that what he was teaching at that stage was slightly different in application from what he taught in his early days. I don't think he tried to teach something totally different but his perception of the art was different because of his age. That's why I decided to use the term "Wing Tsun" instead of Wing Chun or Ving Tsun.

how different is your Wing Tsun method from Wing Chun or Ving Tsun?

Wing Tsun differs from other "Wing Chun" or "Ving Tsun" methods in that the main idea is not to memorize methods of reacting to any kind of attack. Wing Tsun is based on reaction and how to use a certain training to efficiently protect yourself from any kind of attack.

Do the empty hand forms directly relate to the Chi sao training?

Yes, we do have a series of cycles in Chi Sao but these cycles are only a way of organizing the material so the student knows exactly where it comes from and how these techniques belong to certain empty hand forms. Siu Lim Tao has its set of techniques for Chi Sao; Chum Kiu and Biu Jee too and finally the Muk Yan Chong too. So the material is broken down according to each one of the forms for a better comprehension from the students. Your ability to use these techniques will depend entirely on you and how you can actually use these in a practical application under various real circumstances.

What is the meaning of form training in Wing Tsun?

All the Wing Tsun forms are extremely important because they teach certain principles that are unique to each one of them. The first form, Siu Lim Tao I consider to be the 'essential' form because without it basically you can't progress. It contains the basis and the fundamental techniques

"Without Siu Lim Tao basically you can't go anywhere."

that you need to study Chi Sao and to get into the core of the system. Without Siu Lim Tao basically you can't go anywhere. As far as Chum Kiu I can say that 'bridges' some elements found in Siu Lim Tao with a more advanced approach in the practical application of the basic techniques. It also introduces the first elements of footwork and this fact alone alters the application of the 'centerline' theory.

Biu Jee introduces us to what can be called 'emergency' tools showing the student a series of technical resources extremely important in practical self-defense circumstances.

And the Wooden Dummy?

The Muk Yan Chong form teaches us a different set of maneuvers that are extremely effective in combat. There are a series of principles that are intrinsic only to the wooden dummy training and can be used in both Chi Sao and self-defense.

Wing Chun Masters

"Wing Tsun training should be used to build your confidence of dealing with a physical altercation."

Why doesn't Wing Tsun have competitions or tournaments?

Because Wing Tsun is not a sport. Wing Tsun is for fighting and real self-defense. A real fight differs from sport tournaments in that there are no rules, no weight divisions, no regulations, etc. A street fight is not fair. There are no judges. You don't try to win... you try to survive and use all the means in your hands to accomplish that.

When do you know when to fight and when to step back?

You should always avoid the fight. Do not look for it and try to avoid it at all cost. This is what I teach to my students. Sometimes, there are critical situations when there is no other way out and we need to fight. We need to fight when we are truly in danger in a situation where any other solution is not possible.

It is important that as true martial artists we strive to stay away from any physical confrontation that involves hurting any other human being.

I like to think of a Wing Tsun practitioner as a poisonous snake...if you are provoked you analyze the situation and if there is no true danger for you then you simply stay calm and back off, but if you see that you can't avoid the fight, then initiate the attack as fast as you can and try to defeat your aggressor powerfully, without giving him a second chance.

What are the philosophical teachings behind the study of Wing Tsun Kung Fu?

When you learn the art of Wing Tsun or any other martial art for that matter, you are learning fighting techniques but this is not a reason to bully others and to be arrogant about it. Wing Tsun training should be used to build your confidence of dealing with a physical altercation. It is this confidence that eventually will defeat the bullies.

I believe that a true traditional Chinese Kung Fu instructor should teach his students the true morality of martial arts and a sense of knightliness that should be felt in everything he does.

What is the best advice you can give when facing a self-defense situation?

Attack! When you feel the confrontation is inevitable, don't hesitate...attack! Another important principle is not to raise your leg for high kicking...which will put you in a difficult balance. Keep your balance, break the opponent's and finish the fight without giving any chance to the aggressor.

Are there any 'secret' techniques in Wing Tsun?

This is a question that many people around the world always ask. Let me simply say that there are no 'secret' techniques. The 'advanced' techniques are those we use in a real fight. There are no 'secret' moves or applications that will defeat any other technique. Simplicity is the highest level of sophistication. Basic techniques are the ones we should use in real fights...therefore these 'basic' techniques are the true secret of our training. Wing Tsun expertise is based on how you can put these basic and fundamental moves into a practical application under several different circumstances.

"There are no 'secret' moves or applications that will defeat any other technique. Simplicity is the highest level of sophistication."

you were talking about kicking, how does Wing Tsun use the kicking techniques?

Well, let me tell you that there are not many kicks in the Wing Tsun method. Basically we have three fundamental kicking principles that can be applied in relation with footwork, hand movements, etc. the main two concepts used in Wing Tsun when kicks are used are; the kick is always delivered when in close range and second; it is always used in combination with a hand movement which diverts the attention of the opponent and makes it harder to block or counter.

Wing Chun Masters

"Self-defense has nothing to do with a strength and conditioning program involving weights, running, stretching, etc."

Don't kick above the waist even of your ability allows it and make sure your foot travels straight and directly to the target without a chambering action as it can be seen in other martial arts systems.

What is the best method to counter the kicking techniques of other martial arts?

A Wing Tsun practitioner will close the gap and will powerfully attack the opponent's head, disturbing his balance and preventing any kicking action of actually taking place. It is interesting to note that usually people tend to back away from a good kicker when in reality what you have to do is just the opposite. You nullify the kicks by crashing and closing the distance not by stepping back from your opponent.

h ow much strength and physical conditioning is necessary for Wing Tsun training?

Many people these days enjoy the weight training and other kinds of physical conditioning. This is good but we must keep in mind that the kind of power used in Wing Tsun does not come from big muscles and that big muscles actually prevent the kind of 'energy' and 'power' that a good Wing Tsun punch must possess. Self-defense has nothing to do with a strength and conditioning program involving weights, running, stretching, etc. These are all good but you should focus on what is good for you and what is the main goal of your study in Wing Tsun Kung Fu.

g rappling has been one of the latest focuses of martial arts around the world, how does a Wing Tsun practitioner handle a grappling expert?

In Wing Tsun we don't look to grab or grapple with the opponent. The main idea is not to make your body 'hard' but keep it 'soft', re-borrowing the pulling force from the aggressor and hit back before the grappler can actually deliver his technique.

how do you deal with a multiple aggressor situation?

Some people recommend that you should find a wall and put your back against it. I truly think this is a very bad idea. You don't want to block your way out in any direction. I would recommend fighting with all your power until you can escape...find an open angle and run. Don't try to be a hero and defeat all of them.

What about armed attacks and against firearms?

These are two very different situations. When facing a knife or a gun the best solution is to run. Don't try to be a hero. Today we see many instructors trying to teach students techniques against knives and guns. Well, these techniques work perfect in a performance or demonstration but in real life the situation is very different. Don't risk your life against an armed aggressor just because you study Kung Fu. Accepting a meaningless fight like these when you can escape it means that you are a fool posing like a hero!

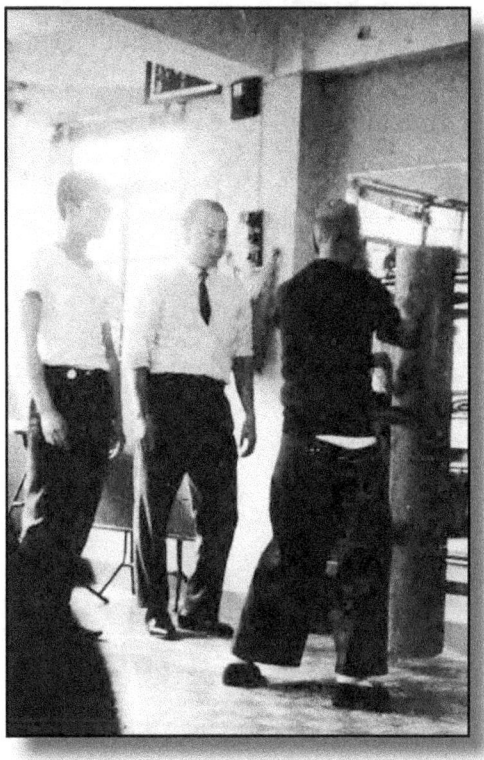

"Train hard but train hard under pressure. They are two different things. Pressure is the key factor that changes everything."

Any final advice?

Train hard but train hard under pressure. They are two different things. Pressure is the key factor that changes everything. Unfortunately, age inevitably diminishes our physical capabilities. Therefore when you are young use your body to train your mind and when you get older...use your mind to train your body.

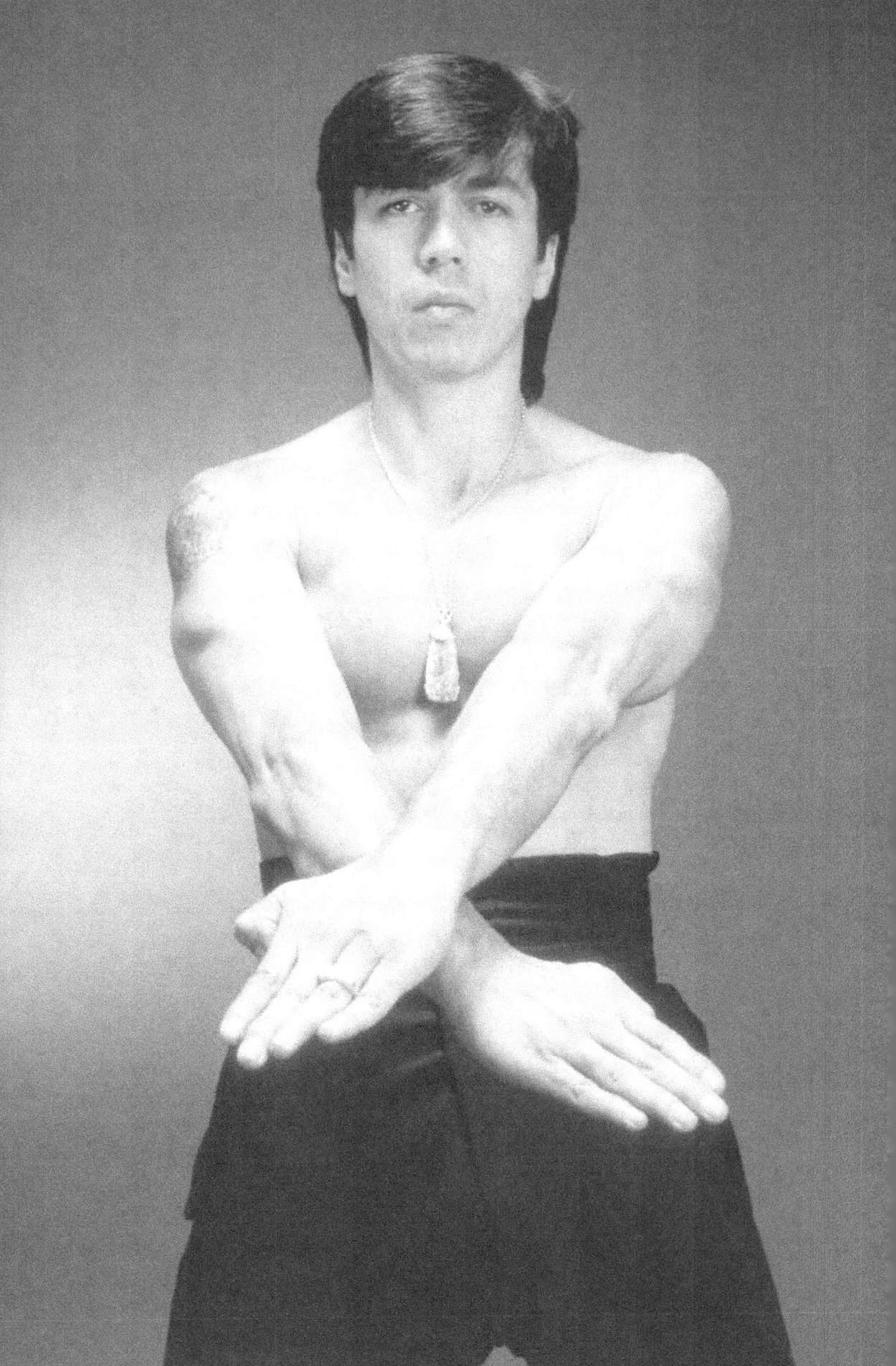

RANDY WILLIAMS

A Wing Chun Crusader

RANDY WILLIAMS IS ONE OF THE MOST PROLIFIC WING CHUN INSTRUCTORS IN THE WORLD. PPRECISION AND ACCURACY-IN EVERY TECHNIQUE HE PRACTICES AND IN EVERY BOOK AND VIDEO HE PRODUCES-ARE HIS SIGNATURE TRADEMARKS. HE IS ONE OF A DISTINGUISHED GROUP OF KUNG-FU MASTERS WHO HAVE BEEN ABLE TO ADAPT AND INTEGRATE MODERN COMBAT ELEMENTS INTO THEIR FIGHTING SYSTEMS WHILE PRESERVING THE TRADITIONAL INTENT AND FLAVOR OF THEIR ANCIENT ARTS. OVER THE PAST THREE DECADES, THOUSANDS OF STUDENTS HAVE LEARNED AND RECEIVED INSTRUCTION UNDER HIM. HIS INDELIBLE MARK ON THE WORLD OF KUNG-FU WILL ALWAYS BE REMEMBERED AND NEVER BE ERASED. WITH A HAPPY-GO-LUCKY ATTITUDE AND KEEN SENSE OF HUMOR, RANDY WILLIAMS HAS TRAVELED THE WORLD VISITING SCHOOLS IN EUROPE, AMERICA, AND ASIA MORE FREQUENTLY THAN MANY OTHER INSTRUCTORS TEACH CLASSES AT THEIR OWN SCHOOLS! RANDY WILLIAMS IS THE PERFECT EXAMPLE OF A TRADITIONAL KUNG-FU MAN FOR WHOM THE STRUGGLES OF THE PAST HAVE BECOME THE SUCCESS OF THE PRESENT.

h ow long have you been practicing the martial arts?

I have been training in martial arts for more than three decades. God, that makes me feel old! Although I enjoy all the martial arts, I have only trained in two systems-wing chun kung-fu and jeet kune do with Sifu Ted Wong.

Who was your first teacher?

Sifu George Yau Chu from Hong Kong. I met him when he walked by and stayed to watch while I was hitting and kicking a bag in my garage. He was my neighbor in LA Chinatown. Coincidentally, so was Sifu Ted Wong. Since I knew he was a member of Bruce Lee's College Street group, I used to beg him to teach me when I was a kid and I'd see him in the neighborhood, but he always refused until many years later. Years later, a friend who trained with him arranged for me to meet him at a private dinner when I was in my early thirties. I said, "Wong Sifu, it's an honor to meet you!" He replied, "What are you talking about? I've known you since you were a kid and you used to pester me to teach you."

What was your early training like?

My sifu was absolutely brutal when he trained me. It seemed like he

Wing Chun Masters

"My sifu was absolutely brutal when he trained me. It seemed like he actually spent time dreaming up new ways to make me quit."

actually spent time dreaming up new ways to make me quit. Like making me stay in yee jee keem yeung ma with my pelvis up and my knees one-fist's distance apart for extended periods. To ensure I didn't waiver, he made me hold my wallet between my knees. And believe me, in those days my wallet wasn't all that thick. When I dropped it, he'd kick me hard in the shins with the sharp inside edge of his shoe and make me start over. I had to endure this kind of torture regularly, but in the end I'm kind of glad he made me do it. To this day, I have a very solid stance and strong footwork, although I went home from many a lesson with bruised, bleeding shins in order to get them that way.

But my favorite war story involving my teacher had to do with jogging. Of course, all of us Bruce Lee fans have been told many times that Bruce considered jogging the "king of all exercises." So of course, I wondered why my own sifu wasn't doing any jogging. Since I jogged regularly, I must have asked him dozens of times why he didn't, and the last straw was when I asked him just before practice at his house. He finally said something like, "OK, Boy" he always called me "Boy," never by my name-since you think jogging so great, you gone take a nice big jog!" He then sent me out to his back yard to pick up two large bricks. He told me to take off my shirt and shoes, and then to hold one brick gripped in the fingers of each hand. He marched me out into his front yard and pointed out some road cones way in the distance and told me to run all the way there and back, and not to stop because he'd be watching. I said, "You've got to be kidding, right?" But he replied that he was dead serious and to "get the hell going." So off I took, barefoot, without a shirt, carrying bricks, running down the street in a drizzle with all the passers-by pointing and laughing at me. By the time I rounded the cones, I was actually whimpering and considered stopping, but a quick glance back at the house revealed the old sifu watching me intently, perhaps with the hint of a smile. So I kept on going.

When I got somewhat near the house, I saw him run inside and shut the door. I made it to the front porch and knocked, but there was no answer for a while. So I stood there, shirtless and barefoot, shivering, hands scraped up and permanently paralyzed into claws. But he finally came to the door, opened it and chucked a pitcher full of ice cold water on me. Then he ordered me to get into the garage and practice siu leem tau on the cold cement floor, which I did for what seemed like hours. Needless to say, point taken, Sifu.

Were you a natural at martial arts?
No, I had to work very hard to develop certain skills, and still do. Plus, I had a language barrier to overcome. My Sifu wasn't going to learn English anytime soon, so he made me learn at least some basic Chinese before he'd even consider taking me on as a student. Again, I'm very glad he made me do that as my ability to speak Chinese has helped me in my business life as well. I overcame my initial awkwardness through sheer stubbornness and repetition training-thousands upon thousands of punches, blocks, kicks and footwork. I still do a siu leem tau or chum kiu, a 45-minute footwork pattern, and a thousand kicks and punches at least once a week to this day. Plus a lot more other drills and exercises since I am now back to full-time teaching and training.

how has your personal martial arts changed over the years?
I have freely used my own common sense and experience to help me derive certain applications and principles of the system that are not as obvious as others, and to use these to help me deal with modern combat situations not encountered and therefore not considered by the founders of the system. As in all other forms of science and technology, I believe that wing chun must move forward. The inventors of the system never had to consider combat against the many modern and non-Chinese arts that a fighter may encounter today, such as Thai boxing, shootfighting, Brazilian jiu-jitsu and sambo just to name but a few. In the past, certain acknowledged ancestors made additions and improvements to the system, and it is my belief that the system will have to be continually modified and

upgraded in order to keep pace with today's ever-changing combat technology.

When you see an effective technique, you can't be afraid to work backwards and to break it down and see why it works-then try to use movements from your own style to create a similar application. I believe you owe it to yourself to be the most effective fighting machine you can. Blindly ignoring the beauty of an effective technique simply because you were never shown it as a "classical" example of the principles of your style is cheating yourself and your style. An old proverb of wing chun says that its techniques are "limitless in their application." That means if you can think of it and it works, it's an application. So what if you didn't think of it first? You didn't think of any of the rest of it first either. And no one owns a style of martial arts they didn't create. Thus, no one can tell you that you can't use the movements of your style in any given way.

With all the technical changes during the last 30 years, do you think there are still pure systems?

Whether we want to believe it or not, almost all systems are modified through the years, even if inadvertently. It can be compared to learning your mother language from parents-you can't help but add your own personal flavor to the language when you speak it. Your voice, the neighborhood you grew up in, the current slang, and other factors creep into your speech patterns. Although your father may have taught you to speak, I still know it's you on the phone when you call and not your father. I believe martial arts is the same. Your expression of the style will be somehow different than your teacher or fellow students regardless of how closely you follow the traditional patterns. If you put bags over ten of my top students' heads, I could still almost immediately tell you which one was Wayne, which was Bert, and which was Jerry simply by watching them move, although I taught them all the same. So in my opinion, nearly every major system is somehow flavored by its various instructors through time, but the essence will remain pure in many cases.

Do you feel that the internet has helped or hurt the martial arts?

Both-it has obviously made martial arts' information much more accessible to the public. When I was beginning, it was very difficult to find anything about wing chun in print. There were few books in English and videos weren't born yet. But on the downside, I think the Internet chat rooms have also given a large number of armchair experts a wide-reaching medium for disrespectful and often libelous criticism and character assassination without having to back up their words. They remain hidden behind their computer screens and user names. Some of my more scrappy students contact many of those people asking for goang sau matches to give them a chance to prove their superior skills, but not surprisingly not a single one of them has ever risen to the challenge. They typically hide behind excuses like, "I'm not famous, so I don't have to be tough," or "A fight like that would be illegal." More common is the, "I'll call the police if you come anywhere near me." Or my favorite-used a lot by pseudo wing chun computer guys-"I'll call your ISP and have your service discontinued if you threaten me." As one of my students so aptly puts it, "Don't let your mouth write checks your butt can't cash!"

The real martial artists are out there training and getting the job done, not just constantly chatting about it on the Net. And if the real guys have a beef with you, you'll know about it, not read about it.

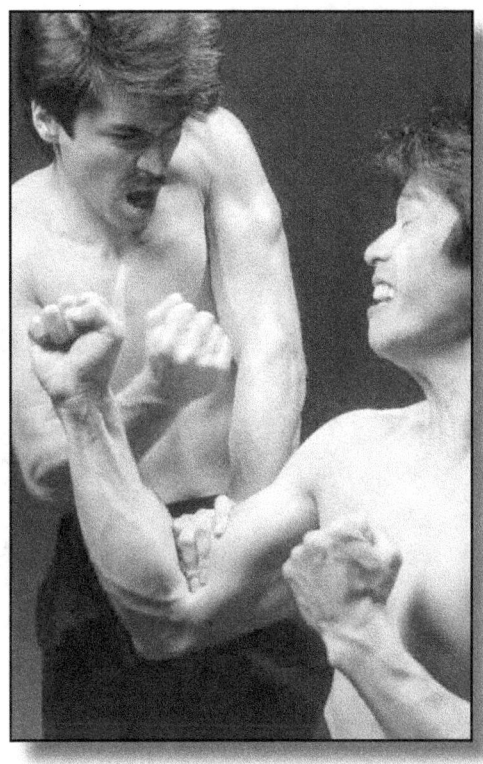

"I have freely used my own common sense and experience to help me derive certain applications and principles of the system."

Do you think different schools or styles of the same method are important?

Yes-after all, why would everyone want to do everything the same? There must be differing slants on each art, and students will tend to gravitate towards the approach that suits them the best. For example, certain instructors place more emphasis on actual combat applications, while others stress the more spiritual or artistic aspects of a system. A potential student can then decide which extreme or middle ground is more applicable to their own situation and desires.

What is your opinion of sport competitions like kickboxing, and fighting events such as the ultimate Fighting Championship?

I think they have brought a much-needed element of reality to the martial arts. In the '70s, you could strike a karate pose and frighten off a number of potential opponents who thought that just because you were trained

"The real martial artists are out there training and getting the job done, not just constantly chatting about it on the Net."

in a martial art you were a deadly fighter. Nowadays, the general public is much more sophisticated in regards to martial arts and is very aware of what works and what doesn't. And the UFC has also forced the martial arts world to take a closer look at what is actually effective in combat. For example, the overall importance of ground fighting skills has been almost universally acknowledged and is now a part of the training regimen of nearly all true combat-minded martial artists.

Do you think that kung-fu in the West has caught up with the East?

It depends on your context. If you mean pure fighting skill, then I would have to say that it is fairly safe to say that Westerners continue to dominate nearly every form of combative competition-be it fencing, boxing, wrestling or MMA fighting. Of course, there have always been, and will always be, many individual exceptions to this. But if you are talking about pure skill in terms of deep-rooted knowledge of concepts and principles, it would be difficult to give a blanket answer. The true skill levels of the originators of the many various styles of martial arts remains largely unknown. For that matter, the same is true of many modern-day masters as well.

Martial arts are often referred to as a sport. Do you agree with this definition?

Not in general, but certainly as the term pertains to various forms of competition, from forms to point fighting to NHB. In fact, the word "art" as part of the term would seem to discern it from sport. I think it would be better to say that sport is only a small facet of the full spectrum of meaning covered by the term "martial arts."

Do you feel that you still have further to go in your studies?

Always-although I'm not sure I will get there. At this point, after so many years of training, I have to struggle to maintain the skill level I have already attained. I constantly review all of my old notes from years gone by and I never fail to pick up on some concept, technique, or drill that I hadn't thought of for decades. The older and more senile I get, the more sense the statement, "I've forgotten more about wing chun than you'll ever learn," makes to me.

Do you think it helps kung-fu practitioners to train with weapons?

Yes, the weight and additional snap of the weapon can help develop empty-hand power. But having said that, I do feel that there are much more efficient methods available today if physical training is the objective-even as it relates to the specific motions of kung-fu.

"The true skill levels of the originators of the many various styles of martial arts remains largely unknown."

Do you think the practitioner's personal training should be different than his teaching schedule as an instructor?

It has to be. Teaching beginning and intermediate level students will keep his basics sharp, but an instructor must also focus on his own personal maintenance and development of advanced techniques, as well as focusing on his own personal weaknesses-which aren't necessarily the most important areas for his students to work on. For example, if the teacher needs work on his stop-kick skills, it would be better for him to focus on that aspect in his own personal regimen, rather than use to large a portion of valuable class time that would be better spent on those things needed by a group that's not ready for such things.

Do you have any general advice you would care to pass on?

Besides the obvious "train hard," "use your knowledge for the right reasons," "respect your elders and superiors in the art," and the old favorite "wax on, wax off," I may have some tips to offer. In your training, try to keep mind, body and spirit in balance. It is easy to train the body with forms, drills, sparring, weight training, et cetera. The mind is a little harder to train, though. But reading, watching videos, learning about the culture and language of the country your art comes from are all ways of improving mental strength.

But to train the spirit is even a much more intricate process. Each person is different, and must strive to find the things that make them stronger spiritually. Some people find it in religion, others in charity work. But whatever it is that you need to do to make yourself feel "clean" and "deserving" will also serve to strengthen your spirit. Some people work extra hard on only the physical aspects, like bodybuilding. Others can literally be rocket scientists, but are extremely out of shape. A religious figure may be both spiritually and mentally strong, but lacking in physical fitness. But a true martial artist should strive to be strong in all three arenas to be complete. In this way, when confronted by an opponent, you will have the strength to deliver effective techniques, the knowledge to make them succeed, and the self-worth to say, "Dammit, I deserve my place on earth as much as you do. I'm not gonna let you harm me."

I would also advise a martial arts instructor to remain a good student for his entire life. If you are a meticulous note-taker and have a great memory, coupled with actually going home and diligently training what you have learned, seen and heard, it is possible to improve your skills even without constant supervision from an instructor. You can even surpass the skills of those that live in the same city with him, but that don't have the same learning potential and drive that you have. For example, I have students in Italy, Germany, Singapore, and many other places whose skill levels are higher than those local students who train with me much more regularly but who aren't as driven.

Lastly, I would advise a student to pick his style and teacher with the utmost care and attention. You must weigh certain factors and decide which are the most important to you. Does this art appeal to me? Will I practice it daily? Is the school in a convenient location? Do I have the time to dedicate? Do I have potential in the art? Am I looking for self-defense, sport, spirituality or all of the above? Is the teacher someone I want to follow? You must also be careful of student/teacher relationships. In my experience, jealousy can unfortunately play a part in driving a rift between student and teacher. At some point, every bird must leave the nest, but it would be nice to pick a teacher who won't push you out and then try to eat you.

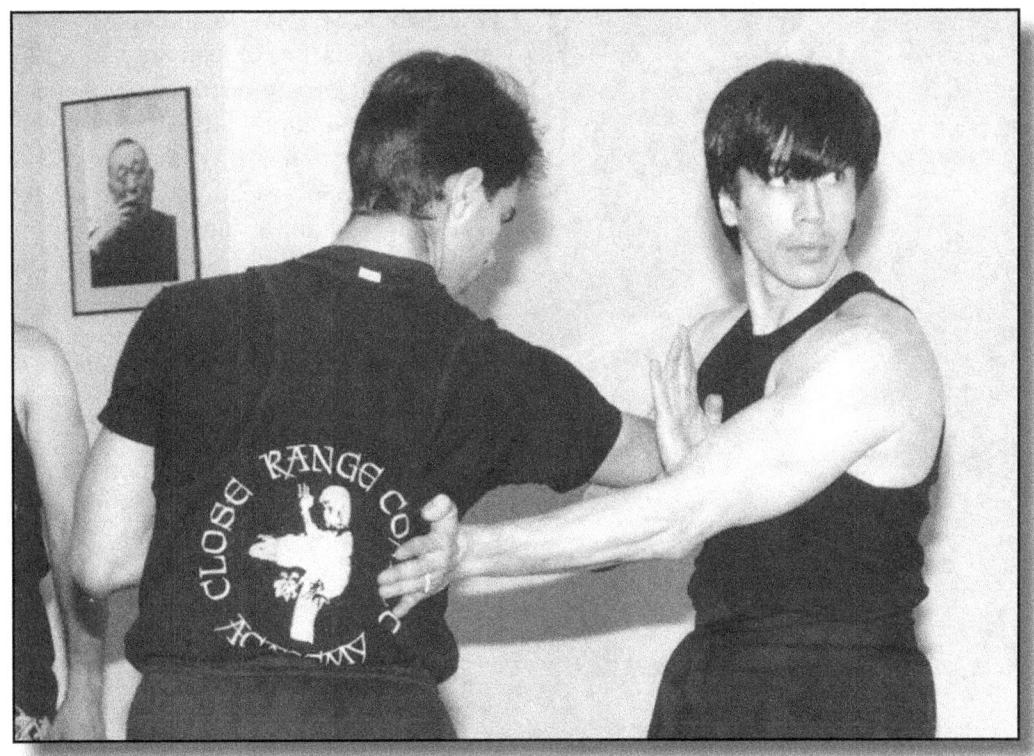

"The older and more senile I get, the more sense the statement, "I've forgotten more about wing chun than you'll ever learn," makes to me."

What do you consider to be the major changes in your art since you began your training?

Widespread availability, not only of more schools and more styles, but also more information available through books, videos, and the Internet. I also feel that competition between many different schools and instructors, as well as MMA-type competition, has raised the bar in terms of quality.

Who would you like to have trained with?

Yip Man, Wong Shun Leung, Moy Yat, and of course, Bruce Lee-like everyone else out there. There is also one guy that I did train with-and put my heart and soul into paying tribute to. But since he now disavows having taught me, I guess I'd have to include him on my list, too. You may be able to figure out who it is, but I can't tell you because it'll just wind him up (laughs).

Wing Chun Masters

"At some point, every bird must leave the nest, but it would be nice to pick a teacher who won't push you out and then try to eat you."

What would you say to someone who is interested in starting to learn martial arts?

If I said it promoted decency, fitness, high moral standards and character, that would imply that I was an example of those virtues. So instead, I would just tell them that it's a lot of fun and will expose you to the most interesting people and places you will ever know.

What keeps you motivated after all these years?

Great students who are also my best friends and practically my extended family. The fact that they want to learn what I have worked so many years to develop makes me want to always be able to satisfy their drive to achieve. So I have to stay at the top of my game in order to live up to their hopes and expectations.

Do you think it is necessary to engage in free-fighting to achieve good fighting skills for the street?

Yes, at some point in your life. At least to experience what it is to hit and to be hit, and to appreciate the importance of fitness and conditioning, as well as crucial elements of distance and timing in actual combat. But I have to qualify that statement by saying that I personally train in the martial arts at least in part not to be beaten up. So it doesn't make a lot of sense to me to purposely expose myself constantly to damaging punches and kicks to the head and body. If my training had included being hit solidly in the head at least once a day, in the course of 30 years of training I would have suffered a whopping 10,950 punches in the head-considerably more damaging blows than I might have suffered not knowing a thing about martial arts and losing even a hundred street-fights in which my opponent had hit me 20 times per fight. The first and foremost purpose of kung-fu is self defense. That doesn't just mean protecting yourself against bullies who want to beat you up, it also involves defending yourself by using your head in your training to avoid injury when you can. This inherent self-preservation is why there are so many revered masters of the martial arts who are still actively training and teaching well into their 70's and 80's but very few boxers can make a similar claim. Muhammad Ali, arguably the best boxer of all time is now unfortunately suffering the ill effects of just such brutal training and competition.

What is your opinion about mixing martial arts styles?

Cross-training has already proven to improve a fighter's effectiveness in a competitive environment. But in terms of keeping an art systematic and preserving its original essence, there have to be dinosaurs like myself who keep the arts separate and to some degree pure and original. Take your pick.

Do you have a particularly memorable experience that inspired you to train?

I have a number, but an experience I had at the San Francisco school of white crane system Sifu Quentin Fong probably had the most impact on me and sticks with me the most. Fong Sifu was on the cover of the very first Inside Kung-Fu magazine I ever read, and to me, he embodied everything that kung-fu was supposed to be. So I convinced my mom to let me take a bus trip all alone from LA to San Francisco to visit his school.

"The first and foremost purpose of kung-fu is self-defense."

After the long bus trip up, I found his school just off the cable car route. When I knocked, a couple of the students who came to the door were really mean to me and wouldn't let me in. But since my bus wasn't leaving until later that night, I decided to sit outside and wait. When Fong Sifu showed up later, he asked me where I was from and why I was sitting outside instead of inside watching the class. When I explained, he took me inside and asked, "Which one of these guys was it? Was it him? What about this one?" He then scolded the guys and made them stand in very low stances until their legs shook. Then he had them clamp quarters between the handles of those springy hand-gripper things and made them throw hundreds of punches, arms fully extended with the grippers held tightly closed so as not to drop the quarters. When they were sufficiently humbled, he had the entire group demonstrate forms for me-empty hand, weapons, and even one with a sawhorse-like work bench.

Afterwards, he took me into his office and picked out a nice T-shirt with a picture of a crane on it and the Chinese characters for white crane kung-fu written in red across the chest, which he gave to me. Then he insisted on driving me back to the bus station and waiting for me to get on before he left, because it was on a bad part of Market Street. He waved goodbye as he drove off. I still have that shirt and the memories of that day, many years ago. Had he not taken the time and effort to treat me with such kindness, I might have lost my passion for kung-fu long ago.

After all your years of training, what does the practice of kung-fu mean to you?

It's a way of unifying mind, body and spirit. A way of building strength, confidence and lifelong relationships. A path to attaining the courage to stand up and fight when it's absolutely necessary, and the courage not to when it isn't, without fear of being called a coward. A constant gauge by which to measure your personal progress and growth. A quest for knowledge. Tapping into the mystique of Asia and its culture. Pride in your students' development and achievements, and pride in passing the art down to another. It's a doorway to countless adventures and journeys around the world. An opportunity to see the world, to meet new people, and to beat them up (laughs). No, seriously, it's all of the above wrapped up into one, plus more that can't be easily put into words.

What are the most important qualities of a successful martial artist?

That depends on what you consider successful. If you mean skillful, I think it's important to set a goal and remain focused. I have always known from a very young age what I wanted to do and be in the martial arts, and I stayed focused on that. So I would advise you to put yourself into a situation conducive to the success you're after. If you want to be an actor, move to Hollywood. In martial arts, it is also very important that you find the right teacher. Then, above all, self-discipline is the most important quality. A martial artist cannot afford to be lazy. To be a good student, and eventually a good teacher, takes many, many hours of hard work and many gallons of sweat.

I have always felt that having a good sense of humor can help you rise to the top of any field, not just kung-fu. In my opinion, you need to have the ability to not take yourself too seriously. I learned something about humility from Sifu Quentin Fong, and I try to follow his example by taking the time to answer every letter, phone call or e-mail I receive, and to treat everyone who contacts me with questions about wing chun with respect and friendliness.

If success for you means commercial success, then I would advise you to put out a good product, be it instruction, books, videos or magazine articles. I can tell you from experience that you will have to look at that article and those photos for the rest of your life, so you better do the best you possibly can, or you'll regret it for many years to come. And although I'm not sure it helps all that much commercially, at least in the short term, you have to be able to guide a student in what he needs-not necessarily what he wants. You must demand from them almost as much as you demand of yourself; this will lead to quality, not quantity.

"There have to be dinosaurs like myself who keep the arts separate and to some degree pure and original."

how do you feel about supplemental physical training?

I am a strong believer in weight training. But you have to be careful how you use weights. It is very possible to train with weights and to actually increase your speed. It may slow you down if you aren't training right for the sport you're in, but I find that most of the guys who say it'll slow you down aren't that fast or strong to begin with (laughs). My rationale is this-if two guys are the same size and skill level, the stronger and fitter one will win nine times out of ten, so it just makes sense to be the strongest and fittest you can be, on top of whatever skill level you are able to achieve. I also believe in jogging.

Why do a lot of students fall away after two or three years of training?

Kung-fu is not as easy to learn as many people might think, and not everyone has the intestinal fortitude to put in the hours of sweat required to achieve a high level of skill. They often come in thinking it'll be like "The Matrix" and quit when they realize they aren't going to be Jet Li anytime soon.

have there been times when you felt fear in your training?

Of course. My first instructor inspired all kinds of fear in me. His teaching methods could be brutal at times, with the result of a missed block being a black eye, a lump on the head and/or a fat lip. And I already told you about his propensity for shin kicking. And there's always fear before a real fight. Of course, you can use that fear and channel it into faster, more powerful techniques. But it never goes away completely, and maybe that's good.

how important is lineage in a martial artist's credentials?

My own view of what is important in wing chun can at times be very different from many other traditional kung-fu instructors. Although I certainly appreciate and respect the history of wing chun and the importance of its lineage as handed down from generation to generation, I am personally more concerned with the more tangible aspects such as skill, knowledge and performance. In other words, I respect my elders and seniors in the system, but I do not necessarily believe that when someone began their study or with whom they studied is the primary criteria for their ranking or status in a system.

Instead, I look at the person's skill level, ability to explain their system in detail and-most importantly-their ability to perform. In other words, I take a more practical approach-almost an American sports attitude. For example, if one looks at the game of football, most fans probably do not care who taught Jerry Rice to catch a football, that he may not know the entire history of football, or that he may not have a genealogy of all of the players which passed it down to him from the founders of the game. What is important to the fans is that he is the best wide receiver of all time. He may have learned from his father, or more likely from just getting out there and playing the game. But above all, he got out there and did the job, head and shoulders above the rest. That is what makes him an all-time great.

It is my belief that wing chun in the modern world has become much the same, and rightfully so. With the abundance of instructional materials available today, virtually anyone with an earnest desire to learn wing chun can do so with relative ease. Personally, I am more interested in watching a player who can do his job with excellence rather than watching a player whose coach, father or grandfather was a star player, but who may himself not be exceptional. Similarly, I respect those that can actually "get out there and do it" much more than those who just talk about it. I feel that martial arts is one of the few fields where many of us are graded by whom

"I am a strong believer in weight training. But you have to be careful how you use weights."

we have trained with, instead of what we have achieved, published or produced.

What are your thoughts on the future of the martial arts?
I believe that martial arts will always move forward with the times, as they must. As in all other forms of science and technology, I believe that wing chun and martial arts in general must move ahead, adapting and improving to keep pace with the rest of the world. After all, would you want to go to a doctor from 300 years ago, from the present, or from 300 years into the future?

LIN XIANG FUK

Hek Ki Boen Wing Chun

KENNETH LIN XIANG FUK, FOUNDER OF THE OFFICIAL "SHAOLIN HEK KI BOEN ASSOCIATION," IS AN INTERNATIONALLY RECOGNIZED GRANDMASTER IN THIS RARE LINEAGE OF WING CHUN. THROUGH HIS EFFORTS, SINCERE PRACTITIONERS ON FOUR CONTINENTS HAVE HAD THE OPPORTUNITY TO BENEFIT FROM THIS UNIQUE SYSTEM. TO SAFEGUARD THE INTEGRITY OF THIS SPECIALIZED INFORMATION, SIFU LIN ESTABLISHED THE ASSOCIATION TO TRAIN, CERTIFY, AND LICENSE PROFESSIONAL MARTIAL ARTS INSTRUCTORS WORLDWIDE, WHO WISH TO BE A PART OF CARRYING THIS INFORMATION INTO THE FUTURE BY PASSING ON THIS LINEAGE. ONE OF THE FASTEST-GROWING SYSTEMS IN THE WORLD, HKB HAS EXPANDED INTO TWELVE COUNTRIES IN TWO YEARS, AND NOW HAS CERTIFIED INSTRUCTORS IN NORTH AND SOUTH AMERICA, ASIA AND EUROPE.

SIFU LIN NOT ONLY WORKS CONTINUALLY TO PRESERVE AND PROMOTE HIS ART, BUT ALSO TO ADVANCE IT, BY INTRODUCING NEW INNOVATIVE APPROACHES TO TRAINING METHODOLOGY. HIS DIRECT, HUMOROUS, ENGAGING TEACHING STYLE HAS PARTICIPANTS – FROM BEGINNER TO ADVANCED – SMILING, LEARNING AND TRAINING HARDER THAN THEY EVER THOUGHT POSSIBLE. HE IS AN APPROACHABLE INSTRUCTOR, FULL OF EXCITEMENT AND JOY, AS HE SHARES THIS ANCIENT TREASURE WITH THE WORLD.

how long have you been practicing the Martial Arts and who were your first teachers?

I have been practicing the Hek Ki Boen system for more than three decades. My first Sifu, who I actually still learn from today, is Senior Grandmaster The Kang Hay. But over the years I also learned from several other seniors of the HKB family in Indonesia.

how many styles of Kung Fu or other methods have you trained in?

As a teenager, I went around and experienced several Kung Fu systems like Tai zu, Hsing Yi to broaden my horizons, as I was, and still am, a real Kung Fu fanatic.

What are the main principles intrinsic to the three forms? Do they interrelate with each other?

Actually, in our family system, these three forms are not necessarily the core forms. We have several others. But to answer your question, Siu Lim

Wing Chun Masters

"Actually, in our family system, these three forms are not necessarily the core forms."

Tao (known as "Siauw Lim Do" in HKB) is an introduction to the ABCs of the system. Chum Kiu (known as "Tim Kiao" in HKB) is to understand the wheel bearing body. Bil Jee (known as "Piao Ki" in HKB) is to acquire the skill of adapting and changing in a combat situation.

Would you tell us some interesting stories of your early days in Kung Fu?

As a boy, even as young as six years old, I had a passion to study Martial Arts. My parents never approved of it. I used to save all of my snack money from my parents, and spend it on Martial Arts books. When I was ten years old, my dad took me to my first Sifu and asked him to accept me as his disciple. That was one of the happiest moments of my life! Soon afterward, I discovered that the exercises were very familiar. The same exercises I had been doing as punishment, whenever my dad had to discipline me, were actually from Hek Ki Boen Eng Chun.

Can you tell us about the lineage and history of the hek Ki Boen Eng Chun (Black Flag Wing Chun)?

Hek Ki Boen Eng Chun came from the Southern Shaolin, out of the Eng Chun Dim Hall (also known as the Weng Chun Dim) and passed down to the Black Flag Lodge of Hung Men (Secret Society) in Fukien Province. Generations later, the Chief Instructor of Black Flag traveled to Indonesia (c. 1907) and passed this treasure down to my Grandmaster, Kwee King Yang, then to My Sifu(s), and finally to me.

Were you a 'natural' at Kung Fu? Did the movements come easily to you?

No, not at all. When I first started to learn, I felt most of my Kung Fu brothers were much more talented in every way. During my early years, my training was very painful as none of my Kung Fu brothers had any mercy, especially the one who was the most senior. Because of that, I was training even harder. I spent most of my time at my Sifu's Bukoan. I would be there right after school during the week, and weekends would be whole days of extreme training.

After a short period of time, my skills dramatically improved. After that experience, I really believe that there's no such thing as talent. Talent is not something you are born with, but it is about how much experience you have. How much time and effort you put in. The sky is not even the limit. Everybody can train as hard as they want, to progress their skill as high as they possibly can. It's a lifelong journey. In the end, I finally understand the real meaning of Kung Fu, which is hard work! So real Kung Fu means real hard work. No hard work means not real Kung Fu.

ho w has your personal Kung Fu developed over the years?

For me, in the beginning, it was combat training and strategy. But over the years, Kung Fu had become a way of life. It exists in every aspect of life. Kung Fu is about achievement with hard work. This should also cover your personal life, your family as well as your career. In Eng Chun training, we focus a lot in becoming empty (nonattached) and therefore adaptable to every situation. This also applies to life, even your career/work.

"Kung Fu is about achievement with hard work."

What are the most important points in your teaching methods? And what are the most important qualities for a student to become proficient in the hek Ki Boen Eng Chun (Blac k Flag Wing Chun) system?

Important points in my teaching methods: humbleness (less ego), honesty, genuine compassion, personal attention to detail toward each student individually, a family-like relationship, maturity, clear and open communication, and recognition given for achievement. Important qualities for students to become proficient: a willingness to empty their cup (have an open mind), hard work, ego control, character/behavior and compassion.

Wing Chun Masters

"Kung Fu is an art that has many different varieties. It's important to find out what fits you best."

With all the technical changes during the last 30 years, do you think there are still "pure" styles of Kung Fu?

The way I see it, there are changes in the areas of training intensity and consistency. Compare today's Martial Arts, where many people may do it more as a hobby, to the intensity of the past, during revolution and in secret societies. In the past, Martial Arts were trained for survival in combat situations. In HKB, we aim for maximum efficiency. Pure or not pure, who knows. None of us lived 300 years ago. Unless there's a time machine, history is just history depending upon which side of the story is being told. What's more important is the quality of the system and the training, and how it can benefit us in our life, even when we become old.

Do you think different 'styles' are truly important to the art of Kung Fu?

Kung Fu is an art that has many different varieties. It's important to find out what fits you best. The style is the person. With all of this variety, it is our collective responsibility to work together to promote Chinese Martial Arts as an essential piece of Chinese culture, without trying to "one-up" one another.

What is your opinion of full contact Kung Fu tournaments?
If this is the person's goal, then he or she should go for it. People can do Martial Arts for many different reasons. Their motivation may be improved health and fitness. Or their goal might be to excel in sports or tournaments. They might study Martial Arts for combat or self-defense. And some study it as a hobby, or enjoy it as entertainment.

h ow different from other Kung Fu styles do you see the principles and concepts of h ek Ki Boen Eng Chun (Black Flag Wing Chun)?
The Hek Ki Boen Eng Chun System focuses on "detachment" as the main goal, through occupying the time, becoming the space, and explosive energy. I am not qualified to speak on other styles or systems.

Do you think that Kung Fu in the West has 'caught up' with the technical level in China?
It depends on who is doing what. Some are and some are not. It really comes down to personal achievement.

Do you feel that there are any fundamental differences in approach or physical capabilities of Chinese practitioners in comparison to European or American practitioners?
There are some similarities as well as differences. It depends on who is doing what. Human is human. People all have unique preferences, character, thinking, motivation and understanding. It really depends on the person. In Shaolin, the method is very important, like the finger pointing to the moon.

Kung Fu nowadays is often referred to as a sport (Wushu). Would you agree with this definition?
Wushu – Wu means Martial, and Shu means Art – so this is technically the correct term to represent Chinese Martial Arts from a language approach. However, the general view of Wushu is more the Chinese government-propagated gymnastic version of Chinese Martial Arts. Chinese Martial Arts in the past were known as Chuan Fa (Fist Method), Kun Tao (Way of fist), Kok Sut (Country Art). In most southern provinces of China as well as Southeast Asia, Chinese Martial Art is more known as Kun Tao

Wing Chun Masters

"Human is human. People all have unique preferences, character, thinking, motivation and understanding."

(Kuen To) "Way of fist." The term "Kung Fu" was popularized around the 1970s in the Bruce Lee era.

Do you feel that you still have further to go in your studies of the art of h KB Wing Chun?

Yes. The moment you think you achieve the top level, that's the time you stop progressing. I don't want to stop at any point. Even seven life incarnations would still not be enough to finish the whole learning when Kung Fu has become your way of life, because Hek Ki Boen Eng Chun is deep and vast. It covers every aspect in the universe.

h ow do you see Eng Chun (Black Flag Wing Chun) Kung Fu in the world at the present time?

HKB is currently growing very quickly. This year, HKB has spread into twelve countries on four continents. My main priority right now is to nurture and identify Instructors "seed" who have the capacity to become leaders representing HKB in the near future, as we make HKB available to people around the world.

Although the inquiries keep increasing, we always keep the door open for the right talented leaders, with the right mindset, at the right time, who meet the criteria we are looking for: Martial Artists who can identify and who want to preserve this treasure, without mixing it or chopping it into pieces.

HKB Eng Chun. It's a rare lineage of Wing Chun that has recently come out to the public which has been classified by the VTM (Ving Tsun Museum) as Wing Chun from the secret society era. Currently, there has been great demand and interest in HKB Eng Chun worldwide. It has sparked the interest of many Sifus and instructors from Wing Chun and other styles to come to us and discover it themselves. Many who have been exposed to our System have become excited and happy with what they have experienced and have converted to HKB Eng Chun.

Does the weaponry aspect of Wing Chun (long pole and butterfly knives) enhance the student's empty hands ability or are those two completely non-related skills?

The weaponry skills are definitely related to the empty hand skill. In HKB, there are Sang To (Double Butterfly sword) and Medium length pole (Not long pole, but eyebrow height). These two weapons are nothing more than extensions of the hands. One must be proficient in empty hand first; otherwise, their "intent" and energy can never reach the tip of the weapon.

how does the hek Ki Boen Eng Chun system differ from other Kung Fu methods when applying the techniques in a self-defense situation?

HKB Eng Chun focuses on maximum efficiency. In a real situation, it will give a smaller opponent an advantage in dealing with a larger and faster aggressor. This is due to the efficiency of time usage, space and energy effort based on HKB Formula.

"The moment you think you achieve the top level, that's the time you stop progressing."

When teaching the art of Kung Fu – what is the most important element; self-defense, health or tradition?

Self-defense, health, and tradition are important elements in HKB Eng Chun, among other things. As a teacher, we must bear the responsibility to pass the system as it is without holding anything back to ensure the preservation to future generation. Sometimes, a student may have a personal preference based on their goal in studying Martial Arts. But as a teacher, we must set aside our preferences and focus on spreading, advancing, and preserving the System for future generations.

Forms and chi sao, what's the proper ratio in training?

Actually, in our family system, Forms and Chi sao are not necessarily the only/main focuses. There are several others as well. This includes Form, Niam Jiu (Chi Sao), Kiao Jiu (Bridging Hand), Skill Challenge (Sparring), Self-defense, Solo Drills, Reaction Drill, Footwork training, stances training and other supplemental training. Each of these training elements and areas bring about many benefits. In HKB, we must practice everything with consistency.

Do you have any general advice you would care to pass on to Martial Arts practitioners in general?

Yes. Consistency of hard work training will guarantee results. Intensity often brings failure. Be aware of your talents; it's a good thing but could easily bring laziness.

It is our collective responsibility to work together to promote, spread and preserve the system for future generations without trying to one-up each other, or wasting time trying to prove which lineage is better, older, more original, etc. We teach, we learn, and we promote traditional Chinese Martial Arts. We are all one big Kung Fu family on four seas and six continents.

some people think going to h ong Kong, China, or Taiwan to train is highly necessary; do you share this point of view?

It's very important to choose the right qualified teacher who is willing to teach with his or her whole heart. But they can be anywhere, not just Hong Kong and China or Taiwan. In fact, there was a big wave of immigrants leaving China in the past due to communism, and among them were many Kung Fu Masters. But this doesn't mean there are none left in China. A good teacher can be anywhere. It depends on their skill, teaching skill and quality of teaching, commitment to the art, and personal motivation behind it. It has nothing to do with their location or even gender.

What do you consider to be the major changes in the art since you began training?

Dedication and the commitment of the younger generation changed a lot. In comparison to 20 or 30 years ago.

Who would you like to have trained with that you have not?

My Grandmaster, Kwee King Yang and his Sifu, Chief Instructor of Black Flag, Cia Fun Tjiao.

What would you say to someone who is interested in starting to learn h ek Ki Boen Eng Chu?

To come to one of our public workshops, to get your first experiential taste of HKB energy and if you find that you are interested, you can then enroll in a class.

If you are a dedicated Martial Artist, you may find it exciting and fulfilling to become part of something greater than all of us. We are engaged in a unique endeavor of creating effective ways to bring knowledge carefully preserved for generations within secret societies into the customs and demands of modern-day life. The HKB opportunity is there for someone truly dedicated to Martial Arts to enter a program in which they would acquire unique skill and knowledge, and be empowered in teaching, business, and living a Martial Arts Life. It comes with seven sacrifices; Hard Work, Time, Energy, Resource, Bruises, Tears and Blood (sometimes!).

What is it that keeps you motivated after all these years?

Three things: my passion in HKB Eng Chun, the commitment to spread and preserve the system to future generations, and my promise to my Sifu to keep training hard and to spread and preserve the system.

"As a teacher, we must bear the responsibility to pass the system as it is without holding anything back to ensure the preservation to future generation."

Do you think it is necessary to engage in free-fighting to achieve good self-defense skills in the street?

I don't recommend that anyone pick a fight in the street to achieve a good skill. However, a real fight is different from a sports tournament. You may have to experience a real fight someday in your life. During a real fight, you must consider every aspect of survival. Therefore, "skill challenge" is an important part of training. It is one of the ways to validate how the body responds under stress.

What is your opinion about mixing Kung Fu styles? Does the practice of one nullify the effectiveness of the other, or on the contrary, it can be beneficial to the student?

Mixing styles is more of a "modern approach." Where it focuses on collecting all technical knowledge that works, this is by all means "Using all ways as the way."

Wing Chun Masters

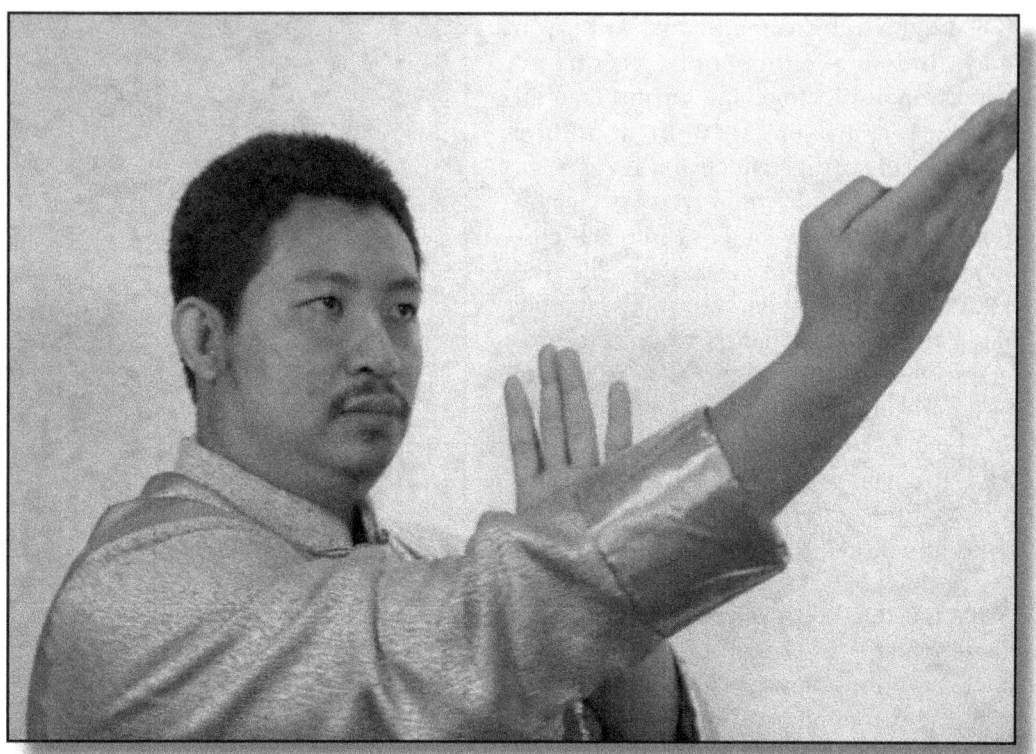

"During a real fight, you must consider every aspect of survival."

I personally don't believe in mixing Kung Fu styles. I am of the Traditional Progressive Mindset. It really depends on what is your goal. There are three kinds of mindsets.

First is "Traditional Conservative," where when the modern MA evolves, the Traditional Conservatives still hold their point of view as written in stone, even if it's no longer valid for working against certain challenges.

Second is "Traditional Progressive," when certain things no longer work – no longer are sufficient in dealing with the new evolution of MA challenge, the Traditional Progressive practitioner will dig deeper and deeper into their own Art to have a better and deeper understanding, instead of looking / borrowing elsewhere (other styles) and find solution from within their own system, instead of borrowing others.

Third is "Modern." This mindset says, collect and combine everything that works. This may result initially, in faster progression, but after it reaches a certain point, it will get stuck at only the technical level and cannot pass beyond it, because of the absence of in-depth training in one style.

I am a believer of Traditional Progressive where "Emptiness" can be achieved through deeper understanding where in the end it becomes "Using no way as the way." Keep adding so many techniques and methods will make "Using all ways as the way." As one goes deeper, style becomes illusion.

What is your philosophical basis for your Kung Fu training?
Only one thing: hard work. Talent is not something that someone is born with. Talent can be developed through experience.

Do you have a particularly memorable Kung Fu experience that has remained as an inspiration for your training?
During my early years, my training was very painful as none of my Kung Fu brother had any mercy, especially one Kung Fu brother who was the most senior. Because of that, I was training even harder. I spent most of my time at my Sifu's bukoan right after school and on the weekend, I sometime spent the whole day on extreme training. After short period of time, my skill level dramatically improved. Afterward, I really believe that there's no such thing as talent. Talent is not something you born with, but it is about how much experience you have. Sky is not even the limit. Everybody can train as hard as they want and progress their skill as high as they can get. In the end, I finally understand the real meaning of Kung Fu, which is hard work. So real Kung Fu means real hard work. No hard work means not real Kung Fu.

After all these years of training and experience, could you explain the meaning of the practice of Eng Chun?
To understand ourselves, others and universe, until in the end our "physical body intelligence" can teach our mind and spirit and achieve emptiness.

h ow is the chi-sao aspects of training related to the practical application of the Wing Chun techniques used in the three empty hands forms?
In the HKB family, Sticky hands is known as "Niam Jiu" (Chi Sao). This is part of important elements of training, but not the most important. The aggressor will not try to chi sao you in the street when they launch an attack. Chi sao develops your sensitivity and reflects once you touch the

Wing Chun Masters

"Talent is not something that someone is born with."

opponent. But there are other aspects as well when it comes to practical application such as during the engagement or the bridging.

is there anything lacking in the way Martial Arts are taught today compared to how they were in your beginnings?

I haven't experienced every other way of MA from past and today, but I can see there are evolutions.

Could i ask you what you consider to be the most important qualities of a successful Kung Fu practitioner?

Hard work, humbleness (Ego Control), compassion, integrity, self-control, and respect.

What advice would you give to students on the question of supplemental training?

In HKB system, we don't focus on muscle development; instead, we focus on Tendons. I can't relate how modern supplemental training can develop HKB Skill. In HKB, we have both main and supplemental training, such as Sam Chian Po form, Iron Palm (Thiat Sei Ciang), Red Palm (Ang Sei Ciang), etc.

What do you see as the most important attributes of a student?

Hard Work, empty the cup (Open-Minded), humbleness (Less Ego), compassion, and a certain degree of Trust.

Why is it, in your opinion, that a lot of students start falling away after two-three years of training?

First; inability to balance the Kung Fu training with the demanding modern life priority (School, Work, Finance demand, etc.) Second, inability to balance their time with their family and third and most importantly, the failure of a Sifu to teach, motivate, and empower the students.

"Everybody can train as hard as they want and progress their skill as high as they can get."

have been times when you felt fear in your Kung Fu training?

No, not really. Maybe when I was a young kid when I first started to learn.

What are your thoughts on the future of the Art?

The necessity for mutual respect and cooperation, so that all human beings can benefit from the experiential knowledge within Martial Arts. For Hek Ki Boen Eng Chun, in the future, with strong support from our large HKB family worldwide and strong leaders within the family, and with the current progression and demand, I can see clearly how HKB will spread to every city in the world. I do want the art to spread so it can be available to people to make their lives safe and happy. And my goal for our organization is that we grow not just big, but so strong in Integrity that we become known for being politic-free, well-managed, doing important work, while maintaining family-oriented relationships. I welcome any sincere seeker who wishes to know more about us.

www.ingramcontent.com/pod-product-compliance
Lightning Source LLC
Chambersburg PA
CBHW081343080526
44588CB00016B/2360